Bullying, Cyberbullying and Student Well-Being in Schools

Comparing European, Australian and Indian Perspectives

School bullying and cyberbullying are widely recognized as an international problem, but publications have focused on the western tradition of research. In India, recognition of these issues and research on the topics have been emerging in recent years. Beginning with cross-cultural differences across Indian, European and Australian contexts, this volume provides direct empirical comparisons between western and Indian situations. It then discusses innovative ways of hearing the views of students, pre-service teachers and teachers, featuring a range of qualitative and quantitative methodologies. The concluding commentaries from North American investigators provide a further international perspective from another region where much progress in researching these areas has been made. Together this ground-breaking collection comprises contributions from four continents on the prevalent issues of bullying, cyberbullying and student well-being.

Peter K. Smith is Emeritus Professor of Psychology at the Unit for School and Family Studies in the Department of Psychology, Goldsmiths, University of London.

Suresh Sundaram is an Associate Professor in the Department of Applied Psychology, Rajiv Gandhi National Institute of Youth Development, Tamil Nadu, India.

Barbara A. Spears is Associate Professor of Education in the School of Education, University of South Australia.

Catherine Blaya is Professor of Education Sciences at the Unit of Special Needs Education at the Haute Ecole Pédagogique du Canton de Vaud, Switzerland.

Mechthild Schäfer is a Professor in the Department of Psychology, Ludwig-Maximilians-Universität Munchen, Germany.

Damanjit Sandhu is an Associate Professor in the Department of Psychology, Punjabi University, Patiala, India.

Bullying, Cyberbullying and Student Well-Being in Schools

Comparing European, Australian and Indian Perspectives

Edited by

Peter K. Smith
Goldsmiths, University of London

Suresh Sundaram
Annamalai University

Barbara A. Spears
University of South Australia

Catherine Blaya
Université de Nice, Sophia Antipolis

Mechthild Schäfer
Ludwig-Maximilians-Universität Munchen

Damanjit Sandhu
Punjabi University, Patiala

CAMBRIDGE
UNIVERSITY PRESS

CAMBRIDGE
UNIVERSITY PRESS

University Printing House, Cambridge CB2 8BS, United Kingdom

One Liberty Plaza, 20th Floor, New York, NY 10006, USA

477 Williamstown Road, Port Melbourne, VIC 3207, Australia

314–321, 3rd Floor, Plot 3, Splendor Forum, Jasola District Centre, New Delhi – 110025, India

79 Anson Road, #06–04/06, Singapore 079906

Cambridge University Press is part of the University of Cambridge.

It furthers the University's mission by disseminating knowledge in the pursuit of education, learning, and research at the highest international levels of excellence.

www.cambridge.org
Information on this title: www.cambridge.org/9781107189393
DOI: 10.1017/9781316987384

First published 2018

Printed in the United Kingdom by Clays, St Ives plc

A catalogue record for this publication is available from the British Library.

Library of Congress Cataloging-in-Publication Data
Names: Smith, Peter K., editor.
Title: Bullying, cyberbullying and student well-being in schools : comparing European, Australian and Indian perspectives / edited by Peter K. Smith and Goldsmiths College, University of London, Suresh Sundaram, Annamalai University, Barbara A. Spears, University of South Australia, Catherine Blaya, Universite de Nice, Sophia Antipolis, Mechthild Schafer, Ludwig-Maximilians-Universitat Munchen, Damanjit Sandhu, Punjabi University, Patiala.
Description: Cambridge, United Kingdom : University Printing House, 2018. | Includes bibliographical references and index.
Identifiers: LCCN 2017055414 | ISBN 9781107189393 (hardback)
Subjects: LCSH: Bullying in schools – Cross-cultural studies. | Cyberbullying – Cross-cultural studies.
Classification: LCC LB3013.3 .B8135 2018 | DDC 371.5/8–dc23
LC record available at https://lccn.loc.gov/2017055414

ISBN 978-1-107-18939-3 Hardback

Contents

Figures

Preface

After China, India is the other major population centre in Asia and indeed the world, with more than 1.2 billion people, about 17.5 per cent of the world population. This book has a focus on pupil well-being in schools in India. While the chapters presented here are mainly centred on bullying and cyberbullying, consideration is also given in this volume to other risk-taking behaviours, and to school safety and school climate. This book focuses especially on adolescent pupils, where the problem is arguably most acute.

The research reported in this book stems in part from a project entitled 'Bullying, Cyberbullying and Pupil Safety and Well-Being', funded by the Indian-European Research Networking Programme in the Social Sciences from 2012 to 2015. This brought together two Indian teams (from Annamalai in Tamil Nadu and from Patiala in the Punjab) and four European teams (from London, the United Kingdom; Nice, France; Munich, Germany; and Amsterdam, the Netherlands).

In addition the project collaborated with researchers from Australia (South Australia and Queensland) who were separately funded by the Australian Academy of Science (Eminent Speakers, 2014), the University of South Australia Division of Education, Arts and Social Sciences Research Performance Fund and the Flinders University Creative Research Fund.

The European, Indian and Australian teams worked closely together over a three-year period from 2012 to 2015. The programme of work involved literature reviews, developing new research tools (cartoon task, questionnaires), trying out innovative techniques (PhotoStory, documentary interviews) and conducting careful comparative studies. Close attention was paid to the nature of cultural differences and developing culturally sensitive instruments, issues that are discussed in most of the chapters.

This book brings together much of the work and findings of this combined network. After an introductory chapter setting the scene for the topic and describing the relevant school systems, there follow twelve quite diverse chapters arising directly from the network activities. We then have two commentaries from North America (Canada and the United States). A final editorial chapter draws together some conclusions and provides suggestions for how further research and collaboration in this area may continue.

The editors are grateful for funding from the Indian Council of Social Science Research (ICSSR, India) in association with the Economic and Social Research Council (ESRC, UK), the Agence Nationale de la Recherche (ANR, France), the Deutsche Forschungsgemeinschaft (DFG, Germany) and the Netherlands Organisation for Scientific Research (NWO, the Netherlands). F.No.ICSSR/IND-EUR/RNP-030/2012/IC.

Peter K Smith
Suresh Sundaram
Barbara A. Spears
Catherina Blaya
Mechthild Schäfer
Damanjit Sandhu

Part I

Issues in Studying Cross-National Differences

1   Introduction

Peter K. Smith, Suresh Sundaram, Damanjit Sandhu,
Catherine Blaya, Mechthild Schäfer, and
Barbara A. Spears

This chapter gives a brief overview of previous work carried out internationally on school bullying and cyberbullying, including evidence for their negative effects. The relatively limited research base in India is then considered. In the second half of this chapter we summarize the kinds of school systems in the four European countries represented in this book (England, France, Germany, the Netherlands), Australia, and India (especially in the states of Punjab and Tamil Nadu). This is to provide a context for the chapters that follow.

Brief History of Research on School Bullying and Cyberbullying

Bullying is generally defined as a form of aggressive behavior (with an intent to harm others) characterized by repetition and imbalance of power (Olweus, 2013). In Western societies, the image of a larger child attacking a smaller one, not just once but on a regular basis, epitomizes this kind of bullying or harassment during the school years.

The origins of research on *bullying* in Western societies (Smith, 2016), as also of *ijime* in Japan (Toda, 2016), have centered on schools and on children and young people. Children at school can be in a vulnerable position; they normally have to attend school, yet they may not have the same awareness of their rights and protections against attacks that adults usually have and expect (Greene, 2006). The majority of research on bullying has been on pupil-pupil bullying in schools, which is also a main focus of this book. However, bullying and related forms of abuse and harassment can occur in many contexts and throughout the lifespan (Monks & Coyne, 2011). Even in schools, bullying between teachers and pupils or between teachers (or other adults) in the school is an important consideration.

Bullying can take many forms. Besides physical attacks (either on a person or by damaging their belongings), verbal threats and insults can be hurtful and frightening; in fact, verbal bullying is usually the most common form (Smith, 2014). These are direct forms of attack, and they have been reported on since the origins of research on bullying in the 1980s. Since the 1990s it has been recognized that aggression, and thus also bullying, can take more indirect (Björkqvist, 1994), social (Galen & Underwood, 1997), or relational (Crick & Grotpeter, 1995) forms. A main form of indirect bullying can be by spreading nasty stories or rumors about someone (to others, rather than face to face). A main form of relational bullying is systematic (direct or indirect) social exclusion, for example from playground games or classroom activities.

Since the 2000s, cyber aggression and cyberbullying have become important issues. This has become noticeable through the increasing penetration of the Internet and the convergence of mobile phones and more recently of smartphones. These of course have brought enormous opportunities and benefits (Costabile & Spears, 2012; Spears et al., 2013), but also risks and dangers (Livingstone & Smith, 2014). Starting with emails and text messages, but now increasingly on social networking sites/platforms and across various devices, multiple kinds of cyber aggression and bullying have been documented. These include attacks and threats, denigration (put-downs), flaming (online verbal fights), cyber-stalking (persistent online intimidation), exclusion (from an online group), masquerade (pretending to be someone else to send/post material to damage someone), outing (sharing embarrassing information or images of someone), and putting up false profiles and distributing personal material against someone's wishes (Willard, 2006).

Definitional Issues

The definition of *cyberbullying* is often taken as being parallel to that of what is now often called *traditional bullying* (i.e., bullying occurring offline rather than online). However, cyberbullying has its own characteristics, and the defining criteria of repetition and imbalance of power are certainly more complex, and arguably more problematic, in the cyber domain. Regarding repetition, one action by a perpetrator (such as putting an insulting or threatening comment on a website) can lead to repetition in the sense of (multiple) viewings or further comments by others. Regarding imbalance of power, the traditional criteria (physical strength, numbers, peer popularity) may be bypassed if the perpetrator is anonymous to the victim, as can often be the case. However, anonymity itself can bestow power on the perpetrator, such that the protective shield provided by being online ensures the victim is helpless in responding. Some researchers regard these issues as sufficiently intractable that they prefer to use the term *cyber aggression* rather than *cyberbullying* (Bauman, Underwood, & Card, 2013), although the use of the cyberbullying construct has also been defended (Smith, Del Barrio, & Tokunaga, 2013).

Definitional issues are not unique to cyber forms of bullying. For traditional bullying too queries have been raised as to the importance of repetition. It can be argued that one significant attack by a more powerful person may leave the victim so fearful of future attacks that there is an implicit fear of repetition, and that imbalance of power can take many forms and be difficult to assess. Furthermore, Finkelhor, Turner, and Hamby (2012) suggest that the focus on bullying may draw attention away from other serious forms of violence that are not repeated or do not involve a power imbalance.

In defense of the research program on bullying, it can be pointed out that imbalance of power can be defined and has been assessed in a number of studies. Furthermore, such studies generally indicate that when imbalance of power is present in an attack, the effects are generally more serious (Hunter, Boyle, & Warden, 2007; Turner et al., 2014; Ybarra, Espelage, & Mitchell, 2014). Indeed Ybarra, Espelage, and Mitchell (2014) concluded that 'Both differential power and repetition are key in identifying youth who are bullied and at particular risk for concurrent psychosocial challenge' (2014, Abstract, p. 293).

Growth of the Research Program on Bullying

Controversies and arguments on definitional issues and on the focus on bullying can be taken as signs of healthy debate. What is indisputable is that the study of bullying, especially among children and young people, has become a major research program over the past 40 years (Hymel & Swearer, 2015). Olweus (2013, figure 3) used the PsycINFO database to locate articles with keywords 'bully', 'bullying', or 'bullied'; these increased from 5 in 1990 to 104 in 2000 and 566 in 2010. Zych, Ortega-Ruiz, and Del Rey (2015) reported a systematic study of publications on bullying and cyberbullying from 1978 to 2013. They used the ISI Web of Science and selected journal articles on school bullying that explicitly referred to and were concerned with bullying (including cyberbullying). This yielded 44 results in 1995, 126 in 2000, 165 in 2005, 438 in 2010, and 689 in 2014. Articles on cyberbullying increased from 4 before 2005 to 41 in 2010 and 139 in 2013.

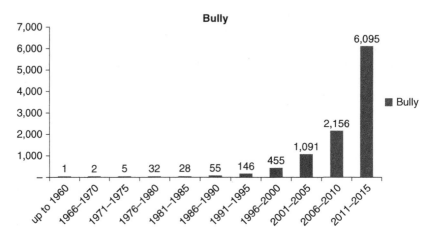

Figure 1.1 Number of articles from keyword 'bully' in searching ISI Web of Science, up to end 2015

Figure 1.1 shows findings using 'bully' as a search keyword in the ISI Web of Science. From a trickle of publications up to the 1980s, there is then an exponential increase, such that more than 6,000 articles appeared in the 5-year period from 2011 to 2016.

Negative Effects of Bullying and Cyberbullying on Pupil Well-Being and School Climate

Much of the research on bullying has focused on its effects. For victims, bullying hurts, and the longer it lasts, the worse the impact. It is well established that being bullied leads to psychosomatic symptoms, poor sleep, and nightmares in the short term, and to such long-term effects as emotional isolation, where a dark picture of oneself and others in relationships emerges, as well as increased difficulties in maintaining friendships, when compared to those not victimized in school (Schäfer et al., 2004). Meta-analyses of many reports from longitudinal studies (Ttofi, Farrington, & Lösel, 2011) show that even after adjustments for a range of other factors, victims at school are at greater risk of later depression. These effects can be substantial and long term (Wolke & Lereya, 2015). Victims are higher on suicidal ideation (Schäfer et al., 2004), and the Environmental Risk Study in the United Kingdom found that exposure to frequent bullying in 12-year-old children predicted higher rates of self-harm, even after taking account of prior emotional problems (Fisher et al., 2012). Suicide, although rare, can be an outcome to which victim experiences can be a significant contributor (Kim et al., 2009).

Research on the consequences of cyberbullying shows similar effects as for traditional or offline bullying. It affects the victims' self-esteem, confidence, and mental health (Kowalski et al., 2014). This is easily understandable since bullying and cyberbullying share some common characteristics (repetition, intention to harm, power imbalance). Also, victims online are quite often also victimized offline, which makes their lives especially challenging since there is no respite (Blaya, 2013). One of the specificities of cyberbullying is that it is difficult to escape. Moreover, the anonymity of the cyberbully is facilitated since the aggression is not face to face, and this can bring some young people to adopt behaviors they would not take on ordinarily. The victim who does not know who is willing to harm them can find it even more challenging to cope with the situation. However, as stressed by Smith and colleagues (2008), the type of cyberbullying may impact the way the victims feel affected.

Given the essential importance of peers for cognitive, emotional, and social development, the victim experience can be devastating for those isolated in the group, including learned helplessness and blaming oneself for the bullying, fueled by peer reactions due to moral disengagement (Bandura et al., 1996). Apart from the effects on mental health, there is some evidence that victims have poorer academic achievement and that bullying contributes to school failure and dropout (Raskauskas & Stolz, 2007; Rothon et al., 2010).

But beyond effects on the victim, bullying causes reduced well-being for classmates who feel stressed by the social polarization in their daily environment (e.g., 'whom should I side with', 'whom do I have to side with'), which also might distract their attention from classwork. Friendships might descend into loyalty conflicts for some while observing the bullying might lead to personal distress for empathetic others (Eisenberg, 2014). Observers of bullying often feel upset and the school climate is adversely affected (Rivers et al., 2009).

Nevertheless, bullying can be functional for the perpetrator (Olthof et al., 2011). It enables the bully to become empowered through the class dynamic, where the goal is power and dominance through achieving elevated status among the peer group. The longer bullying lasts, the more social rejection is reported by the victim, and, at least in secondary school, victims are more rejected than bullies. The bullies are not often high on being liked by classmates (social preference), but typically they are high on perceived popularity. This implies that peers look at and learn from them. In puberty they can serve as a role model for antisocial and norm-breaking behaviors (Moffitt, 1993).

Cultural Issues in Research on Bullying

The great majority of research on bullying that has been carried out, and especially that abstracted in PsycINFO or Web of Science, has been in Western countries – Europe, North America, and Australasia. To some extent this also represents the dominance of the English language in terms of citation analyses. Since the 1980s researchers have conducted significant numbers of studies in countries such as Japan, South Korea, Mainland China, and Hong Kong (see Kwak & Lee, 2016; Lin & Lai, 2016; Toda, 2016; Zhang, Chen, & Chen, 2016), many in the national languages. Some studies have been conducted in Southeast Asian countries (see Sittichai & Smith, 2015). There have also been studies across the globe, in South America, Africa, and other Asian countries. Bullying is an international issue and a worldwide phenomenon. Nevertheless most of the research and intervention base remains Western in origin.

This kind of imbalance was illustrated by Smith and Berkkun (2017) in an analysis of the Web of Science database for articles on cyberbullying. They found a total of 538 articles over the period 2000–2015. Looking at the national affiliation of lead authors, by continent these were North America (n = 197), Europe (including Israel) (n = 190), Asia (including Turkey) (n = 106), Australasia (n = 40), and Other (Africa and South America) (n = 5). Of the Asian contributions, most came from South Korea (52) and Turkey (27). India was represented by only one article.

History of Research on Bullying and Cyberbullying in India

The phenomenon of school bullying is not new in India, and it is a part of the culture of Indian schools (Jaishankar, 2009). Indeed, bullying is embedded in caste hierarchy in India. Those of the 'upper caste' have often bullied the 'lower castes' verbally and physically and by alienating them from the social mainstream (Judge, 2013).

School bullying was traditionally considered a predominantly rural phenomenon, but it has become part of urban Indian culture. Name-calling, threatening, damaging property, and hitting are common ways in which bullying occurs in India. Bullying is known by various names in urban regions (see also Chapters 4 and 13). Two common terms in the English-language media are *ragging* and *Eve teasing*.

Ragging refers to senior students bullying junior students, for example in colleges, where new students are insulted and forced to do things for senior students. Although to some extent accepted as a part of college life in the past, it is now recognized by the Indian government as an 'act that violates or is perceived to violate an individual student's dignity', and in order to eradicate it, the Honourable Supreme Court issued guidelines in 2009 for the setting up of the Central Crisis Hotline and Anti-ragging Database (www.antiragging.in/).

Eve teasing refers to girls bullied by boys, with or without sexual connotations; it is a euphemism used throughout South Asia for public sexual harassment or molestation of women by men.

Recently *groupism* has been recognized as the latest bullying technique, involving groups of students ganging up on classmates whom they consider different by the group's standards; a child may be targeted for being of a different religion, economic background, or social standing.

The dangers of school bullying were first noted by the Raghavan Committee (Jaishankar, 2009) that was constituted to control and prevent ragging in educational institutions. The committee described ragging as a form of bullying, and considered that it started in schools and residential hostels. However, in comparison to the developed countries, school bullying is not well understood in India and is often considered a part of the normal schooling process. Even most teachers and parents fail to understand the seriousness of school bullying. Most bullying cases go unreported, and even if they are reported, the majority of such cases are mediated at an individual level by teachers or die down within a short space of time, rather than being dealt with systematically.

There is a relatively small literature on the prevalence of bullying in Indian schools, but there have recently been alarming headlines, such as 'Every third child is bullied in school, shows study' (*Times of India*, September 3, 2015). In fact, an early study by Kshirsagar, Agarwal, and Bavdekar (2007) assessed the prevalence of bullying among 500 children aged 8–12 years in three schools in the Mumbai area and found 31.4% had been bullied. Teasing was most common, most victims did not tell parents, and victims were more likely to experience psychosomatic symptoms.

A Bullying Research Initiative in Training and Education (BRITE) study at 12 English-medium schools across Dehradun, Munsoorie, and Chandigarh surveyed 1,200 students (aged 14 to 18) and 600 teachers between 2002 and 2005. Some 59% of boys and 65% of girls felt that bullying was present on campus. Common bullying behavior among boys was reported as fights or using abusive language, while in girls it was teasing, name-calling, or avoiding someone (*Daily News & Analysis – Bangalore*, 2008).

Srisiva, Thirumoorthi, and Sujatha (2013) surveyed 300 students aged 11 to 18 years from four schools in Coimbatore City, Tamil Nadu. Only

7% of pupils did not report being bullied; the very high proportion of victims may be because the definition of bullying in this study appeared to include any aggressive acts. Common forms were teasing, intimidating, excluding from the group, and spreading rumors and lies. Common reasons for being bullied were poor performance in studies, appearance, and skin color/complexion.

Jamir and colleagues (2014) surveyed 165 students aged 12 to 17 years in Imphal, Manipur. Again a very large proportion of pupils (about 84%) reported being bullied. Scores for being a victim correlated negatively with self-esteem and positively with depression.

Malhi, Bharti, and Sidhu (2014) assessed physical, verbal, rumor spreading, and extortion forms of bullying among 209 students aged 13–16 years from schools in Chandigarh. About 20% were reported as victims, 13% as bullies (more boys), 20% as bully-victims (more boys), and 45% as controls (more girls). Verbal was the most common form of bullying, followed by physical. The bully-victims scored much worse on academic attainment than the other groups (controls being best). Bully-victims and victims also generally scored the worst on measures of psychosocial adjustment.

One issue with these studies is the varying and often uncertain criteria used for assessing bullying, which could affect the apparently very high prevalence rates. Another common issue is the lack of reporting of the language used in the surveys, and if not English, what words were used to translate bullying. However the general findings regarding types of bullying, sex differences, and negative outcomes of being a victim appear similar to those in Western studies.

As in some European and North American countries, in the past decade, school bullying has extended to extreme forms such as shooting. India's first school shooting took place in December 2007 in an elite school at Gurgaon (near New Delhi), where a student was shot from point blank range by two of his schoolmates. This incident was a planned murder provoked by bullying of the victim (*Times of India*, 2007). A number of school shooting cases have been reported since.

Cyberbullying in India

India is currently one of the most dynamic information and communications technology (ICT) markets in the world and Indians have demonstrated exceptional interest in adopting ICT, particularly mobile phones, spurred by their growing affordability and the convenience they offer in many spheres of life. The ongoing evolution and rapid adoption of social media in this century is affecting Indian society as a whole, including children's lives. Many children now have access to the Internet either at home or in Internet parlors and schools. Even though schools usually restrict students' usage of the Internet solely to academic purposes, children widely use cybercafés, personal computers, and tablets.

As elsewhere, in India too the opportunities afforded by ICT can be abused (see also Chapter 5). The first problem of cyberbullying in India came to light in 2006 when elite schoolboys from Mumbai bullied their principal using the social network Orkut (Chaturvedi, 2007). Many children of elite schools subsequently started using the Internet to vent their frustrations against teachers, school staff, and other pupils. The problem became significantly graver with the reporting of the murder of Adnan Patrawala, a 16-year-old student from the Mumbai region, allegedly as a result of cyber hatred by his friends (Indiatime.com, 2007). This case gained a lot of attention from the public as well as the media as it was the first cyberbullying case in India that we know of that led to the murder of a student.

An early study in Tirunelveli by Jaishanker and Shariff (2008) found that 65% of school students had been victims of cyberbullying, and 60% of students had been involved in bullying others using mobile phones.

More recently, Intel Security (Teens, Tweens and Technology Study, 2015) reported that 81% of 8- to 16-year-olds are active on social media networks. Of these, 22% reported being bullied online, this being the highest in the four countries surveyed (Australia, the United States, and Singapore being the other three). As many as 52% of Indian children indicated that they had bullied people over social media, again the highest of the four countries, with 65% of respondents reporting having witnessed cruel behavior online.

Relatively high rates of cyberbullying in India were corroborated by an international study conducted by Microsoft (Pratap Vikram Singh, 2012) of risks of cyberbullying, getting threatened, or being harassed online. India ranked third highest out of 25 countries in terms of children and youth reporting being bullied online – 53% of respondents (behind only China at 70% and Singapore at 58%). The 2014 report of the Parliamentary Committee on Information Technology recognized that the online bullying of children by their peers was common (Standing Committee on Information Technology, 2013–2014).

Kaur, Kaur, and Sandhu (2014) found that hacking online accounts, receiving vulgar text messages, and posting obscene photographs of someone online and making them public are common ways in which both genders are victimized online. Receiving messages on mobile phones and Facebook ridiculing the victim's body shape, size, and looks are common ways of experiencing cyber victimization. Both girls and boys

were found to be equally targeted by cyber bullies. The major consequences of cyber bullying victimization are feeling sad and helpless,
a depressed mood, anxiety, poor academic performance, high levels of
stress, low self-esteem, loneliness, and suicidal ideation.

On the whole, it is unfortunate that research on school bullying in India
is in its infancy and relatively little empirical research has been conducted
to investigate the nature and prevalence of bullying. The issue of bullying
in India has many parents, psychologists, and counselors very concerned
for the welfare of young students.

School Systems

The nature of educational systems is important to consider as a context for
the ways in which school bullying may be manifested. Aspects such as
school and class size, structure of the school day, break times and supervision, ages of school transfer, grouping by ability, grade retention, and
mainstreaming of children with special needs can all be relevant; these have
been discussed in an international context by Jessel (2016). Attitudes to
bullying and to discipline generally (such as use of physical punishment)
also vary. In addition, countries vary greatly in terms of the resources
available and support for teachers in dealing with bullying. Here, we summarize the main aspects for each of the countries represented in this book.

England

Although homeschooling is possible, almost all pupils in England attend
school by five years of age. These are usually state schools, with about 7%
of pupils attending private (fee-paying) schools (misleadingly often called
public schools). The primary school period covers infant school from
rising 5 to 7 years, and junior school on up to 11 years. The transition
to secondary school at 12 years means typically a much larger school
(jumping from around 300 to 900 pupils; see Jessel, 2016), and a partial
shift from form- or class-based to subject-based teaching. Some schools
group pupils by ability, but grade retention is very rare. Schooling is
compulsory to age 16; after that, pupils continue at school or further
education college, start an apprenticeship or traineeship, or work or
volunteer (for 20 hours or more a week) while in part-time education or
training, until they are 18.

There is a general policy to include or mainstream pupils with specials
needs or disabilities so far as possible. Some schools will have special
facilities for particular kinds of disability. However, there are also special
schools for pupils with severe disabilities. In addition, Pupil Referral

Units exist for very troublesome pupils whom mainstream schools cannot cope with or have excluded.

The school day typically starts around 9:00 AM and continues to around 3:30 PM; there are often one or two short (15–20 minute) break times, plus a longer (typically one hour) break at lunchtime. Break times are not usually supervised by teachers, but by playground assistants (often local people or parents who receive minimal training for the task).

Although attitudes to bullying vary, generally it has come to be seen over the past 20 years as an important social problem. Legally, it has been a requirement for schools to have an anti-bullying policy (either separately, or as part of a broader behavior policy) since 1999. Regular inspections of schools do include questions about bullying and how it is dealt with. Schools are expected to have procedures in place, but these may vary widely – there is no prescribed way or program to be used (Thompson & Smith, 2012). Corporal punishment by teachers is not allowed. Currently the Department for Education (DfE) website (www.gov.uk/government/publications/preventing-and-tackling-bully ing) has several resources on bullying: preventing and tackling bullying; advice for head teachers, staff and governing bodies (July 2017); cyberbullying; advice for head teachers and school staff (November 2014); and advice for parents and carers on cyberbullying (November 2014). There are also many other organizations and charities with websites and resources on the issue, such as the Anti-bullying Alliance (antibullyin galliance.org.uk).

France

The French educational system is characterized by very centralized management with strong influence at the state level. The Ministry of Education defines the overall educational politics and common core curricula at all educational levels: it employs the teachers, who benefit from a civil servant status, it trains the school management, and it controls the quality of education and the way schools work.

Compulsory education is from 6 to 16. However, France has a long tradition of free preschool education and an average of 70% of children attend preschool. Lower secondary school starts at the age of 11 and students enter higher secondary school at 15. Most children attend state schools and 17% of young people attend private schools.

Ability grouping is not allowed and there is a strong policy for mainstream education. Nevertheless, in cases of acknowledged strong disability, students can be schooled in special education needs centers called Instituts Médicaux Educatifs (IME).

The instruction time per student amounts to 932 hours per year, ranking France as one of the European countries where young people spend the most time at school. The average number of students per teacher in primary schools is 18.9, higher than most European countries and the average OECD country rate of 15.3 (but lower than the UK average of 21). In secondary schools, there are an average of 12.5 students per teacher, below the OECD average of 13.5. The average instruction time is 24 hours per week in primary education, 25 hours in lower secondary education, and 30 in higher secondary schools.

Corporal punishment by teachers is not allowed. The focus in France was initially on school violence, with little attention to school bullying. But from 2010, the French Ministry of Education has taken up the issue, setting up a scientific delegation against school bullying. The mission of this delegation is to act as an advisory board and to prevent and combat school bullying. Since then, many actions and awareness campaigns have been undertaken and a website is dedicated to the issue (www .nonauharcelement.education.gouv.fr), as well as a free helpline. Although the law explicitly holds head teachers responsible for the safety of students and staff when at school, there was no specific law against bullying before the year 2014; it is now compulsory for schools to set up explicit anti-bullying policies.

Germany

The German educational system is characterized by decentralized management with strong influence at the federal state level. The cultural sovereignty of federal states implies considerable variance in how compulsory schooling is organized. Nevertheless, there is a constant effort for corporate educational standards carried forward by the conference of the Ministers of Education and Cultural Affairs (KMK), which plays a significant role as an instrument for the coordination and development of education in the country.

Compulsory education starts at 6 years of age and continues for 9 or 10 years, depending on federal state law. The general education system schooling is based on a three-part logic with primary schools, secondary schools on the junior high level, and secondary schools on the gymnasium level. The transition from primary to secondary level is after 4 years in most federal states but after 6 years in others. Higher education entrance level is attained after 12 or 13 years by high school graduation (Abitur), however there are strong efforts for an equalization of those who graduate after 12/13 years at vocational schools. Compulsory education includes children with all kinds of disabilities. There are different types of schools for different forms of physical, mental or behavioral disabilities and medical expertise decides (together with parents) on the kind of allocation offered. However, since the 1990s, the concept of inclusion has been strongly promoted, with new concepts to facilitate this for disabled children. Since then, the range of offers for serious cases of disabilities has reduced, but the system is kept in parallel.

Teachers are employed by the federal states and benefit from a civil servant status. Teacher education comprises a state examination after around four years at university followed by two years of internship with a second state examination.

In 1973, corporal punishment in schools was prohibited and since 2000, the German Civil Code §1631 defines the right of children to an 'education without violence', irrespective of whether at home, in school, or elsewhere.

For most pupils, school starts at around 8:00 AM, in classes with around 25 peers (which might go up to 30 plus on the secondary level) and one teacher. Primary schools close around midday, with after school care offered by many schools, or, alternatively, after school care is organized by parent initiatives. At the secondary school level, pupils are in school around 30 hours a week.

Given the responsibility of federal states for educational issues, there is still no nationally mandated requirement for schools to have a specific anti-bullying policy in Germany. Federal states differ substantially on whether they provide a conceptual framework for prevention of bullying, violence, or other issues regarding children's well-being while in school. There is a great variety of approaches, often launched by school psychologists or ministerial units, initiating, organizing, and promoting initiatives and advanced training; and there is a growing awareness in this sector that conceptual work supported by political will is inevitable in order to tackle bullying in a sustainable way.

Netherlands

The Dutch educational system starts with 8 years of primary school, followed by 4, 5, or 6 years of secondary education. The mandatory age for schooling is from 5 until 16, but most parents send their children to primary school at the age of 4. Parents can choose to send their children to a variety of religiously or philosophically oriented schools, but public schools (without such an orientation) exist as well. All schools are subsidized by the central government.

After primary school, Dutch education is characterized by a binary system. Children attend either more profession-oriented schools (VMBO) or schools preparing for tertiary education, with different pathways for those who go to institutes of higher education (HAVO as secondary education) or to university (VWO as secondary education). Lessons are usually in Dutch, but not exclusively so. Thus, from age 12 children go their separate ways, on the basis of either parental choice or professional advice from the primary school itself, or (most often) on the basis of a national test (CITO-toets). It is possible to switch from one form of education to another. This usually takes place after having acquired a diploma.

There is a general policy to include pupils with specials needs or disabilities in mainstream schools as far as possible. Some schools will have special facilities for particular kinds of disability. However, there are also special schools for pupils with severe disabilities.

The school day may start as early as 8:00 AM, but 8:30 AM and 9:00 AM are more common. As to the rest of the day, the schedule is similar to that in England. Schools that start early often use a short lunchtime break with a view to finishing early. Teachers do supervise during breaks. Corporal punishment by teachers is not allowed.

It took the Dutch government a while to tackle the issue of bullying. In March 2013, the state recognized that bullying was a problem interfering with the safety of pupils/students, that bullying often remained under the radar, and that the staff did not always have the right means available to stop or reduce bullying. The undersecretary of education suggested that norms were necessary to make clear that bullying is not acceptable; parents and teachers need strong support in battling bullying, and school inspectors need more rights to enquire about bullying and to enforce measures when deemed necessary. Schools are expected to have procedures in place, but these may vary widely. Currently, schools are free to choose from among anti-bullying programs, but an empirical evaluation of various programs (including the KiVa and Olweus programs, as well as several others) is under way.

Australia

Australia has three levels of government: federal, state (e.g., New South Wales, Victoria, South Australia), and local. While education is primarily the responsibility of the states and territories, the Australian government's (federal) Department of Education and Training is responsible for formulating national policies, such as the National Safe Schools Framework, which provides Australian schools with a vision and a set of guiding principles to develop positive and practical student safety and well-being policies, as well as other national programs such as those related to curriculum, educational outcomes, and disability.

Overall, government schools are the major provider of school education in Australia, with 65.2% of all students attending, and 34.8% attending nongovernment schools. State and territory governments own and operate their own government schools, develop their own policies (e.g., anti-bullying policies), and monitor and review performance. Nongovernment schools, which are often of religious orientation, receive most of their public funding from the federal government, with supplementary funding from the relevant state or territory. In 2015, Aboriginal and Torres Strait Islander students made up 5.3% of total enrollments, the majority attending government schools.

Compulsory education starts around age 5–6, depending upon the state/territory, and students attend school from Monday to Friday each week, for approximately 6.5 hours per day. Most states and territories have a four-term year, with a short vacation period between terms and the longer summer holidays in December and January. Schooling consists of a three-tier system: early childhood education, not compulsory, but almost always undertaken and delivered through a range of settings, including childcare centers and preschools before full-time schooling commences in grade 1; primary school (grades 1 to 6 or 7); and secondary school (grades 7 or 8 to 12). Class sizes vary, with early years averaging fewer than 20 students, and primary and secondary in the vicinity of 26–30 students. All schools prepare students for the same nationally recognized qualifications in the final years of schooling. These are also used for university entrance.

Supporting students with disability in schooling is a national priority, and the Disability Standards for Education (2005) outlines the obligations of education providers to ensure that students with disability can access and participate in education on the same basis as other students.

Given that the states and territories are largely responsible for their own schools and policies, there is no nationally mandated requirement for schools to have a specific anti-bullying policy. However, all schools do operate under the mantle of the National Safe Schools Framework (www .education.gov.au/national-safe-schools-framework), which emphasizes the policies and procedures required to build safe schools, and provides an overarching vision that all Australian schools are safe, supportive, and respectful teaching and learning communities that promote student well-being. The revamped Student Wellbeing Hub (www.studentwellbeinghub .edu.au/) is also guided by these principles, highlighting the importance of educators, parents, and students working together.

India

Education in India is provided by the public and the private sectors. Under various articles of the Indian constitution, free and compulsory education is provided as a fundamental right to children between the ages of 6 and 14 in government schools. The ratio of public schools to private schools in India is 7:5. The public education system faces serious challenges, including a lack of adequate infrastructure, insufficient funding, a shortage of staff, and scarce facilities.

There are different curricula systems depending on the government or academic organization that sets the curriculum and standards for examinations, usually referred to as School Education Boards. The most common are the Central Board of Secondary Education (CBSE), and the Council of Indian School Certificate Examination (CISCE). The Right to Education Act mandates a pupil-to-teacher ratio of no more than 30:1.

Education is compulsory from 6 to 14 years. The Indian school system is structured as follows:

Preschool: The Montessori system is especially popular at the preschool level. Private play schools cater for children between the ages of 18 months and 3 years.

Kindergarten: Lower kindergarten (3–4 years) and upper kindergarten (4–5 years)

Primary school: First to fifth grade (6–10 years)

Middle school: Fifth to eighth grade (11–14 years)

Secondary school: Ninth to 10th grade (14–16 years)

Higher secondary: 11th to 12th grade (16–17 years). This is when students choose their stream or an academic area to focus on.

Schools in India usually start around 8:00 AM, sometimes with a short assembly period during which students are given moral instruction and information about current events. Regular classes are generally 40 minutes long, and a typical school day consists of eight classes. Most schools give a midday recess or lunch break, while some give another short break as well for water or just stretching a bit.

A private school costs a student about Rs 50,000 per year on average. A government school provides free education with some incentives, the greatest being the Mid-day Meal Scheme, implemented from April 2006, whereby primary school students are provided with a cooked midday meal. It is a flagship program of the Government of India, which is implemented in association with the state governments. The main objective of this scheme is to increase enrollment retention, to enhance the learning abilities of the pupils coming from economically deprived sections of society, to provide nutritious meals to pupils, and to promote friendship and feeling of common brotherhood among children belonging to different castes, colors, or creeds.

Corporal punishment has been banned in the country through a Supreme Court ruling in 2000, also incorporated in the Right to Education Act. Since 2012, according to guidelines issued by the Ministry of Women and Child Development, this practice has also been made a punishable offense. School principals have been made responsible to prevent corporal punishment. Teachers found guilty could be denied promotion, and even increments. Despite being banned, corporal punishment is so internalized in India that students do not even identify it as a problem and it is often accepted as a normal part of school life.

Under India's Disability Act (1995), children with disabilities have the right to free education up to the age of 18. There are more than 2,500 schools for children with special needs in India. Some are run or supported by the government, while many are registered NGOs or private institutions. Nevertheless, a majority of children with special needs do not receive any formal education, in spite of the practice of inclusive education in some schools. Awareness of inclusive education in schools throughout the country is still at an early stage, and educational institutions are skeptical about having mainstream and special needs children studying in the same classroom. Lack of flexibility in curriculum, inability to fend for themselves and thus being bullied by others in the class, and not getting adequate attention from the teacher are common issues.

Bullying is not addressed systematically by parents or institutions. Incidents of bullying in government schools either evoke apathy or on the extreme side, corporal punishment for the perpetrators. There are no relevant laws against bullying. However, in March 2015, the Central Board of Secondary Education (CBSE) directed all its affiliated schools to form an anti-bullying committee comprising the vice principal, a senior teacher, school doctor, counselor, parent-teacher representative, school management representative, legal representative, and peer educators. It also recommended strict actions against anyone found bullying, ranging from a written warning to suspension or expulsion of the student.

India – Punjab

The Punjab state in India is a linguistic unit inhabited largely by Punjabi-speaking people. Male and female literacy rates are 81.5% and 71.3%, respectively. Punjab has 37 scheduled castes (SCs), which constitute 31.9% of the population of the state. Punjab has 52,231 schools in total.

Punjab has an average pupil-to-teacher ratio of 27:1 at the primary school level, 21:1 at the upper primary school level, and 23:1 at the secondary school level. Although the sex ratio and literacy rates are biased against women, the percentage of female teachers to total teachers in schools is 70.8% (primary school), 70.3% (upper primary school), and 55.8% (secondary and higher secondary schools).

The condition of facilities and infrastructure available in the 12,997 government primary schools is pitiable. More than 1,000 schools do not have buildings of their own. Even such basic necessities as drinking water and toilets are conspicuous by their absence in many schools. Students do not have proper sitting arrangements and teachers do not have sufficient numbers of blackboards.

Private schools are definitely better than government schools in terms of infrastructure, teacher-to-student ratio, cleanliness and hygienic facilities, environment for students with a focus on personality development, and extracurricular activities. Nevertheless, admitting a child to a government school is the only option for those who cannot afford private schools, and is a better option than no schooling at all.

Other than the physical infrastructure, the most striking weaknesses in government schools are lack of motivation, outdated teaching methodology, and unskilled teachers. The prevalent teaching-learning process is ineffective for first-generation students, who do not get any academic support at their homes. Further, there is lack of relevance of education to the actual demands of daily life. A commitment toward creating and achieving the specific targets of learning and competence at different stages of education is absent. Again, there is a lack of reliable monitoring or evaluation of the education system at the state level. Although a number of schemes are formulated to improve the education system, the actual implementation and evaluation of the schemes is lacking.

India – Tamil Nadu

Tamil Nadu is India's southernmost state; it is one of the better-off states in India, with an overall literacy rate of 80.3% (female literacy rate 73.9%). It has India's highest student enrollment rate in primary- and upper-primary-level education.

Schools are classified as government, private-aided, and private-unaided. Government schools are run by the Department of Education; private-aided schools receive grant in aid from the government, but private-unaided schools do not. Of 55,667 schools in Tamil Nadu, 36,505 are government, 8,266 are private-aided, and 10,896 are private-unaided. In most government and private-aided schools, the medium of instruction is Tamil; in most private-unaided schools, the medium of instruction is English.

Besides the midday meal scheme, government school students receive welfare benefits such as free textbooks, notebooks, school bags, footwear, a bus pass, a uniform, a cycle, sanitary napkins (girls), and a laptop (grade 12 students). These schemes were launched to address the social disparities among schoolchildren and to enhance enrollment and retention.

From 2004 to 2005, the government introduced a no-grade retention policy for grades 1 to 5 (later 1 to 8) in all government and government-aided schools. This is to combat the lowering of the morale of students who are held in grade, which in many rural cases leads to the discontinuation of education and/or the beginning of child labor.

No full-time psychologists are available in government schools, but the Tamil Nadu government has taken initiatives to set up mobile counseling centers in which the students get counseling from psychologists who visit different schools in a district through mobile counseling vans.

Summary

Bullying and cyberbullying are international issues, and this is just as much so in India as in Australia, France, Germany, the Netherlands, and the United Kingdom. Awareness of the seriousness of the issue and research on these topics is now gathering pace in India, a development this book hopes to contribute to. The description of school systems in the various countries gives a context for the material presented in the following chapters.

References

Bandura, A., Barbaranelli, C., Caprara, G. V., & Pastorelli, C. (1996). Mechanisms of moral disengagement in the exercise of moral agency. *Journal of Personality and Social Psychology, 71*, 364–374.

Bauman, S., Underwood, M. K., & Card, N. (2013). Definitions: Another perspective and a proposal for beginning with cyberaggression. In S. Bauman, J., Walker, & D. Cross (eds.), *Principles of Cyberbullying Research: Definition, Methods, and Measures* (pp. 87–93). New York & London: Routledge.

Björkqvist, K. (1994). Sex differences in aggression. *Sex Roles, 30*, 177–188.

Blaya, C. (2013). *Les ados dans le cyberspace. Prises de risque et cyberviolence.* Bruxelles: De Boeck.

Chaturvedi, S. (2007, March 15). *When tradition ends at 256 kbps*. Retrieved from www.ciol.com/content/news/2007/107031517.asp.

Costabile, A. & Spears, B. A. (eds.) (2012). *The Impact of Technology on Relationships in Educational Settings*. London: Routledge.

Crick, N. R. & Grotpeter, J. K. (1995). Relational aggression, gender, and social-psychological adjustment. *Child Development, 66*, 710–722.

Daily News & Analysis – Bangalore. (2008, October 14). *Bullying high in schools in north India*. Retrieved from www.dnaindia.com/bangalore/report-bullying-high-in-schools-in-north-india-1198011.

Eisenberg, N. (2014). *Empathy-related responding: Conceptualization and relations to moral functioning*. Retrieved from https://cast.itunes.uni-muenchen.de/vod/clips/N1UmrAXqax/flash.html.

Finkelhor, D., Turner, H. A., & Hamby, S. (2012). Let's prevent peer victimization, not just bullying. *Child Abuse & Neglect, 36*, 271–274.

Fisher, H. L., Moffitt, T. E., Houts, R. M., Belsky, D. W., Arseneault, L., & Caspi, A. (2012). Bullying victimisation and risk of self harm in early adolescence: Longitudinal cohort study. *British Medical Journal, 344*, e2683.

Galen, B. R. & Underwood, M. K. (1997). A developmental investigation of social aggression among children. *Developmental Psychology, 33*, 589–600.

Greene, M. B. (2006). Bullying in schools: A plea for a measure of human rights. *Journal of Social Issues, 62*, 63–79.

Hunter, S. C., Boyle, J. M. E., & Warden, D. (2007). Perceptions and correlates of peer-victimization and bullying. *British Journal of Educational Psychology, 77*, 797–810.

Hymel, S. & Swearer, S. M. (2015). Four decades of research on school bullying: An introduction. *American Psychologist, 70*, 293–299.

Indiatime.com (2007, September 21). *Adnan Patrawala, cool dude from Orkut. It's India Time*. Retrieved from www.indiatime.com/2007/08/21/adnan-patrawala-coool-dude-fromorkut/.

Intel Security (2015). *Teens, Tweens and Technology Study*. Retrieved from http://apac.intelsecurity.com/digitalsafety/wp-content/uploads/sites/7/2015/10/Intel-Security_India-TeensTweensTechnology-2015-_National-Datasheet.pdf.

Jaishankar, K. (2009) (ed.), *International Perspectives on Crime and Justice*. New Castle, UK: Cambridge Scholars Publishing.

Jaishankar, K. & Shariff, S. (2008). Cyber bullying: A transnational perspective. In F. Schmalleger & M. Pittaro (eds.), *Crimes of the Internet* (pp. 66–83). Upper Saddle River, NJ: Prentice Hall.

Jamir, T., Devi, N. P., Lenin, R. K., Roshan, L., & Sameeta, N. (2014). The relationship between bullying victimization, self-esteem and depression among school going adolescents. *International Journal in Management and Social Science, 2*, 477–489.

Jessel, J. (2016). Educational systems: A basis for some comparative perspectives. In P. K. Smith, K. Kwak, & Y. Toda (eds.), *School Bullying in Different Cultures:*

Eastern and Western Perspectives (pp. 229–258). Cambridge: Cambridge University Press.

Judge, P. S. (2013). *Readings in Indian Sociology: Volume I: Towards Sociology of Dalits*. New Delhi: Sage Publications.

Kaur, K., Kaur, S., & Sandhu, D. (2014). Cyber bullying: An emerging threat to pupil well-being. *International Journal of Social Sciences Review, 2*, 374–377.

Kim, Y.-S. & Leventhal, B. (2008). Bullying and suicide: A review. *International Journal of Adolescent Mental Health, 20*, 133–154.

Kim, Y.-S., Leventhal, B., Koh, Y.-J., & Boyce, W. T. (2009). Bullying increased suicide risk: Prospective study of Korean adolescents. *Archives Journal of Adolescent Mental Health, 20*, 133–154.

Kowalski, R. M., Giumetti, G. W., Schroeder, A. N., & Lattanner, M. R. (2014). Bullying in the digital age: A critical review and meta-analysis of cyberbullying research among youth. *Psychological Bulletin, 140*, 1073–1137.

Kshirsagar, V. Y., Agarwal, R., & Bavdekar, S. B. (2007). Bullying in schools: Prevalence and short-term impact. *Indian Pediatrics, 44*, 25–28.

Kwak, K. & Lee, S.-H. (2016). The Korean research tradition on *wang-ta*. In P. K. Smith, K. Kwak, & Y. Toda (eds.), *School Bullying in Different Cultures: Eastern and Western Perspectives* (pp. 93–112). Cambridge: Cambridge University Press.

Lin, S.-F. & Lai, C. L. (2016). Bullying in Hong Kong schools. In P. K. Smith, K. Kwak, & Y. Toda (eds.), *School Bullying in Different Cultures: Eastern and Western Perspectives* (pp. 133–150). Cambridge: Cambridge University Press.

Livingstone, S. & Smith, P. K. (2014). Research review: Harms experienced by child users of online and mobile technologies: The nature, prevalence and management of sexual and aggressive risks in the digital age. *Journal of Child Psychology & Psychiatry, 55*, 635–654.

Malhi, P., Bharti, B., & Sidhu, M. (2014). Aggression in schools: Psychosocial outcomes of bullying among Indian adolescents. *Indian Journal of Pediatrics, 81*, 1171–1176.

Moffitt, T. (1993). Adolescence-limited and life-course-persistent antisocial behavior: A developmental taxonomy. *Psychological Review, 100*, 674–701.

Monks, C. & Coyne, I. (eds.) (2011). *Bullying in Different Contexts*. Cambridge: Cambridge University Press.

Olthof, T., Goossens, F. A., Vermande, M. M., Aleva, E. A., & Van der Meulen, M. (2011). Bullying as strategic behavior: Relations with desired and acquired dominance in the peer group. *Journal of School Psychology, 49*, 339–359.

Olweus, D. (2013). School bullying: Development and some important challenges. *Annual Review of Clinical Psychology, 9*, 751–780.

Raskauskas, J. & Stoltz, A. D. (2007). Involvement in traditional and electronic bullying among adolescents. *Developmental Psychology, 43*, 564–575.

Rivers, I., Poteat, V. P., Noret, N., & Ashurst, N. (2009). Observing bullying at school: The mental health implications of witness status. *School Psychology Quarterly, 24*, 211–223.

Rothon, C., Head, J., Klineberg, E., & Stansfeld, S. (2010). Can social support protect bullied adolescents from adverse outcomes? A prospective study on the effects of bullying on academic achievement and mental health of adolescents at secondary schools in East London. *Journal of Adolescence, 34,* 579–588.

Schäfer, M., Korn, S., Smith, P. K., Hunter, S. C., Mora-Merchán, J. A., Singer, M. M., & Van der Meulen, K. (2004). Lonely in the crowd: Recollections of bullying. *British Journal of Developmental Psychology, 22,* 379–394.

Singh, Pratap Vikram (2012, June 27). *53 percent kids in India bullied online: Microsoft survey.* Retrieved from www.governancenow.com/views/think-tanks/53-percent-kids-india-bullied-online-microsoft-survey.

Sittichai, R. & Smith, P. K. (2015). Bullying in South-East Asian countries: A review. *Aggression and Violent Behavior, 23,* 22–35.

Smith, P. K. (2014). *Understanding School Bullying: Its Nature and Prevention Strategies.* London: Sage Publications.

Smith, P. K. (2016). Research on bullying in schools in European countries. In P. K. Smith, K. Kwak, & Y. Toda (eds.), *School Bullying in Different Cultures: Eastern and Western Perspectives* (pp. 1–29). Cambridge: Cambridge University Press.

Smith, P. K. & Berkkun, F. (2017). How research on cyberbullying has developed. In C. McGuckin & L. Corcoran (eds.), *Bullying and Cyberbullying: Prevalence, Psychological Impacts and Intervention Strategies.* Hauppauge, NY: Nova Science.

Smith, P. K., Del Barrio, C. & Tokunaga, R. (2013). Definitions of bullying and cyberbullying: How useful are the terms? In S. Bauman, J. Walker, & D. Cross (eds.), *Principles of Cyberbullying Research: Definition, Methods, and Measures* (pp. 64–86). New York & London: Routledge.

Smith, P. K., Mahdavi, J., Carvalho, M., Fisher, S., Russell, S., & Tippett, N. (2008). Cyberbullying: Its nature and impact in secondary school pupils. *Journal of Child Psychology and Psychiatry, 49,* 376–385.

Spears, B. A., Costabile, A., Brighi, A., Del Rey, R., Pörhölä, M., Sanchez, V., Spiel, C., & Thompson, F. (2013). Positive uses of new technologies in relationships in educational settings. In P. K. Smith & G. Steffgen (eds.), *Cyberbullying through the New Media: Findings from an International Network* (pp.178–200). London: Psychology Press.

Srisiva, R., Thirumoorthi, R., & Sujatha, P. (2013). Prevalence and prevention of school bullying – A case study of Coimbatore City, Tamilnadu, India. *International Journal of Humanities and Social Science Invention, 2,* 36–45.

Standing Committee on Information Technology (2013–2014). *Cybercrime, Cyber Security and Right to Privacy.* 52nd Report. Fifteenth Lok Sabha. New Delhi: Lok Sabha Secretariat.

Thompson, F. & Smith, P. K. (2012). Anti-bullying strategies in schools – What is done and what works. *British Journal of Educational Psychology, Monograph Series II, 9,* 154–173.

Times of India (2007, December 12). 'Yes, I killed Abhishek.' Retrieved from http://timesofindia.indiatimes.com/city/delhi/Yes-I-killedAbhishek/article show/2617934.cms.

Times of India (2015, September 3). 'Every third child is bullied in school, shows study.' Retrieved from http://timesofindia.indiatimes.com/city/chennai/Every-third-child-is-bullied-in-school-shows-study/articleshow/48781789.cms.

Toda, Y. (2016). Bullying (*ijime*) and related problems in Japan: history and research. In P. K. Smith, K. Kwak, & Y. Toda (eds.), *School Bullying in Different Cultures: Eastern and Western perspectives* (pp. 73–92). Cambridge: Cambridge University Press.

Ttofi, M. M., Farrington, D. P., & Lösel, F. (2011). Do the victims of school bullies tend to become depressed later in life? A systematic review and meta-analysis of longitudinal studies. *Journal of Aggression, Conflict and Peace Research, 3*, 63–73.

Turner, H. A., Finkelhor, D., Shattuck, A., Hamby, S., & Mitchell, K. (2014). Beyond bullying: Aggravating elements of peer victimization episodes. *School Psychology Quarterly, 30*, 366–384.

Willard, N. (2006). *Cyberbullying and Cyberthreats.* Eugene, OR: Center for Safe and Responsible Internet Use.

Wolke, D. & Lereya, S. T. (2015). Long-term effects of bullying. *Archives of Disease in Childhood, 100*, 879–885.

Ybarra, M. L., Espelage, D. L., & Mitchell, K. J. (2014). Differentiating youth who are bullied from other victims of peer aggression: The importance of differential power and repetition. *Journal of Adolescent Health, 55*, 293–300.

Zhang, W., Chen, L., & Chen, G. (2016). Research on school bullying in mainland China. In P. K. Smith, K. Kwak, & Y. Toda (eds.), *School Bullying in Different Cultures: Eastern and Western Perspectives* (pp. 113–132). Cambridge: Cambridge University Press.

Zych, I., Ortega-Ruiz, R., & del Rey, R. (2015). Scientific research on bullying and cyberbullying: Where have we been and where are we going? *Aggression and Violent Behavior, 23*, 1–21.

2 Societal and Cultural Considerations in Understanding Peer Bullying in India

Marilyn Campbell, Margaret Kettle and Suresh Sundaram

Bullying as a repeated abuse of power in young people has often been studied from the psychological or individual student standpoint of the roles taken by the perpetrator, victim bully-victim, and bystander. In this chapter, however, we want to present a new perspective – one that foregrounds bullying as a social practice embedded in cultural values and relationships. Bronfenbrenner's *Ecological Systems Theory* states that human beings cannot be accurately understood in terms of their development and behaviours unless the whole ecological system with which they interact is taken into consideration (Bronfenbrenner, 1977). Bronfenbrenner posits four systems. The individual characteristics of students involved in bullying are examined under the *microsystem*, with the interaction between the components of this system referred to as the *mesosystem*. The *exosystem* is made up of the environment, usually the neighbourhood and community, and the *macrosystem* is the 'cultural blueprint', the social and cultural contexts which influence the interactions in the other system levels (Espelage, 2014). This chapter examines the 'cultural blueprint' of school bullying in India. The point here is that the various systems infuse and influence each other; they do not stand in isolation from each other. Recognising the 'cultural blueprint' of bullying provides understanding of the conditions that afford and mitigate persistent abusive behaviours by perpetrators on victims in a particular context.

Bullying by students in schools is a universal phenomenon (Due et al., 2005). However, although bullying has been found in every country and society in which it has been examined, there are different prevalences of student bullying in different countries (Craig et al., 2009). This has led some researchers to consider that these variations may reflect the differences in cultures and societies in which the behaviour takes place. Thus we argue that bullying needs to be viewed within specific sociocultural environments, as a means of understanding the particular definitions and reactions that certain groups bring to the issue. Socially contextualised understandings problematise the habituated practices of groups of people in their relationships to each other and is a productive springboard for change. Integral to this approach is the recognition that social change is associated with shifting norms and expectations of acceptable behaviour. In this chapter we examine normative cultural expectations and their manifestations between social groups in India. Of particular interest is peer bullying in schools. In line with the view of the editors of this volume, we note the shift at an international level towards the individualisation of rights and the right of each student to expect safety, inclusion, well-being, and access to academic achievement at school. The aim of our chapter is to present bullying as a sociocultural phenomenon with particular interest in the Indian context and its alignments and implications for other countries such as Australia.

We start by presenting different perspectives on culture and how culture accounts for the daily practices of people, including their social relationships and behaviours. We then look at the specific case of India: its history, its current dynamism as an economic power, and its cultural traditions and changes. We are interested in the ways that the prevailing cultural conditions might contribute to unrecognised, normalised practices of marginalisation and bullying, but also how identification can make these practices visible and contribute to greater critical awareness. Our argument is that critical awareness constitutes noticing and a type of knowing that is the necessary first step to addressing peer bullying across social groups in Indian schools.

Defining Culture

Culture is a cross-disciplinary, abstract and multifaceted concept which requires alternate explanations to understand its application to the complex social relationship which is bullying. Canvassing around 140 years of Anglo-American thinking, Lo Bianco (2003) maps the following representations and revisions of the culture concept:

- culture as high arts and civilising thoughts that distinguish personal and social existence;
- culture as the province of the exotic and the different, with inventories of categories that differentiate one culture from the next, mostly 'them' from 'us';
- culture as the ordinary, unmarked social life of a collective group: its institutions, arts and taken-for-granted practices that are both historically-derived and dynamically responsive to change (Williams, 1958);

- culture as the shared symbols and meanings of a collective group which are learned and transmitted; human action and behaviour is patterned and imbued with meaning (Geertz, 1973);
- culture with a focus on change, 'travel' and hybridity as fundamental principles (Clifford, 1992);
- culture as a verb, that is, people enacting culture through what they do; culture is constructed in the everyday interactions of people (Street, 1993).

The synthesis of these approaches to culture is that there are universal principles that constitute culture, e.g., it is shared and learned and is therefore a collective activity. However, culture is also unstable, constantly in process and undergoing change from within and from without. In short, culture as a concept refers to 'behaviour that is patterned, learned and social, but also changing, and constructed, sometimes "in the moment" as hybrid compromises of values are produced, such as in interaction between people of widely varying backgrounds interacting with each other' (Lo Bianco, 2003, p. 25).

As culture is a learned and transmitted activity, social relationships and socialisation processes are highly relevant. While the family is considered the primary locus of socialisation, schooling is a prevalent and powerful form of secondary socialisation. A central tool for both of these processes, but not the sole one, is communication, that is, language.

Analysing Culture: Conundrums and Critiques

Culture is avoided in some disciplines because of concerns about reductivism and essentialisation. Yet as shown earlier in this chapter, culture as a concept can accommodate understandings of both tradition and change. At times, it becomes necessary to explore both the universal and culture-specific aspects of meaning, such as in our exploration of bullying in contemporary Indian culture. The approaches to culture presented earlier indicate that we are all embedded in the everyday-ness of our own cultures and it is incumbent on us to recognise this and make it explicit. As authors of this chapter, the three of us are conversant with the cultural practices of the Western academy; two of us enact these practices as everyday actions and interactions while one of us enacts the practices in India.

We acknowledge that since we cannot place ourselves inside every culture, it is crucial that we avoid talking about other cultures through our own. The conundrum is how to talk about other cultures in a way that does not distort them into our own cultural likeness but rather foregrounds their culture-specific features. It is in isolating the universal and the culture-specific that valuable insights can be gained and possibilities for change generated.

Diversity of Indian Culture

While India is a large country by geographical size and population, it is also extremely diverse with 29 different states and seven union territories (Singh et al., 2003). The country also has many languages and has a complex linguistic story, especially post colonialism by the British. While Hindi is the designated official language, English – the former colonial language – has 'associate' official language status (Iyer, Kettle, Luke & Mills, 2014). English was retained as a tool for building a modern, industrial and secular future for India (Sonntag, 2000); it is widely spoken and generally taught in schools. In addition to the national languages, the constitution acknowledges major regional and state languages.

Indian society is also diverse culturally with extremely complex social interactions and values, especially between the north and south (Skrzypiec, Slee & Sandhu, 2015). Indeed, the legislating of English as a national 'associate' official language was also related to the postcolonial search for national unity. The inclusion of English was a language policy decision designed to allay southern Indian concerns about the adoption of Hindi as the official language of India (Iyer et al., 2014). The economic growth of India is also creating more diversity with a greater economic division between rural and urban India. India is a re-emerging economy, as together with China it was one of the biggest economies in the world for the past 2,000 years (Pereiva & Malik, 2015). The following discussion of Indian culture acknowledges this diversity.

Wierzbicka's Cultural Analysis Framework

Several frameworks have been developed which attempt to explain cultures in an independent way. Wierzbicka (2003) proposes a culture-independent analytical framework using speech acts such as advice, opinions and exclamations. Her argument is that cultural values are reflected in speech acts. Cultural values include cordiality, courtesy and objectivism. Cross-cultural comparisons are often made based on labels such as self-assertion, directness, individualism, solidarity or collectivism.

Yet these concepts often derive from Anglo-Saxon cultural values represented through English ways of speaking. In practice the concepts are understood and enacted differently in different cultures. For example, the concept of 'solidarity' in Israeli culture is different from, although related to the Australian concept of 'mateship', but different from the Japanese understanding of 'dependence' and 'groupism' (Wierzbicka, 2003, p. 91). The implication for analysis is that these concepts are practised differently and cannot be simply determined as versions of the cultural value of solidarity.

The Language of Bullying

Controversy over language, that is, the definitions of bullying, are rife among researchers (Espelage & Horne, 2008) and also vary from country to country (Murray-Harvey, Slee & Taki, 2010). As bullying is a complex social relationship problem, there are many different behaviours involved, often grouped by physical, verbal, exclusion and cyber acts. Detail of each possible behaviour is impractical so definitions are usually broad, such as a repeated abuse of power or behaviours intended to hurt, which are usually repeated where there is an imbalance of power between the participants.

The language around bullying is complicated further when the English word for bullying is translated into other languages (Smorti, Menesini & Smith, 2003). We know that this concept may change when it is embedded in different linguistic contexts (even when English is spoken in a particular country) and cultural structures (Smith, Cowie, Olafsson & Liefooghe, 2002). In their study asking children to define bullying using stick cartoon figures, which eliminated language, Smith and colleagues found there were still differences in various countries. In England bullying was related to severe physical and verbal aggression while in other countries it was associated more with social exclusion than with physical acts (Smith et al., 2002). The same stick cartoon figures were used to assess adults' understanding of bullying in a subsequent study, where it was found that although the adults mainly agreed with researchers' definitions of bullying, there were still different emphases in different countries (Smorti et al., 2003).

The word *bullying* is not familiar in the Indian context. Instead, bullying is denoted by different terms specific to physical, verbal and relational forms, such as, in the Tamil language *Tākkutal, Keli* and *Purakanital* are the words used for physical, verbal and relational types of bullying (see Chapter 4 for more details).

Some people use the terms *ragging* and *Eve teasing* to denote bullying-related behaviour in India. However, the term *ragging* is used only in the context of college students where senior students tease and harass junior students, usually at the time of freshers' entry into college, similar to hazing in America. *Eve teasing* is a specific form of teasing where a male teases a female. *Adam teasing* is when a female teases a male, but this is a relatively rare phenomenon. Eve teasing normally happens in public places, not in schools or colleges, as the males and females are not known to each other in this form of bullying. The men intend to seek the females' attention or make fun of them, using vulgar words, unwanted sexual remarks or physical touch, similar to sexual harassment.

Hofstede's Value Dimensions across Cultures

Another way of conceptualising culture is Hofstede's value dimensions. This well-known framework emanated from cross-cultural management studies (Hofstede, 1980, 1991) and originally had four value dimensions that are argued as universal and significantly impactful in all cultures. These dimensions are individualism-collectivism, uncertainty avoidance, power distance, and masculinity and femininity. In subsequent work, the dimensions of long-term orientation, short-term orientation and indulgence-restraint have been added to this framework (Hofstede, Hofstede & Minkov, 2010; Hofstede & Minkov, 2010). These value preferences refer to cultures as a collectivity; they are described as the shared national values of a society. These concepts could also be applied as a framework for the risk and mitigating factors for bullying behaviour in students.

Individualism and Collectivism

The individualism-collectivism value dimension describes the relationship of the individual and the collective or group. *Individualism* recognises the individual as the most important unit in any social setting. An 'I' consciousness prevails. Countries that tend towards individualism include Australia, Canada, France, Germany, Great Britain, the Netherlands and the United States. The focus is on nation states as 'large' cultures (Holliday, 1999). The argument is that these cultures prioritise individual achievement and initiative. *Collectivism*, on the other hand, foregrounds social groups and presents in cultures with rigid social frameworks for distinguishing in-groups and out-groups (Samovar, Porter & Stefani, 1998). Collective societies include Pakistan, China and Peru, where people are born into large groups that support them in exchange for loyalty. India has also been categorised as a collectivist country, more so than Western countries, although not so much as many other Eastern countries (Hofstede, 1980; Kakar & Kakar, 2007).

This dimension of culture on whether more value is placed on individualism or collectivism (e.g. Hofstede, 1980, 1991; Hofstede et al., 2010) has been the one most applied to studies on bullying. Children in individualistic cultures are encouraged to develop autonomy and self-expression and to be competitive (Hofstede et al., 2010), whereas children in collectivist cultures are likely encouraged to exercise behavioural and emotional control, maintain group harmony and avoid confrontation (Green, Deschamps & Paez, 2005). The prevalence of bullying in collectivist countries such as China has been found to be lower than in individualism-orientated countries (Forbes, Zhang, Doroszewicz & Haas, 2009; Ji, Zhang & Jones, 2016). This has also been shown to be the case with cyberbullying (Barlett et al., 2014). However, this cultural dimension applied to bullying has not been extensively researched in India. In Bergmuller's study (2013) of 62 countries and individualism and collectivism's values in relation to aggression, India was not included. A recent study in adults concluded that participants from Turkey, China and India, classed as collectivist cultures, were less affected by social exclusion than participants from the individualistic country of Germany (Pfundmair et al., 2015). Other studies, however, have not found that collectivism and individualism are linked to the incidence of bullying. In a study of students' attitudes to bullying and helping those victimised, there was no correlation between collectivist Japanese students and individualistic Australian students (Nesdale & Nato, 2005). The authors attributed this to Japan not being strongly collectivistic (Hofstede, 1991). Alternatively, they argued that the dichotomous variable of collectivism and individualism is too simplistic and limited and instead there is more within-culture heterogeneity, which can explain cultural variation (Harkness, Super & van Tijen, 2000).

In applying this concept of collectivism and individualistic values to India, it is interesting to note that some researchers maintain that India is both collective and individualistic at both the societal and individual levels (Sinha & Tripathi, 2002; Verma, 2004). Another point of view is that although India was a collectivist country, it is now becoming more individualist because of the economic reforms propelling India as one of the world's fastest-growing economies, which has enhanced the pace of social change and is changing some cultural values (Arulmari, 2007). Thus, while tolerance and connectedness are valued as in other collectivist cultures depending on the demands of the situation, individualism could prevail (Sinha & Tripathi, 2002).

Uncertainty Avoidance

Uncertainty avoidance references the degree to which a culture is susceptible to anxiety about uncertain and ambiguous situations. High-uncertainty-avoidance cultures are those that take measures to avoid ambiguity and uncertainty. Responses include the establishment of formal rules, the seeking of consensus, the belief in absolute truths and the lack of tolerance for deviant ideas. This provides society with stability and predictability (Samovar et al., 1998). In contrast, low-uncertainty-avoidance cultures are those that accept uncertainty and tolerate deviance. There is a dislike of structure associated with hierarchy and a valuing of initiative.

Indian society with industrialisation and British occupation coinciding reflects a combination of traditional Indian values and Western philosophy. Indian society is considered pluralist, but it is not liberal (Beteille, 2006). While the Indian values of tolerance, sensitivity and connectedness are mitigating factors against school bullying (Kukar & Kukar, 2007), the hierarchical system of caste is a risk factor. The caste system traditionally divides India into hereditary, hierarchical groups following specific occupations. The word *caste* comes from the Portuguese *casta*, meaning race (Devi, 1999). Brahims are the highest caste; Scheduled Castes are the lowest, with Scheduled Tribes the original inhabitants (Upreti, 2007). While the caste system is not as strong as it was in the past, social class, based on education, money and status, is now dividing Indian society (Sreekanth, 2009). Tolerance of deviance is not strong in India. However, with globalisation and national assimilation, society is changing (Kudva, 2003).

Power Distance

Power distance is another of Hofstede's cultural value dimensions that pertains to the extent to which a culture accepts that power is distributed unequally in social relationships, organisations and institutions such as schools. In this framework, India is identified as a high-power-distance culture (Samovar et al., 1998; Verma, 2004). The pervasive understanding is that people are not equal and that everyone has their ascribed position in the social hierarchy. Low-power-distance countries, on the other hand, subscribe to the notion that inequality in society should be minimised and that everyone should have access to power.

This cultural dimension in Indian society could be considered a very real risk of the acceptance of bullying as the imbalance of power is a central concept to the understanding of bullying as a subset of aggression (Smith & Sharp, 1994). Power can be positional or personal and can be used for good and the benefit of society. However, having power can also lead to an abuse of such power, especially if the power is gained from ascribed status and based on age, gender, caste, occupation, class or ethnicity (Beteille, 2006; Sundaram & Tendulkar, 2003). This system of society may promote manipulative and corrupt behaviours (D'Cruz, 2012) and together with a fatalistic outlook can lead to apathy and hopelessness in the 'out-groups', which can foster a sense of power-lessness (Verma, 2004). It has been shown that bullying is seen as standard behaviour and more accepted in the workplace in high-power-distance cultures that accepted hierarchically based power disparity (Loh, Restubog & Zagenczyk, 2010).

Social affiliations provide belonging and support, but Indian social networking is also characterised by in-group (*apra*) and out-group (*parya*) distinctions (Kakar & Kakar, 2007; Verma, 2004) based on the hierarchical systems which underpin Indian society. In-groups and out-groups are based on caste, class, ethnicity, kinship, region, religion and occupation (Beteille, 2006). Thus there is much nepotism and favourit-ism, with out-group members being discriminated against, with interper-sonal and intergroup conflict (Agnes, 2002; Hutnik, 2004). There is, furthermore, abuse of power through authoritarianism and coercion (Tripathi, 1990). Although individuals belong to a variety of groups, this cultural dimension could be a risk factor for bullying, although it has not yet been researched.

Masculinity and Femininity

The fourth dimension in Hofstede's model is masculinity and femininity, which refers to the degree to which the culture orientates to so-called masculine or feminine characteristics. Masculinity is associated with behaviours such as achievement, differentiated sex roles and acquisition of money. Femininity is aligned with more fluid sex roles, shared caring roles, modesty and interpersonal harmony. Spiritualism, compassion, duty and service form a large part of the Indian ethos (Verma, 2004), which are cultural values mitigating against bullying. However, paternal-ism is an important cornerstone of Indian culture and society (Sinah, 1982, 1994). Men in particular still espouse patriarchal world views.

Long-Term versus Short-Term Orientation

Later work has seen the inclusion of long- versus short-term orientation (Hofstede & Minkov, 2010; Hofstede et al., 2010). This dimension focusses on whether people's efforts are dynamic and future-focussed or static and focussing on the present and the past. A future focus orientates to perseverance and thrift, while a present/past focus values respect for tradition and fulfilling social obligations. In high-long-term orientation cultures, having humility and a sense of shame are important for both genders. India is classified as a long-term-oriented culture (Hofstede et al., 2010). For school bullying, this could be a protective factor where social obligations and norms discourage bullying, but this has not been researched to date.

Indulgence versus Restraint

The final dimension of indulgence versus restraint appears in later work (e.g. Hofstede et al., 2010) Indulgence is characterised by the perception that acting as one pleases, spending money, having leisure and fun leads to happiness, while at the opposite end of the continuum, restraint involves the perception that one's actions should be restrained by social norms and prohibitions and that indulgence in spending money and having fun is wrong. Indulgence is the belief in enjoyment and fun while restraint is the belief that gratification needs to be controlled and regulated. India has a middle ranking for this dimension, although there is a slight tendency for more hierarchical societies to be more indulgent (Hofstede et al., 2010). Societal cynicism also correlates with indulgence versus restraint where the view is that 'powerful people are arrogant exploiters of less powerful individuals' (Hofstede et al., 2010, p. 289). This could be seen a risk factor for school bullying in India, but there is no existing research.

Not surprisingly, criticisms have been levelled at Hofstede's work. These include a lack of rigour in his original study in the 1980s, as well as the orientation of the study to management studies, as the people Hofstede surveyed were middle managers in large multinational organisations (Samovar et al., 1998). There are also criticisms that the study did not include Arab countries and was not extensive in Africa. Moreover, the study was conducted in the 1980s with questions about its relevance to 21st-century conditions of globalisation, interconnectedness, and mobility being a concern. However, Hofstede's recent work with colleagues in 2010 has addressed many of these criticisms. Finally, as noted earlier in this chapter, there are charges that the framework operates in dichotomies and cannot accommodate heterogeneity and variation (e.g. Harkness et al., 2000). This argument is especially relevant in a context such as India, which is currently undergoing dramatic economic and cultural change.

Holliday's Large and Small Cultures

Wierzbicka and Hofstede's frameworks for investigating cultures deal with what Holliday (1999) calls 'large' cultures: the frameworks reference culture at the national, international and ethnic levels. Holliday's argument is that this large culture approach risks reductionist overgeneralisation and 'otherisation' of difference. Rather he proposes a 'small' culture approach which looks more closely at cohesive social groupings and frees the concept of culture from referencing only nations or ethnic groups.

Small cultures are not subsets of large cultures, that is, they are not so-called subcultures which have an onion-skin type relationship with large cultures. Rather Holliday's conceptualisation of small cultures is that they pertain to types of social groupings and may, indeed, extend beyond the borders of a large culture such as a nation. An example is schools, class-rooms and teachers, small cultures that despite national differences are similar throughout the world. School seating arrangements and teacher–student interactions are similar in many different contexts. The similarities are due to colonial and postcolonial, and more latterly, standardising global influences, and constitute a small culture with its own inherent histories, meanings and practices.

Small cultures become a way of understanding cultural coherence between and within large cultures. Research within a small culture approach is non-essentialising and concerned with processes, that is, interpretation of the discernible behaviours and understandings that exist within the social group. The complex factors that form a small culture include: (i) the purpose of the group as a cohesive unit; (ii) the cultural influences such as the nation, family and institution; (iii) social constructions such as routines; and (iv) products and associated artefacts. A small culture approach provides a means of analysing behaviours and activities of a social group, which means a middle or meso/mezzo-level focus at the level of the institution. This focus on the institution allows for more detailed, nuanced and particular investigations of practices.

Holliday (1999) provides an example of a small culture approach to researching a British Council aid–based textbook project at the University of Pune in India. British and Indian personnel worked together on the project, during which, despite sensitivity to the potential for the imposition of culturally imperialistic foreign ideas, conflicts arose. Holliday argues that a large culture perspective would interpret the problems as national versus international, for example, confrontation between British and Indian ways of thinking and the threat of new forms of Western colonialism. In contrast, a small culture approach was adopted and found that the problems were more complex and unexpected. Most of the personnel involved with the project – British Council staff, university academics, evaluation consultants – were Indian. A key problem was the mismatch between the institutional cultures of the instrumentally oriented British Council and the academically oriented university English department.

The argument is that the small culture approach enabled the various participants to recognise their cultural affiliations and imperatives as a first step towards making decisions and resolving the problems. In the context of this volume and more specifically, our chapter, it is crucial that bullying as a set of behaviours be investigated and understood at a level more intimate than the 'large' nation-based Indian level. A small culture approach will enable deeper understandings at the institutional level of the family and the school. We acknowledge that bullying by students in schools is a universal, cross-national phenomenon (Modecki et al., 2014). Through this approach, analysis can reveal common characteristics within the 'small' culture of families and schools across the world. In addition, it can provide insights into the specific variables (national, institutional, familial) that influence behaviours and actions of bullying in India. Keeping these foci separate goes some way towards avoiding essentialism and new forms of colonialism.

Family and School as 'Small Culture'

The Family

The family is one of the main socialising institutions in society. India, like most other less industrialised, traditional, Eastern societies, is a collectivist society that emphasises family integrity, loyalty and unity. The Indian family is considered strong, stable, close, resilient and enduring (Shangle, 1995). Historically, the traditional, ideal and desired family in India was the joint family (Chekki, 1996) which included three to four generations, of uncles, aunts, nieces, nephews and grandparents living together in the same household (Nandan & Eames, 1980). The types of kinships and opportunities of shared living enabled children to effectively deal with the world outside the home and family, and hence peer relationships were generally considered amiable and were not a concern in traditional Indian society. However, with society changing, the nuclear family is growing (Census of India, 2011), and there seems to be more concern with children's peer relationships. As most parents now work full time outside the family, it has been hypothesised that these children may lack emotional intelligence and community living values. It has been shown that children from nuclear families experience more bullying victimisation than children from joint families (Sundaram, 2014).

The family is also the social institution in which children first learn about relationships. Unfortunately, in India as in many other parts of the world, there is physical violence within the family, with mothers in India reporting the highest rates of severe physical punishment of hitting children with objects, kicking and choking them (Sadowski, Hunter, Bandiwala & Munoz, 2004). Family violence has been shown to lead to increases in physical and non-physical bullying (Low & Espelage, 2013).

Another factor which has been shown to correlate with students' involvement in bullying is witnessing or experiencing inter-parental conflict in the home. In addition, witnessing inter-parental violence and child maltreatment can co-occur in the same families (Casanueva, Martin & Runyan, 2009). There is evidence for the relationship between parental conflict and being a victim and also a perpetrator of traditional bullying (Baker, 2012; Christie-Mizell, 2003). It is proposed that this could occur because of observation and modelling. Children may learn and adopt bullying behaviours in a family environment where parental arguments and conflicts are common.

In the northern Indian state of Uttar Pradesh extremely high levels of domestic violence have been reported (Martin, Tsui, Maitra & Marinshaw, 1999). In another study in north-eastern India in the state of Tripura it was found that out of 320 urban secondary school students, 30% reported witnessing inter-parental violence, while one fifth had experienced physical violence at home, one-fifth psychological violence and 18% sexual violence (Deb & Walsh, 2012). This situation, while not confined to India, could be a risk factor for peer bullying.

The School

Schools are a reflection of society, a microcosm, and thus we would expect to see Indian culture embodied in the schools. India has almost 87 million students attending nearly a million schools (National Council of Educational Research and Training, 2005). While the central government has control over the curriculum, there are two school systems, public and government-run. Public schools, as in England, are privately managed, are usually in urban areas, are established for profit and all subjects are taught in English. Government-run schools have low fees, are mainly in poorer rural areas, enrol children from diverse backgrounds and have a much higher teacher-to-pupil ratio than public schools (Sreekarth, 2009).

In many Indian schools promotion is not by age, it is by merit, and thus there are often varying ages in the same class. Students who struggle academically are often older than their classmates, and many of these students persistently bully others (Jangra, 2005). This practice could be a risk factor for peer bullying in schools. Harsh discipline by teachers in many government-run schools is also a risk factor for peer bullying (Sreekarth, 2009).

The government of India has made free primary education for all children a priority as a means of modernising India and trying to break down the divisions of caste and class (Thirumurthy, 2005). However, girls are often disadvantaged either by not being sent to school by their families or by encountering sexual harassment and bullying when they attend school (Leach & Sitaram, 2007). Boys and girls usually sit separately in classrooms, in rural schools on separate sides of the room and in urban schools on alternative benches. Girls are forbidden to attend school while menstruating. In a qualitative study, secondary school girls in the state of Karnataka, in southern India, identified their main concern about school was bullying by boys. Of even more concern to the girls was the harassment from older boys outside school when they were travelling to and from school. The girls did not tell their parents for fear of being withdrawn from school or their teachers, as the teachers considered the bullying and harassment 'part of growing up', just harmless mild teasing (Leach & Sitaram, 2007). Gender norms relating to female acquiescence and modesty, especially after puberty, combined with concern for family reputation and marriage prospects means these issues are not discussed. Patriarchal attitudes with the social mechanisms of caste, class and religion are risk factors for peer bullying in India.

Conclusion

Bullying amongst students is a universal phenomenon. However, this relationship behaviour is always enacted in the context of culture and thus culture-specific dimensions must be taken into account when researching bullying. Furthermore, prevention and intervention work also needs to be culturally meaningful in order to be effective. In this chapter the 'cultural blueprint' of bullying was examined using Wierzbicka's cultural analysis framework, then at the macro level by Hofstede's model of six value dimensions and at the 'small' culture level using Holliday's theory. These theoretical concepts were applied as risk and protective factors to both research and hypotheses on school bullying in India. We hope this chapter helps the reader to situate the rest of the chapters in this book on bullying within the Indian culture.

References

Agnes, F. (2002). Transgressing boundaries of gender and identity. *Economic and Political Weekly*, 3695–3698.

Arulmani, G. (2007). Counselling psychology in India: At the confluence of two traditions. *Applied Psychology: An International Review*, 56, 69–82.

Baker, S. K. (2012). Peer victimization as it relates to interparental conflict, friendship support and anxiety. ProQuest LLC, PhD Dissertation, Auburn University (ED546664).

Barlett, C., Gentile, D., Anderson, C., Suzuki, K., Sakamoto, A., Yamaoka, A. & Katsura, R. (2014). Cross-cultural differences in cyberbullying behaviour: A short-term longitudinal study. *Journal of Cross-Cultural Psychology*, 45, 300–313. doi: 10.1177/0022022113504622

Bergmuller, S. (2013). The relationship between cultural individualism-collectivism and student aggression across 62 countries. *Aggressive Behavior*, 39, 182–220. doi: 10.1002/ab/21472

Beteille, A. (2006). *Ideology and Social Science*. New Delhi: Penguin.

Bronfenbrenner, U. (1977). Toward an experimental ecology of human development. *American Psychologist*, 32, 513–531.

Casanueva, C., Martin, S. L. & Runyan, D. (2009). Repeated reports for child maltreatment among intimate partner violence victims: Findings from the national survey of child and adolescent well-being. *Child Abuse and Neglect*, 33, 84–93. doi: 10.1016/j.chiabu.2007.04.017

Census of India (2011). Available at www.censusindia.net/.

Chekki, D. A. (1996). Family values and family change. *Journal of Comparative Family Studies*, 27, 409–411.

Christie-Mizell, C. A. (2003). Bullying: The consequences of interparental discord and child's self-concept. *Family Process*, 42, 237–251.

Clifford, J. (1992). Traveling cultures. In L. Grossberg, C. Nelson & P. Treichler (eds.), *Cultural Studies* (pp. 96–112). New York: Routledge.

Craig, W., Harel-Fisch, Y., Fogel-Grinvald, H., Dostaler, S., Hetland, J. … HBSC Bullying Writing Group (2009). A cross-national profile of bullying and victimization among adolescents in 40 countries. *International Journal of Public Health*, 54, S216–S224. doi: 10.1007/s0038-009-5413-9

D'Cruz, P. (2012). *Workplace Bullying in India*. New Delhi: Routledge.

Deb, S. & Walsh, K. (2012). Impact of physical, psychological, and sexual violence on social adjustment of school children in India. *School Psychology International*, 33, 391–415. doi: 10.1177/0143034311425225

Devi, S. (1999). *Caste System in India*. Jaipur: Pointer Publishers.

Due, P., Holstein, B. E., Lynch, J., Diderichsen, F., Gabhain, S. … Currie, C. (2005). Bullying and symptoms among school-aged children: International comparative cross sectional study in 28 countries. *European Journal of Public Health*, 15, 128–132. doi: 10.1093/eurpub/cki105

Espelage, D. L. (2014). Ecological theory: Preventing youth bullying, aggression, and victimization. *Theory into Practice*, *53*, 257–264. doi: 10.1080/00405841.2014.947216

Espelage, D. & Horne, A. (2008). School violence and bullying prevention: From research based explanations to empirically based solutions. In S. Brown & R. Lent (eds.), *Handbook of Counselling Psychology* (pp. 588–606). Hoboken, NJ: Wiley.

Forbes, G., Zhang, X., Doroszewicz, K. & Haas, K. (2009). Relationships between individualism-collectivism, gender, and direct or indirect aggression: A study in China, Poland and the US. *Aggressive Behavior*, *35*, 24–30. doi: 10.1002/ab.20292

Geertz, C. (1973). *The Interpretation of Cultures*. London: Hutchinson.

Green, E., Deschamps, J. & Paez, D. (2005). Variation of individualism and collectivism within and between 20 countries: A typological analysis. *Journal of Cross-Cultural Psychology*, *36*, 321–339. doi: 10.1177/0022022104273654

Harkness, S., Super, C. & van Tijen, N. (2000). Individualism and the 'Western mind' reconsidered: American and Dutch parents' ethnotheories of the child. In S. Harkness, C. Raeff & C. M. Super (eds.), *New Directions for Children Development: No 86. Variability in the Social Construction of the Child* (pp. 23–40). San Francisco, CA: Jossey-Bass.

Hofstede, G. (1980). *Culture's Consequences: International Differences in Work-Related Values*. Beverly, CA: Sage Publications.

Hofstede, G. (1991). *Cultures and Organisations: Software of the Mind*. London: McGraw-Hill.

Hofstede, G., Hofstede, G. J. & Minkov, M. (2010). *Cultures and Organisations: Software of the Mind* (3rd edn.). New York: McGraw-Hill.

Hofstede, G. & Minkov, M. (2010). Long- versus short-term orientation: New perspectives. *Asia Pacific Business Review*, *16*(4), 493–504. doi.org/10.1080/13602381003637609

Holliday, A. (1999). Small cultures. *Applied Linguistics*, *20*, 237–264.

Hutnik, N. (2004). An intergroup perspective on ethnic minority identity. In J. Pandey (ed.), *Psychology in India Revisited: Developments in the Discipline, Vol. 3: Applied Social and Organisational Psychology* (pp. 216–260). Thousand Oaks, CA: Sage Publications.

Iyer, R., Kettle, M., Luke, A. & Mills, K. (2014). Critical applied linguistics. In C. Leung & B. V. Street (eds.), *The Routledge Companion to English Studies* (pp. 317–332). London: Routledge.

Jangra, A. L. (2005). *Education of the Slow Learner and the Retarded*. New Delhi: Arise Publishers.

Ji, L., Zhang, W. & Jones, K. (2016). Children's experiences of and attitudes towards bullying and victimization: A cross-cultural comparison between China and England. In P. K. Smith, K. Kwak & Y. Toda (eds.), *School Bullying in Different Cultures: Eastern and Western Perspectives* (pp. 170–188). Cambridge: Cambridge University Press.

Kakar, S. & Kakar, K. (2007). *The Indians*. New Delhi: Penguin.

Kudva, N. (2003). Engineering elections: The experiences of women in Panchayati Raj in Karnataka, India. *International Journal of Politics, Culture, and Society, 16,* 445–463.

Leach, F. & Sitaram, S. (2007). Sexual harassment and abuse of adolescent school girls in South India. *Education, Citizenship and Social Justice, 2,* 257–277. doi: 10.1177/1746197907081262

Lo Bianco, J. (2003). Culture: Visible, invisible and multiple. In J. Lo Bianco & C. Crozet (eds.), *Teaching Invisible Culture: Classroom Practice and Theory* (pp. 11–35). Melbourne: Language Australia.

Loh, J., Restubog, S. L. & Zagenczyk, T. J. (2010). Consequences of workplace bullying on employee identification and satisfaction among Australians and Singaporeans. *Journal of Cross-Cultural Psychology, 41,* 236–252. doi: 10.1177/0022022109354641

Low, S. & Espelage, D. (2013). Differentiating cyber bullying perpetration from non-physical bullying: Commonalities across race, individual and family predictors. *Psychology of Violence, 3,* 39–52. doi: 10.1037/a0030308

Martin, S. L., Tsui, A. O., Maitra, K. & Marinshaw, R. (1999). Domestic violence in northern India. *American Journal of Epidemiology, 150,* 417–426.

Modecki, K., Minchin, J., Harbaugh, A., Guerra, N. & Runions, K. (2014). Bullying prevalence across contexts: A meta-analysis measuring cyber and traditional bullying. *Journal of Adolescent Health, 55,* 602–611. doi: 10.1016/j.adohealth.2014.06.007

Murray-Harvey, R., Slee, P. T. & Taki, M. (2010). Comparative and cross-cultural research on school bullying. In S. R. Jimerson, S. M. Swearer & D. L. Espelage (eds.), *Handbook of Bullying in Schools: An International Perspective* (pp. 35–47). New York: Routledge/Taylor & Francis.

Nandan, Y. & Eames, E. (1980). Typology and analysis of the Asian-Indian family. In P. Saran & E. Eames (eds.), *The New Ethnics: Asian Indians in the United States.* New York: Praeger.

National Council of Educational Research and Training (2005). *National Curriculum Framework.* New Delhi: National Council of Educational Research and Training.

Nesdale, D. & Naito, M. (2005). Individualism-collectivism and the attitudes to school bullying of Japanese and Australian students. *Journal of Cross-Cultural Psychology, 36,* 537–556. doi: 10.1177/0022022105278541

Pereira, V. & Malik, A. (2015). Making sense and identifying aspects of Indian culture(s) in organisations: Demystifying through empirical evidence. *Culture and Organisation, 21,* 355–365. doi: 10.1080/14759551.2015.1082265

Pfundmair, M., Aydin, N., Du, H., Yeung, S., Frey, D. & Graupmann, V. (2015). Exclude me if you can: Cultural effects on the outcomes of social exclusion. *Journal of Cross-Cultural Psychology, 46,* 579–596. doi: 10.1177/0022022115571203

Sadowski, L., Hunter, W., Bandiwala, S. & Munoz, S. (2004). The world studies of abuse in the family environment (WorldSAFE): A model of a multi-national study of family violence. *International Journal of Injury Control and Safety Promotion*, *11*, 81–90.

Samovar, L. A., Porter, R. & Stefani, L. A. (1998). *Communication between Cultures* (3rd edn.). Belmont: Wadsworth.

Shangle, S. (1995). A view into the family and social life in India. *Family Perspective*, *29*, 423–446.

Singh, S., Barkhordarian, A., Beech, C., Harding, P., Hole, A., Bindloss, J. & Vidgen, L. (2003). *India*. London: Lonely Planet.

Sinha, D. & Tripathi, R. C. (2002). Individualism in a collectivist culture. In A. Dalal & G. Mishra (eds.), *New Directions in Indian Psychology* (pp. 241–257). New Delhi: Sage Publications.

Sinha, J. B. (1982). *The Nurturant Task Leader*. New Delhi: Concept.

Sinha, J. B. (1994). Power dynamics in Indian organizations. In R. N. Kanungo & M. Mendonca (eds.), *Work Motivation* (pp. 213–229). New Delhi: Sage Publications.

Skrzypiec, G., Slee, P. & Sandhu, D. (2015). Using the photostory method to understand the cultural context of youth victimisation in the Punjab. *International Journal of Emotional Education*, *7*, 52–68.

Smith, P. K., Cowie, H., Olafsson, R. F. & Liefooghe, A. P. (2002). Definitions of bullying: A comparison of terms used, and age and gender differences, in a fourteen-country international comparison. *Child Development*, *73*, 1119–1133.

Smith, P. K. & Sharp, S. (eds.) (1994). *School Bullying: Insights and Perspectives*. London: Routledge.

Smorti, A., Menesini, E. & Smith, P. K. (2003). Parents' definitions of children's bullying in a five-country comparison. *Journal of Cross-Cultural Psychology*, *34*, 417–443. doi: 10.1177/022022103254163

Sonntag, S. K. (2000). Ideology and policy in the politics of English language in North India. In T. Ricento (ed.), *Ideology, Politics, and Language Policies: Focus on English* (pp. 133–149). Amsterdam: John Benjamins.

Sreekanth, Y. (2009). Bullying: An element accentuating social segregation. *Education 3–13*, *37*, 233–245. doi: 10.1080/030042708002349463

Street, B. V. (1993). Culture is a verb: Anthropological aspects of language and cultural process. In D. Graddol, L. Thompson & M. Byram (eds.), *Language and Culture* (pp. 23–43). Clevedon, UK: BAAL in association with Multilingual Matters.

Sundaram, K. & Tendulkar, S. D. (2003). Poverty among social and economic groups in India in the 1990s. *Economic and Political Weekly*, 5263–5276.

Sundaram, S. (2014). *Social Skills Training Programme: A Classwide Group Intervention to Combat School Bullying*. Unpublished project final report (2012–2013) submitted to ICSSR, Annamalai University, Tamil Nadu, India.

Thirumuthy, V. (2005). Sensitive classroom issues. *Childhood Education*, *81*, 292.

Tripathi, R. C. (1990). Interplay of values in the functioning of Indian organizations. *International Journal of Psychology*, *25*(3–6), 715–734.

Upreti, H. C. (2007). *Indian tribes – Then and now*. Jaipur: Pointer Publishers.

Verma, J. (2004). Social values. In J. Pandey (ed.), *Psychology in India Revisited* (pp. 60–117). New Delhi: Sage Publications.

Wierzbicka, A. (2003). *Cross-Cultural Pragmatics: The Semantics of Human Interaction* (2nd edn.). Berlin: Mouton de Gruyter.

Williams, R. (1958). *Culture and Society*. London: Penguin.

3   Bullying or Peer Aggression?
A Pilot Study with Punjabi Adolescents

*Grace Skrzypiec, Phillip Slee, Damanjit Sandhu
and Shubhdip Kaur*

Since Dan Olweus (1978) first drew our attention to the phenomenon of bullying in Western schools, scholars have conducted many studies in different countries and contexts investigating bullying. As Slee and Skrzypiec (2016) have noted in countries such as Japan, a considerable history exists of research on the topic. However, research in bullying has been quite sparse in India (Narayanan & Betts, 2014; Chapter 1).

The few studies undertaken in India suggest that bullying is widespread among Indian youth (Malhi, Bharti & Sidhu, 2014). Bullying prevalence rates have been found to range from 60.4% in a study by Ramya and Kulkarni (2011) to 53% in a study by Malhi and colleagues (2014). Compared to some countries such as Australia, where prevalence rates are closer to 20% (Skrzypiec, Askell-Williams, Slee & Rudzinski, 2014), the rates of bullying among Indian schoolchildren appear high and "it is a matter of great concern that why and how in a country like India, where peace and nonviolence are preached has the most aggressive adolescents as compared to any other country" (Mehta & Pilania, 2014, p. 1143). Malhi, Bharti and Sidhu (2015) have suggested that it is possible that "Indian schools consider bullying normative and have a greater tolerance for it" (p. 80). If true, this could explain the high prevalence of bullying in India, as according to Swearer, Espelage, Vaillancourt and Hymel (2010), bullying begets more bullying, as the peer group comes to accept bullying as the norm.

Bullying is conceived as a subset of violence or aggressive behaviour and while it is sometimes difficult to identify, decades of research on bullying has enabled a consensus of what comprises bullying in the Western world (Smith, del Barrio & Tokunaga, 2012). What delineates bullying from other aggressive acts is that bullying involves repeated negative behaviour intended to harm a person in an interpersonal relationship where there is an imbalance of power (Olweus, 1993). Aggressive interchanges and conflicts between people of approximately equal

45

physical or mental strength are not described as acts of bullying. Bullying may be viewed as peer abuse; however, what distinguishes bullying from other forms of abuse is the context in which it occurs and the relationship between the persons involved. Peer abuse differs from child abuse (usually between an adult and a child) and spouse abuse (between adult partners). The bullying criteria of intention to harm, power imbalance and repetitiveness that comprise the definition of what is referred to as traditional bullying have been generally well accepted by researchers working in the field (Olweus, 2013).

Despite the acceptance by most researchers of the definition of bullying, various studies have noted that bullying is not well understood in the school community. Vaillancourt and colleagues (2008) investigated whether students and researchers are talking about the same thing when they refer to bullying; they found significant differences between the two groups in how bullying is perceived. Students aged 8–18 who had been asked to provide their own definition of bullying rarely mentioned the three criteria that define bullying behaviour. Only 1.7% of them mentioned intentionality, while 6% mentioned repetition and just more than one quarter (26%) made reference to power imbalance. Nearly all students (92%), however, emphasised that the behaviour was a negative act. These findings are in accord with a PhotoStory study by Skrzypiec, Slee and Sandhu (2015) which found little reference to bullying criteria by students aged 12–15 years in Punjab, India. Only four (out of 33) PhotoStories sent by students to the researchers about bullying met the definition of bullying. These findings highlight the confusion which exists in school communities about bullying.

Finkelhor, Turner and Hamby (2012) have noted that in colloquial terms, the technical definition of bullying is not understood, and bullying is not being thought of in terms of the three criteria of intentional harm, repeated action and power imbalance between victim and bully. Rather, when asked about bullying, most students think about a time when someone was "mean" to them. In fact, the concept of someone being "mean" was used to determine bullying status in a survey of more than 10,000 Australian students from preschool through to Year 12 by Bernard, Stephanou and Urbach (2007). That study found that 16% of students had bullied or verbally taunted other students, while 37% stated that they had been quite mean to other people.

Finkelhor and colleagues (2012) have argued that as a subset of peer aggression, a more empirical foundation is needed when measuring bullying. Ybarra, Espelage and Mitchell (2014) found an overlap in generalised peer aggression and bullying when assessed separately within the same study, using the same sampling, data collection methodology and measure time frame. They have suggested that research should include a broader range of peer aggression experiences in a manner that distinguishes victims of bullying and victims of generalised peer aggression.

In line with this suggestion, the aim of this study was to quantify and classify different forms of peer aggression and bullying among students in Punjabi schools. The study sought to identify the degree of bullying and peer aggression overlap and acquire clarification to overcome the confusion related to bullying and peer aggression.

Participants

Peer aggression and bullying are known to peak during the middle years (Skrzypiec et al., 2014; Solberg & Olweus, 2003), so a sample of 186 middle school students (58.6% male) was recruited from three secondary schools in the Patiala region. Participation was voluntary and anonymous. The age of participants ranged from 11 to 15 years, average 13.38 (*S.D.* = 0.91). The cultural background of participants was diverse and included students who described themselves as Sikh (30.9%), Hindu (35.2%) and Punjabi (33.3%).

Method

We followed a methodology similar to that used by Ybarra and colleagues (2014), where bullying and peer aggression were assessed separately within the same study, using the same sampling, data collection methodology and time frame measure.

Participants completed a purpose-built questionnaire in English. They first answered 18 questions about the types of peer aggression they had experienced in the past month (e.g. teasing, exclusion, hitting, threatening) and described their experiences according to the level of harm, intention, repetition and power imbalance involved. This allowed different acts of peer aggression to be classified and distinguished bullying from other forms of peer aggression. Questions included eight acts where the student experienced victimisation (e.g. "I was left out by another person[s]"), seven where s/he was aggressive towards others (e.g. "I left someone out") and three being prosocial (e.g. "I helped someone who was being harassed"), as shown in Table 3.1. These were based on previous questionnaires (e.g. Olweus's [1978] Bullying Questionnaire, and Rigby and Slee's [1991] Peer Relations Questionnaire). Students first indicated whether they had experienced the behaviour in question, e.g. "I left someone out," by responding "Yes" or "No." For all questions

Table 3.1 *Student experiences of aggression and prosocial acts, in the past month*

	No		Yes	
	number	per cent	number	per cent
Prosocial				
I shared my things with someone	7	3.9%	174	96.1%
I was kind to someone	21	11.4%	163	88.1%
I helped someone who was being harassed	36	19.5%	149	80.5%
Victim				
I was teased	31	16.8%	153	83.2%
I had things taken from me	97	53.9%	83	46.1%
I got called names	38	21.1%	142	78.9%
I was made fun of	42	23.1%	140	76.9%
Another person(s) spread rumours (false stories) about me	62	33.9%	121	66.1%
I was picked on	67	36.8%	115	63.2%
I was left out by another person(s)	73	40.1%	109	59.9%
I got hit and pushed around	81	45.3%	98	54.7%
Aggressor				
I made another person(s) scared of me	80	44.7%	99	55.3%
I told false stories or spread rumours about another person(s)	82	45.8%	97	54.2%
I got into a fight with someone I could easily beat	97	53.9%	83	46.1%
I left someone out	109	62.6%	65	37.4%
I was part of a group that went around teasing others	130	73.4%	47	26.6%
I picked on someone	128	73.6%	46	26.4%
I enjoyed upsetting a wimp	137	77.0%	41	23.0%

(prosocial, victim and aggressor), if there was an affirmation, students then rated their experiences for harm, intention, repetition and power imbalance.

Harm: Students responded how harmful it was to them (if a victim) or to the other person (in the case of an aggressor) by selecting a response of "not harmful at all", "not very harmful", "harmful", "very harmful" or "extremely harmful" to the question "How harmful was it to you?" (or "How harmful was it to them?"). A harm score for victimisation was calculated by summing all responses to victim questions that students indicated were at least "harmful".

Intention: Students also rated their experiences according to whether they believed the aggressive act was intended by answering the question "did the person(s) intend to do it deliberately to you?" and then selecting a response of "not intentional at all", "slightly intentional", "intentional", "very intentional" or "absolutely intentional".

Repetition: Students responded "never", "once", "2–3 times", "4–5 times" or "more than 5 times" to the question "during the last month, how often did it happen?"

Perceived power imbalance: Students were asked "how powerful are you compared to the person(s)" and judged on a five-point Likert-type scale ranging from "much less powerful", "about the same", to "much more powerful".

In the next section of the questionnaire, students were provided with the following information about bullying: "People sometimes bully others less powerful than themselves by deliberately and repeatedly hurting or upsetting them in some way; for example, by hitting or pushing them around, teasing them or leaving them out of things on purpose. But it is not bullying/harassment when two young people of about the same strength have the odd fight or quarrel," before being asked "How often in the last month have you been bullied or harassed by a student or students at school?" Responses to this question ranged from "everyday", "most days", "1–2 days week", "about once a week", "less than once a week" to "never". Responses were then grouped so that students affirming that they had been bullied once a week or more often were classified as having been "seriously bullied". Students who indicated that bullying had occurred "less than once a week" were classified as having been "mildly bullied", while the remainder of students with "never" responses were classified in the "never been bullied" group. Students also provided demographic information, including their age, gender and cultural background.

Data Analysis

Counts were undertaken of the number of "yes" responses made by respondents to see how many students reported that they had experienced victimisation, acted aggressively towards others or had acted in a prosocial manner. A victimisation score (from 0 to 8), an aggressor score (from 0 to 7) and a prosocial score (from 0 to 3) were obtained by summing all "yes" responses to the relevant experiences. Responses of harm to the eight acts of victimisation were examined and a harm score (from 0 to 8) was calculated based on the number of times participants indicated that the aggressive act was harmful, very harmful or extremely harmful.

Table 3.2 *Student experiences of harmful acts of aggression*

Harm Score (number of harmful experiences)	Number	Per Cent
0	32	17.2
1	35	18.8
2	20	10.8
3	27	14.5
4	27	14.5
5	22	11.8
6	11	5.9
7	8	4.3
8	4	2.2
Total	**186**	**100**

Results

Acts of Victimisation, Bullying and Prosocial Behaviour

Table 3.1 lists the "yes" and "no" responses provided by students about their aggression and prosocial experiences. As shown, prosocial acts were most commonly reported, although more than three quarters of the participants indicated that they had been teased, made fun of or called names. At least one act of prosocial behaviour was reported by nearly all students ("I shared my things with someone"), while more than 80% reported being victimised at least once by being teased and approximately half had made another person scared of them.

Acts of Harm

The distribution of victimisation harm scores is shown in Table 3.2, where only 32 students (17.2%) reported that they did not experience an act of victimisation that they considered harmful to them. This includes the 16.8% of students who indicated that they had not experienced an act of victimisation in the previous month. As shown in Table 3.2, just more than half (53.2%) of the participants reported at least three harmful acts of aggression during the previous 3 months.

Victimisation

The distribution of victimisation scores is shown in Table 3.3. Only a small number of students indicated that they had not had any experiences

Table 3.3 *Number of experiences of victimisation (victimisation score) reported by participants*

Victimisation Score	Frequency	Per Cent	Cumulative Per Cent
0	4	2.2	2.2
1	8	4.3	6.5
2	14	7.5	14.0
3	21	11.3	25.3
4	14	7.5	32.8
5	34	18.3	51.1
6	28	15.1	66.1
7	36	19.4	85.5
8	27	14.5	100.0
Total	**186**	**100.0**	

Table 3.4 *Number of experiences of aggression towards others (aggressor score) reported by participants*

Aggressor Score	Frequency	Per Cent	Cumulative Per Cent
0	30	16.1	16.1
1	34	18.3	34.4
2	43	23.1	57.5
3	24	12.9	70.4
4	20	10.8	81.2
5	17	9.1	90.3
6	5	2.7	93.0
7	13	7.0	100.0
Total	**186**	**100.0**	

of victimisation; nearly all reported at least one type. Nearly half of the respondents had experienced six or more different types of victimisation, and just more than one in seven responded that they had experienced all of the eight different types of victimisation.

Aggression towards Others

The distribution of aggressor scores is shown in Table 3.4. More than four in five students indicated that they had behaved aggressively towards others in one way or other. Only one in six did not act aggressively towards another

Table 3.5 *Number of prosocial experiences (prosocial Score) reported by participants*

Prosocial Score	Number	Per Cent	Cumulative Per Cent
0	1	0.5	0.5
1	14	7.5	8.0
2	41	22.0	30.0
3	130	69.9	99.9
Total	**186**	**100.0**	

using at least one type of aggressive act. A small minority reported being aggressive towards others using all of the different types of aggressive acts.

Prosocial Behaviour

The distribution of prosocial scores is shown in Table 3.5. All but one student had undertaken at least one prosocial action in the previous month and more than two-thirds of respondents had engaged in a prosocial behaviour using all three scenarios.

Bullying Victimisation

Based on the question: "how often have you been bullied in the past month?", students were classified as having been "seriously" (once a week or more often), "mildly" (less than once a week) or "never" bullied. Overall, 59.1% of students reported some level of bullying; 42.5% of victims were classified as having been seriously bullied in the previous month, while 16.7% were mildly bullied and 40.9% reported never having been bullied.

The proportion of students classified in each bullying involvement group did not vary by gender ($\chi^2(2) = 3.85$, p > 0.05, Cramer's V = 0.15). Victimisation scores were compared between bullying involvement groups. Students who reported being seriously bullied had the highest victimisation scores (ANOVA: $F(2) = 9.7$, p < 0.0001) and Kruskal Wallis: $\chi^2(2) = 15.8$, p< 0.0001).

Victimisation and Bullying

As shown in Table 3.6, students who were classified as having been seriously bullied had victimisation scores that were greater than 1,

Table 3.6 *Victimisation scores of different bullying involvement groups*

Victimisation score	Bullying Involvement Group (n = 186)					
	seriously bullied		mildly bullied		never bullied	
	number	per cent	number	per cent	number	per cent
0	0	0.0	0	0.0	4	5.3
1	0	0.0	3	9.7	5	6.6
2	1	1.3	2	6.5	11	14.5
3	9	11.4	5	16.1	7	9.2
4	7	8.9	3	9.7	4	5.3
5	13	16.5	6	19.4	15	19.7
6	12	15.2	4	12.9	12	15.8
7	21	26.6	4	12.9	11	14.5
8	16	20.3	4	12.9	7	9.2
Total	**79**	**100.0**	**31**	**100.0**	**76**	**100.0**

indicating that they had reported two or more experiences of victimisation in the previous month, while mildly bullied students reported at least one experience of victimisation. However, not all students who had experiences of victimisation reported that they had been bullied in the previous month. For example, 45 (24.19%) students who indicated that they had experienced five or more different acts of victimisation (i.e. with victimisation scores greater than or equal to 5) reported that they had "never" been bullied in the previous month.

Harm by Bully Group

The total number of harmful experiences reported by participants was examined for each bullying involvement group by studying harmful victimisation scores. As can be seen in Table 3.7 (top row), only a small proportion of seriously bullied and mildly bullied students reported no harm, compared with just more than one quarter of students who had never been bullied. The proportions in the never-bullied column in Table 3.7 suggest that a large proportion (73.7%) of students who did not consider themselves to have been bullied, reported at least one act of victimisation that they perceived as harmful to them.

Overlap between Experiences of Victimisation and Bullying

Each of the eight acts of victimisation were examined more closely in order to determine how many students experienced at least one

Table 3.7 *Number of harmful acts experienced by participants in each bullying involvement group*

	Bully Involvement Group					
	seriously bullied		mildly bullied		never bullied	
Harm Score	number	per cent	number	per cent	number	per cent
0	9	11.4	3	9.7	20	26.3
1	8	10.1	13	41.9	14	18.4
2	12	15.2	2	6.5	6	7.9
3	14	17.7	3	9.7	10	13.2
4	15	19.0	5	16.1	7	9.2
5	4	5.1	4	12.9	14	18.4
6	9	11.4	1	3.2	1	1.3
7	6	7.6	0	0	2	2.6
8	2	2.5	0	0	2	2.6
Total	**79**	**100**	**31**	**100**	**76**	**100**

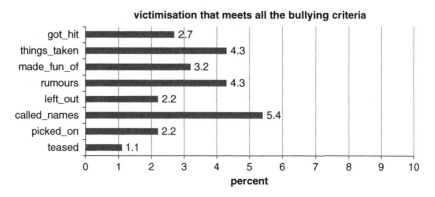

Figure 3.1 Proportion of self-reported victimisation experiences that meet the bullying criteria

victimisation experience which was deliberate, repeated and involved a power imbalance. As shown in Figure 3.1, only a small proportion of victimisation experiences met the three bullying criteria. The most common type of victimisation experience that involved a power imbalance and that was repeated and deliberate was being called names, where 5.4% of the reported experiences could be described as bullying.

Total Sum of Victimisation Experiences Meeting Bullying Criteria (TVB)

The total number of victimisation experiences that were of a type that met the bullying criteria was summed for each student; this is referred to as the Total Victim Bully (TVB) score. The range of such experiences (TVB scores) numbered from 0 to 4. Only two students had more than two different types of victimisation experiences that matched all three bullying criteria, while 17.7% had at least one experience that met the criteria. However, more than four in five (82.3%) described victimisation experiences that did not match all three bullying criteria i.e. had a TVB score of 0.

Bullying Involvement Groups and TVB Scores

The total number of victimisations meeting bullying criteria (recorded as TVB scores) for each bullying involvement group is shown in Table 3.8.

In all groups, most of the students did not have any victimisation experiences that met the bullying criteria (i.e. had a TVB score of 0). This was the case for nearly three-quarters (74.7%) of the students in the "seriously bullied" group, 80.6% of students in the "mildly bullied" group and 90.8% of students in the "never bullied" group. Only one quarter (25.3%) of students who self-reported that they had been seriously bullied had experiences that matched the bullying criteria.

Based on the findings from Table 3.8, it can be concluded that the prevalence of seriously bullied students was 10.8% (n = 20) and not 42.5% (n = 79) as was suggested by the single self-reported level of bullying question. Similarly, the prevalence of mildly bullied students was not 16.7% (n = 31) but 3.2% (n = 6), and the prevalence of never

Table 3.8 *TVB scores by bullying involvement group*

		Self-Reported Bullying Involvement Group					
	TVB Score	seriously bullied		mildly bullied		never bullied	
Not Bullied	0	59	74.7	25	80.6	69	90.8
Bullied	1	13	16.5	5	16.1	4	5.3
↓	2	6	7.6	1	3.2	2	2.6
	3	1	1.3	0	0.0	0	0.0
	4	0	0.0	0	0.0	1	1.3
	Total	79	100.0	31	100.0	76	100.0

bullied students was 82.3%. Furthermore, seven (3.8%) students reported that they had never been bullied yet described experiences that meet the three bullying criteria.

Discussion

If the prevalence of bullying was determined in this study by students' self-reported frequency of bullying, the rate of 59.9% would accord with the 60.4% prevalence rate found by Ramya and Kulkarni (2011). However, this study has shown that when measures of bullying criteria are included, the prevalence rate considerably drops. The great lament of Mehta and Pilania (2014) of the high prevalence rates of bullying can be appeased somewhat with these findings. Rather than bullying prevalence rates that involve the majority of students, this study suggests that the prevalence of bullying defined in terms of the three criteria is much less, in the order of one in ten. Mehta and Pilania's concern, however, might be heightened if aggression between peers was to become the focus of attention, as this study found that acts of aggression were commonly experienced between peers – nearly all students had experienced at least one act of victimisation as well as one act of aggression towards another.

In his pioneering research, Olweus (1993) assumed that bullying was the most damaging form of peer aggression, but he did not establish that position empirically. In his observations of students at school, Olweus noticed that not all peer conflict was equal in seriousness and he sought to highlight bullying as the most damaging part of the spectrum. As Olweus has explained: "I developed the following definition of bullying: 'A student is being bullied or victimised when he or she is exposed, repeatedly and over time, to negative actions on the part of one or more other students ... In order to use the term bullying, there should also be an imbalance in power or strength (an asymmetric relationship): The student who is exposed to the negative actions has difficulty defending himself or herself'" (p. 27).

The importance of power imbalance, although shown to have a negative effect by Hunter, Boyle and Warden (2007), has been queried by Finkelhor and colleagues (2012), who question "whether there are other equally serious types of peer aggression (demarcated by other criteria, for example, the use of a weapon or having sexual content) that should be highlighted along with power imbalance". Nevertheless, Malecki and colleagues (2015) found that the power differential was more important than the frequency of bullying in terms of harm. Furthermore, Juvonen and Graham (2014) have questioned whether repetitiveness is a necessary criterion to define bullying "inasmuch as a single traumatic incident can raise the expectation and fear of continued abuse" (p. 161). In an examination of the three criteria for bullying, Smith and colleagues (2012) accept that one event is sufficient to incite fear of continued abuse and have concluded that "while an important criterion, repetition is not an essential one for bullying in the way that imbalance of power is central; it is more of a probabilistic indicator" (p. 39). With no evidence to suggest otherwise, it may be the case that any one act of peer victimisation could be sufficiently damaging to the individual experiencing it. There are ample reports of studies that show psychosocial maladjustment amongst young people who are bullied (e.g. Sandhu, Kaur & Kaur, 2015; Skrzypiec, Slee, Askell-Williams & Lawson, 2012). However, if the measures of bullying in those studies have not included measures of the three bullying criteria, the extent to which maladjustment is due to "bullying" or "peer victimisation" cannot be known. Such empirical research remains to be undertaken.

Confusion about bullying amongst school students was highlighted by the finding that 75% of "seriously bullied" students did not have any experiences that met the three bullying criteria, although students in this group did report the greatest number of victimisation experiences (Table 3.8). Perhaps the large number of victimisation experiences was the prompt for these students to have considered themselves as victims of bullying. The question which arises therefore is whether the three criteria may be weighted in terms of what matters most to students and what fuels their perception that they have been bullied. An examination of the contribution made by each of the three bullying criteria to an individual's perception of bullying requires further research.

Bullying is currently the main focus of peer aggression programs in schools. This implies that other forms of peer aggression experienced by students may be less important or less harmful. Indeed, "it also needs to be recognized that youth who are victimized but do not meet the criteria of bullying also have elevated rates of psychosocial problems over non-victimized youth" (Ybarra et al., 2014, p. 299). There are suggestions that a focus on bullying, discounting other forms of peer aggression, may hamper efforts to support victims (Finkelhor et al. 2012). For example, there was a case in the United States where school staff failed to respond to an incident (which led to a student committing suicide) because they were waiting for a repeat in victimisation in order to classify the case as bullying and invoke the school's bullying policy (Toppo, 2013).

Bullying is not typically thought of by teenagers in terms of the criteria of intention to harm, repeated action and power imbalance between victim and bully (Cuadrado-Gordillo, 2012). So when asked about bullying, are students' responses in accord with our academic understanding of bullying, or are they referring to different forms of peer aggression? Furthermore, are these different forms of peer aggression differentially harmful to mental health and well-being? These questions require further investigation if we are to understand bullying more fully and if we are to be confident about making comparisons of bullying prevalence rates between countries or before and after interventions. Without clear measures of bullying, the results of comparative studies are cast in doubt.

Caution is needed in generalising the findings from the present study. Only a small number of students were involved in this study and only three schools in one city in India participated. Further studies may explore this issue segregating the genders. Furthermore, the questionnaire was in English and although we were reassured that students had a good command of the English language, English was a foreign language to them. Research assistants were available during questionnaire administration and the assistance students received in completing the questionnaire may have affected their responses. Another limitation of the study was that we did not investigate aggressors in detail. Doing so would have provided further clarity to our understanding of the bullying phenomenon.

In conclusion, our findings suggest that while peer aggression may be normative, bullying is experienced by a much smaller proportion of students than self-reports indicate. The data have shown that there is confusion about the meaning of "being bullied". Better measuring tools are needed if peer aggression is to be distinguished from bullying.

References

Bernard, M. E., Stephanou, A. & Urbach, D. (2007). *The State of Student Social and Emotional Health*. Melbourne, Victoria: Australian Scholarships Group.

Cascardi, M., Brown, C., Iannarone, M. & Cardona, N. (2014). The problem with overly broad definitions of bullying: Implications for the schoolhouse, the statehouse, and the ivory tower. *Journal of School Violence, 13*, 353–276. doi: 10.1080/15388220.2013.846861

Cuadrado-Gordillo, I. (2012). Repetition, power imbalance, and intentionality: Do these criteria conform to teenagers' perception of bullying? A role-based analysis. *Journal of Interpersonal Violence, 27*, 1889–1910.

Fernandes, T., Sanyal, N. & Chadha, S. (2015). Self-esteem and social interaction anxiety in cyberbullied adolescents. *Indian Journal of Health and Wellbeing, 6*(7), 648–655.

Finkelhor, D., Turner, H. A. & Hamby, S. (2012). Let's prevent peer victimization, not just bullying. *Child Abuse and Neglect, 36*, 271–274. doi: 10.1016/j.chiabu.2011.12.001

Hellström, L., Beckman, L. & Hagquist, C. (2013). Self-reported peer victimization: Concordance and discordance between measures of bullying and peer aggression among Swedish adolescents. *Journal of School Violence*, *12*, 395–413. doi: 10.1080/15388220.2013.825626

Hunter, S. C., Boyle, J. M. E. & Warden, D. (2007). Perceptions and correlates of peer-victimization and bullying. *British Journal of Educational Psychology*, *77*, 797–810.

Juvonen, J. & Graham, S. (2014). Bullying in schools: The power of bullies and the plight of victims. *Annual Review of Psychology*, *65*, 159–185. doi: 10.1146/annurev-psych-010213-115030

Kelly, O., Krishna, A. & Bhabha, J. (2016). Private schooling and gender justice: An empirical snapshot from Rajasthan, India's largest state. *International Journal of Educational Development*, *46*, 175–187. doi: 0.1016/j.ijedudev.2015.10.004

Malecki, C. K., Demaray, M. K., Coyle, S., Geosling, R., Yu Rueger, S. & Becker, L. D. (2015). Frequency, power differential, and intentionality and the relationship to anxiety, depression, and self-esteem for victims of bullying. *Child Youth Care Forum*, *44*, 115–131.

Malhi, P., Bharti, B. & Sidhu, M. (2014). Aggression in schools: Psychosocial outcomes of bullying among Indian adolescents. *Indian Journal of Pediatrics*, *81*(11), 1171–1176. doi: 10.1007/s12098-014-1378-7

Malhi, P., Bharti, B. & Sidhu, M. (2015). Peer victimization among adolescents: Relational and physical aggression in Indian schools. *Psychology Studies*, *60*(1), 77–83. doi: 10.1007/s12646-014-0283-5

Mehta, M. & Pilania, V. M. (2014). Bullying in Indian school going adolescents. *Indian Journal of Pediatrics*, *81*(11), 1143–1144. doi: 10.1007/s12098-014-1611-4

Narayanan, A. & Betts, L. R. (2014). Bullying behaviors and victimization experiences among adolescent students: The role of resilience. *Journal of Genetic Psychology*, *175*(2), 134–146. doi: 10.1080/00221325.2013.834290

Nazir, T. & Nesheen, F. (2015). Impact of school bullying on psychological well-being of adolescents. *Indian Journal of Health and Wellbeing*, *6*(10), 1037–1040.

Olweus, D. (1978). *Aggression in the Schools: Bullies and Whipping Boys*. Washington, DC: Hemisphere Press (Wiley).

Olweus, D. (1993). *Bullying at School: What We Know and What We Can Do*. Oxford: Blackwell.

Rajib, L. D. (2012). Why do they bully? Bullying behavior and its implication on the bullied. *Journal of Workplace Behavioral Health*, *27*, 79–99. doi: 10.1080/15555240.2012.666463

Ramya, S. G. & Kulkarni, M. L. (2011). Bullying among school children: Prevalence and association with common symptoms in childhood. *Indian Journal of Pediatrics*, *78*, 307–310. doi: 10.1007/s12098-010-0219-6

Rigby, K. & Slee, P. T. (1991). Bullying among Australian school children: Reported behaviour and attitudes towards victims. *Journal of Social Psychology*, *131*, 615–627.

Sandhu, D., Kaur, M. & Kaur, K. (2015). Bully victimization and pupil well-being. *Indian Journal of Health and Wellbeing*, *6*(3), 260–266.

Singh, V. & Sonkar, N. (2013). Cyber bullying: Experiences, impacts and coping strategies among young adults. *Indian Journal of Health and Wellbeing*, 4(8), 1584–1586.

Skrzypiec, G., Askell-Williams, H., Slee, P. & Rudzinski, A. (2014) IB Middle Years Programme (MYP): Student Social Emotional Wellbeing and School Success Practices. Final report South Australia: Research Centre for Student Wellbeing and Prevention of Violence, Flinders University.

Skrzypiec, G. K., Slee, P. T., Askell-Williams, H. & Lawson, M. J. (2012). Associations between types of involvement in bullying, friendships and mental health status. *Emotional and Behavioural Difficulties*, 17(3–4), 259–272.

Skrzypiec, G. K., Slee, P. T. & Sandhu, D. (2015). Using the PhotoStory Method to understand the cultural context of youth victimisation in the Punjab. *International Journal of Emotional Education*, 7, 52–68.

Slee, P. T. & Skrzypiec, G. K. (2016). *Wellbeing, Positive Peer Relations and Bullying in School Settings*. Dordrecht, The Netherlands: Springer.

Smith, P. K., Cowie, H., Olafsson, R. F. & Liefooghe, A. P. D. (2002). Definitions of bullying: A comparison of terms used, and age and gender differences, in a fourteen-country international comparison. *Child Development*, 73, 1119–1133.

Smith, P.K., del Barrio, C. & Tokunaga, R. (2013). Definitions of bullying and cyberbullying: How useful are the terms? In S. Bauman, J. Walker & D. Cross (eds.), *Principles of cyberbullying research: Definition, methods, and measures* (pp. 64–86). New York & London: Routledge.

Solberg, M. & Olweus, D. (2003). Prevalence estimation of school bullying with the Olweus Bully/Victim Questionnaire. *Aggressive Behavior*, 29, 239–268.

Swearer, S. M., Espelage, D. L., Vaillancourt, T. & Hymel, S. (2010). What can be done about school bullying? Linking research to educational practice. *Educational Researcher*, 39, 38–47. doi: 10.3102/0013189X09357622

Toppo, G. (2013). Researchers: Stop using the word 'bullying' in school. *USA Today*. 1 May.

Vaillancourt, T., McDougall, P., Hymel, S., Krygsman, A., Miller, J., Stiver, K., Davis, C. (2008). Bullying: Are researchers and children/youth talking about the same thing? *International Journal of Behavioral Development*, 32, 486–495.

Ybarra, M. L., Espelage, D. L. & Mitchell, K. J. (2014). Differentiating youth who are bullied from other victims of peer-aggression: The importance of differential power and repetition. *Journal of Adolescent Health*, 55, 293–300. doi: 10.1016/j.jadohealth.2014.02.009

4 Issues in Cross-National Comparisons and the Meaning of Words for Bullying in Different Languages

*Peter K. Smith, Fran Thompson, Adam Rutland, Alice Jones, Suresh Sundaram, Damanjit Sandhu, Kirandeep Kaur, Barbara A. Spears, Silvia Koller, Reda Gedutiene, Ruthaychonnee Sittichai and Yulia Kovas**

Many issues arise in making valid cross-cultural comparisons. These include issues of measurement and bias in quantitative studies, as well as the nature and representativeness of the samples. Another issue important in cross-national studies of bullying is the translation of the word *bullying* into different languages, and how it, or cognate words for it, are understood. This chapter describes a cartoon test, used previously to examine the meaning of words similar to *bullying* but in different languages, and gives findings from a cross-national study within the framework of the Indian-European Network project, including words from Punjabi and Tamil as well as six other languages.

A considerable number of studies have made comparisons of bullying's nature and prevalence between countries, and there are at least four large cross-national surveys of many countries which include questions on this: EU Kids Online, Global School Health Survey (GSHS), Trends in International Mathematics and Science Study (TIMSS), and Health Behaviour of School-Aged Children (HBSC). Of these, GSHS and HBSC explicitly use the word *bullying* in an Olweus-type definition asking about prevalence (EU Kids Online and TIMSS use behaviour-based items). However, it is not made clear how bullying is translated into the various languages used in different countries. In fact, agreement about

* Thanks to Fethi Berkkun, Sophie Bennett, Toby Carslake, Mel Leckie, Roma Simulioniene, Raimonda Sadauskaite, Lina Kantautiene, Luciana Valiente, Ksenia Sharafieva, Alex Miklashevsky, Dina Zueva, Tatiana A. Dolgolrukova, Maxim Likhanov, Sofia A. Mironets, Sarah Quinn, Nureehun Sadara, Aura Kanpanit, Apisit Kruawan, Witoon Sinsirichaveng, Natthapon Songsaeng, Sakdipun Tonwimonrat and Thanapon Peungtippimanchai for help in data gathering. Special thanks to Sampurna Kakchapati for help in analysis.

country differences among these four surveys is modest to low or even non-existent (Smith, Robinson & Marchi, 2016), and variations in the meanings of terms used to translate bullying may be one factor contributing to this, in a largely unknown fashion.

In order to examine the meaning profile of different terms which might be used to translate *bullying*, previous research (see later in this chapter) has used 25-item and 40-item versions of a cartoon test, showing stick-figure scenarios of various situations that might or might not be bullying. Pupils are asked which of these situations represent *bullying*, or the cognate word(s) in their language(s).

As part of the Indian-European Network project, the 40-item cartoons were first revised, to update for examples of cyberbullying on social networks, and also to take account of some particular Indian scenarios (such as taking from a fellow pupil's lunch plate). Pilot work was carried out to find words similar to *bullying* in Punjabi and Tamil. In addition to giving the same cartoon set in England, we also took the opportunity to invite colleagues in a few other countries to participate. This was accepted by colleagues in Australia and Thailand (already associated with the project), and also by colleagues in Brazil, Lithuania and Russia. The same set was given to 14-year-old pupils in all these countries. This chapter describes the process, and some of the findings.

The Cartoon Test

The Cartoon Test was designed to find out more about how different terms used to translate *bullying*, such as, for example, *prepotenze* in Italian or *ijime* in Japan, are understood. Stick-figure cartoons are shown to pupils; Figure 4.1 shows six cartoons from the revision of the set used in the present study. Pupils are asked whether (yes/no) each cartoon is an example of *bullying* (in English-speaking countries), or a similar term that might be used to translate it (in the language of the pupil). Use of stick figures was intended to avoid particular cultural connotations (such as clothes, skin colour, appearance). The pattern of yes/no responses across the cartoon set gives a meaning profile for each term. From this it can be seen what kind of scenarios the term picks up, and how closely it corresponds to the bullying profile.

The cartoon test was initially designed as part of a European Commission (EC)-funded programme of research on bullying which took place between 1997 and 2001. This first version used 25 stick figure cartoons, showing different kinds of scenarios between pupils, mainly but not entirely hostile or 'bullying'. Altogether 14 countries participated, with 13 main languages: Austria (south Germanic dialect), China (Mandarin), England (English),

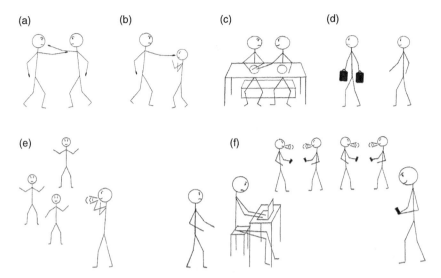

Figure 4.1 Six sample cartoons: these are numbers 1, 2, 8, 9, 25 and 40 in Table 4.2.

France (French), Germany (German), Greece (Greek), Iceland (Icelandic), Italy (Italian), Japan (Japanese), Norway (Norwegian), Portugal (Portuguese), Slovenia (Slovenian), Spain (Spanish) and Thailand (Thai). This constituted 11 European and 3 Eastern countries.

In each of the 14 countries, terms for bullying-like phenomena were found from dictionaries and researchers, and from children's focus groups used to select three to six terms comprehensible to children aged 8 and 14 years. The cartoons were then shown to pupils in sequence, one term 'X' at a time, with pupils asked if each cartoon is an example of 'X'. This was designed to be a move towards a more emic approach – looking at terms used in each culture (such as *bullying, harassment* and *teasing* in English), and their individual profile of meaning – while retaining an etic component in relating these terms to a broad range of common pupil scenarios.

The findings were reported in Smith, Cowie, Olafsson and Liefooghe (2002). Five main clusters of cartoons were identified that got similar responses from the total sample: non-aggressive (four cartoons), physical aggression (two), physical bullying (with imbalance of power) (five), verbal bullying (including rumour spreading as well as direct verbal attacks) (nine) and social exclusion (five).

As an example, Table 4.1 shows the weighting of English *bullying*, Italian *prepotenze*, and Japanese *ijime* on these five clusters from Smith and colleagues (2002). All three terms scored very low on the non-aggressive cartoons, as expected. *Bullying* and *ijime* were low on physical aggression. *Prepotenze* was confirmed as a broader term than *bullying*, with a much higher loading on physical aggression (fighting between equals) compared to either *bullying* or *ijime*. This probably explains why a high incidence of 'bullying' in Italy was reported when it was assessed by *prepotenze* in earlier studies (Menesini, 2000).

Further Studies Using the Cartoon Task

Smorti, Menesini and Smith (2003) used the 25-cartoon set to compare parents' definition of children's bullying in a five-country comparison (Italy, Spain, Portugal, England and Japan). Japanese parents saw the verbal and severe social exclusion cartoons as particularly representative of bullying-related terms such as *ijime*. Besides country comparisons, the cartoon test proved useful for other purposes. Menesini, Fonzi and Smith (2002) compared the attribution of meanings to five terms related to bullying by teachers and pupils in Italy. They found that there was agreement between teachers and pupils as regards

Table 4.1 *Loadings of bullying-related terms from England, Italy, Japan, Portugal and Thailand on five clusters from the original cartoon test (as in Smith et al., 2002; details in text).*

Term	Non-aggressive	Physical aggression	Physical bullying	Verbal (direct + indirect)	Social exclusion
ENGLAND					
Bullying	4	34	94	91	62
Harassment	10	42	88	84	49
Teasing	15	43	35	83	51
ITALY					
Prepotenze	10	71	92	86	90
JAPAN					
Ijime	4	9	50	87	39
PORTUGAL					
Provocação	3	60	69	78	44
THAILAND					
Tum rai	10	38	76	61	48

N.b.: the Portuguese term *Provocação* was incorrectly labelled *Provoção* in the 2002 report.

cartoons showing physical aggression, but that cartoons showing social exclusion and gender exclusion were less often seen by teachers, compared to pupils, as, for example, *prepotenza* or *violenza*. Monks and Smith (2006) used a reduced set of cartoons to examine age-related differences and the role of individual experiences of peer victimisation in the understanding of bullying in a UK sample. Age groups differed in how they characterised bullying: 4- to 6-year-olds and 8-year-olds used one dimension, a distinction between aggressive and non-aggressive acts; 14-year-olds and adults gave a two-dimensional solution, also distinguishing between physical and non-physical (social/relational or verbal) acts. There were no significant differences in how bullying was characterised between boys and girls, or between children involved or not involved in bullying roles.

A First Expanded Cartoon Test

In 2004–2005, an expanded set of 40 cartoons was produced. This was done for three reasons. One was to include an example of cyberbullying; this was a fairly recent but obviously important phenomenon. The caption for this was '*Wendy sends nasty text messages to Linda every break time.*' The second was to include cartoons reflecting some severe kinds of social exclusion which we had found to be important in cultures such as Japan and South Korea. A caption example for this was '*Tatiana and her friends suddenly stop talking and stay silent when Karina enters the classroom.*' A third was to cover examples of use of age or grade to force someone to do something, which might be perceived differently in some cultures. A caption example for this was '*The rest of the team won't let Millie take part in a competition, even though she is one of the best players, because she is from a lower year group.*' The original 25 cartoons were retained (with a few minor wording changes), plus 7 new social exclusion cartoons, 4 new cartoons on abuse of age/grade position, 2 cartoons on new kinds of bullying such as cyberbullying, 1 new ambiguous cartoon and 1 new neutral cartoon.

This cartoon set was given to 8- and 14-year-olds in nine countries: England and Canada (English), Japan (Japanese), South Korea (Korean), Iceland (Icelandic), Mainland China (Mandarin), Hong Kong (Cantonese) and Turkey (Turkish). The feedback from the teams indicated that, overall, the task took some 10–20 minutes with 14-year-olds, and no significant difficulties were encountered. The task took some 20–40 minutes with 8-year-olds, depending on how many terms were studied, and several teams reported problems of concentration at this age, especially if more than one term was used. Thus only the data from 14-year-olds were analysed. Some findings are reported in Smith and colleagues (2016). The term *bullying* was similar in meaning in England and Canada, though generally used more inclusively in England. The South Korean term *wang-ta* was low on physical bullying, but both *wang-ta* and Japanese *ijime* were high on severe social exclusion. But this was not so true in Hong Kong, where Cantonese *ha yan* was low on social exclusion cartoons, and mainland Chinese *qifu* and Turkish *zorbalik* were moderately low as well. As expected, *ijime* and *wang-ta* were low on some age/grade-related cartoons; these were seen as normative rather than bullying-like scenarios. But this did depend on the kind of situation depicted. A detailed analysis of the Turkish data was also made by Ucanok, Smith and Karasoy (2011); this showed that of several Turkish terms, *zorbalik* was the one most closely corresponding to English *bullying*.

A Second Expanded Cartoon Test

As part of the Indian-European network project, it was planned to revise the cartoon set again, and use it in India (as well as other countries, including England, for comparison). It was decided to keep the length to 40 cartoons; this had been found to work satisfactorily with 14-year-olds, but, especially if several terms in a language were to be studied, a longer set might bring about loss of concentration and data quality. However, we did wish to expand the coverage of cyberbullying; this previously had only one cartoon on text messaging, the predominant form of cyberbullying in 2004/2005, when the set was produced (Rivers & Noret, 2010). We also wished to consider the possibility of introducing scenarios particularly relevant for the situation in India. The new set was initially designed and piloted primarily for the comparisons between India (Punjab and Tamil Nadu) and England.

The revised set was discussed as a regular item at early meetings of the Indian-European Network. Indian colleagues suggested specific scenarios. These reflected the nature of school meals in many Indian classrooms (pupils eating from plates in close proximity to each other) and the considerable value put on books (often paid for) and getting good grades. The new scenarios finally included (in the English version using English names) were: *'Lalitha steals food from Eve's dinner plate on most days,' 'Alison rips up Barbara's book,' 'Luke often insults Darren because he is from a lower caste/social class,' 'Felix sneers at the kind of food Trevor eats'* and *'Classmates never speak to Douglas because he always gets bad marks in class.'*

We also added three new cyberbullying items based on social networking to the existing one on text messages: *'Sean films Matt being beaten up and puts it on YouTube for people to see,' 'Richard posts threatening messages about Kwame on Facebook which lots of people can see'* and '*Keely tells everyone on Facebook not to talk to Patricia.*' Some other items had to be dropped; this was to keep the set to 40 cartoons, as prior experience suggested that more than 40 cartoons could lead to loss of concentration.

Piloting the Revised Cartoon Test

The redesigned 40-item set was translated from English into Punjabi and Tamil. It was then back-translated independently, and checked for fidelity with the original English.

The Indian teams in Punjab and Tamil Nadu then ran several focus groups of 14-year-olds to check whether the children understood the cartoons and what words they would use to describe the behaviours shown in the cartoons. These focus groups were of around five to eight pupils, who were not taking part in the main study. All 40 cartoons were presented to them as stimuli and discussed. The researcher running the focus groups asked them to consider firstly whether the words (captions) and pictures made sense, and if it was clear what they meant. Comments were recorded. Then the researcher said to the group that lots of the cartoons show nasty things happening, and asked them '*What words would you use to describe these kinds of behaviours?*' This was important in selecting the terms to examine in the main study. Following this piloting, a few cartoons were slightly revised. The final list of captions (English version) is shown in Table 4.2. Cartoons 1, 2, 8, 9, 25 and 40 are illustrated in Figure 4.1.

Several terms in the native language, similar to *bullying*, were chosen for the main task, based on what pupils had said in the focus groups, as well as terms commonly used by adults, including researchers. This procedure was first carried out at the two Indian sites; a bit later, colleagues in Australia and Thailand, associated with the project, and also colleagues in Brazil, Lithuania and Russia, who expressed interest in it, also took part. At this point it was not intended to change the cartoon set, but piloting in these countries otherwise followed a similar pattern, checking that the translations were correct and understandable by pupils, and establishing what terms similar to bullying were used by pupils and should be adopted for the main data gathering.

Ethical Issues

It was agreed that all investigators should follow ethical guidelines appropriate for their own country/institution, for the piloting and the main

Table 4.2 *The set of 40 cartoon captions used in the current study*

Cartoon captions: [English: female and male version]

1. Michael and Jack don't like each other and start to hit each other.
2. Mary starts to hit Linda, who is smaller.
3. Sinan starts to hit Christopher every break time
4. Serla tells Alison that if she doesn't give her money every day, she will hit her.
5. Andrew and his friends start to hit Robbie.
6. Natalie starts to hit Anne, who is in a lower-year group, because Anne disagreed with Natalie.
7. Jason and Rashid hit each other playfully and laugh.
8. Lalitha steals food from Eve's dinner plate on most days.
9. Mark gets his classmate Ben to carry his school bags every day.
10. Amanda gets Vicky, who is in a lower-year group, to carry her school bags every day.
11. Sean films Matt being beaten up and puts it on YouTube for people to see.
12. Lara borrows Helena's ruler and accidentally breaks it.
13. Ian takes Jimmy's ruler and breaks it.
14. Alison rips up Barbara's book.
15. Simon forgot his pen, so Emeka lends him one of his.
16. Danielle says nasty things to Janet.
17. Paul says nasty things to Alan every week.
18. Julia says nasty things to Lisa about the colour of her skin.
19. Luke often insults Darren because he is from a lower caste/social class.
20. Kim says nasty things to Victoria because she is gay.
21. Chung makes fun of Tim's hair. They both laugh.
22. Elaine makes fun of Sue's hair. Sue is upset.
23. Felix sneers at the kind of food Trevor eats.
24. Wendy sends nasty text messages to Sophie every break time.
25. Kanye spreads nasty stories about Brendan.
26. Susie writes nasty things about Jodie on the walls of the school toilets.
27. Richard posts threatening messages about Kwame on Facebook which lots of people can see.
28. Emma asks Heidi if she would like to play.
29. Kwan won't let Hideo play today.
30. Natalie never lets Jean play with her.
31. Josh and his friends won't let Max play with them.
32. No one wants to be with Julia for a paired activity.
33. No one in his school will make friends with Barry.
34. The girls won't let Mark skip with them because he is a boy.
35. The boys won't let Karen play football because she is a girl.
36. No one will play with Kerry because she has one leg and needs to walk with sticks.
37. Classmates never speak to Douglas because he always gets bad marks in class.
38. Tatiana and her friends suddenly stop talking and stay silent when Karina enters the classroom.
39. Everyone in the class treats Marcus as if he was not there.
40. Keely tells everyone on Facebook not to talk to Patricia.

study. A basic minimum was that (a) informed consent should be obtained from pupils, teachers and parents; (b) pupils should be told of their right to not answer or withdraw, with no negative consequences; (c) an information sheet/ help sheet and/or a resource person should be available for help, should the material bring up actual experiences of bullying or victimisation. Regarding (a), it was perceived as usually sufficient if parents were informed, for example, by a school newsletter, about the task, and could ask for more information or withdraw their child if they wished. If they did not reply, then parental consent was assumed, i.e. passive consent.

Protocol for the Main Data Gathering

It was agreed that the task should be given to a minimum of 20 boys and 20 girls at around 14 years old (with a larger number being desirable). They should be selected from a school or schools deemed reasonably representative of the education system in the country; that is, they should not draw from extreme groups in terms of academic ability or socio-economic status.

The 40 cartoons, each with a caption, should be in the native language. The names in the captions, originally appropriate in England, should be changed in other countries to familiar names in that native language/ country. Different names should be used in each caption; one name should never be repeated. The captions provided alternated male and female names (male:male and female:female). Previously, gender of names had not been found important (Smith et al., 2002).

The task could be given individually to pupils, or to pupils on a class basis provided that pupils could do the task independently. On an individual basis, hard copies of the cartoons could be used. On a group or class basis, overhead transparencies or PowerPoint could be used. The sequence as given in the list of captions was followed. This was done in order to maximise consistency across cultures and to give a 'narrative' line to the task, as the child moves through physical, verbal and more indirect/relational and cyber scenarios. The possible drawback of order effects was recognised, but previous piloting experience suggested that a random order was more confusing for children to follow.

It was agreed a maximum of five terms should be chosen (in fact, the range was three to five). Each pupil was given a score sheet listing the 40 cartoon captions, and a column for each term (X, Y, ...) so that they could write Y (yes) or N (no) in a box corresponding to each cartoon, for each term. Each term (X, Y, ...) was taken in turn. The pupils were shown the first cartoon, with the researcher also reading the caption if this was felt useful. The pupils were asked 'Is this X? Write Y (yes) or N (no) in the appropriate box on your scoresheet.' Then the second cartoon was shown, and so on to the last (40th). Then the researcher said, 'Now we are going to think about Y. We'll start again with the first picture. Is this Y?', going through the 40 cartoons again. This was repeated with each remaining term, in turn. Finally all the pupils were thanked and the score sheets collected for analysis.

Each team also filled in a short questionnaire about sample characteristics, and if there were any comments or feedback from the pupils about the task.

Choice of Terms and Sample Sizes

The terms chosen, and the sample sizes in each country, are shown in Table 4.3. Although terms in the native language were chosen, both the Punjabi and Brazilian teams chose to include the term *bullying*, as it is quite widely used and understood. All data were screened, initially by the host team, and then by the first author and Sampurna Kakchapati, for consistency; a small percentage of responses were removed, where, for example, all cartoons (or no cartoons) were ticked for a particular term.

Findings

The overall findings are presented in Table 4.4 in terms of the percentages for each term, in terms of eight clusters based on previous research and the nature of the captions. The eight clusters are: physical fight (cartoon 1), physical bullying (2, 3, 4, 5, 6), belongings (8, 9, 10, 13, 14), verbal (16, 17, 18, 19, 20, 22, 23), rumours (25, 26), cyber (11, 24, 27, 40), exclusion (29, 30, 31, 32, 33, 34, 35, 36, 37, 38, 39) and non-aggressive (7, 12, 15, 21, 28).

Generally, we would expect all the terms to be low on the non-aggressive cluster. However, it is worth noting that this cluster includes two prosocial scenarios (cartoons 15, 28), one of accidental harm (12), and two of more playful teasing or aggression (7, 21). We would expect terms similar to *bullying* to be low on physical fight, which has no imbalance of power, but high on all the other six clusters. Terms more similar to general aggression would be expected to be high on all seven aggressive clusters. However, within clusters, cartoons do vary on other characteristics, such as presence/absence of repetition or presence of audience, which could be considered in more detailed analysis.

Table 4.3 *Details of terms used and pupil sample, in each country*

COUNTRY	N (Male, Female) AGE SCHOOLS	ETHNICITY	TERMS USED

Australia	50 (22, 28)
	Mostly 14 years, some 15.
	Three schools in the
	    Adelaide area.
		Mixed, but mainly
		    Anglo-European
		    heritage and all
		    spoke English in
		    the classroom
			Bullying
			Harassment
			Teasing
			Conflict

Brazil	95 (57, 38) 14 years most common, but range 10 to 17 years. One school in Porto Alegre.	All Brazilian	*Bullying* *Assédio* *Provocação*

England	77 (44, 32; 1 no response)
	All 13–15 years.
	Two schools, one in north
	    London, one in Exeter.
		36 White, 12 Black,
		    11 Asian, 10
		    Other, 5 Mixed, 4
		    no response; all
		    English speakers
			Bullying
			Harassment
			Teasing

India-Punjab	125 (82, 68)
	Mostly 14 years.
	Four schools, two
	    government and
	    two private.
		All Indian, majority
		    Sikh or Hindu. All
		    understood
		    English as well as
		    Punjabi.
			Dhakeshahi
			Pange laina
			Baar baar
			    tang karna
			
			Bullying

India-Tamil
    Nadu
	150 (68,82)
	Almost all 14 years.
	Two schools, in
	    Puducherry and
	    Chidambaram.
		All Indian, Tamil
		    speaking
			Cintutal
			Keli
			Tunpuruttal

Lithuania	160 (77, 83) mostly 13–14 years. Three schools in Klaipeda.	All Lithuanian	*Patyčios* *Smurtas* *Pažeminimas* *Atstūmimas* *Diskriminacija*
Russia	127 (72, 55) Almost all 14 or 15 years. Three schools in Tomsk.	Almost all ethnic Russian	*Discriminatsia* *Izdevatel'stvo* *Uschemlenie* *Preznenie* *Neuvazhenie*

Thailand	880 (412, 467; 1 no
	    response)
	Almost all 14 years.
	Eight schools, two each from
	    north, south, east and
	    central Thailand.
		All Thai	*Rang khae*
			Lorlen
			Tum rai

Table 4.4 *Mean percentage of children who included the cartoons in each cluster as part of their definition of that term. High and low percentages are shown in bold (HIGH > 80; high > 70; low < 20; LOW < 10).*

COUNTRY	Physical fight	Physical 'bullying'	Belongings	Verbal	Rumours	Cyber	Exclusion	Not aggressive
AUSTRALIA								
Bullying	22	**HIGH 94**	**HIGH 89**	**HIGH 95**	**HIGH 99**	**HIGH 98**	**HIGH 85**	**LOW 2**
Harassment	56	**HIGH 91**	62	**HIGH 89**	**HIGH 85**	**HIGH 90**	61	**LOW 6**
Teasing	**LOW 8**	37	32	**HIGH 83**	66	53	45	low 14
Conflict	**HIGH 98**	**high 78**	33	47	45	47	38	**LOW 9**
BRAZIL								
Bullying	40	**high 79**	69	**HIGH 88**	**HIGH 87**	**HIGH 89**	**high 75**	low 19
Assédio	23	47	36	49	49	56	34	**LOW 8**
Provocação	56	36	53	**high 71**	**high 71**	60	48	33
ENGLAND								
Bullying	low 10	**HIGH 81**	**high 71**	62	**high 78**	**high 78**	54	**LOW 3**
Harassment	47	51	32	35	32	38	**low 15**	**LOW 3**
Teasing	low 17	**LOW 6**	**LOW 9**	37	**low 13**	**low 12**	22	35
INDIA PJ								
Dhakeshahi	42	58	56	34	26	44	59	low 13
Pange laina	57	37	56	47	63	52	42	34
Baar baar tang karna	29	43	50	53	56	43	37	20
Bullying	35	51	49	51	**high 73**	52	42	**Low 10**
INDIA TN								
Cintutal	**high 71**	51	64	68	**high 70**	65	51	**LOW 5**
Keli	25	34	40	59	**high 79**	**high 74**	64	**LOW 4**
Tunpuruttal	**high 77**	68	55	**high 71**	**high 84**	**high 72**	62	**LOW 6**

LITHUANIA								
Patyčios	29	63	67	**HIGH 90**	**HIGH 92**	69	45	**LOW 7**
Smurtas	**HIGH 98**	**HIGH 91**	31	low 12	low 12	low 14	61	**LOW 2**
Pažeminimas	41	high 71	**HIGH 81**	**HIGH 86**	**HIGH 96**	high 70	53	**LOW 6**
Aistinimas	39	49	37	65	69	61	**HIGH 88**	**LOW 2**
Diskriminacija	28	49	47	67	42	34	48	**LOW 4**
RUSSIA								
Discriminatsia	21	58	49	65	43	52	69	**LOW 8**
Izdevatel'stvo	27	**HIGH 82**	high 74	**HIGH 84**	high 70	**HIGH 81**	49	**LOW 6**
Uschemlenie	23	high 78	63	high 71	49	62	54	**LOW 4**
Preznenie	62	51	40	high 79	high 70	65	high 71	**LOW 6**
Neuvazhenie	high 72	**HIGH 81**	**HIGH 87**	**HIGH 86**	**HIGH 89**	**HIGH 83**	high 70	low 12
THAILAND								
Rang khae	34	high 78	high 79	61	high 74	52	46	20
Tum rai	**HIGH 91**	68	low 11	23	31	43	22	low 14
Lor len	**LOW 5**	low 13	32	47	32	32	21	23

The various country profiles are now considered in turn. In three cases comparisons can be made with data from Smith and colleagues (2002), bearing in mind that these data were gathered nearly 20 years earlier, and that linguistic terms can change in meaning over such a time period. The earlier study included data from England, Portugal (Portuguese, to compare with Brazilian Portuguese), and Thailand; findings from this earlier data set for the relevant terms in common are shown in Table 4.1.

Australia

The profile of terms from Australia is very clear and is as expected. All four terms are low on the non-aggressive cartoons. *Bullying* is very high on all six types of bullying, but not on physical fight. *Harassment* has a similar profile, although somewhat less applicable to taking/damaging belongings or to social exclusion; the discrimination from physical fighting is also less good than for *bullying*. This was also the case for *harassment* in England in the earlier study. *Teasing* mainly picks up verbal attacks, consistent with the expected meaning of this term, again consistent with *teasing* in England in the earlier study. Finally *conflict* comes out high on physical attacks rather than other forms.

Brazil

The term *bullying* is used in Brazil, as (like in other Latin-based languages) no Portuguese term very similar in meaning to bullying exists. The profile for *bullying* is considerably higher on all six types of bullying scenarios than on physical fighting; this suggests that it has a broadly similar meaning to that in English-speaking countries. Of the two Portuguese terms, *assédio* has a rather uncertain profile. However, *provocação* is clearly high on verbal attacks and rumours rather than on physical or cyber attacks or on social exclusion.

In the earlier study (Smith et al., 2002) examination was made of six terms in Portugal; the term *provocação* was the term closest to the bullying profile. As here, it was highest on verbal attacks and rumours, and only moderate on other forms of attack (Table 4.1). However, Brazilian Portuguese is quite different from Portuguese spoken in Portugal, and the culture is quite different, especially related to school education and childrearing, which may influence bullying behaviour. The findings here suggest that while Brazilian Portuguese *provocação* is moderately close to English *bullying*, the actual term *bullying* used in Brazilian Portuguese is a closer equivalent.

England

The profile for *bullying* is as expected. It is not quite as high a profile as in the Australian sample, but does have a clear distinction from physical fighting. Although high on most forms of bullying, it is not so high on social exclusion, a pattern also found in the 2002 study (Table 4.1). *Harassment* has a more uncertain profile, different from that in Australia and also from the England data from the 2002 study (Table 4.1). The meaning of *harassment* may have changed somewhat over the past 20 years, now referring more to aggression related to gender or race; in these data at least, it has poor discrimination from physical fighting. The third term, *teasing*, is rather low on all clusters (even if less low for verbal attacks), and, in this sample, does not seem to connote aggressive actions. It is not low on the non-aggressive cartoons, being quite high for the two playful aggression cartoons.

India – Punjabi

The findings from India Punjab were disappointing in the sense that all four terms gave rather indistinct profiles. *Dhakeshahi* was low on non-aggressive cartoons, but scored moderately on all kinds of aggression. *Pange laina* scored moderately across all clusters, even on the non-aggressive cartoons. *Baar baar tang karna* scored moderately on all forms of aggression. Finally, the term *bullying*, which did score low on non-aggressive cartoons, scored quite high on rumours and moderately on other kinds of aggression (least on physical fighting).

From these results, it would seem that none of the Punjabi terms is a very good equivalent to English *bullying*, although the closest is in fact the term *bullying*, at least in this sample. It may be relevant to consider that this participating sample had many middle/upper-class pupils and that *bullying* might not be used in socially deprived contexts where English is not widely spoken.

According to dictionaries, *dhakeshahi* is a word for showing off one's power; *baar baar tang karna* is a word for repetitive harassment; and *pange laina* is a word for getting into an issue/ fight kind of actively, and mostly when it could be avoided, like intentionally starting a quarrel or doing misconduct (see also Chapter 13). The Punjabi team held focus group discussions with two groups of teachers in the schools from where data were collected. The consensus amongst the teachers was that there is no specific term used in a hard and fast manner for behaviour considered bullying. However, of the three terms, the most serious/grave connotation was expressed by *dhakeshahi*, followed by *baar baar tang karna*.

It is possible that the clustering used to simplify the data presentation (as in Table 4.4) does not do justice to the complexity of the Punjabi terms. For example, in the Belongings cluster, where *dhakeshahi* gets 56% yes responses, it is high (95%) for cartoon 9, Mark gets his classmate Ben to carry his school bags every day, but low (17%) for cartoon 8, Lalitha steals food from Eve's dinner plate on most days (these two cartoons are included in Figure 4.1). The Punjabi team explained this apparent discrepancy in terms of audience. In situations like cartoon 8, the pupil is being victimised with few or no audience/spectators around, thus, many pupils did not consider it bullying. In comparison, in cartoon 9, the whole school is the audience and in north India, children are brought up in such a way that social consciousness, social shame and embarrassment in front of others are considered very important. A child's social image is damaged when he/she is repeatedly victimised with many people witnessing him/her.

The Punjabi researchers did comment that although the pupils enjoyed doing the task and found it interesting, they also 'found the task lengthy and time-consuming' (no other teams forwarded such comments), so it is also possible that falling of concentration affected these results.

India – Tamil

Three Tamil terms were selected for study. All three score very low on the non-aggressive cartoons. However *cintutal* is clearly not a good substitute for *bullying*, as it is high on physical fights (as well as on rumours). *Keli* is low on physical fights, and moderate on the other clusters, but high on rumours and cyber. *Tunpuruttal* is high on physical fights, verbal attacks, rumours and cyber, and moderately high on the others, so comes across as a general term for aggression.

There are in fact a plethora of terms in Tamil that describe various kinds of aggression (see Chapter 13). According to dictionaries, *cintutal* refers to a verbal or relational form of disturbing others, *keli* to verbal bullying or teasing and *tunpuruttal* to harassment. In summary, from the cartoon data none of these three terms appears to be a good equivalent for *bullying*. *Tunpuruttal*, and to a lesser extent *cintutal*, describe aggression generally. *Keli* comes closer to *bullying* in discriminating from physical fights, but focuses on rumours and cyber attacks and does not score at all high on physical attacks.

Lithuania

Five Lithuanian terms were selected for study. All five score very low on the non-aggressive cartoons. *Patyčios* scores high on verbal attacks and rumours. *Smurtas* scores high on physical attacks, whether there is a power imbalance or not. *Pažeminimas* scores high on all bullying clusters except for social exclusion, although it does not discriminate physical bullying from physical fighting quite as well as *patyčios*. *Atstūmimas* mainly scores high on social exclusion. *Diskriminacija* has a rather indistinct profile although tending to be highest on verbal attacks.

In summary, of the terms examined, *pažeminimas* is closest to *bullying*, while the other terms have more specialised meanings. *Pažeminimas* is usually translated as *humiliation*. In a book for teachers (Povilaitis & Jasiulione, 2008), the aim of bullying is defined as to humiliate and hurt others, and the president of Lithuania, Dalia Grybauskaite, used the terms *žeminantis elgesys* (humiliating behaviour) and *žeminimas* (humiliation), as well as *patyčios* as synonyms in her Annual Report of 2016 (www.lrp.lt/lt/kalbos/metiniai-pranesimai/2016-m./25366) and in her speech for opening the annual 'Action Week without Bullying' published in the national media portal (www.15 min.lt). Nevertheless, *patyčios* is usually taken as the translation of *bullying*, and was the term used in the HBSC report on Lithuania (e.g. Craig et al., 2009).

Russia

Five Russian terms were selected for study. All five score low or very low on the non-aggressive cartoons. Similar to Lithuanian *diskriminacija*, Russian *discriminatsia* has a rather indistinct profile, although somewhat higher on verbal attacks and social exclusion. *Izdevatel'stvo* has a profile quite similar to that for bullying, although a bit low on exclusion. *Uschemlenie* is high on physical and verbal bullying, but only moderate on other forms. *Preznenie* is high on verbal attacks, rumours and exclusion. *Neuvazhenie* is high on all kinds of attacks, including fights, so appears to be a term for general aggression. In summary, *izdevatel'stvo* appears to be quite a similar term to English *bullying*, except for not scoring so high on social exclusion. The other terms are more specialised, or in the case of *neuvazhenie*, more general.

Thailand

Three Thai terms were used; one, *tum rai*, was also included in the 2002 study (Table 4.1). All three score low on four of the non-aggressive cartoons but get rather high scores (57, 52, 61) on cartoon 7 (playful hitting), suggesting some specific issue around distinguishing playful and real fighting in these Thai pupils. Otherwise, the term *rang khae* has a reasonable match to English *bullying*, although a bit low on social exclusion. *Tum rai* is high on physical attacks, followed by physical bullying; this is a somewhat different finding from that in the 2002 study, where *tum rai* scored highest on physical bullying. Finally, *lor len* scored rather low on all clusters, but moderate on verbal attacks. In summary, of the three terms examined here, *rang khae* appears a reasonable equivalent of English *bullying*.

Discussion

The English term *bullying* has a distinct meaning, generally considered as enshrined in intent to harm, repetition and power imbalance. Given these criteria, it can apply to physical, verbal, relational and cyber forms. The findings regarding bullying from Australia and England are consistent with this interpretation.

Other languages do not always have terms very similar to *bullying*, even if the concept is readily recognised when discussed. Interestingly *bullying* has been introduced into other languages, for example, in Spain, and in Brazil, where the understanding of its meaning is quite concordant (Table 4.4). In Italy, it has been co-opted as *bullismo* (Menesini, 2000). In Punjab, it is used too in schools where English is widely used. However, identifying a word close in meaning to *bullying* proved more difficult both in Punjab and in Tamil Nadu. The situation may be complicated by a considerable variety of dialects in both these Indian regions. It was easier for the other participating countries, as *pažeminimas* in Lithuania, *izdevatel'stvo* in Russia and *rang khae* in Thailand all have quite similar profiles to *bullying* (Table 4.4).

The issue is important when using a term for *bullying* in questionnaires. The Olweus questionnaire uses the term, and although it also gives a definition, it is quite likely that the pupils' natural understanding of the term may influence their responses. In this respect, the data from Lithuania are of particular interest. Lithuania regularly comes out highest or near highest in HBSC surveys of victim and bully rates across mainly European and North American countries (www.hbsc.org); these surveys use Olweus-type questions and a term as a translation of *bullying*. One possibility is that if a general term for aggression was used as the translation for *bullying* in the Lithuanian surveys, then high rates might be obtained because of this – an artefact of the translation.

However if *patyčios* was usually taken as the translation of *bullying*, then this explanation is discredited, as *patyčios* has a generally lower profile than *pažeminimas* across most main bullying clusters (e.g. lower than *bullying* in Australia) (Table 4.4). The high HBSC rates in Lithuania remain a puzzle, as Lithuania does not score high (in fact just below the mean) on the EU Kids online survey of bullying rates in 25 European countries (Livingstone, Haddon, Görzig & Ólafsson, 2011); this survey used a more behavioural description and did not use the term *bullying*. It would nevertheless be good practice if surveys such as HBSC, and other comparative studies that use a *bullying* term, say what actual term was used to translate bullying in the languages concerned.

The data presented here should be considered indicative, in the sense that the samples are fairly small, and not necessarily representative of the countries concerned; indeed in Punjab and Tamil Nadu they may not be representative of the states concerned, especially given dialectical variations within them. Meanings can also change over time; indeed, the term *bullying* has probably come to include more social exclusion situations in more recent decades (Monks & Smith, 2006). Comparing Tables 4.1 and 4.4, some shifts in the meaning of *harassment* and *teasing* are suggested, possibly sample effects (e.g. more pupils of non-white backgrounds in the current sample), possibly actual changes over a time span of about 18 years. The Thai term *tum rai* also has a different profile from the earlier study.

Some questions remain in interpreting the findings from the data, and identifying a concordant term for *bullying* in Punjabi or Tamil was not really achieved. However the study raises serious issues. Choice of terms used to translate *bullying* do matter. Furthermore, such choices should be clearly specified in reports and publications. The cartoon test provides an important way of examining the meanings of terms, to help interpret cross-national and cross-cultural comparisons.

References

Craig, W., Harel-Fisch, Y., Fogel-Grinvald, H., Dostaler, S., Hetland, J., Simons-Morton, B., ... HBSC Bullying Writing Group (2009). A cross-national profile of bullying and victimization among adolescents in 40 countries. *International Journal of Public Health*, 54 (Suppl. 2), 216–224.

Livingstone, S., Haddon, L., Görzig, A. & Ólafsson, K. (2011). *Risks and Safety on the Internet: The Perspective of European Children. Full Findings*. LSE, London: EU Kids Online.

Menesini, E. (ed.) (2000). *Bullismo: Che fare?* Florence: Giunti.

Menesini, E., Fonzi, A. & Smith, P. K. (2002). Attribution of meanings to terms related to bullying: A comparison between teachers' and pupils' perspectives in Italy. *European Journal of Psychology of Education, 17*, 393–406.

Monks, C. & Smith, P. K. (2006). Definitions of 'bullying': Age differences in understanding of the term, and the role of experience. *British Journal of Developmental Psychology, 24*, 801–821.

Povilaitis, R. & Jasiulione, J. R. (2008). *Mokykla gali įveikti patyčias. Rekomendacijos mokytojams [School Can Overcome Bullying. Recommendations for Teachers]*. Vilnius: SMM.

Rivers, I. & Noret, N. (2010). 'I h8 u': Findings from a five-year study of text and email bullying. *British Educational Research Journal, 36*, 643–671.

Smith, P. K., Cowie, H., Olafsson, R. & Liefooghe, A. (2002). Definitions of bullying: A comparison of terms used, and age and sex differences, in a 14-country international comparison. *Child Development, 73*, 1119–1133.

Smith, P. K., Kwak, K., Hanif, R., Kanetsuna, T., Mahdavi, J., Lin, S.-F., Olafsson, R. & Ucanok, Z. (2016). Linguistic issues in studying bullying-related phenomena: Data from a revised cartoon task. In P. K. Smith, K. Kwak & Y. Toda (eds.), *School Bullying in Different Cultures: Eastern and Western Perspectives* (pp. 280–298). Cambridge: Cambridge University Press.

Smith, P. K., Robinson, S. & Marchi, B. (2016). Cross-national data on victims of bullying: What is really being measured? *International Journal of Development Science, 10*, 9–19.

Smorti, A., Menesini, E. & Smith, P. K. (2003). Parents' definition of children's bullying in a five-country comparison. *Journal of Cross-Cultural Psychology, 34*, 417–432.

Ucanok, Z., Smith, P. K. & Karasoy, D.S. (2011). Definitions of bullying: Age and gender differences in a Turkish sample. *Asian Journal of Social Psychology, 14*, 75–83.

Part II

Comparative Data on Bullying

5 Cyberviolence and Cyberbullying in Europe and India
A Literature Review

Catherine Blaya, Kirandeep Kaur, and Damanjit Sandhu

The emergence of the age of the web 2.0, of handheld devices that enable constant connexion and the development of new forms of communication (blogs, photo and video sharing, instant messaging, tweeting, and video calls) has opened up new opportunities under the form of knowledge and culture sharing, of communication and socialization, and has transformed inter-individual relationships. India, just as European countries, has seen a rapid growth in Internet and smartphone usage in recent years. Digital India and other policy initiatives by the Government of India and the contribution of multinational companies in harnessing the potential of the Indian market have promoted the extension of information and communication technologies (ICTs) in the country at a rapid pace (UNICEF, 2016). In Europe, digital communication and tools are included in the school environment for learning purposes and there is a strong incentive from boards of education to promote digital literacy and innovative pedagogies using ICTs (Blaya, 2013). The rapid expansion of ICTs has provided young children and adolescents with new and varied opportunities, but at the same time a lack of online safety measures and digital literacy has put them at a risk of cyberbullying, grooming, and online sexual exploitation (UNICEF, 2016). As a consequence, cyberspace has emerged as a place where young people can be the targets of bullies, well beyond the playground (Hinduja & Patchin, 2009), and new technologies have become a privileged medium for harassment, intimidation, blackmail, discrimination, and harming others.

Research on cyberbullying among young people was initiated in North America (Ybarra & Mitchell, 2004; Li, 2007; Kolwalski, Limber, & Agastston, 2008; Shariff, 2008), while in Europe, research was developed later, mainly by researchers in psychology (Smith et al., 2008), following the path of research on school bullying to start with. In India, there is a dearth of research examining online behaviours of children and cyber victimization patterns of youth. Furthermore, no proper online abuse reporting system is available to Indian children. Thus, cyberviolence and cyberbullying have become public health concerns due to their potential dramatic consequences. These range from anger, frustration, isolation, dropping out of school, and anxiety to suicidal ideation and suicide (Kowalski & Limber, 2013).

Only a few studies take a cross-national approach (Livingstone et al., 2011; HBSC, 2016), and so far, no comparison has been made between Europe and India. The only existing scientific survey we know of is by Wright and colleagues comparing adolescents in China, India, and Japan (Wright et al., 2015a). Here we present a review and synthesis of research on cyberviolence and cyberbullying in Europe and India. We also address the related phenomenon of Internet addiction.

Internet Addiction in Europe

In a world where young people are heavily involved in online activities, research in its early stages focused on risk-taking and negative online experiences. As part of risk-taking, some concern grew about Internet addiction, as a correlation between a large amount of time spent online with victimization and perpetration was found (Ybarra & Mitchell, 2004).

Internet addiction is defined by Young (1998) from the accumulation of five criteria out of eight: mental preoccupation with the Internet; feeling the need to spend more time on the Internet to gain more satisfaction; not being able to control or limit Internet use; feeling frustration, anger, anxiety, or depression when not being able to connect; spending more time online than intended; job opportunities and social relations jeopardized because of the time spent online; lying about time spent online; and using the Internet as a distraction from personal problems. Griffiths (2002) defines Internet addiction as a dependence on electronic devices and identifies different types of addiction, such as Internet gaming addiction and addiction to social networks. There is not yet a consensus definition within the scientific community (Sariyska et al., 2015).

Many expressions are used such as problematic use of the Internet, compulsive use of the Internet, or excessive use of the Internet. In Europe, attention has been put on excessive use of the Internet (Šmahel et al., 2012); that is, a use that is repetitive, compulsive, and uncontrolled and that negatively affects other aspects of life. Findings from EU Kids Online show that among young people aged 11–16 from 25 European countries, 35% stated they had spent less time with family or friends than they should because of their online activities, and 33% acknowledged they had felt bothered when not able to go online. As a whole, 29% of respondents answered "fairly" or "very often" to at least one or more of the questions assessing the excessive use of the Internet; however, the study concluded that very few young people (1%) can be considered as having reached a pathological level of use. The type of excessive use most often quoted was spending time on the Internet with no real interest. The most vulnerable young people are those with emotional problems and with high levels of sensation-seeking. Looking across European countries, the ones where young people reported an excessive use most often were Estonia, Portugal, Bulgaria, and England (p. 18); Cyprus scored the highest rate of young people answering positively to all the assessed behaviours (5%).

Cyberbullying in Europe: The First Stages of Research

As for cyber victimization and cyberbullying, much research has been completed. Much has focused on the definition of cyberbullying (Menesini & Nocentini, 2009; Menesini et al., 2012) and the possible differences or similarities between cyberbullying and traditional or offline bullying (Slonje & Smith 2008; Schultze-Krumbholz & Scheithauer, 2009). Some researchers argue that online and offline bullying are the "same wine in a new bottle" (Li, 2007), while others point out the specific characteristics of what happens online (Heirman & Walrave, 2008; Vandebosch & Van Cleemput, 2008; Corcoran, McGuckin, & Prentice, 2015).

As shown by Berne and colleagues (2012), a great variety of concepts and measuring tools is available to evaluate online aggression, cyberbullying, electronic bullying, online victimization, cyberviolence, cyber aggression, etc. As Corcoran, McGuckin, and Prentice (2015) stress, the way we define and measure online aggression does influence the quality of responses. Some researchers base their research on asking about behaviours, others on asking about the electronic media used to bully. Many researchers use a definition of cyberbullying based on the characteristics defined by Olweus (1993): repetition, intention to harm, and imbalance of power. However, bullying on the Internet and with digital devices has specific characteristics such as great dissemination of power, facilitated anonymity, and distance that can reduce empathy.

Just as in the rest of the world, researchers in Europe do not share the same approach and do not all use the term *cyberbullying*. For example, Grigg (2010) in England, Pyzalski (2012) in Poland, Sticca and colleagues (2013) in Switzerland, and Corcoran and colleagues (2015) in Ireland use the term *cyber aggression*, which relates to a certain number of violent incidents online. Blaya (2013) in France uses the term *cyberviolence*, which has the same meaning as *cyber aggression* and which represents any type of online aggression without limiting it to cyberbullying (that is considered as one specific type of cyberviolence). Corcoran and McGuckin (2014) show the incidence is lower in studies using a more restrictive definition of *cyberbullying*.

The prevalence, frequency, and consequences of cyberbullying have been investigated with a focus on the different forms that cyberbullying can take and on online risk-taking by young people (Gradinger, Strohmeier, & Spiel, 2009; Ortega et al., 2009; Baldry, Farrington, & Sorrentino, 2015). A risk and needs assessment approach can identify children at risk and design better interventions. Very rapidly, research in communication and media, but also in criminology and social sciences, has focused on the risks and harm related to the use of the Internet and electronic media, as well as on the opportunities they could offer. Most research has used self-report methods for assessing victims and perpetrators, based on the Olweus bullying questionnaire and the subsequent version of Smith and colleagues (2008). Findings have shown that prevalence rates range from 6% to 40%.

The first comparative research work on cyberbullying completed across Europe was by EU Kids Online (www2.lse.ac.uk/mediaalse/resea rch/EUKidsOnline/home.aspx) (Hasebrink, Livingstone, & Haddon, 2008); this provided an overview of the digital practices of young people (access, usage, risks taking), of harm online, and of traditional bullying, as well as the mediation of Internet use by parents and teachers; it stressed that there were some large differences between the 21 participating European countries. This research was followed by a second survey in 2010 (Livingstone et al., 2011); together with the HBSC survey (2016), these compare the prevalence of the phenomenon cross-nationally. However, the measures used were different. The EU Kids Online survey asked young people if they had experienced bullying online during the 12 previous months and if this was on the Internet, or by mobile phone calls, texts, or image/video texts. The respondents were also asked if the negative experience took the form of nasty or hurtful messages that were sent to them, nasty or hurtful messages that were passed around or posted publicly, nasty or hurtful things on the Internet, threats on the Internet, online ostracism, or something else. The HBSC survey that included 42 countries (inside Europe and outside Europe), asked if the respondents "had experienced being sent mean messages, emails, texts or wall-postings, or someone had created a website that made fun of them; or someone had taken unflattering or inappropriate photographs of them without permission and posted them online" (2016, p. 24). The respondents could answer "not at all during the last couple of months" to "several times a week".

The analyses of these data show that differences remain in the involvement of young people in cyberbullying across European countries. As highlighted by Smith, Robinson, & Marchi (2016), findings differ greatly from one survey to the other (EU Kids Online and HBSC). The two surveys are hardly comparable due to differences in the research design and in age ranges (HBSC: 11, 13, and 15 years old; EU Kids Online: 9–16 years old). The EU Kids Online survey shows that there can be huge differences across participating countries and that these differences are partly influenced by historical and culturally constructed factors such as post-war situations. The HBSC survey stresses that differences between countries were not as big as for traditional bullying (HBSC, 2016, p. 208). In a few countries, cyberbullying was associated with family affluence (Greenland, Israel, Lithuania, Canada, Slovakia, Croatia, and Sweden; see p. 207). This confirms that cyberbullying is not only related to the use of electronic media, and highlighted the need for further research on the impact of cultural and socio-economic factors and ethical values.

The HBSC survey findings show that as a whole, 3% of the respondents (11–15 years old) reported cyberbullying (victims online at least twice in the two previous months) and that there is no significant gender difference.

Another important research network was the COST Action IS0801 *Cyberbullying: coping with negative and enhancing positive uses of new technologies, in relationships in educational settings* (http://sites.google.com/site/costis0801/). This gathered researchers from 26 European countries. The network was organized into six working groups, whose objectives were to enhance positive uses of new technologies in the relationships area, contribute to the definition of cyberbullying and tools to measure it, assess the input of the outside research community, review existing guidelines, and recommend coping strategies (Smith & Steffgen, 2013).

Both networks produced a lot of literature on the definition and measurement of cyberbullying, the uses of digital skills, prevention, and intervention. An example is the work of Menesini and colleagues (2012) on the definition of cyberbullying in six European countries (Germany, Italy, Spain, France, Estonia, and Sweden), which showed differences, although small, in the representation of the characteristics of cyberbullying for young people across countries. As a whole, in terms of definition, the notion of imbalance of power was relevant in all countries.

Intentionality and anonymity proved less important in Italy and Germany. Whether cyber aggression was private or public did not prove of importance in terms of definition. A set of guidelines for preventing cyberbullying in the school environment applicable in Europe was also designed (Välimäki et al., 2012).

From the mid-2000s, under the impulse of the European Commission and mainly within the frame of the Leonardo Da Vinci/ Lifelong Learning Programme and Daphne projects, some intervention programmes were developed. An early project was implemented by Guarini, Brighi, and Genta (2009) from 2007 to 2009, funded by the Daphne II programme. The objectives were to design measurement tools, to collect data in a cross-national perspective, and to design specific educational material for awareness-raising interventions. This research (as also shown by EU Kids Online) concluded that cyberbullying was a Europe-wide issue, although differences existed, especially where no policy was designed to tackle negative online behaviours. Another important action was the CyberTraining project, undertaken in 2008, coordinated by Thomas Jäger. This two-year project aimed to design a training manual on cyberbullying for training school staff, families, and young people on the nature of, prevalence, and interventions against cyberbullying in Europe. It included Germany, Spain, Portugal, England, Bulgaria, and Switzerland (www.cybertraining-pro ject.org).

Whatever the differences in definitions and prevalence of cyberbullying, research has concluded that, just as for traditional bullying, cyberbullying is to be taken seriously and represents a major health problem for young people. In this regard, the EU Kids Online research has used nationally representative samples and provided some rigorous cross-national insight (Helsper et al., 2013).

There is some evidence that as for traditional bullying, the protagonists of cyberbullying often attend the same school. As a consequence, considerable focus has been on the role of schools to target and prevent cyberbullying (Wölfer et al., 2014; Blaya, 2015). As stressed by Smith and colleagues (2012), many schools still lack policies against cyberbullying, and Blaya (2015) showed that the quality of the overall school climate can be affected by cyberbullying among the students. Whatever policy schools implement, there is little evidence of their positive impact up to now.

Although the European Commission funding of these projects is over, these networks have facilitated continuing cooperation since the mid-2000s. Further research is being done, and the focus of attention has been changing due to the technical and societal evolution.

Research on Sexting in Europe

There is a growing concern about the sexualization of online relationships, and qualitative research has been completed to better understand the underlying process of sexting and cybersexism. Sexting, including sexual solicitations and sexually explicit messages, is quite prevalent (Ringrose et al., 2012). Some studies examine how young people present and build their identity online through the use of social media and the publication of pictures. The development of services such as Instagram and Snapchat has facilitated the publication of private photographs, and pre-teens have become very active in publicizing their self-identity. A survey by Mascheroni, Vincent, and Jimenez (2015) suggests that there are gender differences in the presentation of self online and that girls are more subjected to norms and appraisals from others than boys. Some girls post suggestive and provocative pictures or sexually explicit messages in search of peer acceptance; however, this may lead to rejection and blaming such as the so-called *slut-shaming* effect, revenge porn, and low self-esteem. Cybersexism has developed and girls are subjected to peer pressure to look perfect, to stick to gender stereotypes imposed by their bodies' hypersexualization, or, on the contrary, to look pure and innocent, corresponding then to the recent backlash of puritanism (Renold & Ringrose, 2011). This research concluded that in Europe, mobile devices have facilitated the exposition, distribution, and consumption of sexual-oriented publications and communication and that this is a problematic issue of our contemporary society (Ringrose et al., 2012).

European Intervention Programmes

We now better understand the negative experiences and behaviours of young people online and cyberbullying during the past 10 years. Intervention programmes and their evaluation have now come to the fore; many intervention programmes have been designed, but there is little scientific evidence about their effectiveness in changing behaviours and reducing harm.

Four systematic reviews and meta-analyses offer a review or analysis of interventions against cyberbullying since the early 2000s (Tokunaga, 2010; Mishna et al., 2009; Perren et al., 2012; Blaya, 2015). School-based interventions to prevent and tackle cyberbullying are becoming numerous, but the question that arises is the effectiveness of such interventions from the perspective of an evidence-based approach (Blaya et al., 2006; Nocentini, Zambuto, & Menesini, 2015). Research suggests that more than restrictive approaches, the most effective way to limit harm online is to set up dialogue with young people (Law, Shapka, & Olson, 2010; Livingstone et al., 2011; Nikken & de Graaf, 2013). Moreover, since cyberviolence is often associated with traditional violence, systemic approaches and interventions that aim to improve the social climate of schools and to reduce traditional bullying are likely to contribute to a reduction of cyberbullying too (König, Gollwitzer, & Steffgen, 2010; Perren et al., 2012). Moreover, the synthesis of the aforementioned reviews shows that few interventions are effective in reducing cyberbullying. As for traditional bullying, most of them have a positive impact on awareness raising, but provide few positive outcomes on behaviours (both for risk-taking and for involvement).

Interventions that specifically target cyberviolence and that have been assessed as effective at the European level include the MedienHelden programme in Germany (Schultze-Krumbholz et al., 2012), Noncadiamointrappola in Italy (Palladino, Nocentini, & Menesini, 2012) and ConRed in Spain (Del Rey, Casas, & Ortega, 2011). The common characteristics of these interventions are that they are school-based and offer a systemic approach. They are based on behavioural cognitive techniques and the beneficiaries are actively involved in activities to prevent cyberbullying. Finally, they contribute to the development of social skills such as empathy, self-esteem, and peer support. Staff and parents are included, and the researchers who designed the interventions monitor the programmes.

Two other intervention programmes, whose objectives are mainly to reduce traditional bullying, have shown that they can also reduce cyberbullying. One is the KiVa programme from Finland (Salmivalli, Kärnä, & Poskiparta (2011) and the other is the VisC in Austria (Strohmeier et al., 2012). The effectiveness of these two intervention schemes tends to confirm the conclusions of Perren and colleagues (2012), as well as Modecki and colleagues (2014), that, due to the overlap between traditional bullying and cyberbullying, multimodal interventions that address both types of bullying are recommended for greater effectiveness.

Cyberbullying: A Worldwide Issue and Research Perspectives

Cyberbullying is not specific to a few countries but is a worldwide challenge. Studies are often not comparable due to differences in research design and measurement tools (Smith et al., 2016). For instance, much depends on the definition of what is measured: *cyber aggression, cyberviolence*, and *cyberbullying* in many countries are used as umbrella terms while in others, the researchers make a distinction between repeated cyber aggression or isolated incidents. Differences also exist in the period of time used to measure the phenomenon (last week, last month, last six months, during the academic year, etc.), the specificities of the surveyed population, and the cutting point for deciding when it is cyberbullying or not.

There is little research that investigates cyberbullying and sociological factors such as the socio-economic background of the family, the family functioning, the social structure of society, or acceptance and exposure to violence. Gender and sexting need to be further investigated mainly with the youngest Internet users. The EU Kids Online group has included some sociological variables in its work. The first conclusions are that the differences between children from low, medium, and high socio-economic backgrounds are low. However these aspects need to be thought over more thoroughly so that they are applicable Europe-wide and can reflect accurate situations.

In relation to the issues of violent extremism, racism, and xenophobia, hate online is one of the rising concerns and deserves further investigation. Some studies have been completed about online hate in social media and cyber hate among young people (Hawdon, 2012; Oksanen et al., 2014; Blaya, 2016) and show that exposure to this type of online hate is rather common (67% in Finland; 32% in France), as well as the involvement of young people (32% victims in Finland; 15% victims and 9% perpetrators in France). These researches show the link between violent extremism and online hate activism; it seems of vital importance to better understand what processes lead some young people to adopt extremist ideologies and violence and what role electronic media play.

Even if cross-national research within the European context has been completed, little has been done to compare the European situation with countries outside Europe. The Asia-Pacific region, and, within the area, India, have dedicated some research to better understand the involvement of young people in digital uses and cyberbullying. Wright, Kamble, and Soudi (2015b) have started some work on the impact of cultural values on cyberbullying behaviours among Indian adolescents and shown that individualism was positively associated with cyber aggression while collectivism and peer attachment at an average level acted as a protective factor. Their study highlights the need to further investigate the involvement of Indian students in cyber aggression.

India and Cyberbullying: A Paucity of Scientific Research but Quite a Few Surveys

As in many countries, there has been a rapid growth in the use of ICTs and Internet services among the Indian population (Chapter 1). Although access to ICT is a priority for the Indian government, risks related to being online have received very little attention until recently (UNICEF, 2016). There is a dearth of research of the potential risks associated with the use of electronic media. It can be said that research in India on issues like online behaviours of children and youth, cyberbullying, and various other negative online experiences is still in its infancy.

Recently, Indian researchers from various fields, especially psychology, information technology, and criminology, have started to explore youth access, usage, and negative online experiences. The Indian media have also played a significant role in exposing the impact of cyberbullying and cyber harassment on young people and have helped spread awareness about these issues. For example, the Indo-Asian News Service (IANS, 2016) recently covered the suicide of a 17-year-old Kolkata schoolgirl because someone uploaded her obscenely morphed picture on a social networking site, and this has drawn attention to the possible dramatic consequences of cyberbullying.

An article in *India Today* in 2012 showed the results of a survey done by Ipsos (a global market research company). The poll surveyed 18,000 adults (including 6,500 parents) from 24 countries. The study found that 45% of Indian parents believed that a child they knew was being cyberbullied, while 53% were aware of the issue of cyberbullying. Three out of 10 parents in India say that their children have been victims of cyberbullying; this was most often through informal communication destinations like Facebook (60%). Globally, cell phones and online talk rooms were a far-off second and third, each around 40%; in India, it is equal between long-range interpersonal communication locales like social networking sites (55%) and online talk rooms (54%). Biswarup Banerjee, the head of marketing communications for Ipsos in India, stressed that "the discoveries are very astounding, which uncovered that the prevalence of cyberbullying in India was higher than that of western countries, including the US (15%), Britain (11%) and France (5%). Before this review, there has been little proof to recommend cyberbullying is a noteworthy issue in the nation".

A survey by the Microsoft Corporation (2012) with 8–17-year-olds set out to understand the global pervasiveness of cyberbullying across 25 countries. India was found to have the third highest rate of online bullying. Among the Indian young people who responded, 53% had experienced cyberbullying and 50% had bullied someone online. Girls (53%) were found equally likely to be bullied online as boys (52%). Seventy per cent of the youth knew what online bullying was.

A third survey, entitled *Teens, Tweens and Technology Study* (Lenhart, 2015), examined online behaviours and social networking habits of tweens and teens (aged 8 to 16 years) in India. According to the poll, 90% of parents would monitor all of their children's online activities across all devices if they could. However, the majority of the children (64%) reported hiding (some of) their online activities from their parents, indicating that even parents who do keep a watchful eye are often deceived by what they see. Additionally, while many parents (86%) claimed to know the kind of activities that their children regularly participated in online, more than half of the children (56%) claimed that they would change their online behaviour when they knew their parents were watching, and 43% of children used anonymous names or aliases for their social media profiles. One in four (27%) children knew another person's password, and 61% of them had even accessed those people's accounts without them knowing; the main reasons cited for this were to see if they were talking to an ex-partner (64%), to see their private photos (49%), or to dig up dirt on them (42%). Forty-three per cent of the children active on social media claimed to have witnessed cruel behaviour on social networks, while 52% indicated that they had bullied people over social media themselves. Of these, 27% made fun of others, 24% called someone fat or ugly or made fun of other physical appearances, and 23% tagged mean pictures. Reasons for cyberbullying another child were because the others were mean to them (49%) or they just didn't like the other person (28%).

These surveys conducted by several private companies show that there is an increased concern about cyberbullying and various other negative online experiences among young people. Such surveys help in increasing public awareness regarding the uses of the Internet and their associated risks among the Indian population, but still there is a scarcity of sound scientific research about the prevalence, nature, and consequences of cyberbullying and even less research to provide teachers, schools, and parents with proactive strategies to combat and prevent it. However, some scientific works have been completed and provide preliminary indications on the state of the situation concerning cyberbullying and Indian youth.

Indian Research: A Focus on Digital Practices and Addiction to the Internet but Little Scientific Research on Cyberbullying

Taking into account the current ICT expansion in India, such that India now ranks third in the world for Internet usage (Internet Live Stats, 2015), it has become important to set the basis for an improved understanding of the digital environment in which Indian young people navigate and interact (UNICEF, 2016). Recently, there has been growing concern about whether the Internet usage of Indian children and youth is excessive and, if so, whether it amounts to an addiction; research has been completed to investigate the extent of cyberbullying among young people.

As in other countries, social networking in India is considered as potentially risky activity. For instance, Manjunatha (2013) explored the uses of social networking sites (SNS) by Indian students (aged 18–26) from various colleges and universities throughout the country; 80% spent a significant amount of time on social networks regularly, for 5 to 10 hours per week. Among the total users of SNS, two-thirds were males and one-third were females. Most of the respondents were registered on several networks. Among these students, 48% stated that they used SNS to maintain existing friends/relationships and 19% to find new friends, with 3% using them for dating purposes.

Various other researches have shown widespread SNS usage among Indian youth. Kumar and Kumar (2013) studied the activities and reasons for using SNS by postgraduate students and research scholars (mainly 20–30 years old) of Maharishi Dayanand University, Rohtak; the majority of the respondents from all disciplines had a profile on an online social network. Facebook was the most popular site used by all categories of respondents, followed by Twitter. Most used mobiles for accessing SNS, followed by PCs. The main purpose of using SNS was found to be entertainment, followed by sharing videos and pictures, instant messaging, and finding information. Nearly half had 10–49 friends online, with one-third having 50–100 friends. An important finding of this study was that the use of SNS was time-consuming.

Mahajan (2009) explored the usage, impact, and problems related to SNS and their impact on Indian social and cultural values. Findings from her survey showed that Indians use SNS such as Facebook to combat a rising concern and alertness against activities certain groups feel are not in keeping with the spirit of Indian culture. For example, Sourabh Mishra in Ad Age (Mishra, 2009) reported a group called A Consortium of Pub-Going, Loose and Forward Women, who organized a Pink Chaddi

Campaign on Valentine's Day, in which members were encouraged to send a pair of pink *chaddi* (a slang word for underwear or boxer shorts) to the head of a fundamentalist Hindu group. As a consequence, 40 Hindu activists attacked young men and women in a Mangalore pub, claiming that the women were behaving contrary to traditional Indian values. This attack was posted on YouTube (Pothier, 2009). Its impact on the country's social and cultural values is debatable, as some Indians feel it is a threat while others feel it is not. Its misuse needs to be addressed and resolved by people like site executives, legislators, and members of the regular community before it becomes endemic.

One of the main concerns in India about the Internet and its possible negative impacts is addiction. Internet addiction has been defined as an excessive use of the Internet, mobile phones, and social networking sites, which has detrimental consequences for a person's overall well-being. Its manifestations include obsessively checking one's phone or accessing the Internet very frequently to see if there are any new messages or any new updates, which results in physical, mental, and social health problems like eyesight issues, weight fluctuations, poor hygiene, social isolation, anxiety, stress, and headaches (UNICEF, 2016). Many Indian psychiatrists have reported a substantial increase in the number of people getting involved in Internet addiction to the extent of disrupting their daily functioning (DNA India, 2012; *Hindustan Times*, 2015).

Looking at the growing incidence of Internet addiction, Chakraborty, Basu, and Vijaya Kumar (2010) reviewed the fast-growing literature on the topic; despite no universally accepted definition, researchers seemed to agree that Internet addiction involves problematic computer usage which is time-consuming and causes distress or impairs functioning in important life domains. Several aetiological models have been proposed, from the diverse perspectives of learning theory, cognitive behavioural theory, social learning, reward deficiency, culture, genetics, and neurobiology. Controversies abound, ranging from conceptual (whether behavioural addictions are true addictions), technical (which component of Internet use is a person "addicted" to), and practical (how Internet addiction should be diagnosed, if it exists at all). Using various instruments and populations, Internet addiction has been suggested as having a prevalence of from 0.3% to 38%, with a preponderance of young males. Several screening, diagnostic, and severity assessment instruments are now available, but few have been subjected to rigorous psychometric testing. Psychiatric co-morbidity is common. Treatment modalities lack a firm evidence base, but antidepressants, mood stabilisers, and cognitive behavioural therapy and other psychotherapies have been used.

Nalwa and Anand (2003) investigated the extent of Internet addiction in a small sample of schoolchildren (16–18 years old) in Punjab. Two groups were identified, dependents (18) and non-dependents (21). Dependents, who spent more time on the Internet, were found to delay other work to spend time online, lose sleep due to late-night logons, and feel life would be boring without the Internet. The dependents also scored higher than the non-dependents on a loneliness measure.

Internet addiction and its correlates were explored among high school students in years 11 and 12 from Ahmedaba, India by Yadav and colleagues (2013). Out of the total sample of 621 pupils, 65 (11.8%) had Internet addiction. Age, gender, and self-rated academic performance did not predict Internet addiction. A strong positive correlation was observed between Internet addiction and depression, anxiety, and stress.

Some research has been conducted in higher education. Chathoth and colleagues (2013) examined the prevalence of Internet addiction in undergraduate medical students at Kasturba Medical College, Mangalore. They randomly selected 90 first-year students (18–20 years of age). Students were classified as normal users, mild, moderate, and severe in terms of Internet addiction. The most common online activity was found to be social networking (98%), followed closely by emailing (88%). The prevalence of moderate to severe Internet addiction appeared to be low, with 17 students (19%) classified this way.

Vidyachathoth and colleagues (2014) explored the association between addiction to the Internet and individuals' affect. This cross-sectional study involved 90 individuals from Mangalore, in the south of India, aged 18–20. Participants were selected randomly from the first year of medical undergraduate students. They found a significant positive correlation between Internet addiction and negative affect. Daily duration of Internet use and negative affect also had a positive correlation, highlighting the role of affect in behavioural addictions.

Rural and urban communities in India differ in many respects, including the accessibility and use of the Internet. Koovakkai and Muhammed (2010) focused on the difference in abuse of the Internet among a sample of 145 rural and urban adolescents in Kerala. Internet abuse was more frequent among rural than urban adolescents; this may be because of their ignorance about the seriousness of the matter and also due to a lack of available leisure activities. The rural and urban communities differed in many respects, including the accessibility of the Internet. The level of education and awareness of abuse of the Internet may also be higher among parents in urban areas. Most of the rural parents in Kerala are not exposed much to the Internet and their awareness about its misuse may be limited. Rural adolescents may explore and experiment with the possibilities of the Internet when they are exposed to such modern technology for the first time. Hence, the pattern of abuse of the rural and urban adolescents seems to differ in various aspects.

These research studies, although exploratory and often with small sample sizes, highlight that the prolonged and continuous use of the Internet is habit-forming and can lead to addiction along with various negative effects such as attention deficits and obsessive and compulsive behaviours. Studies have documented the negative impact of excessive Internet use and the potential negative outcomes from widespread SNS usage. Along with other negative outcomes associated with excessive ICT usage, Internet addiction and excessive usage of SNS among Indian children and youth has become a major concern for educators and mental health professionals.

Negative Online Experiences and Cyberbullying

The negative online experiences documented by the limited published research in India on cyberbullying, online harassment, and online risks highlight that Indian educators and researchers need to gain a better understanding of this issue. Research on risk-taking by Halder and Jaishankar (2010, involving 73 adult respondents from different regions of India, showed that the majority did not feel the need to read the policy guidelines or terms and conditions of ISPs and social networking websites before entering into a contract with these sites and opening their accounts. They did not mind sharing their profiles and passwords with their spouses and children either. They liked to participate in virtual socializing, with many unaware of spams, phishing emails, etc., and they often replied to these emails out of curiosity. However, many disliked chatting with strangers in public chat rooms and were aware that such chat friends may be fraudulent; many disliked sharing their personal secrets with chat friends. Social networking sites such as Orkut and Facebook are used to harass women by putting up fake profiles with or without morphed pictures, obscene descriptions, and so on.

Another recent trend in online usage highlighted by research involves using the Internet for watching pornography. Umarhathab, Rao, and Jaishankar (2009) studied people living in Chennai with basic computer (both software and hardware) knowledge. According to this survey, 56% and 46% of the participants spent their free time watching Tamil and English pornographic movies, respectively.

A survey by *Time* magazine, as reported by *Times of India*, revealed that more than 50% of Indians have admitted to sending sexually provocative pictures. Indian doctors have warned that teenagers who blindly ape the

West and who are suffering from lack of impulse control are most vulnerable to acts like sexting (SiliconIndia, 2012).

A study by security technology company McAfee looking at the gender differences in sexting found that 59% of the Indian women polled sent personal and intimate texts and images and that 30% filmed sexual video content. The rates are higher than for males (Ramya, 2014). Indian women of all ages and milieu are in jeopardy with the coming up of the Internet. Halder and Jaishankar (2010) highlighted that women are more likely than men to be victims of sexting and unwanted sexual content and to be submitted to sexual abuse in the form of unwanted requests for friendship or sexual solicitations from males. Revenge porn and cyberbullying from former partners are also part of the negative experiences reported by Indian females. While many women are victimized online, what makes Indian women unique? India is predominantly a patriarchal and orthodox country and women who are victimized are mostly blamed – online victims are no exception (Halder & Jaishankar, 2011a). There are instances where marriages of women victims were stopped due to their online victimization. Also, there is less legal protection for them compared to their Western counterparts and victimized Indian women do not get adequate solutions for their victimization from the ISPs governed predominantly from a Western cultural perspective (Halder & Jaishankar, 2011b). Women with feminist opinions can also be the target of online bullying such as hate messages, sexual messages or nasty teasing, and offensive comments on blogs or forums. However, the Halder and Jaishankar (2010) survey only focused on adult males and females, not adolescents.

Our literature review reveals a high prevalence of cyberviolence among Indian young people, and documents the potentially dramatic consequences it can have on the mental health and well-being of youth. Kaur and Sandhu (2015a) showed significant differences in the depressive affect and loneliness of cyberbullying victims compared to adolescents who were uninvolved in cyberbullying. Kaur and Sandhu (2015b) investigated the relationships of victims of cyberbullying with their parents and peers; they found that they were significantly lower on parental and peer attachment in comparison to their non-cyberbullied counterparts. Similarly, Wright and colleagues (2015b) investigated the moderating effects of peer attachment in Indian adolescents' involvement in cyber aggression. Their research was based on the assumption that Indian society is based on both collectivistic and individualistic values. They found a correlation between low levels of peer attachment and the perpetration of cyberbullying, more specifically when young people showed individualistic values. They concluded that peer attachment could be a protective factor against cyberbullying when associated with collectivistic cultural values. However, the same association with victimization was not found.

These findings, and previous findings related to offline bullying and aggression (Burton, Florell, & Wygant, 2013; Huang, Hong, & Espelage, 2013), are of importance to guide intervention schemes to prevent young people getting into online peer-to-peer aggression. However, further investigation of the issue according to the context in which young people live would be relevant.

When comparing the involvement of Indian adolescents in cyberbullying with other Asian countries such as China and Japan, research shows a higher involvement among Indian youth in both perpetration and victimization (Wright et al., 2015a). A study by Blaya and colleagues (2016) shows a similar difference between secondary school students from Punjab (north of India) and the Côte d'Azur area (south of France).

As far as India is concerned, research about various positive and negative online behaviours and risks among young people has been slower to develop than in Western countries, and needs further investigation. Surveys completed by various ICT private companies and NGOs show that there is a real need for better understanding of the issue. According to a UNICEF (2016) report, the total extent of online crimes and abuses against Indian children and youth is still unknown and there are neither preventive measures nor interventions in place. Although awareness has risen, huge gaps persist in terms of knowledge, reporting mechanisms, support services, law enforcement, and prevention strategies to effectively tackle online abuse, online violence, and exploitation of young people. As for Europe, although awareness is high and policies have been developed to prevent and tackle the issue, measurement and effective intervention issues need further investigation. Moreover, new concerns such as the use of the Internet by very young children, and online identity, race, or religious hate crimes, are emerging due to changes in society, and these urgently need to be addressed.

References

Baldry, A. C., Farrington, D. P., & Sorrentino, A. (2015). "Am I at risk of cyberbullying"? A narrative review and conceptual framework for research on risk of cyberbullying and cybervictimization: The risk and needs assessment approach. *Aggression and Violent Behavior, 23*, 36–51.

Berne, S., Frisén, A., Schultze-Krumbholz, A., Scheithauer, H., Naruskov, K., Luik, P., Katzer, C., Erentaite, R., & Zukauskiene, R. (2012). Cyberbullying assessment instruments: A systematic review. *Aggression and Violent Behavior, 18*, 320–334.

Blaya, C. (2013). *Les ados dans le cyberespace – prises de risque et cyberviolence.* Bruxelles: De Boeck.

Blaya, C. (2015). Cyberviolence et école. *Les Dossiers des sciences de l'Education, 33.*

Blaya, C. (2016). *Digital Uses, Risk-Taking and Online Negative Experiences among Secondary School Students in France and India: A Comparative Study.* Brasilia, Cetic Brazil: ICT Brazil, pp. 47–56.

Blaya C., Farrington, P. D., Petrosino, A., & Weisburd, D. (2006). Revues systématiques dans le champ criminologique et le groupe crime et justice de la collaboration Campbell. *International Journal of Violence and Schools, 1,* 72–80.

Blaya, C. & Fartoukh, M. (2015). Digital uses, victimization and online aggression: A comparative study between primary school and lower secondary school students in France. *European Journal on Criminal Policy and Research, 22*(2), 285–300. doi 10.1007/s10610-015–9293–7.

Burton, K. A., Florell, D., & Wygant, D. B. (2013). The role of peer attachment and normative beliefs about aggression on traditional bullying and cyberbullying. *Psychology in the Schools, 50*(2), 103–114. doi: 10.1002/pits.21663.

Chakraborty, K., Basu, D., & Vijaya Kumar K. G. (2010). Internet addiction: Consensus, controversies, and the way ahead. *East Asian Archives of Psychiatry, 20*(3), 123–132. Retrieved from www.easap.asia/index.php/component/k2/item/113-1003-v20n3-p123

Chathoth, V. M., Kodavanji, B., Arunkumar, N., & Pai, S. D. (2013). Internet behaviour pattern in undergraduate graduate students in Mangalore. *International Journal of Innovative Research in Science, Engineering and Technology, 2*(6), 2133. www.ijirset.com/upload/june/19_INTERNET.pdf.

Corcoran, L., McGuckin, C., & Prentice, G. (2015). Cyberbullying or cyber aggression? A review of existing definitions of cyber-based peer-to-peer aggression. *Societies, 5,* 245–255.

Corcoran, L., & McGuckin, C. (2014). Addressing bullying problems in Irish schools and in cyberspace: A challenge for school management. *Educational Research, 56,* 48–64.

Del Rey, R., Casas J.A., & Ortega, R. (2011). The ConRed Program, an evidence-based practice. *Comunicar, 20*(39), 129–138. doi: 10.3916/C39-2012-03-03

DNA India (2012, June 26). Internet addiction killing personal touch. Retrieved from www.dnaindia.com/mumbai/report-Internet-addiction-killing-personal-touch-1706731.

Goel, D., Subramanyam, A., & Kamath, R. (2013). A study on the prevalence of Internet addiction and its association with psychopathology in Indian adolescents. *Indian Journal of Psychiatry, 55*(2), 140–143.

Gradinger, P., Strohmeier, D., & Spiel, C. (2009). Traditional bullying and cyberbullying identification of risk groups for adjustment problems. *Zeitschrift für Psychologie/Journal of Psychology, 217*(4), 205–213.

Guarini, A., Brighi, A., & Genta, M. L. (2009). Traditional bullying and cyberbullying in Italian secondary schools. In Genta, M. L., Brighi, A., & Guarini, A. (eds.). *Bullying and Cyberbullying in Adolescence.* Roma: Carocci, pp. 77–85.

Griffiths, M. (2002). Occupational health issues concerning Internet use in the workplace. *Work and Stress, 16,* 283–286.

Grigg, D. W. (2010). Cyber-aggression: Definition and concept of cyberbullying. *Australian Journal of Guidance & Counselling, 20,* 143–156. doi:10.1375/ajgc.20.2.143.

Halder, D. & Jaishankar, K. (2010). *Cyber Victimization in India: A Baseline Survey Report.* Tirunelveli, India: Centre for Cyber Victim Counselling. www.cybervictims.org/CCVCresearchreport2010.pdf.

Halder, D. & Jaishankar, K. (2011a). Cyber gender harassment and secondary victimization: A comparative analysis of US, UK and India. *Victims and Offenders, 6*(4), 386–398. doi: 10.1080/15564886.2011.607402.

Halder, D. & Jaishankar, K. (2011b). *Cyber Crime and the Victimization of Women: Laws, Rights, and Regulations.* Hershey, PA: IGI Global.

Hasebrink, U., Livingstone, S., & Haddon, L. (2008). *Comparing Children's Online Opportunities and Risks across Europe: Cross-National Comparisons for EU Kids Online.* London: EU Kids Online.

Hawdon, J. (2012). Applying differential association theory to online hate groups: A theoretical statement. *Research on Finnish Society, 5,* 39–47.

Health Behaviour of School-Aged Children (HBSC) (2016). Growing up unequal: Gender and socioeconomic differences in young people's health and well-being. International Report from the 2013/2014 Survey. Retrieved from www.euro.who.int/__data/assets/pdf_file/0003/303438/HBSC-No.7-Growing-up-unequal-Full-Report.pdf?ua=1.

Heirman, W. & Walrave, M. (2008). Assessing concerns and issues about the mediation of technology in cyberbullying. *Cyberpsychology: Journal of Psychosocial Research on Cyberspace, 2*(2), article 1. www.cyberpsychology.eu/view.php?cisloclanku= 192008111401&article=1.

Helsper, E., Kalmus, V., Hasebrink, U., Sagvari, B., & de Haan, J. (2013). Country classification: Opportunities, risks, harm and parental mediation. Retrieved from http://eprints.lse.ac.uk/52023/.

Hinduja, S. & Patchin, J. W. (2009). *Bullying beyond the Schoolyard: Preventing and Responding to Cyberbullying.* Thousand Oaks, CA: Sage Publications.

Hindustan Times (2015, October 10). Reboot your brain: Phone addiction leads to depression. Retrieved from www.hindustantimes.com/health-and-fitness/rebootyour-brain-phone-addiction-leads-to-depression/story-Rp2jHxPGz6zhsmCi5YIAFO.html.

Huang, H., Hong, J. S., & Espelage, D. L. (2013). Understanding factors associated with bullying and peer victimization in Chinese schools within ecological contexts. *Journal of Child and Family Studies, 22*(7), 881–892. doi: 10.1007/s10826-012-9647-4.

India Today Online (2012, January 19). Indian kids worst victims of cyberbullying: Study. Retrieved from http://indiatoday.intoday.in/story/indian-kids-worst-victims-of-cyberbullying-study/1/169603.html.

Indo-Asian News Service (2016, September 12). Teen allegedly commits suicide over obscene photos on Facebook. Retrieved from www.ndtv.com/kolkata-ne ws/teen-allegedly-commits-suicide-over-obscene-photos-on-facebook-1457626.

Intel Corporation (2015). Intel security study reveals that almost half of Indian children admit to meeting or wanting to meet a stranger they first met online. Retrieved from http://intelsecurityapac.com/digitalsafety/wp-con tent/uploads/sites/40/2015/10/IntelSecurity_India_Press-Release_TeensTwe ensTech_271015.pdf.

Internet Live Stats (2015). Internet live stats. Retrieved from www.internetlive stats.com/.

Kaur, K. & Sandhu, D. (2015a). Studying depression and loneliness amongst the victims of cyber bullying. In M. Irfan, R. Sultana, H. Shafiq, M. Singh, & K. Singh (eds.), *Mental Health, Religion and Culture: A Psychological Paradigm* (pp. 10–18). Patiala: 21st Century Publications.

Kaur, K. & Sandhu, D. (2015b). Cyberbullying among adolescents: Attachment with parents and peers. *Journal of Research: The Bede Athenaeum*, 6(1), 104–118.

König, A., Gollwitzer, M., & Steffgen, G. (2010). Cyberbullying as an Act of Revenge? *Australian Journal of Guidance and Counselling*, 20(2), 210–244.

Koovakkai, D. & Muhammed, P. (2010). Internet abuse among adolescents: A study on the locale factor. *Webology*, 7(1). Article 75. www.webology.org/192 010/v7n1/a75.html.

Kowalski, R. M. & Limber, S. P. (2013). Psychological, physical, and academic correlates of cyberbullying and traditional bullying. *Journal of Adolescent Health*, 53(1), S13–S20.

Kowalski, R., Limber, S., & Agatston, P. W. (2007). *Cyber Bullying: Bullying In The Digital Age*. Malden, MA: Blackwell Publishers.

Kumar, A. & Kumar, R. (2013). Use of social networking sites (SNSs): A study of Maharishi Dayanand University, Rohtak, India. *Library Philosophy and Practice (e-journal)*. Paper 1000. Retrieved from http://digitalcommons.unl.edu/libphil prac/1000.

Kumar, S. N. & Sayadevi, V. (2009). Internet addiction among college students. Retrieved from www.iacp.in/2009/06/internet-addiction-among-college.html.

Law, D., Shapka, J., & Olson, B. (2010). To control or not to control? Parental behaviors and adolescent online aggression. *Computers in Human Behavior*, 26, 1651–1656.

Lenhart, A. (2015). Pew Research Center, "Teen, Social Media and Technology Overview 2015". Retrieved from http://assets.pewresearch.org/wp-content/up loads/sites/14/2015/04/PI_TeensandTech_Update2015_0409151.pdf.

Li, Q. (2007). New bottle but old wine: A research of cyberbullying in schools. *Computers in Human Behavior*, 23, 1777–1791.

Livingstone, S., Haddon, L., Görzig, A., & Ölafsson, K. (2011). *Risks and Safety on the Internet: The Perspective of European Children. Full Findings*. LSE, London: EU Kids Online.

Mahajan, P. (2009). Use of social networking sites in a linguistically and culturally rich India. *The International Information & Library Review, 41,* 129–136.

Manjunatha, S. (2013). The usage of social networking sites among the college students in India. *International Research Journal of Social Sciences, 2*(5), 15–21. Available online at: www.isca.in.

Mascheroni, G. & Ólafsson, K. (2014). *Net Children Go Mobile: Risks and Opportunities.* Second Edition. Milano: Educatt. www.netchildrengomobile.eu/ reports.

Mascheroni, G., Vincent, J., & Jimenez, E. (2015). "Girls are addicted to likes so they post semi-naked selfies": Peer mediation, normativity and the construction of identity online. *Cyberpsychology: Journal of Psychosocial Research on Cyberspace, 9*(1), article 5. doi: 10.5817/CP2015-1-5.

Menesini, E. & Nocentini, A. (2009). Cyberbullying definition and measurement: Some critical considerations. *Zeitschrift für Psychologie/Journal of Psychology, 217*(4), 230–232.

Menesini, E., Nocentini, A., Palladino, B. E., Frisén, A., Berne, S., Ortega Ruiz, R., Calmaestra, J., Scheithauer, H., Schultze-Krumbholz, A., Luik, P., Naruskov, K., Blaya, C., Berthaud, J., & Smith, P. K. (2012). Cyberbullying definition among adolescents: A comparison across six European countries. *Cyberpsychology, Behavior, and Social Networking, 15*(9), 455–463.

Microsoft Corporation (2012). *Bullying among Youth 8–17 Years Old – India.* Cross-Tab Marketing Services & Telecommunications. Research Group for Microsoft Corporation.

Mishna, F., Cook, C., Saini, M., Wu, M.-J., & MacFadden, R. (2009). *Interventions for Children, Youth and Parents to Prevent and Reduce Cyber Abuse.* Oslo: Campbell Systematic Reviews.

Mishra, S. (2009). Newest tools in India's culture wars: Facebook and pink underwear. Advertising age. Retrieved from http://adage.com/globalnews/arti cle?article_idZ134573.

Modecki, K., Minchin, J., Harbaugh, A. G., Guerra, N. G., & Runions, K. C. (2014). Bullying prevalence across contexts: A meta-analysis measuring cyber and traditional bullying. *Journal of Adolescent Health, 5,* 602–611.

Nalwa, K. & Anand, A. P. (2003). Internet addiction in students: A cause of concern. *Cyberpsychology & Behavior, 6*(6), 653–656.

Nikken, P. & de Graaf, H. (2013). Reciprocal relationships between friends' and parental mediation of adolescents' media use and their sexual attitudes and behavior. *Journal of Youth and Adolescence, 42,* 1696–1707. doi: 10.1007/ s10964-012-9873-5.

Nocentini, A., Zambuto, V., & Menesini, E. (2015). Anti-bullying programs and information and communication technologies (ICTs): A systematic review. *Aggression and Violent Behavior, 23,* 52–60.

National Sample Survey Office (2014). *Key Indicators of Social Consumption in India: Education, 71st Round.* NSS KI (71/25.2), New Delhi. Retrieved from http://mospi.nic.in/mospi_new/upload/nss_71st_ki_education_30june15.pdf.

Oksanen, A., Hawdon J., Holkeri, E., Näsi, M., & Räsänen, P. (2014). Exposure to online hate among young social media users. *Sociological Studies of Children & Youth, 18*, 253–273.

Olweus, D. (1993). *Bullying at School: What We Know and What We Can Do.* Oxford: Blackwell.

Ortega, R., Elipe, P., Mora-Merchán, J. A., Calmaestra, J., & Vega, E. (2009). The emotional impact on victims of traditional bullying and cyberbullying: A study of Spanish adolescents. *Zeitschrift für Psychologie/Journal of Psychology, 217*(4), 197–204.

Palladino, B. E., Nocentini, A., & Menesini, E. (2012). Online and offline peer led models against bullying and cyberbullying. *Psicothema, 24*(4), 634–639.

Perren, S., Corcoran, L., Cowie, H., Dehue, F., Garcia, D., McGuckin, C., Ševčíková, A., Tsatsou, P., & Völlink, T. (2012). Tackling cyberbullying: Review of empirical evidence regarding successful responses by students, parents, and schools. *International Journal of Conflict and Violence, 6*(2), 283–293.

Pyżalski, J. (2012). From cyberbullying to electronic aggression: Typology of the phenomenon. *Emotional and Behavioural Difficulties, 17*, 305–317.

Pothier, R. (2009, February). Indian culture war takes to the Web. Retrieved from www.talkibie.com/socialnetworking/indian-culture-war-takes-to-the-web.

Ramya, M. (2014, February 10). Indian women outdo men in sexting and filming sexual video content: Survey. Retrieved from: http://timesofindia.indiatimes.com/india/Indian-women-outdo-men-in-sexting-and-filming-sexual-video-content-Su rvey/articleshow/30172628.cms.

Renold, E. & Ringrose, J. (2011). Schizoid subjectivities: Re-theorising teen-girls' sexual cultures in an era of sexualisation. *Journal of Sociology, 47*(4), 389–410.

Ringrose, J., Gill, R., Livingstone, S., & Harvey, L. (2012). *A Qualitative Study of Children, Young People and "Sexting".* London: National Society for the Prevention of Cruelty to Children.

Salmivalli, C., Kärnä, A., & Poskiparta, E. (2011). Counteracting bullying in Finland: The KiVa program and its effects on different forms of being bullied. *International Journal of Behavioral Development, 35*, 405–411.

Sariyska, R., Reuter M., Lachmann, B., & Montag, C. (2015). Attention deficit/ hyperactivity disorder is a better predictor for problematic Internet use than depression: Evidence from Germany. *Journal of Addiction Research & Therapy, 6*(1), 1–6. http://dx.doi.org.proxy.unice.fr/10.4172/2155–6105.1000209.

Schultze-Krumbholz, A. & Scheithauer, H. (2009). Social-behavioral correlates of cyberbullying in a German student sample. *Zeitschrift für Psychologie/Journal of Psychology, 217*(4), 224–226.

Shariff, S. (2008). *Cyber-bullying: Issues and Solutions for the School, the Classroom and the Home.* London and New York: Routledge.

SiliconIndia (2012, August 20). "Sexting" on the rise among Indian teens. Retrieved from www.siliconindia.com/news/general/-Sexting-on-the-Rise-Am ong-Indian-Teens-nid-126841-cid-1.html.

Slonje, R. & Smith, P. K. (2008). Cyberbullying: Another main type of bullying? *Scandinavian Journal of Psychology, 49*, 147–154.

Šmahel, D., Helsper, E., Green, L., Kalmus, V., Blinka, L., & Olafsson, K. (2012). *Excessive Internet use among European children*. EU Kids Online. www .eukidsonline.net.

Smith, P. K. & Steffgen, G. (2013). Cyberbullying through the New Media. Findings from an international network. New York: Psychology Press.

Smith, P. K., Kupferberg, A., Mora-Merchan, J. A., Samara, M., Bosley, S., & Osborn, R. (2012). A content analysis of school anti-bullying policies: A follow-up after six years. *Educational Psychology in Practice, 28*, 47–70. doi: 10.1080/02667363.2011.639344.

Smith, P. K., Mahdavi, J., Carvalho, M., Fisher, S., Russell, S., & Tippett, N. (2008). Cyberbullying: Its nature and impact in secondary school pupils. *Journal of Child Psychology and Psychiatry, 49*, 376–385. doi: 10.1111/j.1469-7610.2007.01846.x.

Smith, P. K., Robinson, S., & Marchi, B. (2016). Cross-national data on victims of bullying: What is really being measured?. *International Journal of Developmental Science, 10*(1–2), 9–19.

Sticca, F., Ruggieri, S., Alsaker, F., & Perren, S. (2013). Longitudinal risk factors for cyberbullying in adolescence. *Journal of Community & Applied Social Psychology, 23*, 52–67.

Strohmeier, D., Hoffmann, C., Schiller, E. M., Stefanek, E., & Spiel, C. (2012). ViSC Social Competence Program. In D. Strohmeier & G. G. Noam (eds.), *New Directions in Youth Development* (133):71–84. doi: 10.1002/yd.20008.

Tokunaga, R. S. (2010). Following you home from school: A critical review and synthesis of research on cyberbullying victimization. *Computers in Human Behavior, 26*, 277–287.

Umarhathab, S., Rao, G. D. R., & Jaishankar, K. (2009). Cyber crimes in India: A study of emerging patterns of perpetration and victimization in Chennai City. *Pakistan Journal of Criminology, 1*(1), 51–66.

UNICEF (2016). Child online protection in India – an assessment. Retrieved from http://unicef.in/Uploads/Publications/Resources/pub_doc115.pdf.

Välimäki, M., Almeida, AN., Cross, D., O'Moore, D., Berne, S., Debouotte, G. Heiman, T., Olenik-Shemesh, D., Fulop, M., Fandrem, H., Stald, G., Kurki, M., & Sygkollitou, E. (2012). Guidelines for preventing cyber-bullying in the school environment: a review and recommendations. Retrieved from http://sit es.Google.com/site/costis0801/.

Vandebosch, H. & Van Cleemput, K. (2008). Defining cyberbullying: A qualitative research into the perceptions of youngsters. *Cyberpsychology & Behavior, 11*(4), 499–503.

Vidyachathoth, B. K., Kumar, N. A., & Pai, S. R. (2014). Correlation between affect and Internet addiction in undergraduate medical students in Mangalore. *Journal of Addiction Research & Therapy, 5*(1). http://dx.doi.org/10.4172/2155-6105.1000175.

Wölfer, R., Schultze-Krumbholz, A., Zagorscak, P., Jäkel, A., Göbel, K., & Scheithauer, H. (2014). Prevention 2.0: Targeting cyberbullying @ school. *Prevention Science, 15*(6), 879–887.

Wright, M., Aoyama, I., Kamble, S. V., Li, Z., Soudi, S., Lei, L., & Shu, C. (2015a). Peer attachment and cyberbullying involvement among Chinese, Indian, and Japanese adolescents. *Societies, 5*(2), 339–353. doi: 10.3390/soc5020339.

Wright, M., Kamble, S., & Soudi, S. (2015b). Indian adolescents' cyber aggression involvement and cultural values: The moderation of peer attachment. *School Psychology International, 36*(4) 410–427. doi: 10.1177/0143034315584696.

Yadav, P., Banwari, G., Parmar, C., & Maniar, R. (2013). Internet addiction and its correlates among high school students: A preliminary study from Ahmedabad, India. *Asian Journal of Psychiatry, 6*(6), 500–505.

Ybarra, M. L. & Mitchell, K. J. (2004). Online aggressors, victims, and aggressor/victims: A comparison of associated youth characteristics. *Journal of Child Psychology and Psychiatry, 45*(7), 1308–1316.

Young, K. S. (1998). Internet addiction: The emergence of a new clinical disorder. *Cyberpsychology & Behavior, 3*, 237–244.

Young, K. S. (2004). Internet addiction: A new clinical phenomenon and its consequences. *American Behavioral Scientist, 48*, 402–415.

6 Cyberbullying in Higher Education in India and France

An Empirical Investigation

Catherine Blaya, Kirandeep Kaur,
Damanjit Sandhu and Suresh Sundaram

Opportunities that digital technologies offer to young people are huge in terms of social interactions and access to knowledge (Livingstone et al., 2011). The Internet has become an indispensable means to access information and a core instrument for young people's social life. However, risks and harm are also part of the online experience of some of them. Research on cyberbullying and cyberviolence has been developed worldwide these past decades, and, after having focused on secondary school (Mishna et al., 2009; Tokunaga, 2010), some investigations are being completed within tertiary education and mostly with undergraduate students. As stressed by Chapell and colleagues (2006), many young people who were bullied in primary and secondary school are bullied later on at university. This leads us to think that as far as cyberbullying is concerned, the pattern is similar and that online behaviours learnt from the youngest age might carry on to early adulthood.

The first studies on cyberbullying in the university environment were completed by Finn (2004) and Alexy and colleagues (2005). They showed that the phenomenon does not stop at the university gates and that further research on the issue was relevant. Since then, quite a few research works have been dedicated to the issue, but, up to now, none was completed in a cross-national perspective between a Western country and an Asian country (Barlett & Coyne, 2014).

This chapter sets out to present the findings from a comparative survey completed in France (south-eastern France) and India (Punjab and Tamil Nadu). It investigates the prevalence and characteristics of cyberbullying among higher education students. The cross-cultural perspective is considered here as a means to gain knowledge of others' potential differences, to feed thought for informed prevention (Craig, 2004) and to help accommodate people from different cultural contexts. What we refer to when using the expression "cultural contexts" is the social environment, that is the physical setting in which people live and the culture they were raised in, as well as the groups they interact with. We adopt a cultural relativist approach in the sense that the comparisons between the two countries do not serve the objective to privilege some values from one country over the other, but to promote cultural diversity and to better understand the situation in each participating country (Geertz, 1973). Ethnocentricity is one of the major pitfalls of doing cross-national comparative work, and to create some kind of neutrality in trying to understand other systems or the issues surveyed is challenging.

Cyberbullying in Higher Education

The first two studies about negative online behaviours at university, by Finn (2004) and Chapell and colleagues (2005), were completed in the United States. Finn's work showed that 10% to 15% of students had received unpleasant or threatening instant messages and that more than half of the respondents had been exposed to unwanted pornography. Chapell and colleagues more specifically studied cyberstalking, and they found a rate of 3.7% victimized students. Further research was conducted to investigate the involvement of university students in cyberbullying (Adams & Lawrence, 2011; Akbulut & Eristi, 2011; Dilmaç, 2009; Faucher, Jackson & Cassidy, 2014; Finn, 2004; Francisco et al., 2015; Kraft & Wang, 2010; Vance, 2010; Walker, Sockman & Koehn, 2011). According to the research by Dilmaç in Turkey (2009), 55.3% of students reported being victims of cyberbullying, and one out of five acknowledged cyberbullying others. Also in Turkey, Akbulut and Eristi (2011) showed that cyberbullying affected the majority of students who took part in their survey, completed in a state college of education. Similar results come from Turan and colleagues (2011) in Turkey, with 55% of students reporting cyberbullying. Perpetrators are also more numerous, with 23% in Dilmaç's study. In Australia, Zhang, Land and Dick (2010) found similar percentages, with 62% of students reporting victimization and 40% reporting perpetration.

Kraft and Wang (2010) in the United States conducted a study with college students in which 10% of college students stated they were cyberbullied. This last percentage is very similar to the one from Walker and colleagues (2011), who also completed their study in the United States and found 11% of college students reporting victimization. However this should be considered cautiously in the sense that the participants in the survey were asked to answer some items specifically linked to cyberbullying, as well as other questions related to unwanted or obsessive communication, for which 34% students answered they received such messages.

The authors explain that the students do not consider these forms of abusive communication cyberbullying and that they are linked to online social life (Walker et al., 2011, p. 36). MacDonald and Roberts-Pittman (2010) found that among the college students they surveyed, more than one out of five (21.9%) was a victim and 8.6% admitted being perpetrators. Other research has mainly surveyed freshmen and reported some rather low cyberbullying percentages (between 1% and 7%), which is understandable since the survey asks about their college experience.

In India, there is no other research but that from Kumar and Sayadevi (2009), who tried to explore the patterns of Internet usage among Indian college students (for more details, see Chapter 5). As a consequence, this gap in scientific knowledge needs filling. The interest in researching the issue is growing, though, and three scientific studies have recently investigated the issue at the secondary school level (we do not consider polls completed by stakeholders such as Microsoft or McAfee; see Chapter 5). For a presentation of their results, see Blaya and colleagues (2016).

In France, the issue of cyberbullying at university has also been little explored. A survey among college students by Berthaud and Blaya (2014, 2015) indicated that 50.8% of the respondents were victims at least once during the previous 12 months and that 14% had cyberbullied others. One student out of 10 (10.8%) reported being both victim and perpetrator, and being a victim was significantly related to becoming a perpetrator (being a perpetrator increased the risk to become a victim by 3.4). More than one student out of 10 (11.8%) were targeted repeatedly.

The prevalence of cyberbullying varies greatly from one study to the other, including within the same country, and it is challenging to get an accurate estimate for both victimization and perpetration. This is probably due to methodological issues such as definitions, sampling, time frames, and measurement discrepancies (Rivers & Noret, 2010). Some researchers use the term *cyberbullying* (Dilmaç, 2009; Molluzzo & Lawler, 2012; Turan et al., 2011; Walker et al., 2011), others refer to *cyberstalking* or *cyber harassment* (Alexy et al., 2005; Vance, 2010), and others only measure different specific types of online behaviours (such as harassing, threatening and stalking) and do not consider other forms of cyberbullying such as insults, rumours or identity theft (Kennedy & Taylor, 2010). Most studies focus on victimization rather than perpetration.

Whatever the discrepancies in the rates of cyberbullying victims and perpetrators, research shows evidence that cyberbullying does not stop at the gates of university and that the issue should be taken seriously. Students from higher education tend to be victims of insults, threats and harassment (Kennedy & Taylor, 2010; Molluzzo & Lawler, 2012;

Turan et al., 2011; Vance, 2010; Zhang et al., 2010) but also of obscene content or grooming (Kennedy & Taylor, 2010; Vance, 2010). The most used platforms for cyberbullying are social networks such as Facebook (Berthaud & Blaya, 2014; Francisco et al., 2015). Cyberbullying that involves images and videos as well as phone calls is perceived as having a greater negative impact than other forms of online aggression.

Research in secondary education tends to show that females have a greater tendency to post private information and suggestive pictures of themselves (Mascheroni, Vincent & Jimenez, 2015), and are more affected by certain forms of cyberbullying such as revenge porn and sexting (Ringrose et al., 2012). However, there is no consistency in gender-related findings and reviews by Kowalski and colleagues (2014) and Barlett and Coyne (2014) showed that there was no gender difference as a whole. As for university, the situation is rather similar. Francisco and colleagues (2015) found that the largest percentages of victims and aggressors were women. Chapell and colleagues (2006), but also Hong and colleagues (2007) in China and Akbulut and Eristi (2011) and Dilmaç (2009) in Turkey, showed that male students were more likely to be involved as perpetrators. Faucher and colleagues (2014) found that females were more affected by cyberbullying from a person they already knew, while males reported more cyberbullying from strangers. Female students, more than males, reported that it occurred through social networks and SMS. However, MacDonald and Roberts-Pittman (2010) did not identify any gender difference for victimization or perpetration. A consistent finding is that minority groups are more subjected to cyberbullying (Finn, 2004; Molluzzo & Lawler, 2012; Wensley & Campbell, 2012).

Social networking sites and smartphones are the most frequent media for cyberbullying among students in higher education (Lindsay & Krysik, 2012; Walker et al., 2011). As for cyberbullying in secondary education, spending much time online, risky online behaviours such as disclosing personal information to strangers, meeting unknown people online or sharing passwords characterize both victims and perpetrators (Baker & Tanrikulu, 2010; Turan et al., 2011; Vandebosch & Van Cleemput, 2008). As for traditional bullying, low empathy towards the victims of cyberbullying has been identified as one of the predictors, as well as favourable attitudes towards cyberbullying and the approval of peers. Students with higher empathy towards the victims also showed lower positive attitudes towards cyberbullying and thought that it was not an acceptable behaviour, including among their group of peers (Doane, Pearson & Kelley, 2014). These last points agree with some previous research results for students in secondary education (Renati, Berrone, & Zanetti, 2012; Schultze-Krumbholz & Scheithauer, 2009; Steffgen et al., 2011).

The Present Study

While scholars have completed much research on cyberbullying-related phenomena in Japan, South Korea, China and Hong Kong (Hong et al., 2007; Lin & Lai, 2016; Smith, Kwak & Toda, 2016; Toda, 2016; Wright et al., 2015; Zhang, Chen & Chen, 2016), little has been done up to now in India except for research on Internet addiction (Chakraborty, Basu & Vijaya Kumar, 2010; Chathoth et al., 2013; Goel, Subramanyam & Kamath, 2013; Kumar & Sayadevi, 2009; Nalwa & Anand, 2003; Vidyachathoth et al., 2014; Yadav et al., 2013; and see Chapter 5).

Aims

The overall objective was to compare possible differences in online risk-taking and negative experiences between France and India.

This study set out to investigate and compare (a) the prevalence of cyberbullying (victimization and perpetration) between France and India; and (b) the different typologies of protagonists (victims, perpetrators, victims/perpetrators and witnesses). Because cultures and their influence on human behaviours vary from one context to the other, this research was carried out in close collaboration between Indian and French researchers. Field trips were organized within the overall project to get a perspective of each other's environment, and the measurement tool was tested in both areas. Close collaboration was also involved in the interpretation of the findings.

Participants

A total of 1,355 college students participated, aged 18–37 years ($M = 20.30$, $SD = 2.44$).

In India, there were 904 students (450 males, 49.8%; 454 females, 50.2%) aged 18–24 ($M = 20.19$, $SD = 1.89$). The sample was recruited from Annamalai University (Tamil Nadu) and Punjabi University (Punjab), aiming to achieve a gender balance. Some 44% of the participants were from a rural background.

In France, there were 451 students (163 males, 36.1%; 278 females, 61.6%) aged 18–37 ($M = 20.52$, $SD = 3.26$). There were a few doctoral students, and 3.5% of the sample were mature individuals, older than 26;

however, the difference in ages between the Indian and French samples was not significant. This was a convenience sample; only students who wished to complete the questionnaire did so. The sample was mainly (79.6%) from an urban background.

Methods

A cyberbullying anonymous self-report questionnaire survey was used. In France the questionnaire was administered online, after campus advertising through the university student mailing list. In India, once authorization from the HOD/principal of the college/university had been obtained, a research assistant personally met the students in their classrooms during their leisure hours and distributed a paper version of the questionnaire. The purpose of the research and instructions for completing the questionnaire were given to the group, as well as individually when required. Once completed the questionnaires were collected back on the same day or the next day. Translation of the questionnaire into the mother tongue of the students was not necessary, as all the students were able to read and write English fairly fluently.

The survey was based on the questionnaires of Smith and colleagues (2008), EU Kids Online (2011) and Blaya (2013). It investigated digital uses of and negative experiences on the Internet. Since the final questionnaire did not assess the traditional criteria for the definition of bullying, such as repetition, power of imbalance, intent to harm and duration, we refer to *negative experiences* rather than *cyberbullying*. The term *negative experiences* is taken from the EU Kids Online research (Livingstone et al., 2011) and is close to the definition proposed by Grigg (2010, p. 152), namely "intentional harm delivered by the use of electronic means to a person or a group of people irrespective of their age, who perceive(s) such acts as offensive, derogatory, harmful, or unwanted".

The questionnaire thus asked about experiences and behaviours having potential negative effects on the participants. It was drafted in English by the first author (from France) and then tested and discussed with the Indian team. We found that there was no need to translate it into Tamil or Punjabi, but it was translated into French. The translation of the questionnaire was performed using the front and back translation method and the English version was submitted to the whole research group. After piloting the instrument in each university to assess understanding, it was amended to optimize relevance to the cultural and national contexts involved.

The questionnaire referred to the previous 12 months. In this chapter we focus on the different categories of young people involved (cyber

victims, cyber victims and perpetrators, cyber perpetrators and witnesses), risky behaviours, and addiction to the Internet, as well as offline
victimization.

Cyber victimization: victims (received nasty or hurtful messages on
the Internet or on the phone; nasty or hurtful messages were passed
around or posted where others could see; were left out of or excluded
from a group or activity on the Internet; were threatened online; humiliating pictures of the respondents were posted on the Internet).

Perpetration: perpetrators (same questions as for victimization but as
perpetrators).

For each experience (victimization and perpetration), questions were
asked about frequency (how often did this happen? several times
each day, daily or almost daily, at least every week; less often, never;
I do not know) and duration (how long did it last? a few days, about
a month, six months, the whole year, for several years).

Exposure to Harmful Online Content   We asked the respondents to the
survey if they had witnessed cyber victimization. The question was: in the
past 12 months, have you witnessed cyberbullying? The possible answers
were: yes; no; I do not know; I prefer not to say.

Risky behaviours: Four questions were used: looking for a new friend
on the Internet, sending personal information (full name, address, phone
number) to someone never met face to face, adding new friends that were
never met face to face, pretending to be a different kind of person on the
Internet. Each item was scored on a four-point scale: 4. Very often;
3. Fairly often; 2. Not very often; 1. Never/almost never. Dimension
scores were calculated by taking the mean of the respective items.

Attitudes to the Internet and addiction: we used questions based on the
Internet Addiction Test (IAT), which is the most used assessment scale for
Internet addiction measurement (Young, 1998). The questions to assess
excessive use were also used in the EU Kids Online 2010 survey
(Livingstone et al., 2011); they asked if young people had tried unsuccess-
fully to spend less time on the Internet, if their online activities were
performed at the expense of family activities or healthy living (sleep, eating), if they were compulsive users, and if they were annoyed when not able
to get online. The Cronbach alpha is 0.8. The scale was as follows: 4. Very
often; 3. Fairly often; 2. Not very often; 1. Never/almost never.

Offline victimization: we asked the students if they had been
victimized in real life. The questions asked if at college, in the previous

12 months, the students had been victims of bullying. The possible answers were: yes; no; I do not know. We also asked what type of victimization they had experienced: nasty or hurtful messages; bad jokes/teasing; exclusion from a group; insults; physical aggression; threats/intimidation; petty theft (school material, snack, etc.); serious theft (money, phone, etc.); rumours spread about you; harassment; something else; none of these; I do not know.

Findings

Prevalence of Cyberbullying Victimization and Perpetration

Altogether, 36.1% of the Indian students reported cyber victimization while victims were fewer in France with 22.4% of the respondents involved as victims (Chi2 = 26.04, df = 1, p < 0.001). Table 6.1 shows the different types of students' involvement in cyberbullying. The authors identify a higher percentage of French students who reckoned they were perpetrators only (8.4% vs. 2.1%) while there were twice as numerous Indian students as the French to report being both victim/author (20.9% vs. 10%). The Indian and the French participants were similarly involved as witnesses as the difference between the two countries is not statistically significant.

The participants were asked to specify which type of cyber victimization they were subjected to. There was no difference between the two countries for receiving nasty or hurtful messages on the Internet with, respectively, 12.3% and 12.2% of the French and Indian students reporting such experiences. However, as shown in Table 6.2, the Indian participants more commonly reported victimization through SMS, having had nasty or hurtful messages passed around or posted where others could see. They were also more numerous in declaring they were subjected to exclusion from a group or an activity online and to online threats, and in

Table 6.1 *Types of cyberbullying involvement in France and India*

TYPOLOGY	VICTIMS ONLY	VICTIM AND PERPETRATOR	PERPETRA- TORS ONLY	NOT INVOLVED	WITNESS	TOTAL
FRANCE	12.4%	10.0%***	8.4%	69.2%***	18.6%	100%
INDIA	15.2%	20.9%***	2.1%	61.8%***	21.1%	100%

*p < 0.05; **p < 0.01; ***p < 0.001.

Table 6.2 *Comparison of the different types of victimization and perpetration in India and France (%)*

TYPES OF VICTIMIZATION AND PERPETRATION/ COUNTRY	VICTIMI-ZATION INDIA	VICTIMI-ZATION FRANCE	PERPETR-ATION INDIA	PERPETR-ATION FRANCE
NASTY OR HURTFUL MESSAGES ON THE INTERNET	12.20	12.30	33.3	23.6
NASTY OR HURTFUL MESSAGES ON SMS	15.20	9.30***	13.5	26.5**
NASTY OR HURTFUL MESSAGES PASSED AROUND OR POSTED PUBLICLY	14.70	4.90***	7.20	1.10***
ONLINE SOCIAL EXCLUSION	17.10	2.40***	12.20	5.50***
THREATENED ONLINE	15.00	4.70***	10.60	1.01***
HUMILIATING PICTURES OF SELF POSTED ON THE INTERNET	13.20	2.70***	10.60	3,33***

*p < 0.05; **p < 0.01; ***p < 0.001.

stating that humiliating pictures of themselves were posted on the Internet. In terms of perpetration, the survey shows no significant difference in the percentages of students who reported having perpetrated at least one of the cyberbullying experiences included in the questionnaire. However, when studying the types of cyber aggression, the Indian students reported more often than the French having posted or passed around nasty or hurtful messages where others could see, as well as excluding others from a group or activity and threatening others online, while the French students seemed more prone to spread nasty or hurtful messages by SMS.

As presented in Tables 6.3 and 6.4, the Indian victims were also significantly more likely to report repeated victimization with one out of four victims who stated that happened every day or almost every day and 16.5% who stated it happened at least once a week. In terms of duration, the Indian students were more likely to say that the problem lasted about a month (28.5% vs. 12.1%), or several years (13.9% vs. 1.9%).

Table 6.5 reveals that the frequency and duration of perpetration show similar patterns as for victimization, with 23.1% of the Indian

Table 6.3 *Frequency of cyber victimization for Indian and French students*

FREQUENCY CYBER VICTIMIZATION	EVERYDAY OR ALMOST EVERYDAY	AT LEAST ONCE A WEEK	LESS OFTEN	I DO NOT KNOW	TOTAL
FRANCE	3.9%	9.1%	68.8%	18.2%	100%
INDIA	26.8%	16.5%	19.0%	37.6%	100%
TOTAL	23.1%	15.3%	27.1%	34.5%	100%

Table 6.4 *Duration of cyber victimization for Indian and French students*

DURATION CYBER VICTIMIZATION	ONCE	A FEW DAYS	ABOUT A MONTH	ALL YEAR LONG	SEVERAL YEARS	TOTAL
FRANCE	63.6%	14.0%	12.1%	8.4%	1.9%	100%
INDIA	39.0%	10.4%	28.5%	8.4%	13.7%	100%
TOTAL	43.3%	11.5%	23.6%	8.4%	10.1%	100%

Table 6.5 *Frequency of perpetration for Indian and French students*

FREQUENCY PERPETRATION	SEVERAL TIMES A DAY	EVERYDAY OR ALMOST EVERYDAY	AT LEAST ONCE A WEEK	LESS OFTEN	I DO NOT KNOW	TOTAL
FRANCE	0.0%	0.0%	16.2%	83.8%	0.0%	100%
INDIA	4.8%	19.3%	51.7%	19.3%	4.8%	100%
TOTAL	3.8%	15.4%	44.5%	32.4%	3.8%	100%

perpetrators reckoning they were involved as authors of cyberbullying every day or almost every day versus 0% of the French respondents; 16.2% of the French respondents cyber-aggressed at least once a week while among the Indians, the percentage was 51.7%. The vast majority of the French aggressors responded they were involved less often versus 19.3% of the Indians.

As for the duration of their involvement, the French perpetrators were twice as likely as the Indian ones to declare they cyber-aggressed once while the Indian perpetrators were more likely to state they were authors for longer periods of time with more than one out of three bullying for a few days and one out of four bullying for about a month. However, it seems that a small percentage of the perpetrators in France (6.1%) have

Table 6.6 *Duration of perpetration for Indian and French students*

DURATION PERPETRATION	ONCE	A FEW DAYS	ABOUT A MONTH	Six MONTHS	ALL YEAR LONG	SEVERAL YEARS	TOTAL
FRANCE	61.2%	26.5%	4.1%	0.0%	2.0%	6.1%	100%
INDIA	30.1%	34.1%	27.1%	5.7%	3.1%	0.0%	100%
TOTAL	35.6%	32.7%	23.0%	4.7%	2.9%	1.1%	100%

developed a "career", since they reported their behaviour had lasted several years, which is not the case for the Indian ones.

These findings seem to reflect that the Indian students are more involved in what could be called *cyberbullying* here, that is to say online victimization through electronic means of communication that is repeated and lasts for a period of time.

As a whole, results show Indian college students are more likely to be cyber victimized than French ones. Moreover, their online negative experiences as victims but also as perpetrators seem to be more frequent and to last longer, but for a small percentage of French perpetrators who reckoned they had been involved for several years. It is important to note that 11.2% of Indian students ticked the "I do not know" box for perpetration and even more puzzling, 5.5% did so for victimization. We probably can attribute this to Indian students' denial of the situation and fear of being sanctioned by the perpetrators, or to the fact that it could be too painful to be consciously recollected on the victim's side. For females, *Eve teasing* (see Chapter 1) in India has many times resulted in violence and serious situations to avenge the family honour that remains based on patriarchal values (Bohra et al., 2015; Saha & Srivastava, 2014). Among the ones who responded they do not know if they were victims, 43.9% are males and 56.1% are females. In India, females are often told by their mothers not to talk about their victimization, including with their fathers. If a girl shares it with her family, the family does not report it to the police, but asks the girl to ignore it (Gadekar, 2016). As a consequence, although the questionnaires were anonymous, we can be led to think that the law of silence is stronger than any form of reassurance on the part of the researchers.

We also asked the respondents to the survey if they had witnessed cyber victimization Altogether, 18.6% of the French students witnessed some cyberbullying during the academic year and 21.1% of the Indians, the difference between the two countries not being significant.

Characteristics of Victims and Perpetrators in Terms of Risky Behaviours and Addiction to the Internet: Cross-National Comparison

In order to better understand who were the victims and the perpetrators we cross-compared risky behaviours within the victims and perpetrators subgroups for each country. We did not find any significant difference as far as age and gender are concerned.

Risky Behaviours

As shown in Figure 6.1, significant differences exist between the scores obtained by the French and Indian students. The Indian students take more of all risks than the French students, both as perpetrators and as victims. However, in each country victims and perpetrators tend to adopt similar online behaviours. The Indian victims significantly tend to have more risky behaviours for all items, and the difference is particularly significant for looking for new friends online (t = 7.02, p < 0.001), posting personal information and pretending to be someone else when online (t = 8.26, p < 0.001). As for adding strangers, the difference is less significant with t = 2.22 (p < 0.05). The pattern is similar for perpetrators: (looking for new friends [t = 3.16, p < 0.001];

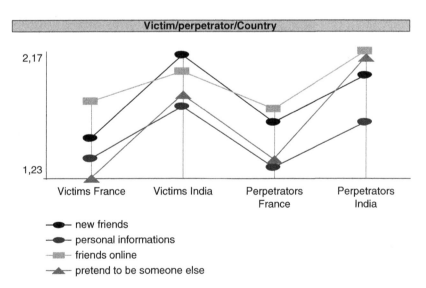

Figure 6.1 Cross-national comparison across France and India of risky online behaviours by victims and perpetrators

posting personal information [t = 3.87, p < 0.001]; pretending to be someone else when online [t = 7.18, p < 0.001]; adding strangers [t = 3.87, p < 0.001]).

Internet Addiction

When cross-comparing within the victims and perpetrators subgroups the addiction characteristics for each country for which a means calculation was performed (t test) in the same way as for the previous analysis for risk-taking, we can see from Table 6.7 that there is no overall significant difference between France and India; that is to say that the Indian and French victims and perpetrators show similar levels of addiction. The scale was: 4. Very often; 3. Fairly often; 2. Not very often; 1. Never/almost never. Therefore, the nearer the result is to 4, the higher the addiction.

However, some specific items are significantly different from one country to the other. The French victims tend to surf more with no particular interest, but the Indian ones declare greater difficulties in controlling their time online (tried to spend less time on the Internet) and that they find more comfort when online. They also report more unhealthy practices such as eating or sleeping less to be online. Moreover, the Indian victims stated they find comfort in using the Internet. As far as the perpetrators are concerned, they are online at the expense of eating or sleeping, they surf more with no interest, they find it difficult to manage their time online and they are more likely to be bothered when they cannot connect than the French perpetrators. There is no difference in terms of time dedicated to family, friends or doing homework between the French and Indian victims and perpetrators.

As most research on cyberbullying has found, there is a substantial overlap between traditional bullying and cyberbullying (Hinduja & Patchin, 2008; Mishna, Saini & Solomon, 2009), with 83% of the traditional bullying victims also victimized online and 12% of the online victims online also victimized offline. We sought to examine possible differences between the two countries in the possible association between online and offline victimization. Our findings do not show any significant difference.

However, the percentage of Indian respondents, either victims or perpetrators, who answered they did not know is rather puzzling, since for both subgroups they are one out of four respondents. We cannot conclude that this is because they did not want to answer, since they had the option not to answer, which was the case for one French respondent.

Table 6.7 *Cross-national comparison of Internet addiction among victims and perpetrators, comparing France and India. Mean values and significance levels for victims and perpetrators from both countries.*

VICTIMS/ PERPETRATORS/ COUNTRY	VICTIMS INDIA	VICTIMS FRANCE	PERPET- RATORS INDIA	PERPET- RATORS FRANCE	TOTAL
DO NOT EAT/SLEEP BECAUSE OF INTERNET	2.00	1.68***	2.08	1.66***	1.94
FEEL BOTHERED WHEN CONNECTION IS NOT POSSIBLE	2.03	2.10	2.11	2.11	2.07
SURF WITH NO REAL INTEREST	2.99	1.92***	2.13	3.14***	2.27
SPEND LESS TIME WITH FRIENDS OR FAMILY	1.88	2.05	2.17	2.00	2.06
SPEND LESS TIME DOING SCHOOLWORK	2.40	2.25	2.61	2.62	2.37
TRIED TO SPEND LESS TIME ONLINE	2.04	1.63***	2.88	3.33***	1.96
FIND COMFORT USING THE INTERNET	2.82	2.56**	2.45	2.56	2.66
FEEL BOTHERED WHEN PHONE NOT CONNECTED	2.06	2.17	3.15	2.72***	2.04
USE PHONE WHEN NOT APPROPRIATE	2.30	2.47	2.4	2.37	2.60
OVERALL ADDICTION SCORE	2.18	2.19	2.22	2.26	2.20

$*p < 0.05$; $**p < 0.01$; $***p < 0.001$.

Discussion

This survey investigated the possible differences in the experiences of cyberbullying of young people in France (south-eastern region) and in India (Punjab and Tamil Nadu). The difference between the two countries as far as victimization is concerned is significant, with a greater number of Indian participants reporting cyber victimization. This confirms previous findings for secondary schools that showed that the Indians were more involved in cyberbullying than their Chinese or Japanese counterparts (Blaya et al., 2016; Wright et al., 2015). It is interesting to note, though, that our survey did not find any significant difference for perpetrators. Two explanations are possible: cyberviolence in India is more a group issue than in France, or the Indian respondents are more reluctant to declare that they were involved as perpetrators.

An issue already raised is that many more Indian than French students gave "don't know" responses as regards negative experiences. This could be due to greater reluctance to report they were perpetrators or victims, or it could reflect the lack of information about cyberbullying and knowledge about this type of bullying and its underlying process. Indian legislation provides a legal framework to protect victims and to discourage cyber aggression (Section 66A of Information Technology Act on 17.10.2000 N 21 [as amended on 23 December 2008]); the law prohibits sending by means of a computer resource or a communication device any offensive or threatening content that is likely to cause harm to the target. It is also prohibited to send any electronic content that shows the private parts of anyone without his/her previous consent (Section 66 E) and to post or transfer obscene material online. Section 509 of the Indian Criminal Code prohibits words, gestures or acts intended to insult the modesty or privacy of a woman (Halder & Jaishankar, 2013). Thus Indian society acknowledges the importance of dealing with the issue. As expressed earlier, this could also be a consequence of a heavier law of silence, mainly for female students, due to a treatment of women's victimization that is rather based on the shaming of the victim at the societal level (Awasthi, 2015; Saha & Srivastava, 2014), or because female victims fear retaliation from perpetrators if they complain (Halder & Jaishankar, 2010), or they think that they will be refused any help due to the lack of acknowledgement or awareness from the police services (Halder & Jaishankar, 2009).

Our findings confirm the overlap between the status of victims and aggressors in higher education (Berthaud & Blaya, 2014). It could mean that those who receive aggressive messages are less informed and thus less skilled to handle the situation, so that they reply in a similar tone and thus escalate the conflict and increase the risk of experiencing repeated victimization (Patchin & Hinduja, 2011).

When considering the differences between French and Indian victims, the latter report more risky online behaviours. Although the scores for Internet addiction are similar as a whole, some forms of addictive behaviours are different. The Indian participants more frequently reported indulging in health-risk behaviours because of excessive Internet and mobile phone use. Many of them surf at the expense of eating and sleeping and declare greater difficulties in managing the amount of time spent online, and it seems they have a stronger psychological link to the Internet in the sense that they more often find comfort in surfing online.

They feel it easier to be themselves on the Internet and they can talk more freely about private things. They also adopt more risky behaviours such as pretending to be someone else when online or posting personal information and getting in touch with strangers. In India, the role of family is very strong and the society is based on a patriarchal model in which young people are under the control of the family group and have to behave in order not to jeopardize group cohesion and family reputation (Mandelbaum, 1970). Social control is thus rather strong, and the Internet might be a way to escape the weight of family and social control and to give greater space to individual identity and independence.

Adolescents use media, technology and expensive gadgets as an identity development and enhancement tool. Especially in the case of females, who are allowed limited physical mobility, their contact with the outside world is mainly through the Internet; this has become a way to the outside world and to get support outside family domination (Halder & Jaishankar, 2011; Saha & Srivastava, 2014). Actual emotional sharing within families is very low in India and family times either revolve around some religious activity or parents end up giving moral lectures to the children. Young people feel more comfortable using the Internet and sharing their feelings and intimate secrets online (Meena, Mittal & Solanki, 2012; Saha & Srivastava, 2014). Moreover, as Halder and Jaishankar (2010, p. 1) stated in their study about awareness of cyberbullying in India, "awareness of cyber victimization has remained limited to several informative and useful tips on how to save one's personal computer and personal data from identity frauds, emotional blackmailers, etc."

In France awareness campaigns about online risks, positive online behaviours, possible negative online experiences and how to handle online conflicts have been going on since 2005 and the respondents to this survey are students who have been informed from secondary school. The difference in victimization with India could be explained by positive effects of such awareness-raising activities. However, the findings show that French higher education is not clear from cyberviolence and that risk-taking and victimization are not the "privilege" of pre-teens or younger people.

More students from the Indian sample came from a rural area than in the French sample. This could explain some of the difference in risk-taking, victimization and perpetration. Koovakkai and Muhammed (2010) focused on the locale factor in the abuse of the Internet by the young people, and they concluded that Internet abuse was more prevalent among rural teenagers and that the level of education and risk awareness was higher among urban teenagers. Although their study was assessing Internet abuse, it is not unreasonable to think that the same process could apply to cyberviolence. Another study by Halder and Jaishankar (2010) on cyber victimization in India found that the majority of the respondents did not feel the need to read the policy guidelines or terms and conditions of ISPs and social networking websites before entering into a contract with these sites and opening their accounts. This confirms the need for awareness campaigns, with maybe a special focus for rural areas towards young people, but also for schools and university staff. In India, a national youth policy was adopted by the Ministry of Youth Affairs and Sports in 2014, which includes the promotion of equity and social values, and has education and health as priority areas of intervention, as well as the development of a strong and healthy generation (www.youthpolicy.org/national/India_2014_National_Youth_Policy.pdf). This public policy could support such awareness campaigns.

Moreover, in both countries, universities might set up cyberviolence and cyberbullying protocols to support victims, since there is concern in both countries about the phenomenon and university campuses are not immune to interpersonal violence, either offline or online (Berthaud & Blaya, 2014).

There are several limitations to this study. The French sample had a majority of female participants, which might constitute a bias, especially as only students who wished to complete the questionnaire did so. It is also possible that only the students who had a negative online experience or involvement with cyberviolence participated. On the other hand, in India, the students were required to participate and did not have much choice. That might explain why so many ticked the box "I do not know." The results from this study are consistent with the conclusions of many other studies on cyberbullying both in secondary and in higher education.

Conclusions

This research was the first to compare the involvement of university students in cyberviolence in France and in India. Along with previous studies it shows that cyberbullying does not stop at the entrance to college and is an ongoing issue (Adams & Lawrence, 2011; CDC, 2011; Zalaquett & Chatters, 2014). It also stresses that both countries are affected by the phenomenon. The study did not reveal any gender differences, in alignment with previous findings from Chapell and colleagues (2006), Hong and colleagues (2007), MacDonald and Roberts-Pittman (2010), or Berthaud and Blaya (2014). Cyberbullying as bullying is not explained and limited to individual characteristics only or to the relationship between two or several individuals. It is shaped also by the context and cultural environment of the protagonists (Bronfenbrenner, 1979; Mishna, 2012). Wright and colleagues (2015) showed that cyberbullying behaviours are moderated by culture and peer attachment; and Boulton and colleagues (2012) and Doane and colleagues (2014) have shown the association between low cyberbullying and low acceptance of this type of behaviour. This leads us to conclude that it is important to reinforce a culture of interpersonal positive attitudes as a whole. This could take the form of guidelines for the university environment (Crosslin & Golman, 2014) on how to behave positively online and make the most out of the opportunities technology offers.

However, more research is needed to respond effectively to cyberbullying among young adults at both the prevention and intervention levels. It should be taken into account that India is a huge country with strong regional characteristics among which are linguistic and religious diversity and different traditions (Devaki & Kou, 2000). Further research should focus on assessing more precisely and in depth the impact of culture on cyber aggression, and the possible differences due to the social structure, status and social class of the respondents, the way appropriate relationships and behaviours between individuals and groups are culturally impacted or smoothed due to e-globalization and how this interacts with individual values and aspirations.

References

Adams, F. D. & Lawrence, G. L. (2011). Bullying victims: The effects last into college. *American Secondary Education, 40*(1), 4–13.

Akbulut, Y. & Eristi, B. (2011). Cyberbullying and victimisation among Turkish university students. *Australasian Journal of Educational Technology, 27*(7), 1155–1170.

Alexy, E. M., Burgess, A. W., Baker, T., & Smoyak, S. A. (2005). Perceptions of cyberstalking among college students. *Brief Treatment and Crisis Intervention, 5*(3), 279–289.

Awasthi, D. (2015). *Eve-Teasing: A Social Epidemic*. Delhi: Kalpaz Publications.

Baker, Ö. E. & Tanrıkulu, İ. (2010). Psychological consequences of cyber bullying experiences among Turkish secondary school children. *Procedia-Social and Behavioral Sciences, 2*(2), 2771–2776.

Barlett, C. & Coyne, S. M. (2014). A meta-analysis of sex differences in cyber-bullying behavior: The moderating role of age. *Aggressive Behavior, 40*, 474–488.

Barlett, C. P., Gentile, D. A., Anderson, C. A., Suzuki, K., Sakamoto, A., Yamaoka, A. & Katsura, R. (2014). Cross-cultural differences in cyberbullying behavior: A short-term longitudinal study. *Journal of Cross-Cultural Psychology, 45*(2), 300–313 [United States and Japan].

Berthaud, J. & Blaya, C. (2014). *Premiers résultats de l'enquête française Cyberviolence à l'université.* Adjectif, Analyses et Recherches sur les TICE. www .adjectif.net/spip/spip.php?article279.96.

Berthaud, J. & Blaya C. (2015). Pratiques numériques, perception de la violence en ligne et victimation chez les étudiants. *Recherches en éducation, Hors série, 7,* 146–161.

Blaya, C. (2013*).* *Les ados dans le cyberespace – prises de risques et cyberviolence.* Bruxelles: De Boeck.

Blaya, C., Sundaram, S., Kaur, K. & Sandhu, D. (2016). Digital uses, risk-taking and online negative experiences among secondary school students in France and India: A comparative study. TIC Kids Online Brazil 2015, pp.47–55. [in Portuguese] http://www.lse.ac.uk/media@lse/research/EUKidsOnline/Partici patingCountries/PDFs/BZTIC-Kids-2015.pdf

Bohra, N., Sharma, I., Srivastava, S. et al. (2015). Violence against women. *Indian Journal of Psychiatry, 57*(2). S333–S338. doi: 10.4103/ 0019-5545.161500.

Bronfenbrenner, U. (1979). Basic concepts. In U. Bronfenbrenner (ed.), *The Ecology of Human Development* (pp. 3–15). Cambridge, MA: Harvard University Press.

Boulton, G., Campbell, P., Collins, B., Elias, P., Hall, W., Laurie, G., O'Neill, O., Rawlins, M., Thornton, J., Vallance, P. & Walport, M. (2012). *Science as a Public Enterprise.* London: Royal Society Science Policy Centre.

Chakraborty, K., Basu, D. & Vijaya Kumar, K. G. (2010). Internet addiction: Consensus, controversies, and the way ahead. *East Asian Archives of Psychiatry, 20*(3), 123–132.

Chapell, M. S., Blanding, Z. B., Siverstein, M. E., Takashi, M. N. B., Newman, B., Gubi, A. & Mccain N. (2005). Test anxiety and academic performance in undergraduate and graduate students. *Journal of Educational Psychology, 97*(2), 268–274.

Chapell, M. S., Hasselman, S. L., Kitchin, T., Lomon, S. N., MacIver, K. W. & Sarullo, P. L. (2006). Bullying in elementary school, high school, and college. *Adolescence, 41*(164), 633–648.

Chathoth, V. M., Kodavanji, B., Arunkumar, N. & Pai., S. R. (2013). Internet behaviour pattern in undergraduate students in Mangalore. *International Journal of Innovative Research in Science, Engineering and Technology, 2*(6), 2133.

Craig, A. D. (2004). Human feelings: Why are some more aware than others?. *Trends in Cognitive Sciences, 8*(6), 239–241.

Crosslin, K. & Golman, M. (2014). "Maybe you don't want to face it" – College students' perspectives on cyberbullying. *Computers in Human Behavior, 41*, 14–20.

Dilmaç, B. (2009). Psychological needs as a predictor of cyber bullying: A preliminary report on college students. *Educational Sciences: Theory and Practice, 9*(3), 1307–1325.

Devaki, L. & Kou, O. N. (2000). *Linguistic Heritage of India and Asia.* Central Institute of Indian Languages.

Doane, A., Pearson, M. & Kelley, M. (2014). Predictors of cyberbullying perpetration among college students: An application of the theory of reasoned action. *Computers in Human Behaviour, 36,* 154–162.

Faucher, C., Jackson, M. & Cassidy, W. (2014). Cyberbullying among university students: Gendered experiences, impacts, and perspectives. *Education Research International.* Article ID 698545. http://dx.doi.org/10.1155/2014/698545.

Finn, J. (2004). A survey of online harassment at a university campus. *Journal of Interpersonal Violence, 19*(4), 468–483.

Francisco, S. M., Veiga Simão, A. M., Ferreira, P. C. & Martins, M. J. D. D. (2015). Cyberbullying: The hidden side of college students. *Computers in Human Behaviour, 43*(0), 167–182. http://dx.doi.org/10.1016/j.chb.2014.10.045.

Gadekar, U. (2016). Eve teasing and its psychosocial influences among the adolescent girls. *International Journal of Current Advanced Research, 5*(6), 1028–1031.

Geertz, C. (1973). *The Interpretation of Cultures: Selected Essays.* New York: Basic Books.

Goel, D., Subramanyam, A. & Kamath, R. (2013). A study on the prevalence of Internet addiction and its association with psychopathology in Indian adolescents. *Indian Journal of Psychiatry, 55*(2), 140–143.

Grigg, D. (2010). Cyber-aggression: Definition and concept of cyberbullying. *Australian Journal of Guidance and Counselling, 20*(2), 143–156.

Halder, D. & Jaishankar K. (2009). Cyber socializing and victimization of women. *Temida – The Journal on Victimization, Human Rights and Gender, 12*(3), 5–26. Reprinted as Online social networking and women victims. In K. Jaishankar (ed.), *Cyber Criminology: Exploring Internet Crimes and Criminal Behavior* (pp. 301–320). Boca Raton, FL: CRC Press, Taylor and Francis Group.

Halder, D. & Jaishankar, K. (2010). Cyber victimization in India. A baseline survey report. Tirunnelveli, Tamil Nadu, India. Centre for Cyber Victim Counselling.

Halder, D. & Jaishankar, K. (2011). *Cyber Crime and the Victimization of Women: Laws, Rights, and Regulations.* Hershey, PA: IGI Global.

Halder, D. & Jaishankar, K. (2013). *Use and Misuse of Internet by Semi-urban and Rural Youth in India: A Baseline Survey Report.* Tirunelveli, India: Centre for Cyber Victim Counselling.

Hinduja, S., & Patchin, J. W. (2008). Cyberbullying: An exploratory analysis of factors related to offending and victimization. *Deviant Behavior, 29*(2), 129–156.

Hong, Y., Li, X., Mao, R. & Stanton, B. (2007). Internet use among Chinese college students: Implications for sex education and HIV prevention. *Cyberpsychology & Behavior, 10,* 161–169.

Kennedy, M. A. & Taylor, M. A. (2010). Online harassment and victimization of college students. *Justice Policy Journal, 7*(1), 1–21.

Kraft, E. & Wang, J. (2010). An exploratory study of the cyberbullying and cyberstalking experiences and factors related to victimization of students at a public liberal arts college. *International Journal of Technologies, 1*(4), 74–91.

Koovakkai, D. & Muhammed, P. (2010). Internet abuse among the adolescents: A study on the locale factor. *Webology, 7*(1).

Kowalski, R. M., Giumetti, G. W., Schroeder, A. N. & Lattanner, M. R. (2014). Bullying in the digital age: A critical review and meta-analysis of cyberbullying research among youth. *Psychological Bulletin, 140*, 1073–1137.

Kraft, E. & Wang, J. (2010). An exploratory study of the cyberbullying and cyberstalking experiences and factors related to victimization of students at a public liberal arts college. *International Journal of Technologies, 1*(4), 74–91.

Kumar, S. N. & Sayadevi. (2009). Internet addiction among college students. Retrieved from www.iacp.in/2009/06/internet-addiction-among-college.html.

Lin, S.-F. & Lai, C. L. (2016). Bullying in Hong Kong schools. In P. K. Smith, K. Kwak & Y. Toda (eds.), *School Bullying in Different Cultures, Eastern and Western Perspectives* (pp. 133–150). Cambridge: Cambridge University Press.

Lindsay, M. & Krysik, J. (2012). Online harassment among college students: A replication incorporating new Internet trends. *Information, Communication & Society, 15*(5), 703–719.

Livingstone, S., Haddon, L., Görzig, A. & Ólafsson, K. (2011). *Risks and safety on the internet: The Perspective of European Children. Full Findings*. LSE, London: EU Kids Online.

MacDonald, C. D., & Roberts-Pittman, B. (2010). Cyberbullying among college students: Prevalence and demographic differences. *Procedia-Social and Behavioral Sciences, 9*, 2003–2009.

Mandelbaum, D. G. (1970), *Society in India, Vol. 1*. Berkeley: University of California Press.

Mascheroni, G., Vincent, J. & Jimenez, E. (2015). "Girls are addicted to likes so they post semi-naked selfies": Peer mediation, normativity and the construction of identity online. *Cyberpsychology: Journal of Psychosocial Research on Cyberspace, 9*(1), article 5. doi: 10.5817/CP2015-1-5.

Meena, P. S., Mittal, P. K. & Solanki, R. K.(2012). Problematic use of social networking sites among urban school going teenagers. *Industrial Psychiatry Journal, 21*(2), 94–97.

Mishna, F. (2012). *Bullying: A Guide to Research, Intervention, and Prevention*. New York: Oxford University Press.

Mishna, F., Saini, M. & Solomon, S. (2009). Ongoing and online: Children and youth's perceptions of cyber bullying. *Children and Youth Services Review, 31*(12), 1222–1228.

Molluzzo, J. C. & Lawler, J. P. (2012). A study of the perceptions of college students on cyberbullying. *Information Systems Education Journal, 10*(4), 84–109.

Nalwa, K. & Anand, A. P. (2003). Internet addiction in students: A cause of concern. *Cyberpsychology & Behavior, 6*(6), 653–656.

Patchin, J. W. & Hinduja, S. (2011). Traditional and nontraditional bullying among youth: A test of general strain theory. *Youth & Society, 43*(2), 727–751.

Renati, R., Berrone, C. & Zanetti, M. (2012). Morally disengaged and unempathic: Do cyberbullies fit these definitions? An exploratory study. *Cyberpsychology, Behavior, and Social Networking, 15,* 391–398.

Ringrose, J., Gill, R., Livingstone, S. & Harvey, L. (2012). *A Qualitative Study of Children, Young People and "Sexting": A Report Prepared for the NSPCC.* London: National Society for the Prevention of Cruelty to Children.

Rivers, I. & Noret, N. (2010). "I h8 u": Findings from a five-year study of text and email bullying. *British Educational Research Journal, 36,* 643–671.

Saha, T. & Srivastava, A. (2014). Indian women at risk in the cyberspace: A conceptual model of reasons for victimization. *International Journal of Cyber Criminology, 8*(1), 57–67.

Schenk, A. M. & Fremouw, W. J. (2012). Prevalence, psychological impact, and coping of cyberbully victims among college students. *Journal of School Violence, 11,* 21–37.

Schultze-Krumbholz, A. & Scheithauer, H. (2009). Social-behavioral correlates of cyberbullying in a German student sample. *Zeitschrift Für Psychologie/Journal of Psychology, 217,* 224–226.

Smith, P. K., Kwak. K. & Toda, Y. (2016). *School Bullying in Different Cultures, Eastern and Western Perspectives.* Cambridge: Cambridge University Press.

Smith, P. K., Mahdavi, J., Carvalho, M., Fisher, S., Russell, S. & Tippett, N. (2008). Cyberbullying: Its nature and impact in secondary school pupils. *Journal of Child Psychology and Psychiatry, 49*(4), 376–385.

Steffgen, G., König, A., Pfetsch, J. & Melzer, A. (2011). Are cyberbullies less empathic? Adolescents' cyberbullying behavior and empathic responsiveness. *Cyberpsychology, Behavior, and Social Networking, 14,* 643–648.

Stocking, G. W. (ed.). (1974). *The Shaping of American Anthropology 1883–1911: A Franz Boas Reader.* New York: Basic Books.

Toda, Y. (2016). Bullying (*ijime*) and related problems in Japan: History and research. In P. K. Smith, K. Kwak. & Y. Toda, (eds.), *School Bullying in Different Cultures, Eastern and Western Perspectives* (pp. 73–92). Cambridge, Cambridge University Press.

Tokunaga, R. S. (2010). Following you home from school: A critical review and synthesis of research on cyberbullying victimization. *Computers in Human Behavior, 26*(3), 277–287. doi: 10.1016/j.chb.2009.11.014.

Turan, N., Polat, O., Karapirli, M., Uysal, C. & Turan, S. G. (2011). The new violence type of the era: Cyber bullying among university students – violence among university students. *Neurology, Psychiatry and Brain Research, 17,* 21–26. doi: 10.1016/j.npbr.2011.02.005.

Vance, J. W. (2010). Cyber-harassment in higher education: Online learning environments. Doctoral dissertation, University of Southern California. Retrieved from http://digitallibrary.usc.edu/cdm/compoundobject/collection/p15799coll127/id/309077/rec/19.

Vandebosch, H. & Van Cleemput, K. (2008). Defining cyberbullying: A qualitative research into the perceptions of youngsters. *CyberPsychology & Behavior, 11*(4), 499–503.

Vidyachathoth, K. B., Kumar N. A. & Pai S. R. (2014). Correlation between affect and Internet addiction in undergraduate medical students in Mangalore. *Journal of Addiction Research & Therapy*, 5(1), 175. doi: 10.4172/2155–6105.1000175. www .omicsonline.org/open-access/correlation-between-affect-and-internet-addiction-in-undergraduate-medical-students-in-mangalore-2155–6105.1000175.pdf.

Walker, C. M., Sockman, B. R. & Koehn, S. (2011). An exploratory study of cyberbullying with undergraduate university students. *TechTrends: Linking Research and Practice to Improve Learning*, 55(2), 31–38.

Wensley, K. & Campbell, M. (2012). Heterosexual and nonheterosexual young university students' involvement in traditional and cyber forms of bullying. *Cyberpsychology, Behavior, and Social Networking*, 15(12), 649–654. doi: 10.1089/cyber.2012.0132.

Wright, M. F., Aoyama, I., Kamble, S. V., Li, Z., Soudi, S., Lei, L., & Shu, C. (2015). Peer attachment and cyberbullying involvement among Chinese, Indian, and Japanese adolescents. *Societies*, 5(2), 339–353. doi: 10.3390/soc5020339.

Yadav, P., Banwari, G., Parmar, C. & Maniar, R. (2013). Internet addiction and its correlates among high school students: A preliminary study from Ahmedabad, India. *Asian Journal of Psychiatry*, 6(6), 500–505.

Young, K. S. (1998). Internet addiction: The emergence of a new clinical disorder. *Cyberpsychology & Behavior*, 1, 237–244.

Zacchilli, T. L. & Valerio, C. Y. (2011). The knowledge and prevalence of cyberbullying in a college sample. *Journal of Scientific Psychology*, 5, 12–23.

Zalaquett, C. P. & Chatters, S. J. (2014). Cyberbullying in college: frequency, characteristics, and practical implications. *Sage Open*, 4(1). doi: 10.1177/2158244014526721.

Zhang, A. T., Land, L. P. W. & Dick, G. (2010). Key influences of cyberbullying for university students. PACIS 2010 Proceedings Paper 83. http://aisel.aisnet.org/pacis2010/83.

Zhang, W., Chen, L. & Chen, G. (2016). Research on school bullying in Mainland China. In P. K. Smith, K. Kwak & Y. Toda (eds.), *School Bullying in Different Cultures, Eastern and Western Perspectives* (pp. 113–132). Cambridge: Cambridge University Press.

7 Participant Roles in Bullying
What Data from Indian Classes Can Tell Us about the Phenomenon

Mechthild Schäfer, Manuel Stoiber, Tamara Bramböck, Hannes Letsch, Klaus Starch, and Suresh Sundaram

It is widely accepted that bullying is a group phenomenon: it occurs in classes under certain conditions, namely:
- group members cannot freely choose whom they are with;
- an external rule keeps them in the group on a regular, often daily basis;
- the chance to leave the group when not treated well is virtually non-existent; and
- the group is surrounded by or part of a hierarchical structure, where norms like accepted behavior are transferred from the top down.

Bullying itself is a group process, with the bully(s), who incite the bullying, supported by assistants who follow through on what others plan, and by reinforcers who applaud or cheer on the bullying thereby defining the bullying as within norms for others in class. The pro-bully group represents around 30% in a typical Western class (Salmivalli, 2010). Some 50% to 60% are opposed to bullying; around half of those are defenders who actively try to stop the aggressive attacks, search for help from teachers or supervisors, or console the victim, while the other half are outsiders who keep away from the bullying or do nothing to support the victim(s). The victims represent around 10% of a typical class.

Bullying is functional, inspired and initiated by the bully's search for dominance and accomplished by strategies that shed a better light on the bully's aggressive actions than the desperate attempts of the victim to avoid the bullying (see also Chapter 8). Many children may be torn between what they perceive as morally right, and the developmental task to keep/maintain their role within the group. For them, moral disengagement (Gini, Pozzoli, & Hymel, 2014) can be an easy way out, and the longer the process lasts, the more the group of those standing against the bullying is likely to diminish, leaving the victim more and more isolated. Meta-analyses on evaluations of intervention programs support the view that bullying is in part resistant to intervention: this is supported as well as contrasted by the finding that highly efficient intervention can come from within the class (Polanin, Espelage, & Pigott, 2012). Peer defending happens in one of three cases and is successful in around 60% of those (O'Connell, Pepler, & Craig, 1999).

Given that bullying is functional as well as adaptive behavior (Sutton, Smith, & Swettenham, 1999), and expected to appear in classes under certain conditions, we should not be too optimistic about finding intercultural differences when Indian and European (German) classes are compared. Most studies on bullying are from a more or less homogeneous "Western" cultural background (Europe, North America, Australasia) and thus relatively high on similarities, as societal norms translate into the structure as well as shared values of and within the school system. On an administrative/structural level, Indian schools are not that different, but what about divergent cultural values, and how do they translate into Indian schooling (see also Chapter 1)? We would like to explore the idea that bullying phenomena may appear similar on the surface, but that peer reactions might differ depending on the cultural framework they are embedded in. Thus we assume variance in social norms that translate values into behavior. If we postulate that cultural differences between India and Germany impact the bullying process, we need to verify these cultural differences within some sociological or psychological framework. Two questions seem appropriate to gain inspiration about bullying by an intercultural comparison: *why* can/should we learn from Indian data, and *what* can/should we learn from Indian data?

Why Can We Learn from Indian Data?

There is a long tradition of studying cultural differences. How we understand the world influences Eastern and Western systems of thought. Social organization is assumed to translate into cognitive processes both indirectly, as attention might be focused on different parts of the environment, and directly, as certain communication patterns are more acceptable than others (Nisbett, Peng, Choi, & Norenzayan, 2001).

Western societies are generally described as individualistic; by contrast, India exemplifies a collective culture. But collectivism and individualism should not be seen as opposites of a uniform dimension. Experiments have shown that people from a collectivist (e.g., Asian) society are characterized by an holistic view and are better able to orientate in relation to context, while people from an individualistic (e.g., North American) society share an analytic view and are better able to orientate to individual objects (Choi, Nisbett, & Norenzayan, 1999).

However, does this translate into Indian data on how children perceive bullying or specify certain behaviors as part of the bullying in their class?

And can we consider India even as one culture? In *Culture and Leadership across the World*, Chhokar (2008) titles a chapter "India: Diversity and Complexity in Action" and cites "yet the sameness of the traditions on which all of them have been reared cannot be overlooked" (Bose, 1967, p. 9). With reference to the development of the country since the 1950s, the political situation is described as the "sharing of environment and ethos by communities and their vibrant participation in political and economic processes and ritual roles (and) a sense of harmony ... in spite of conflicts and contradictions" (Singh, 1992, pp. 101–102). Chhokar (2008) concludes that India should score high on societal collectivism as a core value.

Hofstede, Hofstede, and Minkov (2010), in contrast, characterize India as both collectivistic and individualistic (it comes in the middle of their individualism/collectivism dimension), but quite high on power distance (hierarchy). Suppose there is high popularity assigned to a bully role in Indian and German classes. This could be explained by acceptance of the bully's behavior, as in India hierarchy is highly appreciated and a top-down structure – linked to the expectation of obedience and loyalty by those on top – is socialized. It could also result from the individualistic search for power, valued by those who observe it as a model behavior (Moffitt, 1993) probably more common in individualistic societies such as Germany. Thus a similar pattern (high popularity attributed to dominance) might originate in culture, but might display divergent patterns, if perception and group mechanisms are analyzed more deeply. More precisely, the intercultural comparison might bring to light the ambivalence of potential interpretations, if evaluated in the respective context of a dynamic process. Could this amplify our mind-set about how to convert empirical evidence into successful interventions?

What Can We Learn from Indian Data?

Given the complexity of potential relations to be considered when bullying happens in a class of 25 or more, we can gain safer knowledge about what originates from social psychological processes in groups of humans per se and what is variable, if an external factor like culture varies. Does socialization based on collective values support a peer reaction to bullying that favors the perception of bullying as a strong situation (cf. Krueger, 2009)? Bullying as a strong situation implies that the behavior shown orientates more from shared values, namely collectivism. This would lead to convergent behavior guided by the situation, which is a group member being attacked for the sake of another individual's striving for dominance and suffering. We should expect Indian peers to be more perceptive about the context (the group) when someone is increasingly isolated from the group. However, given that it is the function of a group to provide space for the developmental necessity to stick to group norms, to keep the individual's status within the group (class) safe, would this undermine the individual's perception if bullying happens, and translate values into adequate behavior, as "determined" by the situation? This might best describe the situation in Western societies: the majority of children perceive bullying as unfair and unacceptable (O'Cornell et al., 1999), but when it happens in their class, this attitude or conviction seems no longer applicable. On the behavioral level, peer reactions to bullying predominantly follow the criteria of a so-called weak situation. Automatized behavior follows no emotional perception and no reflection of what happens in the situation (e.g., Mischel, 1977). In contrast, a strong situation is identified by a pause for reflection, that results in emotional activation when kids are fully alert to the situation.

But what about the perceptual level? If we expect differences or variant patterns linked to culture, what level of analysis should be approached, if the final goal is to uncover reliable evidence about where to start intervention/prevention that comes out of the group itself? In this chapter we will explore the Indian data with reference to external (e.g., hierarchy, rules) and internal (values) motivations that frame the background for social norms to work in groups. We will use a German sample extended by a larger dataset for comparisons, to unearth where similarities should be explained by the robustness of the phenomenon, or offer alternative interpretations due to cultural background, and finally try to fix differences that are meaningful to tell us more about new pathways to tackle bullying.

Methodological Issues

To explore the potential of the Indian data, we start the analyses based on data gathered in Tamil Nadu in spring 2015. Altogether, 911 8th to 10th graders from 16 classes of two schools, situated in Annamalai Nagar and Puducherry, filled in the Participant Role Questionnaire (PRQ: Salmivalli et al., 1996); pupils could choose Tamil or English versions. To guarantee anonymity, children nominated classmates by using their numbers from the class list. The PRQ was supplemented by two questions to derive sociometric status (from Coie, Dodge, & Coppotelli, 1982), two questions on perceived popularity (Parkhurst & Hopmeyer, 1998), and several questions on resource control, coercive strategies, and prosocial strategies (Hawley, 2003; n.b. Resource Control Theory data are not part of the findings reported here). Around the same time, 583 7th to 10th graders from 19 classes of a Munich school responded to the same set of questionnaires under identical conditions. For reasons of gender balance, we extended the sample up to N = 1,646 by data from three other German schools.

Empirical Findings

Figure 7.1 presents a typical picture of the social reality in Indian classes. Two blocks of forms divided by a passage for the teacher to move up and down makes the typical picture of an Indian classroom – all the girls on one side and all the boys on the other side. This spatial picture defines territories, as boys and girls are not permitted to interact and teachers are advised to ensure that this norm is accepted both in class and on the playground. It is thus predictable that this norm is reflected in the patterns of nominations, as Figure 7.2 shows.

Figure 7.1 Indian girls and boys within one classroom

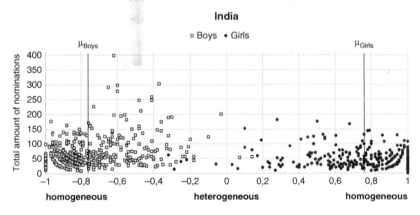

Figure 7.2 The ratioX-spectrum of nominations by boys and girls in the Indian sample

Perceiving and Being Perceived – the Indian Sample

Figure 7.2 presents the total number of nominations received, differentiated by gender. Dots around 0 show nominations given in equal share by girls and boys (heterogeneous nominations), while those at -1 are homogeneous nominations only by/to boys, and those at +1 those given only by/to girls. We calculated each ratioX-value as follows:

$$ratioX = \frac{-\,sumNOMboys + sumNOMgirls}{sumNOM}$$

Indian boys and girls both receive around 88% of nominations within gender and 10% across gender. The blue line (boys) and the green line (girls) represent the ratioX-means with $\mu_{\text{Indian boys}}$ = -0.77 (SD = 0.21) for boys and $\mu_{\text{Indian girls}}$ = 0.76 (SD = 0.30) for girls, thus without any difference due to gender. On first glance, this suggests that the administrative rule of no interaction across gender reproduces itself in the majority of nominations about bullying behaviors perceived, with nominations on liking, not liking, and popularity included. But to confirm this, the typicality of nominations patterns has to be examined.

Two Societies: Girls' and Boys' Perspective – and How This Compares to German Pupils

An intercultural comparison of within- and across-gender nomination patterns is shown in Figure 7.3. Clearly, the right graph seems at first sight more colorful as boys' nominations (blue) and girls' nominations (green) mix up for the German pupils, while on the left graph they are clearly separated for the Indian pupils. The central box identifies the area of heterogeneous nominations defined as being one standard deviation above the respective ratioX-mean. RatioX-means for German pupils are μ_{bG} = -0.28 (SD = 0.38) for boys and μ_{gG} = 0.43 (SD = 0.35) for girls. These are significantly different from the values for Indian pupils, for boys $t(502)$ = -53.22, p < 0.001; d = 1.54, and for girls, $t(393)$ = 26.09, p < 0.001; d = 1.20. The effect size confirms a substantial intercultural difference for within/across gender nominations; in Indian classes both sexes nominate primarily within sex, while in German classes boys and girls nominate prioritized across sex. These differences appear to be related to an absence of regulation on gender interactions in Germany, but a clear regulation against interactions between boys and girls in India.

The perceptions of behavior shown in a group normally translate into peer reactions. This is one way by which social norms of a group are

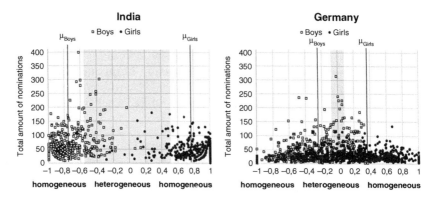

Figure 7.3 Comparison of the ratioX-spectrums and area of heterogeneity in the Indian and German samples

		Peer-reactions comparing heterogeneous to homogeneous gender nominations	
Nominations		to boys	to girls
Social acceptance (L$_{ike}$ M$_{ost}$)	from boys	–	↑
	from girls	↑	↓
Reciprocal friendships		–	↓
Social rejection (L$_{ike}$ L$_{east}$)	from boys	↑	↑
	from girls	↑	–
Exclusion	from boys	↑	↑
	from girls	↑	–

Figure 7.4 Overview of significant effects of different qualities of peer reactions if homogeneous and heterogeneous nominations are compared (Indian sample only) (exclusion was represented by nominations on the item "Who often gets left out of the group on purpose?")

constituted. Figure 7.4 represents peer reactions as indexed by social acceptance (like most), reciprocal friendship (these are reported only within gender), social rejection (like least), and exclusion. We compared children nominated across gender (heterogeneous) to those nominated within gender (homogeneous). Girls nominated heterogeneously are more accepted by boys, and less accepted by girls. Like girls, boys are more accepted by the other sex too, but neither more nor less accepted by their own sex when heterogeneously nominated. That reciprocal friendships are less for girls might derive, at least in part, from fewer girl-to-girl like most nominations.

Peer reactions, namely peer rejection, are surprising: both girls and boys score high on social rejection by the other sex, and boys too get more rejection from their own sex, which does not apply for girls.

Finally, exclusion replicates the pattern already stated for social rejection (exclusion was represented by nominations on the item "Who often gets left out of the group on purpose?"). The other sex is more excluded when peer reactions to those heterogeneously nominated are compared to those homogeneously nominated and again boys are more excluded by their own sex. Given the huge difference in nomination patterns between India and Germany, it appears surprising that children from the Indian and German samples are assigned to participant roles with similar prevalence rates.

The Prevalence of Bullying in India and Germany

Calculating prevalence rates, the differences in how many bullies, assistants, and reinforcers (pro-bully roles) are identified in the Indian and German samples are as small as for defenders, outsiders, and victims (anti-bully roles). Note that of all children being nominated, in the Indian sample the "no role" category is significantly more extended due to a higher number of children, identified due to a uniform nomination pattern with no peak for any bullying role (Abenthum, 2016). However, as we could not assign the correct sex to the children who were not active respondents in the study by nominating their peers, we corrected the sample for these children and the category "no role" diminished substantially (see Figure 7.5).

But does the quality of bullying behaviors have an impact on within or across nominations? In order to specify this, we extended the analyses and checked whether pro-bullying (bully, assistant, reinforce) or anti-bullying (defender, outsider, victim) behaviors differ on within- or across-gender nominations.

As shown in Figure 7.6, the Indian data present a difference particularly for boys. If girls nominate boys, it's more on pro-bullying behaviors than on anti-bullying behaviors; boys get significantly more across-gender nominations on pro-bullying behaviors (**boys**, India, **pro-b**ullying beha-vior, μbIpbb = 0.53(SD =0.16); **boys**, India, **anti-b**ullying **b**ehavior, μbIabb = 0.66 (SD = 0.16) / t(202.76) = 3.39, p < 0.01; d = 0.40). For girls no such difference is found.

Comparing boys and girls across gender nominations, no significant gender difference can be found in pro-bullying and anti-bullying behaviors.

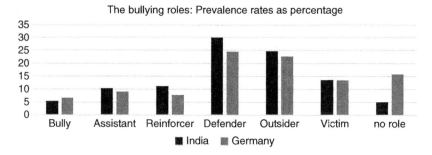

Figure 7.5 Prevalence rates for participant roles in India and Germany

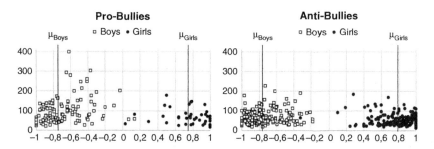

Figure 7.6 Nomination Spectrum for pro-bully and anti-bully roles from Indian boys and girls

Altogether the Indian pattern is described best by a focus on exclusively aggressive behaviors (but not so nonaggressive behaviors) and only when perceived/reported by girls.

The German data provide a divergent, somehow extended pattern: across-gender nominations differ between pro-bullying and anti-bullying behaviors within both boys ($t(511,223) = 2.22$, p < 0.05, d = 0.19) and girls ($t(64,822) = 3.14$, p < 0.01; d = 0.46). Like in India, pro-bullying behaviors get more across-gender nominations than anti-bullying behaviors, but unlike in India, this is irrespective of gender. This is not so if we compare boys and girls on pro-/anti-bullying behavior nominations: German boys (μbG = 0.32 (SD = 0.24)) get more across-gender nominations than girls (μgG = 0.52 (SD = 0.28)) on pro-bullying behaviors ($t(66,77) = -4.68$, p < 0.00; d = 0.80) with no difference on anti-bullying behaviors (μbG = 0.39(SD = 0.27); μ_{gG} = 0.41 (SD = 0.24)/$t(697) = -10.16$, n.s.). In all, German girls appear to be more observant and reporting than German boys, thus a knowledgeable source as far as (pro-)bullying behaviors are concerned. Indian girls show this too, but to a lesser extent.

Focusing on the participant roles in the Indian sample, there is no difference in the extent of across-gender nominations except for the victim role: boys get significantly more across-gender nominations ($t(83) = -2.22$, $p < 0.05$, $d = 0.50$) than girls do. Similarly, German victims get slightly more across-gender nominations when boys ($t(152) = -1.86$, $p = 0.065$), but there are significantly more across-gender nominations when pupils are nominated as reinforcers ($t(87) = -3.18$, $p < 0.001$, $d = 0.95$) or assistants ($t(103) = -3.79$, $p < 0.001$, $d = 0.98$). This might reveal a clear perspective on and a recognition of the behaviors supporting the bully actions (and intentions?) apart from his individual attacks. The bully's actions and motives behind their behaviors might not be on Indian girls' radar.

Outsiders: A Heterogeneous Group by Itself?

The final analysis focuses on outsiders and subgroups, namely behavioral tendencies as identified by a secondary role, which is the role given to pupils due to the second highest nomination value if it is above average on the respective scale. Figure 7.7 presents peer reactions as social preference indices (vertical) and the perceived popularity indices (horizontal) assigned by Indian girls, Indian boys, and German boys and girls (together) to outsiders in total and outsiders differentiated by subgroups. Outsiders in total (black) are rather average on social preference and perceived popularity, and without difference whether assigned by boys or girls. However, if differentiated by secondary role, two differences are striking: on the one hand those outsiders who are also nominated as victims by secondary role are negative on perceived popularity and on social preference if assigned by Indian boys and girls, but substantially lower on both when nominated by German pupils. On the other hand, those outsiders perceived as popular (and socially preferred) due to their secondary role are outsider/defenders in the Indian sample and outsider/pro-bullies in the German sample. Indian outsider/defenders are not just the most popular outsiders but at least twice as high on social preference as the German outsider/pro-bullies, whose popularity value is highest of all. Where do these nominations on social preference and perceived popularity come from? "From defenders" if the high social preference values for Indian outsiders/defender are considered and "from all the class" if the high perceived popularity value of German outsiders/pro-bullies is considered.

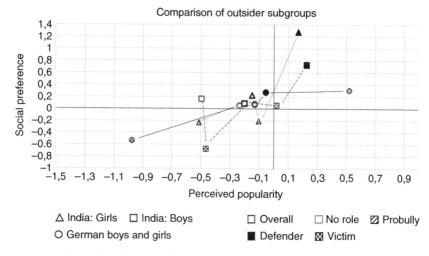

Figure 7.7 Social preference and perceived popularity of outsiders and outsider subgroups differentiated by Indian boys/girls and German pupils (mixed).

Discussion

The findings presented here are exploratory. They aim at a deeper understanding of the group dynamics behind bullying and extend the "who is who" in the bullying process to "who nominates whom" by zooming in on the perceptual level, its homogeneity and on subgroup analyses. As such we started with the very obvious: the gender segregation in Indian classes. The administrative rule, that boys and girls should not interact while in school, proves decisive as an external factor and separates boys and girls even on the level of perception. However, whenever it is overruled by across-gender nominations, patterns from the Indian sample point at what we find for German classes: girls are more observant and probably more knowledgeable about (bullying) behaviors in class; and aggressive behaviors are more clearly perceived than defending or trying to stay outside the bullying (outsiders).

It is important to note that we have found an external cultural norm to have a forceful effect. Given that the idea of a whole-school approach is perceived as absolutely essential/mandatory for efficient prevention/intervention to tackle bullying, the data from India prove the effectiveness of an external norm impressively.

But the external norm in India is not against bullying but against interaction of boys and girls who share a classroom. Around 80% follow social norms set as rules within school, as shown by the number of gender-homogeneous nominations. In contrast, in German classes, pupils identify by around 40% of within-gender nominations, which might be seen as typical, if no external gender segregation rule is in place. Nominations represent perception and perceiving within and across gender and imply the chance to learn on a broader basis. This might influence group processes in both good and bad ways. If within-group socialization is considered, the chance to reflect on observed behavior and learn to decide about one's own behavior is based in a more extended variety of information if a class is represented as one entity. One might postulate that the advantages outnumber the disadvantages (loss of tradition) if a society heads toward an equal rights community for men and women.

Cross-gender nominations might provide an idea about the first steps. While assessing the data in Indian schools we were often asked by the children if cross-gender nominations are permitted or even invited: we confirmed that they are invited. Thus around 20% of heterogeneous nominations provide a first step as those children with nominations from boys and girls receive similar peer reactions from both sides. They are more accepted, more rejected, and more excluded by the other sex, and while girls are less accepted by their own sex, boys are more rejected and excluded by their own sex. In other words, they are controversial as they "look over the fence" and while some of their peers show an externalized reaction (sanctioning), some might react in a more internalizing (accepting) way, as a broader frame of perception was confirmed by permission from the researchers: you can nominate any child in your class.

What Can We Learn from Indian Data?

That groups in a hierarchical system are easy to abuse is known worldwide – India is no exception, as prevalence rates for the participant roles in bullying are similar to the German sample and to what we know from other Western countries. However, with India high on power distance (Hofstede et al., 2010), this construct/tradition might still serve as a supporting/justifying factor for social power in class and its abuse (cf. Lewin, Lippitt, & White, 1939). In consequence, we see the exploitation of a well-chosen victim and the potential power of the group to resist the bullying.

Below the surface, the use of aggressive means to educate a child is still controversial in India, but it appears as a collectivistic value that it is wrong to pick on a member of one's group by downgrading his or her personality. Bullying in India unfolds among these two norms. Still, reports from within schools tell us that the reaction to victimization in India points more to ignoring and even hiding the phenomenon of bullying than toward the claim of safety for all.

In contrast to Western societies, in India a bully abuses the group for his/her individual sake and the sensitivity of peers to recognize that they are part of that game is still not shaped as necessary to provide a natural support for respect for everyone in class. Still, dominance taken is looked at differentially and admired by those who affiliate and disliked by those who see the suffering of the victim as outside accepted norms (Schäfer & Starch, 2015).

We leave it for discussion, as to whether the acceptance of hierarchy contradicts the idea of collectivism when groups are the unit to learn with and learn from (e.g., Ladd & Kochenderfer, 1996). Therefore, we slightly doubt that the idea that the "best interventions come out of the group" (Polanin et al., 2012) can come true for India as long as a class is not perceived as a group with the full range of group mechanisms possible. And from both samples we learn that girls outnumber boys on different levels with perspective taking and sensitivity toward behaviors shown.

A further zooming in on the intercultural data led to the subgroup analyses for outsiders. They focus on complexity of behavior, as the outsider group is not as homogeneous as supposed for other participant roles. Outsiders represent a substantial part of the class and are often seen as those who tip the scale when majorities for or against bullying are considered. Secondary roles thus might indicate a behavioral option or the direction for behavioral orientation, when bullying gets worse. Not surprising, in German classes outsiders are well perceived by the pro-bully group and often nominated by them as outsiders. In contrast, defenders don't seem to like them (few social preference nominations). Knowing this, the comparative analysis of Indian and German data might serve as a hint for how behavior is to be understood in the respective cultural frameworks.

Highest popularity and social preference scores for outsider/defenders are assigned by those Indian boys or girls who themselves favor anti-bullying behaviors – defenders (and outsiders). In contrast, in German classes highest popularity scores are assigned to outsider/pro-bullies and come from all peers irrespective of the role held. Does this – for India – represent a kind of accumulated focus on "positive" behaviors (collective approach) as "the behavior of the individual should be guided by the expectations of the group" (Nisbett et al., 2001, p. 292) and in-group harmony? In German classes outsiders with a secondary role as defender are, similar to those with a secondary role as pro-bully, equally liked slightly above average. We speculate that this might be guided by the primary focus on outsider behaviors instead of secondary role behaviors. However, the highest popularity score for outsider/pro-bullies speaks against this as it seems to mirror perceptions of "motives" behind (secondary role pro-bully) behaviors. We benchmark these findings as preliminary evidence for a perspective on bullying behaviors in class that reflects an interculturally divergent socialization about the role of the individual within the context and about the significance of personal agency in the bullying process.

From an intervention/prevention perspective, analyzing secondary roles could also serve as a predictor of children's performance, if the context is convenient, i.e., no bullying in class is salient. In India outsider/pro-bully children are average by peer reaction, but those outsiders who show defending now and then are well liked and this preferably by defenders (and outsiders). Thus a majority against bullying might be much easier to achieve in India than in Germany – if awareness for dynamics of a group and a shaping of opinion is stimulated toward coalition building in defenders and outsiders. The same is needed in Germany, but the situation is more complicated. With outsiders not well liked by defenders, their awareness needs to be raised for why outsiders don't step in directly (Schäfer, Starch, Stoiber, & Letsch, 2017) or why they shy away when bullying happens although they might be able to offer support (Pronk et al., 2013).

Finally the question "*Why* can we learn from Indian data" finds an easy response: because we can empirically show that a divergent cultural framework for bullying influences the perception of bullying and the behaviors involved. This inspires new pathways to prevention by changes to the framework. However, the results also confirm that the repeated systematic abuse of social power is found wherever group membership is not freely chosen in a hierarchical system and where no option to avoid the group is in place (Smith & Brain, 2000). It is the framework and the respective importance given to social relationships and cooperation that can make a difference.

References

Abenthum, M. (2016). *Bullying als kulturabhängiges Phänomen? – Eine Vergleichsstudie zwischen Deutschland und Indien [Bullying as a Culture-Dependent Phenomenon? A Comparative Study between Germany and India]*. Zulassungsarbeit im Studiengang Schulpsychologie, Department Psychologie der LMU München.

Bose, N. K. (1967). *Culture and Society in India*. Bombay: Asia Publishing House.

Chhokar, J. S. (2008). India: Diversity and complexity in action. In J. S. Chhokar, F. C. Brodbeck, & R. J. House (eds.), *Culture and Leadership across the World. The GLOBE Book of In-Depth Studies of 25 Societies* (S. 971–1020). Mahwah, NJ: Lawrence Erlbaum Associates.

Choi, I., Nisbett, R. E., & Norenzayan, A. (1999). Causal attribution across cultures: Variation and universality. *Psychological Bulletin, 125,* 47–63.

Coie, J. D., Dodge, K. A., & Coppotelli, H. (1982). Dimensions and types of social status: A cross-age perspective. *Developmental Psychology, 18*(4), 557–570.

Gini, G., Pozzoli T., & Hymel, S. (2014). Moral disengagement among children and youth: A meta-analytic review of links to aggressive behavior. *Aggressive Behavior, 40*(1), 56–68.

Hawley, P. H. (1999). The ontogenesis of social dominance: A strategy-based evolutionary perspective. *Developmental Review, 19,* 97–132.

Hawley, P. H. (2003). Strategies of control, aggression, and morality in preschoolers: An evolutionary perspective. *Journal of Experimental Child Psychology, 85,* 213–235.

Hofstede, G., Hofstede, G. J., & Minkov, M. (2010). *Cultures and Organisations: Software of the Mind* (3rd edn.). New York: McGraw-Hill.

Kochenderfer, B. J. & Ladd, G. W. (1996). Peer victimization: Cause or consequence of school maladjustment? *Child Development, 67,* 1305–1317.

Krueger, J. I. (2009). A componential model of situation effects, person effects, and situation-by-person interaction effects on social behavior. *Journal of Research in Personality, 43,* 127–136.

Lewin, K., Lippitt, R., & White, R. K. (1939). Patterns of aggressive behavior in experimentally created "social climates." *Journal of Social Psychology, 10,* 271–299.

Mischel, W. (1977). The interaction of person and situation. In D. Magnusson & N. S. Endler (eds.), *Personality at the Crossroads: Current Issues in Interactional Psychology* (pp. 333–352). Hillsdale, NJ: Lawrence Erlbaum Associates.

Moffitt, T. E. (1993). Adolescence-limited and life-course-persistent antisocial behavior: A developmental taxonomy. *Psychological Review, 100*(4), 674–701.

Nisbett, R. E., Peng, K., Choi, I., & Norenzayan, A. (2001). Culture and systems of thought: Holistic versus analytic cognition. *Psychological Review, 108*(2), 291–310.

O'Connell, P., Pepler, D. J., & Craig, W. (1999). Peer involvement in bullying: Insights and challenges for intervention. *Journal of Adolescence, 22,* 86–97.

Parkhurst, J. T. & Hopmeyer, A. (1998). Sociometric popularity and peer-perceived popularity: Two distinct dimensions of peer status. *Journal of Early Adolescence, 18*(2), 125–144.

Polanin, J. R., Espelage, D. l., & Pigott, T. D. (2012). A meta-analysis of school-based bullying prevention programs' effects on bystanders intervention behavior. *School Psychology Review, 41*(1), 47–65.

Pronk, J., Goossens, F. A., Olthof, T., De Mey, L., & Willemen, A. M. (2013). Children's intervention strategies in situations of victimization by bullying: Social cognitions of outsiders versus defenders. *Journal of School Psychology, 51,* 669–682.

Salmivalli, C. (2010). Bullying and the peer group: A review. *Aggression and Violent Behavior, 15,* 112–120.

Salmivalli, C., Lagerspetz, K., Björkqvist, K., Östermann, K., & Kaukiainen, A. (1996). Bullying as a group process: Participant roles and their relations to social status within the group. *Aggressive Behavior, 22,* 1–15.

Schäfer, M. & Starch, K. (2015). Changing perspective is changing the system – A moral foundation perspective on how to approach the group dynamics behind bullying. *Presentation at the VI World Congress on School Violence and Public Policies: From Violence to School Well-being,* Lima, Peru.

Schäfer, M., Starch, K., Stoiber, M., & Letsch, H. (2017). Changing perspective is changing the system – Bullying as "strong situation." *Journal of Addiction Research & Therapy, 8*(1). doi: 10.4172/2155–6105.1000305

Singh, K. S. (1992). *People of India: An introduction* (National Series Vol. 1). Calcutta: Anthropological Survey of India.

Smith, P. K. & Brain, P. (2000). Bullying in schools: Lessons from two decades of research. *Aggressive Behavior, 26,* 1–9.

Sutton, J., Smith, P. K., & Swettenham, J. (1999). Bullying and theory of mind: A critique of the "social skills deficit" view of anti-social behaviour. *Social Development, 8,* 117–127.

8 Bullying, Defending and Victimization in Western Europe and India

Similarities and Differences

Frits Goossens, Jeroen Pronk, Nikki Lee, Tjeert Olthof, Mechthild Schäfer, Manuel Stoiber, Suresh Sundaram, Sajeeth Kumar Gopalakrishnan, Damanjit Sandhu, Kirandeep Kaur and Shubhdip Kaur

Evolutionary psychology attempts to understand human behavior by applying Darwin's (1968) evolutionary theory. Darwin suggested that species are in a continual process of adaptation through reproduction and the success of this reproduction is driven by natural selection. Both Axelrod (1984) and Hawley (1999) suggested that all species, including humans, use two strategies to get ahead. These two strategies – using prosocial and aggressive (coercive) behaviors – are both considered adaptive. This chapter concerns a study on bullying as an example of an aggressive or coercive strategy, and defending as an example of a prosocial strategy. Bullying is defined as repeated and intentional aggression from a more powerful person toward a weaker victim (Olweus, 1993). As victims are the objects of aggression in the form of bullying and prosocial behavior in the form of defending, we also look at victimization.

Evolutionary theoretical perspectives suggest that individuals' social status can be equated with their control over the resources available in social groups (Hawley, Little & Card, 2008). According to Hawley's resource control theory (RCT) (1999, Hawley, Little & Rodkin, 2007), groups provide several resources, such as social contacts, attention, affection, cognitive stimulation and novelty. There are also material resources as the individuals comprising the group may differ in their individual possessions (money, clothes and toys). Individuals are differentially motivated by these resources. Those who are motivated by the group's resources or who covet individual resources are willing to compete for them. Both Hawley (2003) and Olthof and colleagues (2011) demonstrated that children can use either aggressive (coercive) or prosocial strategies to obtain resource control, but those who combine both strategies, the so-called bistrategic children, acquire the most resources and are seen as dominant in the group. Olthof and colleagues also showed that bullies are often bistrategics, although bullying itself can be seen as a coercive strategy to gain access to resources (cf. also Archer, 2001; Griskevicius et al., 2009; Reijntjes et al., 2013). Nevertheless, bullies also help their friends (Huitsing et al., 2014).

Bullying promotes access to physical, social and/or sexual resources (Volk et al., 2015). The latter may be the ultimate goal of bullying, as only procreation guarantees the continuation of one's genes. Volk and colleagues (2015) provide considerable evidence to support the idea of bullying as adaptive behavior. First, bullying is common not only in the human species but also in many social animals. Second, Western adolescent bullies have more dates with members of the other sex and are more likely to have experienced sexual intercourse (Arnocky & Vaillancourt, 2012; Connolly et al., 2000; Dane et al., 2016; Volk et al., 2015). Third, bullying is ubiquitous, having been found in every modern society in which its measurement has been undertaken. Fourth, bullying has been suggested to be resistant to intervention (Garandeau, Lee & Salmivalli, 2013; Ttofi & Farrington, 2011; Yeager et al., 2015), presumably because bullying is rewarding and giving it up may not be. Finally, Ball and colleagues (2008) found bullying to be heritable, that is, it has genetic roots.

Given the ubiquitous nature of prosocial behavior, a genetic basis of prosocial behavior is to be expected. Certainly, genetic twin research as well as molecular genetic studies support this assumption (Israel, Hasenfratz & Knafo-Noam, 2015; Knafo-Noam et al., 2015). As to cooperation or altruism, evolutionary theorists have made several suggestions why behavior that seems to benefit others, but not the persons themselves, could exist. They first came up with kin selection theory, which explains altruism to relatives but cannot explain why altruistic acts are directed at non-kin members of the species. Trivers's view of reciprocal altruism ("if you scratch my back, I'll scratch yours") may explain the behavior of bullies, who, as calculating individuals, buy the loyalty of their cronies by defending them (Huitsing et al., 2014).

However, in the bullying process, we also encounter children who defend other children, but who do not have the reputation of being bullies. It would seem unlikely that these (defending) children operate on the principle of reciprocal altruism, given that the victims (disliked and powerless) may not have much to offer in return. As reciprocal altruism cannot properly explain all human altruistic behavior, Hardy and van Vugt (2006) put forth the competitive altruism hypothesis, which they describe as the process through which individuals attempt to outcompete each other in terms of generosity. "It emerges because altruism enhances the status and the reputation of the giver" (p. 1403).

They mention some conditions that need to be fulfilled in order to result in benefits for the altruistic actor. First, the behavior must be costly for the actor to display. Defending victims can be costly as bullies may decide that the defender should be victimized too. Second, the behavior must be easily observable to others. We know that defenders exist and can reliably be found by way of nomination procedures within classrooms (Salmivalli et al., 1996). Finally, the signal (defending) must be a reliable indicator of some underlying desirable trait. Defenders have been found to be well liked by their peers (Goossens, Olthof & Dekker, 2006; Pronk, Olthof & Goossens, 2015), and to be empathic (Gini et al., 2008).

This chapter has two aims. The first aim is to study the links between the roles of bully, defender and victim and adolescents' social rank in their group's social hierarchy in terms of preference (i.e. likeability) and dominance (popularity and resource control). We will test this in two European countries (the Netherlands and Germany) as well as in India (in the provinces of Punjab and Tamil Nadu). India is different from Europe in culture, religion and economic wealth. Nevertheless, given the basis of our reasoning in terms of evolutionary theory, we expect to find similar results. The second aim concerns a comparison of prevalence (visibility) rates of bullying, defending and victimization between Europe and India. Here, we expect differences, because poverty and adverse social circumstances are not conducive to prosocial behavior, but they are to aggression and bullying.

As to the first aim, based on the link that evolutionary theory makes between bullying and social dominance, we expect that bullies will occupy high positions in the dominance hierarchy, although they are less likely to score high on preference. The behavior of bullies is harmful to others and therefore less likely to be appreciated, although they may be liked by their in-group members. Similarly, consistent with the competitive altruism hypothesis, defending should go with high scores for dominance and preference. After all, the behavior of defenders is to the benefit of others. Being a victim tends to go with low scores for dominance (Olthof et al., 2011) and affiliation (Goossens et al., 2006; Salmivalli et al., 1996). We expect to replicate such findings in both continents.

We also refer to a recent study by Pronk and colleagues (2016), who used a variable-centered approach to test the links between bullying, defending and victimization and preference and dominance in both the Netherlands and India (Punjab). The present study differs from the one by Pronk and colleagues (2016) in several respects. First, we added data collected in Germany and elsewhere in India (Tamil Nadu), made available by colleagues from Munich and Chidambaram. Second, we applied a person-centered approach instead of the variable-centered approach employed by Pronk and colleagues.

To summarize, we formulate the following hypotheses: (1) bullying will be positively associated with popularity and resource control and will not or only moderately be associated with preference; (2) defending will be positively associated with popularity and resource control, and will be strongly associated with preference; (3) being victimized will be negatively associated with popularity, resource control and preference.

As to the second aim, we expect differences in prevalence scores (i.e. visibility) of bullying, defending and victimization between the continents. There is some debate as to whether classifications into participant roles (such as bully, victim and defender) are the best measure for assessing prevalence. Certainly, Solberg and Olweus (2003) argued that they are not. Among the objections against peer nominations of such roles, they mention the skewed distribution of the data and the fact that number of nominations given does not add up to a frequency. We nevertheless prefer peer nominations to self-reports, as self-reports can be biased (Gromann et al., 2013). Bullies downplay their involvement in bullying, while victims often exaggerate the frequency of their victimization. We will use the term *visibility* for our measure of prevalence.

Hofstede (1980) suggested that variability in individuals' tendency to emphasize personal versus collective gains differs by culture. Some cultures have a more individualistic orientation and others (such as India) a more collectivistic orientation (see Chapter 2). We do not, however, think that such collectivistic orientations will have an impact on bullying (Pronk et al., 2016). First of all, the collectivistic orientation usually covers the relations with members of the (extended) family, and this domain is not or only marginally at stake in bullying at school. Few peers at school are likely to be members of the extended family. Second, bullying within the family is not uncommon, at least in Western cultures (Wolke & Samara, 2004), while there is some evidence supporting a link between bullying at home and at school (Duncan, 1999). Third, our main argument is that adverse social and economic circumstances are not conducive to prosocial behavior (defending), but to aggression, and thus to bullying. Such adverse circumstances are more likely to be encountered in India than in Western Europe.

Daly and Wilson (1988) suggest that males may be less likely to find a sexual partner when they lack resources that can attract females. This fact makes males more prone to engage in competitive risk-taking, which reaches its zenith in adolescence (Cairns & Cairns, 1994; Kolbert & Crothers, 2003). Evolutionary theory predicts that males without resources (those residing in impoverished communities) would engage in higher levels of risk-taking and violence against other males, but presumably also against females (cf. also Arnocky & Vaillancourt, 2012). In line with this way of thinking, two Indian studies (Ksirsagar, Agarwal & Bavdekap, 2007, in Maharashtra, and Ramya & Kulharni, 2011, in Karnataka) reported high prevalence figures for victimization of more than 30% and more than 60%, respectively, using self-report measures. Khatri and Kupersmidt (2003, in Gujarat), who used a peer report measure, did not find such high visibility figures. All studies found that boys were more involved in bullying than girls. Khatri and Kupersmidt also looked at preference (being liked) and rejection (being disliked), and found both bullies and victims to be lower on preference and higher on rejection than the remaining group. The first two studies (Ksirsagar et al., 2007; Ramy & Kulharni, 2011) expected higher prevalence rates than those reported for Western samples. They based their expectations on the prevalence of aggression throughout Indian society. Khatri and Kupersmidt expected lower visibility figures because of the collectivistic nature of Indian culture. We have already argued against a strong influence of the collectivistic cultural orientation in India. We suggested instead that general wealth differences within India will influence visibility rates of bullying, defending and victimization and that we will find more bullying and victimization and less defending in India than in Europe. We will use peer nominations to assess the visibility of these behaviors.

Method

Sample

Students were recruited from the first and second year of public secondary schools (equaling the seventh and eighth grades in the US schooling system) in Europe (Amstelveen, the Netherlands; Munich, Germany) and from equivalent schools in India (Patiala, Punjab and Chidambaram, Tamil Nadu). Final data were collected from 2,050 pupils in a total of 59 classrooms. The European and Indian schools differed in classroom size. The average classroom size was considerably smaller in Europe than in India. We present descriptive sample information (for each of the four sites) in Table 8.1.

Table 8.1 *Descriptive sample information for the total sample and separately by location*

| | N | % boys | M_{age} (SD_{years}) | Classes | | |
				N	M (SD)	Range
Total sample	2,050	60.7	13.9 (1.2)	59	41.6 (13.7)	19 – 61
Amsterdam	219	53.4	13.9 (0.7)	8	27.7 (3.1)	19 – 30
Munich	536	69.4	14.2 (1.5)	23	25.6 (2.5)	21 – 32
Tamil Nadu	815	56.8	13.6 (1.1)	16	56.4 (3.5)	48 – 61
Patiala	480	69.4	14.2 (1.0)	12	40.6 (4.5)	28 – 46

Measures

Behavioral reputation: An adapted version of the Participant Roles Scales, originally developed by Salmivalli and colleagues (1996), was used to measure participants' bullying-related behavioral reputation. First, students were given a definition of bullying (i.e. bullying is repeatedly executed, goal-directed, aggressive behavior characterized by a power imbalance between perpetrator[s] and victim). Subsequently, they completed 18 peer nominations pertaining to the bullying-related behavioral reputations of their classmates: (1) *bully* (five items, one item each for physical, verbal, direct relational, indirect relational and cyberbullying); (2) *victim* (five similar items); (3) *follower* (four items for helping and supporting the bullying); (4) *outsider* (two items for refraining from involvement); and (5) *defender* (two items, one item each for direct and indirect defending). Peer-nomination procedures are based on information provided by all members of the group (classroom). This provides an assurance that the behavioral assessment of each individual within a classroom is obtained reliably (Pellegrini & Long, 2002). Students could nominate a maximum of 10 classmates for each of the questions (no self-nominations) from a list that contained all classmates' names.

As the literature suggests that some bullies specialize in particular forms of bullying, computing a grand mean across five forms of bullying could underestimate the extent to which students are bullying or being victimized. Following procedures used by Witvliet and colleagues (2010) and by Olthof and colleagues (2011), we therefore averaged students' two highest scores out of all five bullying (and victimization) items to obtain an overall measure of bullying (or victimization) that reflects the frequency of their most used forms of bullying (or victimization). Spearman-Brown coefficients were 0.95 for bully and 0.92 for victim. For defender (two items only), the Spearman-Brown coefficient was 0.75. Continuous scores were computed per class for each type of nomination by dividing the number of received nominations by the number of nominators. The scores themselves ranged from 0 to 1, with the latter score indicating that all participating classmates nominated the particular participant. We normalized the data with the SPSS Rankit procedure over the whole sample (i.e. all percentage scores irrespective of location or gender). This was done in order to compare the visibility of these bullying-related behaviors between the continents.

Classifying participants in terms of bullying roles: We first checked if the five-factor (bullying-related behavior) structure was supported by an acceptable model fit through Confirmatory Factor Analysis (CFA). This appeared to be the case, although the Root Mean Square Errors of Approximation (RMSEA) fit indexes were slightly higher than generally recommended (0.09 or less). The results of the CFA for all participants as well as per continent are presented in Table 8.2. As we were mainly interested in bullying, defending and victimization, we distinguished only between the roles of bully, defender and victim. Students were classified into a particular bullying role if their score for one of the bullying roles described earlier was at least 10% and exceeded all other role scores with at least 1%. Previous research (Goossens et al., 2006) had demonstrated the viability of the 10% criterion. Students scoring lower than 10% on all dimensions were considered uninvolved in bullying. For ease of presentation we left out those who could be assigned other classifications than those of bully, defender or victim.

Table 8.2 *Confirmatory Factor Analysis outcomes for the five-factor structure of bullying-related behavioral reputation for the total sample (N = 2,050) and separately for Europe (n = 755) and India (n = 1,295)*

	Fit indices					
	χ^2 (125)	RMSEA	CFI	SRMR	TLI	λ_{range}
Total sample	2,378.63	0.09	0.95	0.06	0.94	0.53 –0.99
Europe	1,101.84	0.11	0.95	0.07	0.93	0.40 –0.99
India	1,607.84	0.10	0.95	0.07	0.93	0.32 –0.94

Note. All models were significant at p < 0.001. RMSEA = Root Mean Square Error of Approximation; SRMR = Standardized Root Mean Square Residuals; CFI = Comparative Fit Index; TLI = Tucker-Lewis Index.

Social status: We assessed both preference status and popularity status. Standard procedures were used for both.

For preference status, students completed peer nominations (maximum 10 nominations) indicating which classmates they liked most (positive nominations) and which they liked least (negative nominations). Final preference status was calculated as the within-classroom standardized difference between the within-classroom standardized "like most" and "like least" nominations (Coie, Dodge & Coppotelli, 1982).

For popularity status, students responded to *"Which children in your class are popular?"* and *"Which children are not popular?"* Popularity status was determined by subtracting the standardized number of unpopular votes (again a maximum of 10) received from the standardized number of popular votes received. This last measure was standardized again by classroom (Parkhurst & Hopmeyer, 1998).

Finally, three items were adapted from Hawley's procedures to measure peer reported *resource control*. These were: (1) *"Which children in your class ... have the nicest items or the best place when something is happening?"*; (2) *... usually get what they want?"*; and (3) *... usually get the best roles in games?"* (Hawley, 2003). Based on the number of nominations received, continuous scores were computed that were subsequently averaged to yield a measure of peer-reported resource control (coefficient alpha = 0.72). To correct for differences between classes in terms of students' characteristics as reporters about each other's behavior, these scores were standardized by classroom.

Because popularity and resource control correlated fairly highly (r = 0.52), we combined these scores by averaging across the two measures. (We also analyzed our data with popularity and resource control separately, with very similar results.) We refer to this new measure as *dominance*. This combined score was also expressed as a standardized score.

Procedure

In agreement with Faculty Ethical Review Board guidelines, the parents of the Dutch participants were notified about the study via an informed passive consent letter. Parents who did not want their children to participate returned a preprinted objection note in a stamped addressed envelope. The parents in Munich were approached in a similar manner. The parents of the Indian participants were notified about the study via the school's principal. Parents who did not want their children to participate informed their children's classroom teachers about this decision, who subsequently notified the testing assistants. The students themselves were also offered the opportunity to opt out of the study before they started the testing procedure. At all sites the testing procedure was administered in a classroom setting, supervised by at least two research assistants who followed a written research protocol to ensure consistent and correct response collection. Students were given a questionnaire package on which they answered all peer nominations, were informed about the confidentiality and anonymity of their responses and were urged not to talk with each other during the testing procedure. On average, the testing procedure took one hour to complete. However, there were slight differences in the various procedures. In Patiala, the questionnaires were in English, but one assistant also translated back into Punjabi on the spot. The questionnaires in Chidambaram were in Tamil, while in Munich they were in German, and in the Netherlands they were in Dutch.

Results

In Table 8.3 we present distributions across the three relevant roles for the total sample and for both continents separately. There were only a few children who could not be classified, because of conflicting nominations. Percentages of bullies never exceeded 10%. Almost all samples were characterized by more defenders than bullies and by more victims than bullies.

The first research question concerned similarities in the associations between bullying, defending and being victimized on the one hand and the status variables of preference and dominance on the other. In Table 8.4 we present the means and standard deviations of both variables (Status and Role) for the total sample. We subjected the data to profile analysis by way of a mixed design ANOVA with Role (bullies, defenders and victims), Continent (Europe and India) and Gender as the between-subject factors and Status as the within-subjects factor.

We present an overview of all outcomes in Table 8.5. We had predicted similar associations between the Role and Status variables, irrespective of Continent, and this is indeed what we found. Specifically, the Role by Status interaction was highly significant, without being qualified by significant higher-order interactions including Continent. The different bullying roles' status profiles suggest the following: defenders were preferred and quite dominant; bullies were dominant, but not preferred; victims were neither preferred nor dominant. Tukey HSD post hoc analyses showed that victims scored lower than both bullies and defenders on dominance, but bullies and victims did not differ from each other on preference. Defenders scored higher than either bullies or victims on

Table 8.3 *Frequency distributions of bullies, defenders and victims for the total sample and separately for Europe and India; percentages are of Total rows at bottom, including other roles and unclassified*

Role	Total sample			Europe			India		
	N (%)	N_{boys} (%)	N_{girls} (%)	n (%)	n_{boys} (%)	n_{girls} (%)	n (%)	n_{boys} (%)	n_{girls} (%)
Bully	138	111	27	48	40	8	90	71	19
	(6.7)	(8.9)	(3.3)	(6.4)	(8.2)	(3.0)	(6.9)	(9.4)	(3.5)
Defender	195	76	119	120	33	87	75	43	32
	(9.5)	(6.1)	(14.8)	(15.9)	(6.7)	(32.7)	(5.8)	(5.7)	(5.9)
Victim	182	134	48	71	44	27	111	90	21
	(8.9)	(10.8)	(6.0)	(9.4)	(9.0)	(10.2)	(8.6)	(11.9)	(3.9)
Total	2,050	1,244	806	755	489	266	1,295	755	540
	(100)	(100)	(100)	(100)	(100)	(100)	(100)	(100)	(100)

Table 8.4 *Descriptive statistics (means and standard deviations) for peer-group status (dominance and social preference) for all bullying roles (bully, defender and victim) for the total sample (in bold) and separately for Europe versus India (N = 515)*

	Dominance		Social preference	
	M	*SD*	*M*	*SD*
Bully	**0.74**	**1.05**	**−0.52**	**1.05**
Europe	0.83	1.16	−0.60	0.86
India	0.70	0.99	−0.48	1.14
Defender	**0.61**	**1.03**	**0.92**	**0.87**
Europe	0.32	0.89	0.73	0.84
India	1.07	1.08	1.24	0.82
Victim	**−0.48**	**0.79**	**−0.71**	**0.99**
Europe	−0.71	0.80	−1.00	0.91
India	−0.33	0.75	−0.52	1.00

Table 8.5 *Outcomes of the 2 (Gender: boy, girl) × 2 (Continent: Europe, India) × 3 (Role: bully, defender, victim) × 2 (Status: dominance vs social preference) Repeated Measures ANOVA (N = 515)*

	F	*df*s	η_p^2
Main effects			
Gender	0.23	(1, 503)	0.00
Continent	9.35**	(1, 503)	0.02
Role	172.72***	(2, 503)	0.41
Status	54.46***	(1, 503)	0.10
Two-way interactions			
Gender × Continent	1.11	(1, 503)	0.00
Gender × Role	4.62*	(2, 503)	0.02
Gender × Status	1.06	(1, 503)	0.00
Continent × Role	5.07**	(2, 503)	0.02
Continent × Status	0.15	(1, 503)	0.00
Role × Status	44.53***	(2, 503)	0.15
Three-way interactions			
Gender × Continent × Role	5.72**	(2, 503)	0.02
Gender × Continent × Status	4.15*	(1, 503)	0.01
Gender × Role × Status	1.58	(2, 503)	0.01
Continent × Role × Status	0.72	(2, 503)	0.00
Four-way interaction			
Gender × Continent × Role × Status	0.42	(2, 503)	0.00

Note. * p < 0.05; ** p < 0.01; *** p < 0.001

preference, but the latter did not differ from each other, despite the lower scores of victims on preference.

The second research question concerned potential differences in peer visibility of bullying, defending and victimization between Europe and India. In other words, we were looking for a Continent effect here. We subjected the data to a MANOVA with Gender and Continent (Europe versus India) as between factors. The Ms and SDs are presented in Table 8.6. The overall effect of the MANOVA was significant, $F(3, 2,044) = 969.25$; Pillai's Trace $=.59$; $p < 0.001$. We found univariate effects for Gender, and for Continent, for all three roles; as well as an interaction effect of both Gender and Continent for two roles (after Bonferroni correction; Table 8.7; we did not find a Gender by Continent effect for bullying).

For the univariate Gender effect, we found that boys scored higher on bullying and on victimization; girls scored higher on defending. For the univariate Continent effect, we found more bullying and victimization, but less defending, in India. This is what we predicted. The two Gender x Continent interactions showed that for defending, the gender difference was more strongly present in Europe (girls defend more often) and virtually absent in India. For victimization, the gender differences between boys (more often victimized) and girls, were stronger in India than in Europe.

Table 8.6 *Descriptive statistics (means and standard deviations) for peer visibility (behavioral frequency proportion scores) of bullying, defending and victimization*

		Gender					
		Boy		Girl		Total	
		M	SD	M	SD	M	SD
	Europe	0.056	0.090	0.025	0.039	0.045	0.078
Bullying	India	0.071	0.087	0.032	0.038	0.055	0.073
	Total	0.065	0.088	0.030	0.038	0.051	0.075
	Europe	0.033	0.059	0.093	0.089	0.054	0.076
Defending	India	0.042	0.040	0.042	0.037	0.042	0.039
	Total	0.038	0.048	0.059	0.064	0.046	0.056
	Europe	0.048	0.101	0.042	0.070	0.046	0.091
Victimization	India	0.074	0.076	0.038	0.040	0.059	0.066
	Total	0.064	0.087	0.040	0.052	0.054	0.076

Note. $N_{total} = 2,050$ ($N_{boys} = 1,244$); $n_{Europe} = 755$ ($n_{boys} = 489$), $n_{India} = 1,295$ ($n_{boys} = 755$).

Table 8.7 *Outcomes of the MANOVA investigating gender and continent differences in peer visibility of bullying, defending and victimization (bullying-related behavioral frequency proportion scores; N = 2,050)*

	Pilai's Trace	F	dfs	η_p^2
Gender	0.11	85.01*	(3, 2,044)	0.11
Bullying		102.91†	(1, 2,046)	0.05
Defending		144.54†	(1, 2,046)	0.07
Victimization		35.47†	(1, 2,046)	0.02
Continent	0.04	27.69*	(3, 2,044)	0.04
Bullying		10.20†	(1, 2,046)	0.01
Defending		68.46†	(1, 2,046)	0.03
Victimization		9.83†	(1, 2,046)	0.01
Gender × Continent	0.07	54.84*	(3, 2,044)	0.07
Bullying		1.23	(1, 2,046)	0.00
Defending		145.21†	(1, 2,046)	0.07
Victimization		17.60†	(1, 2,046)	0.01

Note. * $p < 0.001$; † significant at Bonferroni-corrected $p < 0.016$.

Discussion

The data supported our predictions. Regardless of Continent, both bullying and defending were linked to dominance in the classroom, but bullies were not preferred, while defenders were. Victims were neither seen as dominant nor were they preferred.

While evolutionary theory would predict such results for bullies, we are left with the question of why more children do not behave as defenders, given the resulting rewards in terms of social status. It may be that bullies directly aim for dominance (here measured as popularity and resource control), while defenders may be more strongly motivated by the urge to relieve distress. In other words, defenders acquire status as a result of respect for their behavior, as suggested by Hardy and van Vugt (2006). Henrich and Gil-White (2001) suggest that there are two pathways to status, one based on coercion aimed at dominance, and one based on excellence in domains of activity valued by other members of the group. It is our view that such (prosocial/altruistic) excellence may well be demonstrated by defenders. Those who rise to the front on the basis of excellence acquire prestige. We could call the first pathway (coercive) the bully pathway, and the second the defender pathway.

When Hardy and van Vugt (2006) describe competitive altruism as the process through which individuals attempt to outcompete each other in terms of generosity, they assume intention, but it is not clear whether this intention is there right from the start or originates after the first successes of the altruistic behavior. What we also do not know yet is what the developmental course is of competitive altruism. Could it be that under certain adverse circumstances, this form of altruism disappears because coercive strategies have become exclusively successful, while this form of altruism (defending the victims) becomes overlooked (Cheng, Tracy & Henrich, 2010)? Many studies into bullying (Pozzoli & Gini, 2013; Pozzoli, Gini & Vieno, 2012) seem to indicate a decrease in defending once pupils get older. It could be that the classroom climate changes, thereby becoming less conducive to any appreciation of defending. At least, it would appear that later on in adolescence, defending no longer gets awarded with social dominance.

We also found support for the prediction that there would be more bullying and victimization, and less defending, in India. We pointed to both empirical data supplied by others and to the presumed influence of adverse social and economic circumstances, which would increase aggression (bullying) and decrease prosocial behavior (defending). We suggested an increase in risky behavior as a potential explanation for the effects of adverse circumstances. According to life history theory (Belsky, Schlomer & Ellis, 2012; Belsky, Steinberg & Draper, 1991; Ellis et al., 2012), gene survival will be prioritized when environmental cues suggest a shorter and/or (cyclic) uncertain life expectancy (i.e. harshness and/or unpredictability). Translated to the behavior of adolescents in social groups, harsher and/or unpredictable environments increase adolescents' battle for social dominance as this proximately enhances their reproductive success and ultimately increases the chance of gene survival in later generations.

Other explanations are possible. Studies of aggression and violence in adult populations suggest that adolescent bullying might also be closely related to income inequality (rather than to overall wealth such as country GDP). This was supported by a study from Elgar and colleagues (2009), who demonstrated a strong link between income inequality and bullying in 37 predominantly European countries. One sociological explanation is that inequality has a corrosive effect on social relationships and the availability of social resources to the individual in communities (Kawachi & Kennedy, 2002). Drawing upon evolutionary psychology, Wilkinson and Pickett (2009) describe inequality as a form of structural violence that elicits shame, humiliation and violent retaliation. They suggest that as income inequality increases, status competition intensifies as more people are deprived of access to markers of status and success. Among adolescents, who are acutely aware of class differences, income inequality might increase social distance between individuals and foster a harsh social environment that is rife with teasing, rejection and humiliation.

A psychological approach on how social inequality might contribute to antisocial behavior was presented by Arsenio and Gold (2006). According to their model, children internalize social norms, including the notion that life does not revolve around equality and reciprocity, but around power and domination. Exposure to inequality biases how social information is processed, such that instrumental goals are valued more than relational goals and violence is seen as an effective way to succeed. We did not include any measures of income inequality, but the Gini index (an economic indicator of income inequality) of India (World Bank data) confirms that there is more income inequality in India than in either of the two European countries.

Some Limitations

First of all, a limitation is that this study was cross-sectional in nature. We can offer explanations for our findings, but we need longitudinal studies to tease social behaviors and status components apart, and to make the causal assumptions more probable. Next, classroom sizes may also have had an effect. These were considerably larger in India than in Europe. It may be more difficult for students to assess other students' reputations in the larger classroom. In addition, at least in Punjab, the questionnaires were presented both in English and in the native tongue for Indian students. While the definitions for the bullying role behaviors and peer-group status measures were evaluated by the researchers to ensure consistency between the Dutch, German, Tamil, English and Punjabi translations, slight definitional differences cannot be ruled out. Such differences may have had an impact on the present findings (Smith et al., 2002).

We used Salmivalli and colleagues' classifications (1996) in combination with peer nominations. We prefer peer nominations to self-reports, as self-reports can be biased. Bullies downplay their involvement in bullying, while victims often exaggerate the frequency of their victimization. Also, self-reports generally limit themselves to questions about bullying and victimization, while we also wanted to know about defending. It is for this reason that we opted for the Participant Role Scales. However, when using nominations, it seems more exact to use the term *visibility* instead of *prevalence*. Another weakness is that the Participant Role Scales, which have been used often in Europe, still need validation for use in India. Certainly, our predictions concerning the links between status on the one hand, and bullying, defending and victimization on the other hand, were confirmed. We also replicated some of Khatri and Kupfersmidt's results concerning the low scores of bullies and victims for preference. As to the visibility ("prevalence") figures reported by us, they are in line with other (self-report) data collected in India (Kshirsagar, Agarwal & Bavdekar, 2007; Ramya & Kulkarni, 2011), but given the sheer size of India, we cannot assume that these figures are accurately representative of the whole subcontinent. In order to estimate that, we would need larger and more representative samples.

In short, we set out to test an evolutionary hypothesis about the adaptive nature of bullying, while we also tested whether defending was linked to status, as could be expected on the basis of the competitive altruism hypothesis. The data supported our hypotheses. We also predicted that bullying and victimization would occur more often in India than in Europe and that defending would occur less often.

References

Archer, J. (2001). A strategic approach to aggression. *Social Development*, *10*, 267–271. doi:10.1111/1467-9507.00163.

Arnocky, S. & Vaillancourt, T. (2012). A multi-informant longitudinal study on the relationship between aggression, peer victimization and dating status in adolescence. *Evolutionary Psychology*, *10*, 253–270. doi: 10.1177/147470491201000207.

Arsenio, W. F. & Gold, J. (2006). The effects of social injustice and inequality on children's moral judgments and behavior: Towards a theoretical model. *Cognitive Development*, *21*, 388–400. doi: 10.1016/cogdev.2006.06.005.

Axelrod, R. (1984). *The Evolution of Cooperation*. New York: Basic Books.

Ball, H. A., Arseneault, L., Taylor, A., Maughan, B., Caspi, A. & Moffitt, T. E. (2008). Genetic and environmental influences on victims, bullies and bully-victims in childhood. *Journal of Child Psychology and Psychiatry*, *49*, 104–112. doi: 10.1111/j.1469–7610.2007.01821.x.

Belsky, J., Schlomer, G. L. & Ellis, B. J. (2012). Beyond cumulative risk: Distinguishing harshness and unpredictability as determinants of parenting and early life history strategy. *Developmental Psychology*, *48*, 662–673. doi: 10.1037/a0024454.

Belsky, J., Steinberg, L. & Draper, P. (1991). Childhood experience, interpersonal development and reproductive strategy: An evolutionary theory of socialization. *Child Development*, *62*, 647–670. doi: 10.2307/1131166.

Cairns, R. B. & Cairns, B. D. (1994). *Lifelines and Risks: Pathways of Youth in Our Time*. New York: Cambridge University Press.

Cheng, J., Tracy, J. L. & Henrich, J. (2010). Pride, personality, and the evolutionary foundations of human social status. *Evolution and Human Behavior*, *31*, 334–347. doi: 10.1016/j.evol.humbehav.2010.02.004.

Coie, J. D., Dodge, K. A. & Coppotelli, H. (1982). Dimensions and types of social status: A cross-age perspective. *Developmental Psychology*, *18*, 557–570. doi: 10.1037/0012–1649.18.4.557.

Connolly, J., Pepler, D., Craig, W. & Taradash, A. (2000). Dating experiences of bullies in early adolescence. *Child Maltreatment*, *5*, 299–310. doi: 10.1177/1077559500005004002.

Crick, N. & Dodge, K. A. (1994). A review and reformulation of social information-processing mechanisms in children's social adjustment. *Psychological Bulletin*, *115*, 74–101. doi: 10.1037/0033–2909.115.1.74.

Daly, M. & Wilson, M. (1988). *Homicide*. New York: Aldine.

Dane, A. V., Marini, Z. A., Volk, A. A. & Vaillancourt, T. (2016). Physical and relational bullying and victimization: Differential relations with adolescent dating and sexual behavior. *Aggressive Behavior*, *43*, 111–122. doi: 10.1002/ab.21667.

Darwin, C. (1968/1985). *On the Origin of Species*. London: Penguin.

Due, P., Merlo, J., Harel-Fisch, Y., Damsgaard, M. T., Holstein, B. E., ... & Lynch, J. (2009). Socioeconomic inequality in exposure to bullying during adolescence: A comparative, cross-sectional, multilevel study in 35 countries. *American Journal of Public Health*, *99*, 907–914. doi: 10.2105/AJPH.2008.139303.

Duncan, R. D. (1999). Peer and sibling aggression: An investigation of intra- and extra-familial bullying. *Journal of Interpersonal Violence*, *14*, 871–886.

Elgar, F. J., Craig, W., Boyce, W., Morgan, A. & Vella-Zarb, R. (2009). Income inequality and school bullying: Multilevel study of adolescents in 37 countries. *Journal of Adolescent Health*, *45*, 351–359. doi: 10.1007/s00038-012–0380-y.

Ellis, B. J., Del Giudice, M., Dishion, T. J., Figueredo, A. J., Gray, P., Griskevicius, V., ... Wilson, D. S. (2012). The evolutionary basis of risky adolescent behavior: Implications for science, policy, and practice. *Developmental Psychology*, *48*, 598–623. doi: 10.1037/a0026220.

Garandeau, C. F., Lee, I. A. & Salmivalli, C. (2013). Differential effects of the KiVa anti-bullying program on popular and unpopular bullies. *Journal of Applied Developmental Psychology*, *35*, 44–50. doi: 10:1016/jappdev.2013.10.004.

Gini, G., Albiero, P., Benelli, B. & Altoè, G. (2008). Determinants of adolescents' active defending and passive bystanding behavior in bullying. *Journal of Adolescence*, *31*, 93–105. doi: 10.1016/j.adolescence.2007.05.002.

Goossens, F. A., Olthof, T. & Dekker, P. H. (2006). New participant role scales: Comparison between various criteria for assigning roles and indications of their validity. *Aggressive Behavior*, *32*, 343–357. doi: 10.1002/ab.20133.

Griskevicius, V., Tybur, J. M., Gangestad, S. W., Perea, E. F., Shapiro, J. R. & Kenrick, D. T. (2009). Aggress to impress: Hostility as an evolved context-dependent strategy. *Journal of Personality and Social Psychology*, *96*, 980–994. doi:10.1037/a0013907.

Gromann, P. M, Goossens, F. A., Olthof, T., Pronk, J. & Krabbendam, L. (2013). Self-perception but not peer reputation of bullying victimization is associated with non-clinical psychotic experiences in adolescents. *Psychological Medicine*, *43*, 781–787. doi.org/10.1017/S003329171200178X.

Hardy, C. L. & van Vugt, M. (2006). Nice guys finish first: The competitive altruism hypothesis. *Personality and Social Psychology Bulletin*, *32*, 1402–1413. doi: 10.1177/0146167206291006.

Hawley, P. H. (1999). The ontogenesis of social dominance: A strategy-based evolutionary perspective. *Developmental Review*, *19*, 97–132. doi: 10.1006/drev.1998.0470.

Hawley, P. H. (2003). Strategy of control, aggression, and morality in preschoolers: An evolutionary perspective. *Journal of Experimental Child Psychology*, *85*, 213–235. doi:10.1016/S0022-0965(03)00073-0.

Hawley, P. H., Little, T. D. & Card, N. A. (2008). The myth of the alpha male: A new look at dominance-related beliefs and behaviors among adolescent males and females. *International Journal of Behavioral Development*, *32*, 76–88.

Hawley, P. H., Little, T. D., & Rodkin, Ph. C. (eds.). (2007). *Aggression and Adaptation: The Bright Side to Bad Behavior*. London: Routledge.

Henrich, J. & Gil-White, F. J. (2001). The evolution of prestige. Freely conferred deference as a mechanism for enhancing the benefits of cultural transmission. *Evolution and Human Behavior*, *22*, 165–196. doi: 10.1016/S1090-5138(00)00071-4.

Hofstede, G. (1980). *Culture's Cconsequences*. Beverly Hills, CA: Sage.

Huitsing, G., Snijders, T. A. B., van Duijn, M. A. J. & Veenstra R. (2014). Victims, bullies, and their defenders: A longitudinal study of the coevolution of positive and negative networks. *Development and Psychopathology*, *26*, 645–659. doi: 10.1017/S0954579414000297.

Israel, S., Hasenfratz, L. & Knafo-Noam, A. (2015). The genetics of morality and prosociality. *Current Opinion in Psychology*, *6*, 55–59. doi: 10.1016/j.copsyc.2015.03.027.

Kawachi, I. & Kennedy, B. P. (2002). *The Health of Nations: Why Inequality Is Harmful to Your Health*. New York: New Press.

Khatri, P. & Kupfersmidt, J. B. (2003). Aggression, peer victimization, and social relationships among Indian youth. *International Journal of Behavioral Development*, *27*, 87–95. doi: 10.1080/01650250244000056.

Knafo-Noam, A., Uzefovsky, F., Israel, S., Davidov, M. & Zahm-Waxler, C. (2015). The prosocial personality and its facets: Genetic and environmental architecture of mother-reported behavior of 7-year-old twins. *Frontiers in Psychology*, *6*, 1–9. doi: 10.3389/fpsyg.2015.00112.

Kolbert, J. B. & Crothers, L. M. (2003). Bullying and evolutionary psychology. *Journal of School Violence*, *2*, 73–91. doi: 10.1300/1202/v02n03 05.

Kshirsagar, V. Y., Agarwal, R. & Bavdekar, S. B. (2007). Bullying in schools: Prevalence and short-term impact. *Indian Pediatrics, 44,* 25–28. Retrieved from http://indianpediatrics.net/jan2007/jan-25-28.htm.

LaFontana, K. M. & Cillessen, A. H. N. (2002). Children's perceptions of popular and unpopular peers: A multimethod assessment. *Developmental Psychology, 38,* 635–647. doi: 10.1037/0012-1649.38.5.635.

Olthof, T. & Goossens, F. A. (2008). Bullying and the need to belong: Early adolescents' bullying-related behavior and the acceptance they desire and receive from particular classmates. *Social Development, 17,* 24–46. doi: 10.1111/j.1467–9507.2007.00413.x.

Olthof, T., Goossens, F. A., Vermande, M. M., Aleva, E. A. & Van der Meulen, M. (2011). Bullying as strategic behavior: Relations with desired and acquired dominance in the peer group. *Journal of School Psychology, 49,* 339–359. doi: 10.1016/j.jsp. 2011.03.003.

Olweus, D. (1993). *Bullying at School: What We Know and What We Can Do.* Cambridge, MA: Blackwell.

Parkhurst, J. T. & Hopmeyer, A. (1998). Sociometric popularity and peer-perceived popularity. *Journal of Early Adolescence, 18,* 125–144. doi: 10.1177/0272431698018002001.

Pellegrini, A. D. & Long, J. D. (2002). A longitudinal study of bullying, dominance and victimization during the transition from primary school to secondary school. *British Journal of Developmental Psychology, 20,* 259–280. doi: 10.1348/026151002166442.

Pickett, K. E. & Wilkinson, R. G. (2007). Child wellbeing and income inequality in rich societies: ecological cross-sectional study. *British Medical Journal, 335,* 1080–1087. doi: 10.1136/bmj.39377.580162.55.

Pozzoli, T. & Gini, G. (2013). Why do bystanders of bullying help or not? A multidimensional model. *Journal of Early Adolescence, 33,* 315–340. doi: 10.1177/0272431612440172.

Pozzoli, T., Gini, G. & Vieno, A. (2012). The role of individual correlates and class norms in defending and passive bystander behavior in bullying: A multilevel analysis. *Child Development, 83,* 1917–1931. doi: 10.1111/j.1467–8624.2012.01831.x.

Pronk, J., Lee, N. C., Sandhu, D., Kaur, K., Kaur, S., Olthof, T. & Goossens, F. A. (2016). Associations between Dutch and Indian adolescents' bullying role behavior and peer-group status: Cross-culturally testing an evolutionary hypothesis. *International Journal of Behavioral Development.* Advance online publication November 24, 2016. doi: 10.1177/0165025416679743.

Pronk, J., Olthof, T. & Goossens, F. A. (2015). Differential personality correlates of early adolescents' bullying related outsider-behavior and defender-behavior. *Journal of Early Adolescence, 35,* 1069–1091. doi: 10.1177/0272431614549628.

Ramya, S. G. & Kulkarni, M. L. (2011). Bullying among school children: Prevalence and associations with common symptoms in childhood. *Indian Journal of Pediatrics, 78,* 307–310. doi: 10.1007/s12098-010-0219-6.

Reijntjes, A., Vermande, M. M., Goossens, F. A., Olthof, T., van der Schoot, R., Aleva, E. A. & Van der Meulen, M. (2013). Developmental trajectories of bullying and social dominance in youth. *Child Abuse & Neglect*, *37*, 224–234. doi: 10.1016/j.chiabu.2012.12.004.

Salmivalli, C., Lagerspetz, K. M. J., Björkqvist, K., Österman, K. & Kaukiainen, A. (1996). Bullying as a group process: Participant roles and their relations to social status within the group. *Aggressive Behavior*, *22*, 1–15. doi: 10.1002/(SICI)1098–2337.

Smith, P. K., Cowie, H., Olafsson, A. P. D., Liefooghe, A., Almeida, A., Araki, H. & Wenxin, Z. (2002). Definitions of bullying: A comparison of terms used, and age and gender differences, in a fourteen-country international comparison. *Child Development*, *73*, 1119–1133. doi: 10.1111/1467–8624.00461.

Solberg, M. E. & Olweus, D. (2003). Prevalence estimation of school bullying with the Olweus Bully/Victim Questionnaire. *Aggressive Behavior*, *29*, 239–268. doi: 10.1002/ab.10047.

Ttofi, M. M. & Farrington, D. P. (2011). Effectiveness of school-based programs to reduce bullying: A systematic and meta-analytic approach. *Journal of Experimental Criminology*, *7*, 27–56. doi: 10.1007/s11292-010–9109-1.

Volk, A. A., Dane, A. V., Marini, Z. A. & Vaillancourt, T. (2015). Adolescent bullying, dating and mating: Testing an evolutionary hypothesis. *Evolutionary Psychology*, *13*, 1–11. doi: 10.1177/1474704915613909.

Volk, A. A., Della Cioppa, V., Earle, M. & Farrell A. M. (2015). Social competition and bullying: An adaptive socioecological perspective. In V. Zeigler-Hill, V., Welling, L.L.M. & Shackelford, T. K. (eds.), *Evolutionary Perspectives on Social Psychology* (pp. 387–399). Switzerland: Springer International Publishing.

Vreeman, R. C. & Carroll, A. E. (2007). A systematic review of school-based interventions to prevent bullying. *Archives of Pediatrics & Adolescent Medicine*, *161*, 78–88. doi: 10.1001/archpedi.161.1.78.

Wilkinson, G. & Pickett, K. E. (2009). *The Spirit Level: Why More Equal Societies Almost Always Do Better*. London: Penguin.

Witvliet, M., Olthof, T., Hoeksma, J. B., Goossens, F. A., Smits, M. S. L. & Koot, J. M. (2010). Peer group affiliation of children: The role of perceived popularity, likeability, and behavioral similarity in bullying. *Social Development*, *19*, 285–303. doi: 10.1111/j.1467–9507.2009.00544.x.

Wolke D. & Samara, M. M. (2004). Bullied by siblings: Association with peer victimization and behavior problems in Israeli lower secondary school children. *Journal of Child Psychology and Psychiatry*, *45*, 1015–1029. doi: 10.1111/j.1469–7610.2004.t01-1–00293.x.

Yeager, D. S., Fong, C. J., Lee, H. Y. & Espelage, D. L. (2015). Declines in efficacy of anti-bullying programs among older adolescents: Theory and a three-level meta-analysis. *Journal of Applied Developmental Psychology*, *37*, 36–51. doi: 10.1016/j.appdev.2014.11.005.

9 Defining the Relationship between Risk-Taking and Bullying during Adolescence
A Cross-Cultural Comparison

Nikki Lee, Jeroen Pronk, Tjeert Olthof, Damanjit Sandhu, Shubhdip Kaur and Frits Goossens

During adolescence interactions between psychological, biological and environmental changes place adolescents on a trajectory towards both adaptive and maladaptive developmental outcomes. A frequently cited problem in adolescents' behaviour is their propensity for risky and irresponsible actions. This drive is well documented, and examples abound from drug use to reckless driving and unsafe sexual behaviours. Given the dangers arising from these actions, it is tempting to regard them as maladaptive. Bullying, a behaviour which peaks during adolescence, has often been considered an example of a maladaptive risky behaviour (e.g. Laslett, 1980). However, the links between bullying and risk-taking tendencies have received little attention in the literature, and therefore the first aim of this chapter is to characterise the interplay between bullying and risk-taking during adolescence. Furthermore, in recent years this characterisation of adolescent risk-taking as a maladaptive behaviour has started to shift, and has been reframed by some researchers as a behavioural phenotype that may play a functional role in the transition towards adulthood (Ellis et al., 2012). These accounts, often grounded in evolutionary theory as well as increased insights into the neural development during adolescence, posit that risk-taking occurs in environments where this behaviour is beneficial to the adolescent. This suggests that while risk-taking may occur cross-culturally due to evolutionary drives, the dynamics of the process may differ. Therefore, the second aim of this chapter is to examine how interactions between bullying and risk-taking may differ between a European country such as the Netherlands, and India.

Recent empirical work has enabled the development of a model of age-related changes in behaviour during adolescence, and supports the idea of a developmental window characterised by increases in risk-taking behaviour. Neuroimaging studies have shown that the brain continues to develop both structurally and functionally during this time (Giedd et al., 2009; Giedd et al., 2012; Mills et al., 2016). The areas of the brain involved in processing social and emotional rewards become increasingly active, resulting in a reorientation towards those risky and novelty-seeking behaviours which enable attainment of these rewards. These drives are strengthened by the slower development of the regions of the brain involved in self-regulation and impulse control. These regions are not fully developed until late adolescence or early adulthood, and the self-regulatory abilities they support are therefore also still in development (for reviews of this process, see Casey, 2015; Crone & Dahl, 2012; Mills et al., 2014). This so-called maturational gap between affective and control regions is thought to be an underlying cause of the drive adolescents show towards risk-taking, enabling them to leave the childhood safety net of their immediate family by encouraging them to explore and experience the world around them as they progress towards adulthood (Dodge & Albert, 2012). The degree to which these behaviours are exhibited is influenced by context; factors such as peer pressure and the value of specific rewards impact the degree to which adolescents take risks.

Taking greater risks entails greater variability and therefore more uncertainty about outcomes, but can often also lead to larger rewards. While adolescents are cognitively able to comprehend the potential costs of negative behaviours such as drinking, smoking or bullying, the rewards they could obtain in the form of higher social approval may make this a worthwhile risk to take. For example, though adolescents generally show age-related increases in their ability to delay short-term gratification in favour of larger long-term reward (Lee et al., 2013), they shift their preferences towards short-term rewards in the presence of their peers (O'Brien et al., 2011), and make more risky decisions than they do when making similar decisions alone (Gardner & Steinberg, 2005; van Hoorn et al., 2016).

The behavioural flexibility seen during adolescence is thought to be a crucial skill that enables adolescents to understand and adapt to their changing social environment (Crone & Dahl, 2012). This supports the idea that adolescent risky behaviour cannot simply be categorised as either adaptive or maladaptive. Evolutionary theories of development (see e.g. Ellis et al., 2011; Ellis et al., 2012) propose that risk-taking occurs in environments where this behaviour is of benefit to the adolescent. While certain risky behaviours may expose adolescents to danger and/or inflict harm on others, they may also have important signalling functions for establishing social status, prestige and dominance. Studies have shown that most adolescents find status enhancement more important than adhering to rules (LaFontana & Cillessen, 2010). Consequently, risk-taking can be beneficial to the adolescent in achieving a higher position within their peer group, something that is particularly relevant during this time.

Bullying can be seen as an example of a risky behaviour driven by status goals. It is a dynamic group process, defined by repeated and intentional aggression from one or more powerful individuals towards a weaker victim (Olweus, 1993). The continuous nature, combined with the power difference between bully and victim, distinguishes bullying from more general forms of aggression. Though harming others involves the risk of retaliation, research has shown that successful bullies can increase their social standing and access to resources (Olthof et al., 2011). Bullying increases social dominance and status, and is often accompanied by a strong desire to achieve and maintain dominance within the social group (Huitsing et al., 2014; Reintjes et al., 2013a). Adolescent bullies are perceived as popular by their classmates (Olthof et al., 2011; Vaillancourt, Hymel & McDougall, 2003), and have high levels of resource control, meaning that they have access to the best social and material resources (e.g. attention from others, the best materials in the classroom; Hawley, 1999). As a result, they are more likely to be in a romantic relationship, start dating earlier and report more dating opportunities than adolescents who do not bully (Connolly et al., 2000). In spite of the described advantages, bullies also run the risk of suffering negative consequences of their actions. Internalising problems appear to be linked to bullying (Vaillancourt et al., 2003), and it has been suggested that bullying leads to higher levels of depression (Seals & Young, 2003). Moreover, despite being popular, bullies are often not liked by their classmates (Reintjes et al., 2013b), especially if they bully others for prolonged periods of time (Scholte et al., 2007).

Studies of bullying have shown that it is a group process, in which various behavioural roles can be distinguished. Six roles have been proposed: 1) bullies, who take the initiative to bully others; 2) assistants, who join in the bullying; 3) reinforcers, who provide assistance and reinforcement to the bullies (this category is often combined with the assistants and defined as followers); 4) outsiders, who avoid involvement in the bullying; 5) defenders, who support and provide help to the victims and try to stop the bullying; and finally, 6) victims, those who are bullied (Salmivalli et al., 1996). This group view recognises the individual differences between the participants in the bullying dynamic, and suggests that the underlying attitudes and motivations differ between the group members.

These differences can interact with environmental influences, such as cultural norms, to determine the role that individuals play in the process (Salmivalli, 2010). Furthermore, these roles also influence the individual's social status within their peer group. In many situations the potential social advantages of bullying may make it an attractive proposition, especially during adolescence, when behaviour seems oriented towards improving social status, and the brain is wired to encourage risk-taking behaviour. Adolescents with a strong inclination to take risks may therefore be more inclined to bully others than those who are less inclined towards risk-taking. Yet as far as we are aware, these relationships have not previously been examined in detail.

Both risk-taking and bullying may prove most valuable when resources are scarce, and therefore competition to obtain these resources is greater. This competition can be focussed on material resources, but also on the roles that lead to these resources (e.g. in competitive educational programmes). In these situations those individuals who are prepared to take risks may more frequently resort to bullying as a way of utilising this tendency, as this is a strategy with high potential gains. Certain environmental circumstances may trigger or promote adolescents to take the risk of engaging in the various bullying roles. Studies relating income inequality and bullying prevalence have found positive correlations, showing that environments with higher inequality also show increased victimisation through bullying (Elgar et al., 2009; Pickett & Wilkinson, 2007).

Our earlier work, comparing bullying in India and the Netherlands, has shown a higher prevalence of bullying in India, a country where adolescents generally grow up in harsher and more unpredictable surroundings (Pronk et al., 2016). Other studies comparing Western countries to India have also shown this increased prevalence in India (e.g. Kshirsagar, Agarwal & Bavdekar, 2007). If risk-taking is also influenced by environmental factors in a similar way to bullying, it follows that risk-taking behaviour may also be more frequent in India. Due to biological similarities in the patterns of adolescent (brain) development, Indian adolescents may not have a higher propensity towards taking risks (i.e. at a trait level), but they may be more inclined to do so due to environment pressures. This may strengthen the relationship between risk-taking behaviour and bullying. Interestingly, a recent study found that bullies anticipated increased involvement in risky activities compared to a group of same-age controls, despite also viewing these events as more risky than the control group did (Poon, 2016). This suggests that bullies knowingly engage in increased levels of risk-taking behaviour.

Risk-taking may also influence the other behavioural roles within the bullying process. The patterns for followers may be similar to those for bullies, as they engage in similar risks to bullies. Though defending is often seen as a prosocial behaviour, it could also be defined as a risky behaviour. It requires the individual to actively involve themselves in the bullying process and to stand up to the bullies and their followers, who are often popular with their peers. Therefore, defending may also be related to higher levels of risk-taking behaviour, especially in India, where bullying occurs more frequently than in the Netherlands. Conversely, outsiders, who avoid involvement in the bullying process, may show low levels of risk-taking behaviour. Finally, recent work has suggested that victims may underestimate the consequences of taking risks, as well as demonstrating high levels of impulsivity. Consequently, they may be more likely to engage in risk-taking behaviour (Poon, 2016). However, these hypotheses require further investigation.

In this chapter we examine the associations between risk-taking behaviours and bullying in samples of Dutch and Indian adolescents as well as examining cross-cultural differences in this relationship. In doing so we are building on our earlier work (Pronk et al., 2016; see also Chapter 8). We examine if adolescents in India and the Netherlands differ in the frequency of their risk-taking behaviour, but not in their underlying risk-taking propensity. Furthermore, we examine how risk-taking behaviour affects adolescents' role in the bullying process.

Method

Participants

Participants were recruited as part of a research project conducted within the Indian-European Research network on Bullying, Cyberbullying, Pupil Safety and Well-Being. To this end a total of 699 adolescents were recruited from schools in the Netherlands and India. Participants ($n = 46$) who failed to complete all questionnaires (e.g. due to testing complications) were removed from the current study. This resulted in a final sample of $N = 653$ (Mage = 13.77, $SD = 0.90$, range = 11.28 – 16.10, 58% boys). The Dutch sample comprised 211 participants (Mage = 13.81, $SD = 0.72$, range = 12.43 – 15.73, 60% boys) enrolled in the first and second years of a secondary school in Amsterdam. These participants were divided over eight classrooms. The Indian sample consisted of 442 participants (Mage = 13.76, $SD = 0.98$, range = 11.25 – 16.10, 60% boys) enrolled in equivalent year levels of a Punjabi-Indian English-language secondary school in Patiala, Punjab province, and were divided over 12 classrooms. The classroom size differed greatly between locations: classrooms in

Amsterdam contained an average of 27.4 students (range: 19–31), compared to 40 (range: 28–46) in Patiala.

The current sample is a subset of data used in our earlier work; further details of the sample have been described elsewhere (see Pronk et al., 2016 and Chapter 8).

Materials

Bullying role behaviour. Salmivalli and colleagues' (1996) Participant Role Scale was used to measure participants' bullying role behaviour. The original questionnaire was adapted for the current study. Participants were presented with a definition of bullying, followed by 20 peer nomination questions. For each question they were asked to nominate up to 10 classmates from a class list. Thus each classmate could be nominated for multiple roles. The 20 questions covered each of five bullying roles: (1) bully (six items, one item each for physical, material, verbal, direct relational, indirect relational and cyberbullying); (2) follower (four items addressing various aspects of assisting and reinforcing bullying); (3) outsider (two items about avoiding involvement in the bullying process); (4) defender (two items, one for direct and one for indirect intervention); (5) victim (six items addressing the same behaviours as the bullying questions). The victim nominations were not used in the current study. Pronk and colleagues (2016) confirmed this five-factor bullying role behaviour structure through confirmatory factor analysis in both the Dutch and Indian datasets.

Scores on each of the bullying roles were calculated using the number of nominations each participant received, divided by the number of within-classroom nominators. This resulted in scores ranging from 0 (no nominations) to 1 (nominated by all classmates). For the bully and follower variables, the scores were calculated using the average of the two items on which the participants were most frequently nominated (i.e. two of the six bullying items and two of the four follower items). This approach was taken to ensure that the participants' reputations were not underestimated due to the larger number of items used for these roles compared to the outsider and defender roles (see also Witvliet et al., 2010). To correct for differences between classrooms and to correct the positive skews in the data due to many children receiving no nominations on certain variables, all variables were within-classroom normalised prior to inclusion in the analyses.

Risk Propensity Scale. The seven-item Risk Propensity Scale (Meertens & Lion, 2008) was used to measure general risk-taking tendencies. This questionnaire requires participants to rate their behaviour on a nine-point Likert scale using domain-general questions. Thus, participants are asked about their attitudes towards risk-taking rather than their engagement in risk-taking behaviours (e.g. "I take risks regularly"). Higher scores on the questionnaire indicate a higher level of risk-taking tendencies. Previous research has shown the questionnaire has good internal reliability and test-retest coefficients, based on Cronbach's alpha values of around 0.77 (Meertens & Lion, 2008), and that scores on the questionnaire are significantly correlated with behaviour on risk-taking tasks (e.g. Lion & Meertens, 2005). In the current sample the Cronbach's alpha was 0.52, a value which could potentially indicate a lack of internal consistency. However, as alpha levels are affected by the length of the questionnaire (Schmitt, 1996), and the Risk Propensity Scale consists of just seven items, each item was additionally correlated with the total score on the questionnaire to examine the unidimensionality of the examined construct (Tavakol & Dennick, 2011). All items were significantly correlated with total score (lowest: $r = 0.436$, $p < 0.001$), suggesting that the items measure a common latent trait.

Risk-taking behaviour questionnaire. In addition to the Risk Propensity Scale, an additional measure was created to measure the frequency of domain-specific risk-taking behaviours. Though a number of risk-taking measures exist, the behaviours in these questionnaires were not deemed relevant or suitable for use in the Indian sample, suggesting that translation of these questionnaires for use in India would not result in an adequate measure of risk-taking behaviour. As others have argued (e.g. Kloep et al., 2009), cultural differences in how risk-taking is defined have often been ignored during the development of risk-taking instruments.

Therefore, a new measure was developed for use in the Indian sample in the current study. To this end four focus groups were run in India, comprising 8–12 adolescents aged between 12–18 years. The discussions concentrated on the types of risk behaviours adolescents and their friends engage in and encounter in daily life. Through transcript analysis five main risk-taking domains were identified: (1) risk of unintentional injuries (e.g. getting on/off moving train, fighting); (2) rule-breaking behaviours (illegal behaviours, e.g. stealing, carrying weapons); (3) peer-influenced risks (e.g. doing something dangerous when dared to by friends); (4) technology and media-related risks (e.g. excessive use of computers or phones); and (5) health risk behaviours (e.g. lack of exercise, overeating). As expected, the examples given by the focus group participants differed from many of the behaviours described in Western questionnaires. Based on the examples given by the participants, a new 25-item questionnaire was created, comprising five questions per domain. In order to compare data from the Dutch and Indian samples, a Dutch version of the questionnaire was also created. This used the domains identified in the Indian sample but different, culturally relevant, examples within the domains. See Appendix 9.A for an overview of the questionnaires.

Participants were asked to indicate on a six-point scale (from 1 = never to 6 = every day) how often they engaged in specific risk-taking behaviours. A higher mean score indicated a higher tendency to take risks. The Cronbach's alpha of the scale was 0.83 in the current sample.

Procedure

Participants were recruited through schools participating in the study. Prior to testing all participants' parents were notified about the project. The parents of the Dutch participants were sent written information and asked to return a form to the research team by post if they did not wish for their children to participate. The Indian participants' parents were informed about the research by the school's principal, and asked to inform the researchers via their children's classroom teachers if they would not permit their children to participate. Additionally, the participants provided written informed consent prior to participation.

Data collection took place during normal class time and was supervised by the classroom teacher and a minimum of two trained research assistants. A written research protocol was used to ensure standardisation of procedures. Participants were informed that their participation was voluntary, that they could stop at any time and that all responses were confidential. If they agreed, they were then asked to sign the informed consent form. As described earlier, questionnaires were presented in the language spoken at each of the schools. To ensure that the Indian participants fully understood all questions the items were also presented orally in Punjabi-Indian by a research assistant who is a native Punjabi-Indian speaker. Completion of the questionnaires took approximately 50 minutes, with 20–30 minutes of this time spent on the questionnaires described in the current study. All procedures were approved by the Vrije Universiteit Amsterdam institutional ethical review board.

Analyses

Initial MANOVA analyses were used to examine differences between the locations (the Netherlands and India) on the risk-taking measures.

Subsequent linear multiple regression analyses were used to examine the relationship between risk-taking (both propensity and reported behaviours) and bullying role behaviours, while accounting for sex and country. The model comprised three steps: sex was entered in the first step of the model, location and risk-taking were entered in step two and the location x risk-taking interaction was entered in the third step. Regression analyses were conducted separately for risk-taking propensity and risk-taking behaviour.

Results

Cross-Cultural Differences in Risk-Taking   Inspection of the data revealed a low frequency of risk-taking behaviour was reported across locations on the risk-taking behaviour questionnaire, with none of the categories receiving a mean score higher than 2.3. This corresponds to occasional engagement in the listed behaviours. However, across both locations, higher levels of risk-taking behaviour were associated with higher reported risk-taking propensity (India: $r = 0.353$, $p < 0.001$; the Netherlands: $r = 0.402$, $p < 0.001$). This suggests that though the adolescents in our study may have underreported their engagement in risk-taking behaviours, the variance in our sample was still indicative of differences within the group in risk-taking propensity. Furthermore, it strengthens the ecological validity of the Risk Propensity Scale.

Table 9.1 shows descriptive statistics for the risk-taking measures. A two-way (Location: the Netherlands versus India) MANOVA examining differences in risk-taking behaviours on both risk-taking measures revealed

Table 9.1 *Descriptive statistics (means and standard deviations) for the risk-taking measures.*

	Total sample (653)	The Netherlands ($n = 211$)	India ($n = 442$)
	M (SD)	*M (SD)*	*M (SD)*
Risk of unintentional injuries	2.26 (1.05)	2.22 (0.76)	2.31 (1.16)
Rule-breaking behaviours	1.55 (0.65)	1.50 (0.55)	1.57 (0.70)
Peer-influenced risks	1.65 (0.80)	1.39 (0.39)	1.82 (0.88)
Technology and media-related risks	2.21 (0.97)	1.94 (0.73)	2.34 (1.04)
Health risks	1.47 (0.53)	1.32 (0.36)	1.53 (0.58)
Total risk-taking behaviour	1.82 (0.59)	1.64 (0.39)	1.91 (0.63)
Risk-taking propensity	4.41 (1.44)	4.60 (1.32)	4.32 (1.49)

Table 9.2 *Summary of findings from multiple regression analyses on five different roles. βs are given for significant relationships between roles and risk-taking measures*

	Bully	Follower	Outsider	Defender	Victim
Country	ns	NL > India*	ns	ns	ns
Gender	Boys > Girls**	Boys > Girls**	ns	Girls > Boys**	Boys > Girls**
RTP	0.108**	0.097*	ns	ns	0.117*
RTP x Country	ns	ns	−0.29*	ns	ns
RTB	0.219**	0.24**	−0.10*	0.274*	0.276*
RTB x Country	ns	ns	ns	ns	ns

Note. RTP = Risk-taking propensity, RTB = Risk-taking behaviour; *p < 0.05, **p < 0.001

a main effect of Location for both variables (Pillai's Trace = 0.077, F (2, 633) = 26.47, p < 0.001). Univariate ANOVAs showed that Indian adolescents reported higher levels of risk-taking behaviours than Dutch adolescents (F (1, 634) = 30.62, p < 0.001). Conversely, Dutch adolescents scored higher on risk-taking propensity than those from India (F (1, 634) = 5.94, p = 0.015). Cross-cultural differences in bullying role behaviours are reported in Chapter 8 and our previous work (Pronk et al., 2016).

The Effects of Risk-Taking on Bullying Role Behaviour

Bullies. Results of the multiple regression analysis with risk-taking propensity revealed that the overall model was significantly able to predict bullying (R^2 = 0.079, F (3, 652) = 18.49, p < 0.001). Across locations greater risk-taking propensity resulted in increases in bullying (β = 0.108, t (649) = 2.83, p = 0.005), and boys exhibited significantly more bullying behaviour than girls (β = 0.245, t (649) = 2.83, p < 0.001).

The results for risk-taking behaviour were similar: the significant overall model (R^2 = 0.011, F (3, 652) = 26.82, p < 0.001) showed that adolescents who reported engaging in higher levels of risk-taking behaviour were also more frequently named as bullies (β = 0.219, t (649) = 5.49, p < 0.001) and this effect was consistent across both countries.

Followers. Following behaviour was also significantly predicted by the risk-taking propensity regression model (R^2 = 0.13, F (3, 652) = 33.55, p < 0.001). As with bullying, an increase in risk-taking propensity (β = 0.097, t (649) = 2.63, p = 0.009) was positively related to following behaviour, and higher levels of following behaviour were reported for boys compared to girls (β = 0.34, t (649) = 9.23, p < 0.001). These effects were similar in both the Netherlands and India.

Analyses using risk-taking behaviour also significantly predicted following behaviour (R^2 = 0.18, F (3, 652) = 46.37, p < 0.001). Higher reported levels of risk-taking were related to increased following behaviour (β = 0.24, t (649) = 6.26, p < 0.001). Levels of following behaviour were higher in the Netherlands than in India (β = 0.08, t (649) = 2.17, p = 0.030), and among boys than girls (β = 0.30, t (649) = 7.89, p < 0.001).

Outsiders. The regression model significantly predicted outsider behaviour (R^2 = 0.02, F (4, 652) = 3.34, p = 0.01). There was a significant interaction between location and risk-taking propensity (β = -0.29, t (648) = -2.40, p = 0.017), suggesting that the effects of risk-taking on outsider behaviour differed between India and the Netherlands. Subsequent simple slope analyses showed that outsider behaviour was significantly negatively related to risk-taking propensity in the Netherlands (β = -0.16, t (206) = -3.282, p = 0.001), but not in India. These effects did not differ between boys and girls.

The overall model examining risk-taking behaviour also significantly predicted outsider behaviour (R^2 = 0.01, F (3, 652) = 2.68, p = 0.046). Outsider behaviour was negatively related to self-reported risk-taking behaviour in both the Netherlands and India (β = -0.10, t (649) = -2.38, p = 0.018).

Defenders. The regression model significantly predicted defending (R^2 = 0.03, F (4, 652) = 6.09, p < 0.001). Girls showed more defending behaviour than boys (β = -0.17, t (648) = -4.37, p < 0.001), but levels of defending were not influenced by risk-taking propensity or location.

Risk-taking behaviour showed a different pattern: the overall model was significant (R^2 = 0.04, F (4, 652) = 5.99, p < 0.001), and higher levels of defending were significantly associated with higher levels of reported risk-taking behaviour (β = 0.274, t (648) = 1.98, p = 0.048). To further examine this relationship, the question probing direct defending was analysed separately from that examining indirect defending. Results showed that indirect defending was significantly related to risk-taking behaviour (model: R^2 = 0.06, F (4, 652) = 9.56, p < 0.001; indirect defending: β = 0.343, t (648) = 2.52, p = 0.012), but direct defending was not.

Victims. The overall model significantly predicted victimisation (R^2 = 0.06, F (3, 652) = 14.58, p < 0.001). Levels did not differ between countries, but the more frequently adolescents were named as victims, the higher their risk-taking propensity (β = 0.117, t (649) = 3.04, p = 0.002). Boys were reported as victims more frequently than girls (β = 0.207, t (649) = 5.39, p = 0.001). These effects were similar in India and the Netherlands.

Similar results were evident in the model using risk-taking behaviour ($R^2 = 0.08$, $F(4, 652) = 14.18$, $p < 0.001$): higher reported levels of risk-taking behaviour were related to higher levels of victimisation ($\beta = 0.276$, $t(648) = 2.05$, $p = 0.040$). As studies have shown that victims are also often bullies (the so-called hybrid bully-victims), the analyses were repeated with bullying included as a control variable. The results did not differ from those without the additional control variable, suggesting that the significant relationship between victimisation and risk-taking cannot be attributed to the victims' bullying behaviours.

Discussion

The current study demonstrates that increased risk-taking during adolescence is associated with higher levels of both bullying and following behaviour and victimisation, while outsider behaviour is associated with lower levels of risk-taking. Increased defending is related to increases in risk-taking behaviour, but is not affected by risk-taking propensity. Furthermore, the observed effects were largely similar across both the Dutch and Indian groups, though the strength of the associations differed. Finally, both bullying and risk-taking appear to be more prevalent in India than in the Netherlands. These findings will now be discussed in more detail.

Our results showed that Indian adolescents more frequently engage in risk-taking behaviours than those in the Netherlands. This is in line with our expectation that the harsher environmental circumstances in India would lead to increased risk-taking. While neurobiological accounts of adolescence have stressed the commonalities in adolescent behaviour by elucidating the underlying neural changes which lead to increases in risk-taking, these models also suggest that these tendencies are moderated by environmental influences (Crone & Dahl, 2012; Dodge & Albert, 2012). This assumption is supported by evolutionary theories, which posit that adaptive fitness requires leveraging environmental resources in both positive and negative ways (Ellis et al., 2012). These theories suggest that developmental systems have evolved to respond differently in situations of stress compared to those characterised by support (Pollak, 2008). Accordingly, in a high-stress environment, if there is little to lose, there may be more to gain from taking risks to improve your position. In evolutionary terms, if the chances of survival are lower, high-risk but low-investment reproductive strategies, i.e. aimed at fast genetic transmission, should be prioritised over low-risk, high-investment strategies.

The observed increases in risk-taking among the Indian sample did not result in cross-cultural differences in the relationship between bullying and risk-taking: higher levels of risk-taking behaviours were associated with increases in bullying and following in both India and the Netherlands. This is in line with our general expectation that both bullies and followers are more inclined to take risks, and also fits into evolutionary models of both risk-taking and bullying (e.g. Ellis et al., 2012; Volk et al., 2012; Volk et al., 2014). These models suggest that while risk-taking behaviours, such as bullying, may expose adolescents to danger, they offer benefits in terms of increased social status and access to resources. Previous work has focussed on behavioural strategies used by bullies (and followers), suggesting that their high-status position in the group can be attributed to their use of both coercive and prosocial behaviours (Olthof et al., 2011; Pronk et al., 2016). However, this comes at a cost: as has previously been shown, bullies and followers are perceived as popular, but they are not well liked (Olthof et al., 2011). But as both bullying and risk-taking increase social dominance, these behaviours may be adaptive strategies for individuals growing up in difficult circumstances, where the advantages of the central position in the group afforded to those who are perceived as popular outweigh the drawbacks of not being liked.

In contrast to bullying and following, analyses of outsider behaviour revealed a possible cultural difference. While in the Netherlands lower risk-taking propensity was related to increased outsider behaviour, this was not the case in India. It is unclear why this relationship was not found in the Indian sample, as a negative relationship between risk-taking behaviour and outsider behaviour was observed in both countries. This is in line with previous work suggesting that outsiders may be more selective, and potentially risk-averse, when selecting situations in which they are willing to intervene. Research among Dutch adolescents has suggested that outsiders do occasionally intervene when their classmates are bullied, but perhaps not frequently enough to be viewed as defenders by their peers (Goossens, Olthof & Dekker, 2006). In fact, outsiders have a tendency towards avoiding problems rather than attempting to solve them (Pozzoli & Gini, 2010). This may be due to their decreased risk-taking propensity: when weighing up the costs and benefits of intervening, they may decide that avoiding the situation is the best solution. Further research is needed to examine the discrepancy in the role of propensity and behaviours among the Indian outsiders.

In contrast to outsider behaviour, defending could come at a personal cost. By standing up to bullies, defenders run the risk of retribution. We therefore expected that higher risk-taking would also lead to more defending, as a prosocial way of utilising risk-taking tendencies. This was confirmed by the results of the current study, which showed that risk-taking behaviour is positively related to defending, and this relationship seems to be cross-culturally similar. In our study defending was operationalised as a hybrid behaviour, combining both direct and indirect forms of defending (see Olthof et al., 2011; Pouwels, Lansu & Cillessen, 2016). Therefore, we also ran post hoc analyses to separately examine the direct and indirect defending items. These analyses showed that the relationship between risk-taking behaviour and defending is specific to indirect defending. This may initially seem counter-intuitive, as direct defending involves actively confronting bullies, which seems a risker proposition than indirectly intervening in the process, for example by helping the victim or alerting a teacher. However, it fits within the behavioural profile of defenders, who generally show low levels of aggression (Camodeca & Goossens, 2005), have high levels of empathy (Gini et al., 2008) and are generally well liked by their peers (Goossens et al., 2006). However, further work is needed to examine this relationship in more detail: both direct and indirect defending were measured with a single item in the current study and more extensive questionnaires could shed additional light on this relationship. Interesting, no relationship was found between risk-taking propensity and defending. It seems that only active risk-taking is related to defending behaviours.

The final group we examined were those adolescents who were identified as victims by their classmates. Results showed higher levels of risk-taking were associated with victimisation by bullies. Previous work has suggested that victims may take risks due to impulsivity combined with an impaired understanding of the consequences and benefits of the risks they take (Poon, 2016). Their impaired self-control may cause friction in relationships with peers, increasing the chances of being bullied. This is also seen in children with ADHD, who frequently experience impairment in peer relationships due to their impulsive behaviour, as well as being bullied by their peers (Hoza, 2007). This finding could prove an interesting insight for current anti-bullying interventions, which may benefit from including risk evaluation or self-control training in order to improve victims' relationships with their classmates.

Strengths, Limitations and Implications

The current work should be viewed in light of a number of strength and weaknesses. This study is one of the first examining the influence of risk-taking on bullying roles, as well as comparing these results cross-culturally. However, it is important to note that it was conducted in a single location in both India and the Netherlands. While the results give us interesting insights into possible cross-cultural differences and similarities, it would be too early to generalise these to differences between Eastern and Western cultures. Furthermore, it has been reported that drug abuse and violence among adolescents are higher in Punjab than in other states in India (Kaur, 2017), supporting the suggestion that these results cannot be generalised nationally.

Collecting data cross-culturally poses unique challenges to researchers. Key concepts such as bullying and risk-taking need to be similarly defined in each country. However, the results also need to reflect the potential differences in how behaviours manifest. We aimed to address this issue by creating a separate measure of risk-taking behaviour for each country, and combining it with a more culturally neutral measure of risk-taking propensity. As the current study was conducted collaboratively by an international team of researchers whose backgrounds reflected the cultural diversity of the participants in the study, all measures and definitions were discussed within the team before implementation. However, differences in cultural definitions cannot be completely ruled out (Smith et al., 2002).

Factors at a more practical level may also have influenced the results. Classroom sizes in India were much larger than in the Netherlands, meaning that adolescents had a larger group of classmates to nominate from. Due to methodological and time constraints participants were able to nominate a maximum of 10 classmates per question. Thus, those individuals nominated in the Indian sample may have been those whose behaviour is most salient, while in the Netherlands there may have been more room to nominate those who show the examined behaviours to a lesser degree. Future research should consider the possibility of using an unrestricted nomination procedure.

In sum, we have shown that risk-taking plays an integral part in the dynamics of the various roles in the bullying process and that these relationships are generally similar in both India and the Netherlands. Though the dynamics are comparable, risk-taking occurs more frequently in India, possibly due to the harsher and more unpredictable environment Indian adolescents grow up in. Future work should examine these relationships in more detail, to further define these relationships in a culturally sensitive manner. Furthermore, we have demonstrated that the risk-taking profiles of victims may be a risk factor that compromises their ability to fit in with classmates, thereby increasing their chances of being victimised. This should be considered in future interventions.

References

Bandura, A. (1978). Social learning theory of aggression. *Journal of Communication, 28*, 12–29.

Camodeca, M. & Goossens, F. A. (2005). Children's opinions on effective strategies to cope with bullying: The importance of bullying role and perspective. *Educational Research, 47*, 93–105.

Casey, B. J. (2015). Beyond simplistic models of self-control to circuit-based accounts of adolescent behaviour. *Annual Review of Psychology, 66*, 295–319.

Coie, J. D., Dodge, K. A. & Cappotelli, H. (1982). Dimensions and types of social status: A cross-age perspective. *Developmental Psychology, 18*, 557–570.

Connolly, J., Pepler, D., Craig, W. & Taradash, A. (2000). Dating experiences of bullies in early adolescence. *Child Maltreatment, 5*, 288–310.

Crone, E. A. & Dahl, R. E. (2012). Understanding adolescence as a period of social-affective engagement and goal flexibility. *Nature Reviews Neuroscience, 13*, 636–650.

Dodge, K. A. & Albert, D. (2012). Evolving science in adolescence: Comment on Ellis et al. (2012). *Developmental Psychology, 48*, 624–627.

Elgar, F. J., Craig, W., Boyce, W., Morgan, A. & Vella-Zarb, R. (2009). Income inequality and school bullying: Multilevel study of adolescents in 37 countries. *Journal of Adolescent Health, 45*, 351–359.

Ellis, B. J., Boyce, W. T., Belsky, J., Bakermans-Kranenburg, M. J. & van Ijzendoorn, M. H. (2011). Differential susceptibility to the environment: An evolutionary neurodevelopmental theory. *Developmental and Psychopathology, 23*, 7–28.

Ellis, B. J., Del Giudice, M., Dishion, T. J., Figueredo, A. J., Gray, P., Griskevicius, V., . . . & Wilson, D. S. (2012). The evolutionary basis of risky adolescent behavior: Implications for science, policy, and practice. *Developmental Psychology, 48*, 598–623.

Gardner, M. & Steinberg, L. (2005). Peer influence on risk taking, risk preference, and risky decision making in adolescence and adulthood: An experimental study. *Developmental Psychology, 41*, 625–635.

Giedd, J. N., Lalonde, F. M., Celano, M. J., White, S. L., Wallace, G. L., Lee, N. R. & Lenroot, R. K. (2009). Anatomical brain magnetic resonance imaging of typically developing children and adolescents. *Journal of the American Academy of Child and Adolescent Psychiatry, 48*, 465–470.

Giedd, J. N., Raznahan, A., Mills, K. L. & Lenroot, R. K. (2012). Magnetic resonance imaging of male/female differences in human adolescent brain anatomy. *Biology of Sex Differences, 3*, 19.

Gini, G., Albiero, P., Benelli, B. & Altoe, G. (2008). Determinants of adolescents' active defending and passive bystanding behavior in bullying. *Journal of Adolescence, 31*, 93–105.

Goossens, F. A., Olthof, T. & Dekker, P. (2006). The new participant role scales: A comparison between various criteria for assigning roles and indications for their validity. *Aggressive Behavior, 32*, 343–357.

Hawley, P. H. (1999). The ontogenesis of social dominance: A strategy-based evolutionary perspective. *Developmental Review*, *19*, 97–132.

Hoza, B. (2007). Peer functioning in children with ADHD. *Journal of Pediatric Psychology*, *32*, 655–663.

Huitsing, G., Snijders, T. A. B., van Duijn, M. A. J. & Veenstra, R. (2014). Victims, bullies, and their defenders: A longitudinal study of the coevolution of positive and negative networks. *Development and Psychopathology*, *26*, 645–659.

Kaur, K. (2017). Drug abuse! Problem is intense in Punjab, India. *Human Biology Review*, *6*, 20–29.

Kloep, M., Güney, N., Çok, F. & Simsek, Ö. F. (2009). Motives for risk-taking in adolescence: A cross-cultural study. *Journal of Adolescence*, *32*, 135–151.

Kshirsagar, V. Y., Agarwal, R. & Bavdekar, S. B. (2007). Bullying in schools: Prevalence and short-term impact. *Indian Pediatrics*, *44*(1), 25–28.

LaFontana, K. M. & Cillessen, A. H. N. (2010). Developmental changes in the priority of perceived status in childhood and adolescence. *Social Development*, *19*, 130–147.

Laslett, R. (1980). Bullies: A children's court in a day school for maladjusted children. *Journal of Special Education*, *4*, 391–397.

Lee, N. C., de Groot, R. H. M., Boschloo, A., Dekker, S., Krabbendam, L. & Jolles, J. (2013). Age and educational track influence adolescent discounting of delayed rewards. *Frontiers in Psychology*, *4*, 993.

Lion, R. & Meertens, R. M. (2005). Security or opportunity: The influence of risk-taking tendency on risk information preference. *Journal of Risk Research*, *8*, 283–294.

Meertens, R. M. & Lion, M. (2008). Measuring an individual's tendency to take risks: The risk propensity scale. *Journal of Applied Social Psychology*, *38*, 1506–1520.

Mills, K. L., Goddings, A.-L., Clasen, L. S., Giedd, J. N. & Blakemore, S.-J. (2014). The developmental mismatch in structural brain maturation during adolescence. *Developmental Neuroscience*, *36*, 147–160.

Mills, K. L., Goddings, A.-L., Herting, M. M., Meuwese, R., Blakemore, S.-J., Crone, E. A., . . . Tamnes, C. K. (2016). Structural brain development between childhood and adulthood: Convergence across four longitudinal samples. *Neuroimage*, *141*, 273–281.

O'Brien, L., Albert, D., Chein, J. & Steinberg, L. (2011). Adolescents prefer more immediate rewards when in the presence of their peers. *Journal of Research on Adolescence*, *21*, 747–753.

Olthof, T., Goossens, F. A., Vermande, M. M., Aleva, E. A. & van der Meulen, M. (2011). Bullying as strategic behaviour: Relations with desired and acquired dominance in the peer group. *Journal of School Psychology*, *49*, 339–359.

Olweus, D. (1993). *Bullying at School: What We Know and What We Can Do.* Cambridge, MA: Blackwell.

Pickett, K. E. & Wilkinson, R.G. (2007). Child wellbeing and income inequality in rich societies: Ecological cross-sectional study. *British Medical Journal*, *335*, 1080–1087.

Pollak, S. D. (2008). Mechanisms linking early experience and the emergence of emotions. *Current Directions in Psychological Science, 17,* 370–375.

Poon, K. (2016). Understanding risk-taking behaviour in bullies, victims, and bully-victims using cognitive- and emotion-focused approaches. *Frontiers in Psychology, 7,* 1838.

Pouwels, J. L., Lansu, T. A. M. & Cillessen, A. H. N. (2016). Participant roles of bullying in adolescence: Status characteristics, social behaviour, and assignment criteria. *Aggressive Behaviour, 42,* 239–253.

Pozzoli, T. & Gini, G. (2010). Active defending and passive bystanding behavior in bullying: The role of personal characteristics and perceived peer pressure, *Journal of Abnormal Child Psychology, 38,* 815–827.

Pronk, J., Lee, N. C., Sandhu, D., Kaur, K., Kaur, S., Olthof, T. & Goossens, F. A. (2016). Associations between Dutch and Indian adolescents' bullying role behavior and peer group status: Cross-culturally testing an evolutionary hypothesis. *International Journal of Behavorial Development, 41,* 735–742.

Reintjes, A., Vermande, M. M., Goossens, F. A., Olthof, T., van der Schoot, R., Aleva, E. A. & van der Meulen, M. (2013a). Developmental trajectories of bullying and social dominance in youth. *Child Abuse & Neglect, 37,* 224–234.

Reintjes, A., Vermande, M. M., Olthof, T., Goossens, F. A., van der Schoot, R., Aleva, L. & van der Meulen, M. (2013b). Costs and benefits of bullying in the context of the peer group: A three wave longitudinal analysis. *Journal of Abnormal Child Psychology, 41,* 1217–1229.

Salmivalli, C. (2010). Bullying and the peer group: A review. *Aggression and Violent Behaviour, 15,* 112–120.

Salmivalli, C., Lagerspetz, K. M. J., Björkvist, K., Österman, K. & Kaukiainen, A. (1996). Bullying as a group process: Participant roles and their relations to social status within the group. *Aggressive Behavior, 22,* 1–15.

Schmitt, N. (1996). Uses and abuses of coefficient alpha. *Psychological Assessment, 8,* 350–353.

Scholte, R. H. J., Engels, R. C. M. E., Overbeek, G., van de Kemp, R. A. T. & Haselager, G. J. T. (2007). Stability in bullying and victimisation and its association with social adjustment in childhood and adolescence. *Journal of Abnormal Child Psychology, 35,* 217–228.

Seals, D. & Young, J. (2003). Bullying and victimization: Prevalence and relationship to gender, grade level, ethnicity, self-esteem, and depression. *Adolescence, 38,* 735–747.

Smith, P. K., Cowie, H., Olafsson, A. P. D., Liefooghe, A., Almeida, A., Araki, H., … Wenxin, Z. (2002). Definitions of bullying: A comparison of terms used, and age and gender differences, in a fourteen-country international comparison. *Child Development, 73,* 1119–1133.

Tavakol, M. & Dennick, R. (2011). Making sense of Cronbach's alpha. *International Journal of Medical Education, 2,* 53–55.

Vaillancourt, T., Hymel, S. & McDougall, P. (2003). Bullying is power: Implications for school based intervention strategies. *Journal of Applied School Psychology, 19,* 157–176.

Van Hoorn, J., Fuligni, A. J., Crone, E. A. & Galván, A. (2016). Peer influence effects on risk-taking and prosocial decision-making in adolescence: Insights from neuroimaging studies. *Current Opinion in Behavioural Sciences, 10,* 59–64.

Volk, A. A., Camilleri, J. A., Dane, A. V. & Marini, Z. A. (2012). Is adolescent bullying an evolutionary adaptation? *Aggressive Behavior, 38,* 222–238.

Volk, A. A., Dane, A. V. & Marini, Z. A. (2014). What is bullying? A theoretical redefinition. *Developmental Review, 34,* 327–343.

Walden, L. M. & Beran, T. N. (2010). Attachment quality and bullying behaviour in school-aged youth. *Canadian Journal of School Psychology, 25,* 5–18.

Witvliet, M., Olthof, T., Hoeksma, J. B., Goossens, F. A., Smits, M. S. I. & Koot, H. M. (2010). Peer group affiliation of children: The role of perceived popularity, likeability, an behavioural similarity in bullying. *Social Development, 19,* 285–303.

APPENDIX 9.A

The Risk-Taking Behaviour Questionnaire

(Questions for the Netherlands sample were the same as for India, except where indicated.)

In the past few months, how often have you ...

	India	The Netherlands	Domain
1.	... used your cell phone while riding a two-wheeler?		I
2.	... been involved in a physical fight?		I
3.	... taken things from a shop without paying?		R
4.	... done something dangerous because your friends dared you to?		P
5.	... spent less time with friends and family or doing your schoolwork because you were on your computer, tablet or cell phone?		M
6.	... ignored traffic lights when riding a two-wheeler?		I
7.	... drunk alcoholic drinks, such as beer?		H
8.	... watched more than 2.5 hours of TV on a school day?		M
9.	... gotten on or off a moving bus or train?	... speeded while riding a scooter?	I

(*cont.*)

	India	The Netherlands	Domain
10.	. . . intentionally caused damage to other people's or public properties?		R
11.	. . . done something dangerous to show other people how brave you are?		P
12.	. . . been physically active for more than 30 minutes a day (e.g. walking, running, cycling, sports)?		H
13.	. . . carried things like a knife, or a stick, or some other weapon to school?	. . . travelled on public transport without paying?	R
14.	. . . missed school lessons (bunked off)?		P
15.	. . . taken things from one of your friends or family members without their permission?		R
16.	. . . taken medication that was prescribed to someone else?		H
17.	. . . sent personal information to someone you have never met via the Internet?		M
18.	. . . taken money from your parents, because your friends expected you to be able to spend money?		P
19.	. . . smoked cigarettes?		H
20.	. . . spent so much time on your computer, tablet or cell phone that you have gone without eating or sleeping?		M
21.	. . . gotten into a fight to impress your friends?		P
22.	. . . taken credit for another person's schoolwork?		R
23.	. . . sent revealing photographs of yourself to other people via the Internet?		M
24.	. . . taken diet pills or made yourself vomit in order to lose weight?		H
25.	. . . ridden on a two-wheeler without a helmet?	. . . practised an extreme or dangerous sport?	I

Note. Questionnaire consists of two subscales, 1) Risk-taking, consisting of Risk of Unintentional Injuries (I); Rule-Breaking Behaviours (R); Peer-Influenced Risks (P); and 2) Well-being, consisting of Technology and Media-Related Risks (M); Health Risks (H).

Part III

Working with Students and Teachers

10 PhotoStory

A Legitimate Research Tool in Cross-Cultural Research

Phillip Slee, Grace Skrzypiec, Damanjit Sandhu, Kirandeep Kaur and Marilyn Campbell

PhotoStory is a research method using photography to illustrate a story that conveys the perspectives of individuals about a particular issue. Australian and Indian researchers participating in the three-year India–European Network project and an Australian Research Council grant devised and assessed the use of PhotoStory procedures to better understand Indian and Australian students' experiences of bullying. Using iPads, the PhotoStory study involved students capturing visual images of situations related to their experiences of school bullying and attaching a story to their pictures. The research was designed to give children a voice in understanding their perceptions of school safety, particularly in relation to their experiences of school bullying and its impact on them. The data were collected from students in Indian schools in the Punjabi region and students in south Australian schools in Adelaide. In this chapter consideration is given to the procedures used and the challenges faced in gathering these PhotoStories. Suggestions for the analysis of the data gathered and recommendations regarding its use in cross-cultural research are provided.

To best understand the context and background for this chapter it is important to identify the influence of a number of converging themes, namely the research paradigm used, a focus on community action and a participatory empowering co-learning research process (Minkler, 2004). In their critical examination of child development theories, Shute and Slee (2015) have drawn attention to the influential factors of history, culture and the philosophy of science shaping research paradigms.

Research Paradigm

It is important to appreciate the view expressed by Aries (1962) that childhood, as it is understood today in Western society, is a relatively recent phenomenon (Slee, Campbell & Spears, 2012). Throughout history children and childhood have been more or less valued, and more or less recognised, but have been typically regarded as a property of God, the state or the parents (particularly the father). In Western society child labour laws were enacted, first in Britain in 1833, to protect children from the excesses and exploitation of the Industrial Revolution. Whilst it is now true that children and childhood have become the focus of greater attention, as recently as 1977 Bronfenbrenner noted that developmental psychology was 'the study of the strange behaviour of children, in strange situations, with strange adults for the briefest possible period of time' (1977, p. 513). He was critical of the 'artificial' conditions under which the study of children's and young people's behaviour is conducted.

In relation to culture, Kessen (1979) even spoke of children and child psychology as 'cultural inventions', highlighting that we cannot easily separate the influence of culture from any discussion of the nature of children and families. Bruner and Haste emphasised that 'It can never be the case that there is a "self" independent of one's cultural-historical existence' (1987, p. 91). In developmental psychology influential theorists such as Bronfenbrenner and Erikson have identified culture as an overarching influence on development, with Vygotsky highlighting the role of culture on the developing child. All too often, though, as Shute and Slee (2015) have noted, the influence of culture is regarded in research as a variable to be 'controlled' rather than something to be studied in order to understand its influence on development.

Castleden and Garvin (2008) have presented a strong case for an alternative approach to that of mainstream empirical research involving cross-cultural research and in particular research with Indigenous peoples. They have noted that during decades of research with Indigenous people researchers have 'parachuted' into the communities, gathered their data and left, frequently contravening basic principles of ethical guidance including informed consent and communicating their findings back to the communities themselves. In this regard they have argued strongly for community-based participatory research with its philosophy and methodology which highlights the importance of engaging with participants as co-researchers in the endeavour extending to the definition of the issue to be explored, the methodology for examining the issue and communication of the findings to the community.

Presently, the dominant Western model of 'reality' draws heavily upon a belief in a particular view of the scientific method as the only valid approach to the acquisition and understanding of a systematic body of knowledge. The basis for the prevailing scientific method is drawn from the world view of empiricism, a philosophy of science that has exerted a powerful influence on scientific practice. In a very direct way, it has shaped how we have conducted the science of child study. Thus, in modelling itself upon the natural sciences such as physics and chemistry, the empirical method of child study has placed a great deal of importance on the search for causes of behaviour, with an emphasis on reducing the complexity of behaviour to its basic components. As Slee and colleagues (2012) have noted, the conduct of the mainstream scientific study of child development:

> went hand in hand with the development of an empirical methodology which clearly separated the 'observer' from the 'observed' in the best interests of the scientific endeavour. The infant/child/adolescent was 'objectified', in the spotlight of this critical 'gaze'. (p. 8)

Contrasting with a positivist view encapsulated in empirical inquiry, a postmodern view represents a markedly different outlook. Tierney (1996) identifies five features of a postmodern outlook. The first relates to the idea that knowledge is not 'discovered' but rather it is 'constructed'. The second concerns the challenge it directs to an absolute faith in science. The third relates broadly to the image of the neutral, dispassionate scientist in contrast to the engaged and involved researcher. The fourth is postmodernism's embrace of chaos and disequilibrium versus the linear causality of positivism. Finally, different sources of knowledge, apart from that emanating from universities, is a feature of a postmodern outlook.

A related point, highly relevant to the present chapter, is the claim that Shute and Slee (2015) have made that 'in developmental research specifically, the voices of children are even more silent than those of women' (p. 212). Shute and Slee (2015) considered at length the extent to which children's voices had a part to play in research, concluding that it was within the discipline of sociology that the most serious consideration had been given to the idea that children's voices should be heard. They cited the writings of Matthews (2007) around the new sociology of childhood where strong advocacy was made for an alternative outlook on research with young people that did not foster a view of them as passive, vulnerable and acted upon but rather recognised them as active social agents in their own development. Kellett (2010) has argued that:

> Voice is a social construct operating in a cultural context where shared meaning is negotiated. This immediately raises problems for children's voice because in order to have influence, their voice has to transcend the cultural boundaries of childhood and negotiate a shared understanding in the adult world, yet much of children's voice is not expressed in words – least of all adult words – and the rich tapestry of their non-verbal communication frequently goes unheard. (p. 196)

A significant issue, then, is *how* the voices of children may transcend the constraints placed upon them by historical perceptions of what constitutes childhood, its embeddedness in culture and the influence of the dominant positivist paradigm in mainstream Western research regarding the conduct of research. Shute and Slee (2015) have considered at some length the importance of capturing the voices of children and young people as part of developmental psychology's postmodern mandate. With this background in mind we turn to a consideration of the use of PhotoStory as a research tool in cross-cultural research. To that end we must have some appreciation of the method and its development.

Drawings, Visual Images and Photos in Research

Alternative ways of gathering data regarding children and their development have a long history (Slee et al., 2012). For example, art has long been used as a medium, typically in relation to therapy, to better understand young people's perspectives of a situation. The study of children's drawings has occupied researchers for a number of decades, although much of the early work, particularly on emotional expression in children's drawings, had its roots in psychoanalysis. Nic Gabhainn and Sixsmith (2006) noted that 'task-centred activities with children, such as the use of art have been used to elucidate children's perceptions and ideas and enable them to express their views to adult researchers' (p. 250).

Slee and Skrzypiec (2015) describe research where primary school students' drawings were used to examine their experience of bullying. Bullying in schools is an international problem impacting negatively on children's well-being, and children's drawings can provide an insight into their emotional states. The authors concluded that students' drawings could be useful in counselling young people to help offset the negative effects of bullying. The use of children's drawings as a research tool is not without its critics. That is, children might feel more or less constrained by perceptions of their artistic capabilities. Alternative means of gathering information have been explored, including the use of photography and the advent of mobile phones with cameras, and relatively cheap photographic equipment, including iPads, has enhanced the attractiveness of this medium.

Using the medium of photography in research also has a long history, particularly in the disciplines of anthropology and sociology (e.g. Mason 2005). Wang and Burris (1997) have researched and written extensively about the use of this medium; they have argued that photographic data can provide an accurate reflection of participants' worlds, arguing that photographic data provided by participants are more likely to reflect their world. Bessell, Deese and Medina (2007) have argued photography has 'the unique ability to help individuals convey inner thoughts' (p. 558).

There are a range of approaches that essentially employ visual images. One such approach that has been used is 'photo-novella'. As described by Wang, Burris and Ping (1996), 'the theoretical and practical underpinnings of photo novella are empowerment education, feminist theory and documentary photography' (p. 1391). A characteristic feature of this approach is the requirement that the photographs are taken by the participants themselves and not the researcher. This outlook is consistent with the underpinning concept of empowerment education and is a basis of the PhotoStory.

Another approach is usually referred to as photo 'language'. The procedure was initially employed in counselling and clinical psychology. Typically the approach used selected photographs, for example of the family, to trigger therapeutic processes. The photographs may elicit memories and feelings, and clients would discuss aspects of the image they were looking at (Bessell et al., 2007).

'Photovoice' is yet another distinct approach using images. As generally described, 'photovoice' is intended to promote a conversation or critical evaluation of a topic. Similar to photo novella, the photography is in the hands of the participants themselves. Generally, the photographs capture something of the issues which are of greatest significance to the participants. Having taken the photographs, the group will come together to discuss and develop titles or themes. A distinguishing feature is that the photographs are displayed for the purpose of inviting the wider community to see the display with the intention of influencing policy and practice.

The PhotoStory Approach

Yet another approach, less widely known, is 'PhotoStory' (Skrzypiec, Murray-Harvey & Krieg, 2013). PhotoStory is a research method that uses visual images to express the perspectives of individuals about a particular issue. Underpinning this approach is an emphasis on participatory research. A participatory approach considers the 'power differential' that may exist between the researcher and the participants in mainstream empirical research paradigms (Shute & Slee, 2015). In mainstream research, the researcher is positioned as the 'expert' and the participant as the 'informant' from whom knowledge is sought, such as by using questionnaires or interviews or experimental conditions. In contrast a 'participatory' method emphasises equitable partnerships engaging community members (e.g. students and teachers), organisations (e.g. schools or education departments) and researchers in all aspects of the research process (Israel et al., 2001). The researchers and the participants work together as equal partners in co-creating the understanding of the phenomenon that is the focus of the research. The thinking underpinning a participatory approach is that the knowledge gleaned is most closely centred on the experiences of the individuals who are the focus of the research. The method involves engaging with the participants in the research, providing them with cameras and instructions concerning the task, and encouraging the telling of a 'story' about the photograph they took and its personal meaning for them.

To briefly summarise the main characteristics of the PhotoStory approach:

- PhotoStory is a research method using photography to illustrate a story that conveys the perspectives of individuals about a particular issue.
- The approach emphasises contextualising child development issues in relation to history, culture and the philosophy underpinning scientific inquiry.
- Emphasis is given to placing the child/young person at the centre of the investigative process.
- The use of film/visual images as part of the research process has a strong history.
- Empowerment education lies at the heart of the process inasmuch as the process emphasises a participatory outlook whereby the research and participant are considered part of an equal research endeavour.
- Somewhat different approaches to the use of photographs and visual images in the research process are identifiable.

Previous Research Using PhotoStory

The PhotoStory method has been used to investigate a wide range of phenomena. For example, in rural Australia it has been employed to understand issues regarding water resource allocation and the emotions and values associated with this topic (Keremane & McKay, 2011). The PhotoStory method has also been employed as a qualitative component of a mixed-method evaluation of the KidsMatter Early Childhood (KMEC) framework to enhance young children's well-being (Skrzypiec et al., 2013). One hundred family and staff at 10 early childhood education and care (ECEC) services across Australia participated in a PhotoStory study by taking 162 photographs to illustrate children's social and emotional learning. Educators provided photographs to show how KMEC had affected them and their work practices. Analysis of the photos and stories underscores the importance of social cultural aspects of children's social and emotional learning. Findings provided evidence of the personal as well as professional changes that staff attributed to KMEC. The PhotoStory method was an effective and powerful research tool providing unique, rich and informative qualitative data as part of the evaluation study. This information was then used to inform practice regarding the development of a programme to address mental health amongst young children in day-care and long day-care centres in Australia (Slee et al., 2012).

PhotoStory and School Bullying

The present authors have used PhotoStory in previous research to investigate mental health and well-being and have also used it in a cross-cultural context to investigate the phenomenon of school bullying (see Skrzypiec, Slee & Sandhu, 2015). In this study it was found that in India physical acts of aggression between peers were common inside and outside school. The findings were discussed in relation to definitional issues and the need to implement anti-violence programmes in Indian schools. The purpose behind this current study was to use the information generated to better understand the nature of bullying and coping strategies that children/young people used in order to inform effective prevention strategies for schools. Information was gathered from Australian and Indian students. Before we describe the application of PhotoStory, some consideration is needed of the phenomenon of school bullying.

Definition of Bullying

Heinemann (1973) discussed the issue of bullying using the Norwegian term *mobbing*, which highlighted violence against a deviant individual that occurs suddenly and subsides suddenly, that is, the group against the individual. Olweus (1978, 1993) subsequently extended the definition to include systematic one-on-one attacks of a stronger child against a weaker child. Smith and colleagues' (2002) study of 8- and 14-year-olds across 14 countries concluded that the younger children had a less differentiated understanding of the components of bullying than the older children. In the Australian context Hemphill, Heerde and Gomo (2014) concluded that:

School-based bullying is a systematic abuse of power in a relationship formed at school characterised by: 1. aggressive acts directed (by one or more individuals) toward victims that a reasonable person would avoid; 2. acts which usually occur repeatedly over a period of time; and 3. acts in which there is an actual or perceived power imbalance between perpetrators and victims, with victims often being unable to defend themselves effectively from perpetrators. (p. 15)

Slee and colleagues (2003) reviewed the matter of definition in five countries in the Asia-Pacific region, noting considerable differences in whether countries had a word for *bullying* and how it was defined. Slee and Skrzypiec (2016) have examined cross-cultural definitions of bullying, noting that different cultures have different words (e.g. in Japan it is *ijime* and in Korea it is *wang ta*) and that different meanings are attached to these words. For example, in Japan *ijime* refers to indirect and exclusionary features of the behaviour rather than emphasising the physical aspects. Smith, Kwak and Toda (2016) perform an in-depth analysis of the nature of school bullying from Eastern and Western perspectives, providing fascinating insight into how bullying is defined cross-culturally. In the Indian context there is no obvious word for *bullying*, as it is understood in Western countries, but the nearest equivalent terms are discussed in Chapters 4 and 13.

While bullying is an international issue, it is only just beginning to be researched in India. Research using the PhotoStory method by Skrzypiec and colleagues (2015) noted the high frequency with which Indian females report that sexual harassment, or 'Eve teasing', is a common occurrence. *Eve teasing* is defined by the Cambridge Dictionary (2017) as the act of annoying a woman or women in a public place. According to Kuruvilla and Suhara (2014), 'Eve teasing' generally occurs in pre- or early adolescence when girls are sexually maturing. It can take various forms such as catcalling, lewd gestures, stalking or groping, and might lead to sexual assault as well.

As Slee and Skrzypiec (2016) have noted, the issue of cross-cultural research is problematic when the matter of definition varies, the meaning of the term *bullying* is different and the matter of measuring and assessing bullying is complicated by the assessment instruments themselves. These factors influenced the decision to use PhotoStory to explore the issue of school bullying with a focus on how students cope in Australian and Indian schools.

The PhotoStory approach reduces cultural barriers as young people are given the opportunity to express their thoughts through a photograph that they take. Young people who may lack confidence or feel disempowered through a limited means of expression may be able to use an iPad to take a photo of something that triggers their memory about bullying. They may then use this photo to express their feelings and thoughts about bullying as well as how they cope with bullying.

Coping with Bullying

The question of the nature and type of strategies students use to cope with bullying and their effectiveness is a critical one. The answer to these questions will help students understand how to cope and more broadly also inform schoolwide policies and practices to reduce the incidence of bullying. Lazarus and Folkman's (1984) theory of coping dichotomises coping into problem-focussed (responses resolving a given stressor) and emotion-focussed (responses reducing negative emotions that arise as a result of stress) strategies. Kanetsuna, Smith and Morita (2006), in an examination of primary and secondary school students, report that the more successful strategies include telling a teacher, asking a friend for help and ignoring or nonchalance, while less successful strategies are fighting back or passive, helpless behaviour.

There is, however, no definitive set of strategies found to apply for all students, or for coping with all bullying incidents. This is largely because 'coping-strategy use is guided by the way an individual perceives, or appraises, the situation' (Hunter, Mora-Merchan & Ortega, 2004, p. 4). In a study of 1,223 Australian adolescents Murray-Harvey, Skrzypiec and Slee (2012) identified five coping styles:

- Productive Other-Focussed (e.g. talk to a teacher)
- Productive Self-Focussed (e.g. think of a way to solve the bullying)
- Non-productive Avoidance (e.g. 'wish for a miracle')
- Relationship Improvement (e.g. try to make friends with the bully)
- Aggressive/Assertive Response (e.g. fight back).

They concluded that 'effective and ineffective strategies can be clearly differentiated, providing practitioners at all levels within the school community with a strong base on which to design prevention and/or intervention programs' (p. 136).

Using PhotoStory to Understand School Bullying Cross-Culturally

This research project sought to investigate different views on traditional and cyberbullying using a PhotoStory procedure. We were working with schools to try and obtain a picture of what happens when bullying occurs and also investigate students' coping strategies. The overall aim of the project was to use PhotoStory as a medium to understand young people's experiences of bullying and their coping strategies in two different cultures, namely Australia and India.

Obtaining PhotoStories

Approximately 15 student volunteers from each of three schools in India and Australia were engaged in the project. Students and their teachers were invited to participate in this research, as it was important that the views of school students were heard and that the findings represented students' voice. Ethical approval was obtained from both the Australian and Indian universities and relevant education departments.

Participants were asked to attend an informal student briefing session conducted at the school where the researcher explained the project purpose and procedure. Students and teachers were instructed in the use of an iPad to take the picture and attach a story using Pic Collage, a free downloadable app. They were instructed in the use of Pic Collage to edit and add their 'story' regarding the photo, adding 'stickers' if they wished to embellish their picture and story. No pictures of identifiable students, teachers or family were allowed. Finally, instructions were provided regarding downloading the image and story and emailing it to one of the researchers, ensuring their confidentiality.

Students were instructed to use a photograph or picture to illustrate something that they would like to tell the researchers about bullying and coping: 'What you might like to tell us might just be an opinion that you have, or it may involve telling us about something that you have witnessed or experienced. If you tell us about a bullying incident try and tell us how it made you feel and about what you or others did or should have done, about it.'

Students in the Australian classrooms booked out the iPad for 7–10 days, during which time they took the photo and wrote a story about it and emailed it to the researchers. In the Indian schools the conditions were altered to suit the needs of the school, but essentially the students had access to the iPad for a period of days. In both groups the pictures and stories were emailed directly to the researcher to ensure the confidentiality of the picture and story. The PhotoStories were then coded using Murray-Harvey and colleagues' (2012) schema of Productive Other-Focused, Productive Self-Focussed, Non-productive Avoidance, Relationship Improvement, Aggressive/Assertive Response or not applicable. Having coded the data, a second researcher also coded and differences were resolved by discussion.

Examination of the findings showed that with regard to the Australian students and their coping strategies, the largest proportion (11/16) was rated as 'Productive Other-Focussed', for example talking to a trusted adult or peer. In one of the Australian PhotoStories the caption by the student read, 'You are not alone, there is help out there' (Figure 10.1).

You are not alone, there is help out there.

Figure 10.1 Productive Other-Focussed coping strategy

This suggestion to *seek help from outside sources* would be regarded as a 'Productive Other-Focussed' strategy.

In a further example of a 'Productive Other-Focussed' strategy, one of the Indian students described being repeatedly 'teased' on a road. *After asking the perpetrator to stop, the victim told a teacher and then the teasing stopped*; see Figure 10.2.

A photo from India was accompanied by the student's story depicting being excluded by boys from playing with them as he was new to the school. His solution was to make friends with the girls and play with them; see Figure 10.3.

In the Indian sample 9 out of 15 PhotoStories depicted 'Non-productive' coping strategies, for example feeling helpless in the face of the act depicted. In Figure 10.4 an Indian student describes his 'prickly' experience of being verbally abused by senior boys in the cricket club and subsequently feeling helpless and weak.

Generally the findings highlighted differences between the Australian and Indian students in the nature of coping strategies used. Consistent with the PhotoStory methodology, a PhotoStory book was produced for the Indian schools depicting the de-identified photographs and stories and the researchers travelled to the schools to present the books to the teachers and students (Slee et al., 2014). In relation to the Australian schools a written report of the findings was provided to the participating schools.

Figure 10.2 Productive Other-Focussed strategy

Interviews with a Second Group of Indian Students

In addition to the collection and collation of photos and stories from India, another 10 Indian students who were not involved in providing the photos and stories were interviewed regarding their explanation/interpretation of the pictures and stories. This component of the study was undertaken by the Australian researchers in order to better help them understand the experience of bullying from an Indian school student's perspective. The procedure involved showing a randomly selected set of the PhotoStories from the first part of the study and asking them a series of questions including what the scene in the PhotoStory depicted and how the person would feel. The words the students used most commonly to describe the PhotoStory depictions were *harassment* and *teasing*, and only one of the students described the behaviour as *bullying*. In all, six of the students identified the victim as feeling sad and unhappy – two of the students thought the victims would be both angry and sad.

Figure 10.3 Productive Self-Focussed strategy

The findings from the PhotoStories described here highlight a number of points regarding cross-cultural research, research with school students and research relating to school bullying. In reviewing the literature relating to PhotoStory it is clear that the approach embodies a different methodological outlook from mainstream empirical research. We have drawn attention to the use of visual images (photos) to assist students to depict in their own way their negative peer experiences in the school context. It honours the experiences of the students who are viewed as 'experts' on their own world, allowing them to communicate on a more or less equal footing with the adult researchers who are seeking to collaborate with them.

Spears and colleagues (2011) examined the role of young people as co-researchers in anti-cyberbullying initiatives. It was argued that giving youth voice to such initiatives highlights young people's understandings of the issue. Importantly, Spears and colleagues argued that in adopting such an outlook it positions young people identifying them as change agents and as allies in the research process. In a cross-cultural context the approach using iPad technology is admirably suited to the interests and

Figure 10.4 Non-productive coping

needs of young people, including their familiarity with and ability to use ICT technology. As a multimodal medium with the possibility for text, image, video and sound, iPad technology is a particularly attractive medium for children and young people (Spears et al., 2013).

In a cross-cultural context where language and custom may significantly limit the use of more traditional means of data gathering (e.g. questionnaires or interviews) and where direct observation may be problematic in terms of interpreting the behaviours, PhotoStory offers a great deal of potential. In the present research the written content provided by both the Australian and Indian students was limited, but this could be addressed in future research by providing the students with clearer guidelines for the production of the stories.

In relation to the focus of the research which addressed the issue of how students cope with bullying, the conclusions are limited by the small sample from India and Australia. The PhotoStories suggested a limited understanding of the concept of bullying by all students in relation to its defining features, including repetition, intent and power imbalance; these findings are similar to those in research conducted by Skrzypiec and colleagues (2015). Skrzypiec and colleagues found that physical harassment, name calling and Eve teasing were commonly described by students in their stories, who indicated that it had left them feeling sad, embarrassed, depressed and helpless. However, of the stories described only four met the definition of bullying i.e. that the incident involved repetitive, hurtful behaviour perpetrated by a person or persons that could be considered more 'powerful' than the victim. This suggests that developmentally there may be limitations to how young people distinguish between bullying and other forms of aggression. This was highlighted in the interview component of the research with a small group of Indian students who were shown a random selection of Indian PhotoStories and asked to explain what was happening in the story. The Indian students typically referred to *harassment* and *teasing* with limited reference to the concept of *bullying*.

In relation to coping there was a strong indication that it was possible, using the PhotoStory method, to identify how young people cope with bullying and aggression. The predominant coping strategy Australian students used was 'Productive Other-Focussed', indicating key strategies included talking to others: teachers, parents, peers or other trusted individuals. The present finding contrasts somewhat with previously reported research. Murray-Harvey and colleagues (2012), in their research involving young Australian adolescents' coping strategies, reported the underutilisation of 'Productive Other-Focussed' strategies by bullied students; suggesting the reason was they were not convinced that teachers would be supportive. One possible explanation for the disparity in the findings is that in the present research, information was not collected on whether the students providing the PhotoStories were themselves victims of bullying. In the research reported by Murray-Harvey and colleagues (2012) informed adults and students who had not been bullied advocated for 'Productive Other-Focussed' strategies. Another possible explanation is that the students in the present study were drawn from schools where there were quite active anti-bullying policies and practices in place at the school and classroom levels so that the students were aware of the need to report any bullying.

In contrast the Indian school students predominantly used 'Non-productive' strategies and reported feeling helpless in the face of bullying. It was quite clear from the Indian students' PhotoStories that they had been teased, harassed or bullied, so in this case their use of the 'Non-productive' coping strategies is quite consistent with the research involving Australian students who had been bullied (Murray-Harvey et al., 2012).

In summary, we have argued for the efficacy of using a PhotoStory approach in cross-cultural research to understand something of the nature and coping strategies students use to address bullying. As a preliminary study the method itself appears to be productive and useful, as the technology is appealing to young people, the methodology engages them as co-researchers in understanding the phenomenon of bullying and the findings do suggest that the approach has some merit.

References

Aries, P. (1962). *Centuries of Childhood*. New York: Vintage Books.

Bessell, A. G., Deese, W. B. & Medina, A. L. (2007). Photolanguage: How a picture can inspire a thousand words. *American Journal of Evaluation, 28,* 558–569. doi: 10.1177/1098214007306372.

Bronfenbrenner, U. (1977). Toward an experimental ecology of human development. *American Psychologist, 7,* 513–531. doi: 10.1037//0003-066X.32.7.513.

Bruner, J. & Haste, H. (1987). *Making Sense: The Child's Construction of Reality*. London: Methuen.

Cambridge Dictionary (2017). *Eve-teasing*. Retrieved on March 19, 2017 from http://dictionary.cambridge.org/dictionary/english/eve-teasing.

Castleden, H. & Garvin, T. (2008). Modifying Photovoice for community-based participatory Indigenous research. *Social Science & Medicine, 66,* 1393–1405. doi: 10.1016/j.socscimed.2007.11.030.

Heinemann, P. P. (1973) *Mobbing: Gruppevold blant barn og voksne [Bullying: Group Violence among Children and Adults]*. Oslo: Gyldendal.

Hemphill, S. A., Heerde, J. A. & Gomo, R. (2014). *Defining Bullying for the Australian Research and Academic Community*. Canberra: Australian Research Alliance for Children and Youth.

Hunter, S. C., Mora-Merchan, J. & Ortega, R. (2004). The long-term effects of coping strategy use in victims of bullying. *Spanish Journal of Psychology, 7*(1), 3–12.

Israel, B., Schultz, A. J., Parker, E. A. & Becker, A. B. (2001). Community-based participatory research: Policy recommendations for promoting a partnership approach in health research. *Education for Health, 14,* 182–197. doi: 10.1080/13576280110051055.

Kanetsuna, T., Smith, P. K. & Morita, Y. (2006). Coping with bullying at school: Children's recommended strategies and attitudes to school-based interventions in England and Japan. *Aggressive Behavior, 32*, 570–580. doi: 10.1002/ab.20156.

Kaur, K., Kaur, S. & Sandhu, D. (2014). Cyber bullying: An emerging threat to pupil well-being. *International Journal of Social Sciences Review, 2*, 374–377.

Kellett, M. (2010). *Rethinking Children and Research: Attitudes in Contemporary Society.* London: Bloomsbury Academic.

Kelly, J. G., Dassoff, N., Levin, I., Schreckengost, J., Stelzner, S. P. & Altman E. (1988). A guide to conducting prevention research in the community: First steps. *Prevention in the Human Services, 6*, 1–174. doi: 10.4324/9781315791678.

Kelly, J. G, Mock, L. O. & Tandon, D. S. (2001). Collaborative inquiry with African-American community leaders: Comments on a participatory action research process. In P. Reason & H. Bradbury (eds.), *Handbook of Action Research* (pp. 348–355). London: Sage.

Keremane, G. B. & McKay, J. (2011). Using PhotoStory to capture irrigators' emotions about water policy and sustainable development objectives: A case study in rural Australia. *Action Research, 9*, 405–425. doi: 10.1177/1476750311409598.

Kessen, W. (1979). The American child and other cultural inventions. *American Psychologist, 34*, 815–882. doi: 10.1037/0003-066X.34.10.815.

Kuruvilla, M. & Suhara, F. (2014). Response patterns of girl students to eve-teasing: An empirical study in a university setting. *International Journal of Education and Psychological Research, 3*(3), 60–64. doi: 10.5897/IJSA2013.0445.

Lazarus, R. S. & Folkman, S. (1984). *Stress, Appraisal, and Coping.* New York: Springer.

Mason, P. (2005). Visual data in applied qualitative research: Lessons from experience. *Qualitative Research, 5*, 325–346. doi: 10.1177/1468794105054458.

Matthews, S. H. (2007). A window on the 'new' sociology of childhood. *Sociology Compass, 1*, 322–334. doi: 10.1111/j.1751–9020.2007.00001.x.

Meacham, J. (1999). Riegal, dialectics and multiculturalism. *Human Development, 43*, 134–144.

Minkler, M. (2004). Ethical challenges for the 'outside' researcher in community-based participatory research. *Health Education & Behavior, 31*, 684–697 doi: 10.1177/1090198104269566.

Murray-Harvey, R., Skrzypiec, G. & Slee, P. T. (2012). Effective and ineffective coping with bullying strategies as assessed by informed professionals and their use by victimised students. *Australian Journal of Guidance and Counselling, 22*(1), 122–138.

Nic Gabhainn, S. & Sixsmith, J. (2006). Children photographing well-being: Facilitating participation in research. *Children & Society, 20*(4), 249–259. doi: 10.1111/j.1099–0860.2005.00002.x.

Olweus, D. (1978). *Aggression in the Schools: Bullies and Whipping Boys.* Washington, DC: Hemisphere.

Olweus, D. (1993). Victimization by peers: Antecedents and long-term outcomes. In K. H. Rubin & J. B. Asendorf (eds.), *Social Withdrawal, Inhibition, and Shyness in Childhood* (pp. 315–341). Hillsdale, NJ: Lawrence Erlbaum.

Peppard, J. L., Lewis, F. A., McMillan, J. M., Palmer, C. D., Lawson, M. J. & Slee, P. T. (2008). *Family Wellbeing: The Family Learning Network: An Evaluation.* Adelaide, SA: Shannon Press.

Punch, S. (2002). Research with children: The same or different from research with adults? *Childhood, 9,* 321–341. doi: 10.1177/0907568202009003005.

Shute, R. & Slee, P. T (2015). *Child Development: Theories and Critical Perspectives.* East Sussex: Routledge.

Skrzypiec, G., Murray-Harvey, R. & Krieg, S. (2013). PhotoStory method as a legitimate research tool in evaluations: More than a nice story. *Australasian Journal of Early Childhood, 38,* 25–35.

Skrzypiec, G., Slee, P. & Sandhu, D. (2015). Using the PhotoStory method to understand the cultural context of youth victimisation in the Punjab. *International Journal of Emotional Education, 7*(1), 52–68.

Slee, P. T. (2017). *School Bullying: Teachers Helping Students Cope.* London: Routledge.

Slee, P.T., Campbell, M. A. & Spears, B. (2012). *Child, Adolescent & Family Development.* Melbourne: Cambridge University Press.

Slee, P. T., Ma, L., Hee-og, S., Taki, M. & Sullivan, K. (2003). School bullying in five countries in the Asia-Pacific region. In J. Keeves & R. Watanage (eds.), *The Handbook on Educational Research in the Asia Pacific Region* (pp. 425–438). The Netherlands: Kluwer Academic Publishers.

Slee, P. T, Murray-Harvey, R., Dix, K., Russell, A., Skrzypiec G., Askell-Williams, H., Dix, K. L., Lawson, M. J. & Krieg, S. (2012). *KidsMatter Early Childhood Evaluation Report.* Adelaide: Shannon Research Press.

Slee, P. T. & Skrzypiec, G. (2015). No more bullying: An analysis of primary school children's drawings of school bullying. *Educational Psychology, 36*(8), 1487–1500. doi: 10.1080/01443410.2015.1034089.

Slee. P. T. & Skrzypiec, G. (2016). *Wellbeing, Positive Peer Relations and Bullying in School Settings.* London: Springer.

Slee, E., Skrzypiec, G., Spears, B., Campbell, M., Slee, P. T. & Wotherspoon, A. (2014). *Bullying in Schools: An Indian Perspective.* Adelaide: Flinders University.

Smith, P. K., Cowie, H., Olafsson, R. F. & Liefooghe, A. P. (2002). Definitions of bullying: A comparison of terms used, and age and gender differences, in a fourteen-country international comparison. *Child Development, 73,* 1119–1133. doi: 10.1111/1467–8624.00461.

Smith, P. K., Kwak, K. & Toda, Y. (eds.) (2016). *School Bullying in Different Cultures: Eastern and Western Perspectives.* Cambridge: Cambridge University Press.

Spears, B. A., Costabile, A., Brighi, A., Del Rey, R., Pörhölä, M., Sanchez, V. & Thompson, F. (2013). Positive uses of new technologies in relationships in educational settings. In P. K. Smith & G. Steffgen (eds.), *Cyberbullying through the New Media: Findings from an International Network* (pp. 178–201). Hove: Psychology Press.

Spears, B., Slee, P., Campbell, M. A. & Cross D. (2011). *Educational Change and Youth Voice: Informing School Action on Cyberbullying.* Melbourne: CSE Occasional Papers.

Tierney, W. G. (1996). The academic profession and the culture of the faculty: A perspective on Latin American universities. In K. Kempner & W. G. Tierney (eds.), *The Social Role of Higher Education: Comparative Perspectives* (pp. 11–26). New York: Garland Publishing.

Wang, C. & Burris, M. A. (1997). Photovoice: Concept, methodology, and use for participatory needs assessment. *Health Education and Behaviour, 24,* 369–387. doi: 10.1177/109019819702400309.

Wang, C., Burris, M. A. & Ping, X. Y. (1996). Chinese village women as visual anthropologists: A participatory approach to reaching policymakers. *Social Science & Medicine, 42,* 1391–1400. doi: 10.1016/0277–9536(95)00287–1.

11 Pre-service Teachers' Understanding of Bullying in Australia and India

Implications for Practice

Barbara A. Spears, Carmel Taddeo, Lesley-Anne Ey,
Alexander Stretton, Toby Carslake, Colette Langos,
Damanjit Sandhu and Suresh Sundaram

The dominant discourse regarding bullying and cyberbullying research to date has emphasised a strong Western-centric perspective. Whilst an increasingly substantial amount of research has emerged from non-Western countries regarding the prevalence and nature of bullying and cyberbullying (see Smith, Kwak & Toda, 2016 for an overview), a dearth of information remains about pre-service teachers' (PSTs') knowledge about bullying and cyberbullying in non-Western settings, and what the implications might be for prevention and intervention strategies in those contexts. PSTs are those who are enrolled in a teacher-education/training programme that prepares them to become teachers (in-service teachers, or ISTs). Such programmes can range from a 12-month qualification added to a previous certificate or degree, to a comprehensive four-year degree programme in an area of specialisation, each with a set number of practicum/placement days in school settings which are required to be undertaken successfully during the qualification/training period.

Studies involving PSTs have been undertaken in several Anglo-European contexts: the United Kingdom (Boulton, 1997; Boulton et al., 2014; Nicolaides, Toda & Smith, 2002), continental Europe (Begotti, Tirassa & Acquadro Maran, 2017; O'Moore, 2000), the United States (Alvarez, 2007; Bauman & Del Rio, 2005, 2006; Kahn, Jones & Wieland, 2012; Novick & Isaacs, 2010), Canada (Beran, 2005; Craig, Bell & Lescheid, 2011; Li, 2008; Lopata & Nowicki, 2014) and Australia (Lester et al., 2018; Spears, Campbell et al., 2015). But only a few are available in English from non-Western contexts. Yilmaz (2010), for example, examined PSTs' perceptions of cyberbullying in Turkey and also undertook comparative studies involving Canadian and Turkish PSTs (Thomas, Kariuki & Yilmaz, 2011). Studies of ISTs' approaches and perspectives are also beginning to emerge from non-Western settings. Yoon and colleagues (2011), for example, reported on Korean teachers' handling of an incident of school bullying, and similarly Huang and Chou (2013) explored Taiwanese teachers' perspectives of cyberbullying. This chapter extends this body of research through exploring PSTs' knowledge and understanding of bullying and cyberbullying from within and across two cultural contexts: Australia and India.

The Extent of the Problem: Prevalence Estimates in Australia and India

It is important to understand the scope of the issue in terms of why it is important for PSTs to have knowledge and understanding, particularly in relation to the two contexts for this chapter: Australia and India.

Australia

The first nationally representative cross-sectional study, the Australian Covert Bullying Prevalence Study (ACBPS) (Cross et al., 2009), found that in 2007 approximately 25% of young people in Years 4 to 9 reported experiencing traditional forms of bullying (overtly or covertly) during the past/previous term, '*every few weeks or more often*' (considered frequent), and 7% reported experiencing cyberbullying; around 10% reported perpetrating traditional bullying, and 4% reporting cyberbullying others.

Spears and colleagues (2014) examined seven major Australian studies and government-commissioned reports released between 2009 and 2014. After extrapolating across all frequencies, time frames, methodological approaches and definitions, they concluded 'that the general prevalence figure for Australian minors experiencing cyberbullying in a year is approximately 20 per cent, with a range from 6 per cent to 44 per cent' across different studies (p. 37). Rigby and Johnson (2016) examined the prevalence and effectiveness of anti-bullying strategies in Australian schools, and noted that there appeared to be a small decline in the prevalence of traditional bullying, noting 15% of students reported being bullied at the time of the inquiry (2014–2015). Determining the extent of the issue is fraught with measurement issues, but clearly many children and young people are frequently at risk in terms of their exposure to bullying within Australian schools, and PSTs should be adequately prepared upon graduation to manage bullying in schools.

India

Investigations into bullying and cyberbullying are currently limited in India, but a number of studies are reviewed in Chapters 2 and 5 of this volume, including the Intel Security study *Teens, Tweens and Technology* (2015) and the Microsoft (2012) study into online bullying. Collectively these studies indicate that young people in India are experiencing high levels of bullying and cyberbullying, and that there is an opportunity to do more to inform and educate teachers about this phenomenon so they can put mechanisms in place to support young people.

Ramya and Kulkarni (2011) explored the prevalence of bullying amongst 500 randomly selected students aged 8–14 years from five schools, finding that 60% reported bullying experiences. Of the 20 teachers who were interviewed, 8 reported no bullying in their schools. Teachers felt that victims were 'usually the academically weak, physically weak, and quiet students' (p. 310). They described the bullies as 'usually the popular, physically strong and wealthy' students and noted changes in attendance, confidence, participation and general performance amongst those victimised. They concluded that bullying was a major problem among schoolchildren in India, and that 'teachers must be adequately trained to tackle this problem' (p. 309).

Pre-service Teachers

PSTs are a crucial part of the teaching profession's regeneration and renewal processes. Teachers' knowledge of and concern for students' well-being are central to most anti-bullying initiatives (Kallestad & Olweus, 2003), but Ramya and Kulkarni (2011) found teachers in their study who believed that bullying did not occur in their schools, and if it did, justified it through blaming the victims: they were the weak students.

Building PSTs' capacity to recognise and manage bullying and cyberbullying is therefore important as both an intervention and prevention strategy: to change teacher perceptions so they first of all acknowledge there is a problem, and then to recognise that they have to do something about it. This is especially important not only for their own professional development as they transition from pre-service student to early career, IST professional, but also in terms of the role they play in the continuity of a school's anti-bullying initiatives and strategies during their practical placements and later when they are employed in a new school setting (Lester et al., 2018; Spears et al., 2015). However, the opposite is also true: without adequate knowledge, they run the risk of not being industry-ready to commence their professional careers as teachers if they arrive at a school lacking awareness, understanding or knowledge about bullying and how to deal with it, potentially undermining any existing (whole) school strategy.

Whilst students and their parents expect teachers to deal with bullying and cyberbullying, collectively, the existing body of work relating to PSTs' knowledge and understanding has found them generally *lacking* knowledge, confidence and competence in their capacity to deal with bullying (e.g. Bauman & Del Rio, 2005, 2006; Li, 2008; Nicolaides et al., 2002) and cyberbullying (Craig et al., 2011; Ryan & Kariuki, 2011; Yilmaz, 2010).

Alvarez (2007), Kochenderfer-Ladd and Pelletier (2008), and Mishna and colleagues (2005) found that both PSTs and ISTs reported not only having inadequate knowledge about bullying, but also inadequate mastery of personal intervention strategies when faced with abusive behaviours. These and other Western-oriented studies related to how teachers perceive, act and respond to bullying provide a clear message to teacher education training programmes and policymakers: that PSTs want and need to have information about bullying/cyberbullying embedded within their degree/training courses and valued as an important tool in their repertoire for managing classroom behaviour generally.

By comparison, Spears and colleagues (2015) found that 700 Australian PSTs from three universities demonstrated a level of clarity in relation to their understanding and knowledge of bullying which was not evident in earlier studies. The PSTs reported that they understood the construct of bullying and cyberbullying; largely felt informed and capable of taking action; and, when presented with different scenarios, could readily discern bullying and cyberbullying behaviours from other, non-cyber/bullying behaviours. These different findings, compared with previous studies internationally, may relate to the use of vignettes which reflected real-life scenarios and which had been verified as legitimate examples of bully/cyberbullying by an expert panel prior to use. Similar vignettes were used for the current study into Indian and Australian PSTs' knowledge and understanding (not reported here).

Similarly, Lester and colleagues (2018) found that 248 PSTs from two universities in Australia reported high levels of knowledge about bullying and cyberbullying, and again, could correctly identify cyberbullying and bullying scenarios from other behaviours, such as conflict, for example. However, whilst the PSTs from both these studies reported that their knowledge and understanding of bullying were high, they also noted that more was needed to prepare them for the reality of actually working with students in schools.

Spears and colleagues (2017), in a study for a local education authority on bullying and well-being resources, found that 98% of PSTs and 96% of ISTs wanted more information in the degree/training programme prior to employment. The majority of these PSTs felt they had been able to identify actual instances of bullying when on placement/practicum; however, two thirds were unsure when it came to their ability to identify newer forms, such as cyberbullying or sexting in the school setting. When considering how capable they felt in actually dealing with bullying when on placement, however, 47% of those who responded reported not feeling very capable. Amongst the plethora of concerns for PSTs during their practicum/placement which created stress, key challenges were having confidence and skills in recognising bullying and understanding the peer dynamic.

PSTs highlighted that knowing how to intersect with the rules and policies of the school setting, in order to deal with bullying, was especially challenging, as each school has its own culture and approach. Whilst they may have been inducted into schools' global approach to managing behaviour during their placement, they did not receive direction in how the schools chose to explicitly address bullying, and therefore how *they* would be required to act whilst in situ. The PSTs in this study noted that these challenges and stresses were also at risk of being exacerbated by poor modelling by the mentor/supervisory teacher in how to deal with bullying and cyberbullying, and by the lack of adequate resources related to that specific educational/cultural context (Spears et al., 2017).

PSTs' confidence and competence in managing student learning environments more generally has been found to predict their actual behaviours and actions, having direct implications for the effectiveness of a school's anti-bullying initiatives (Boulton et al., 2014). This relationship between one's beliefs and behaviours rests on Bandura's self-efficacy theory of behavioural change (Bandura, 1977), which contends that there are two dimensions: an 'outcome' and an 'efficacy' expectation. Outcome expectancy refers to 'a person's estimate that a given behaviour will lead to certain outcomes', whereas efficacy expectancy relates to the 'conviction that one can successfully execute the behaviour required to produce the outcomes' (p. 193).

Ensuring that PSTs have the knowledge to fuel their conviction and desire to act to stop bullying in schools is behind the call for greater education at the PST level. However, inconsistency in teacher self-efficacy in coping with student bullying in schools has been found (Beran, 2005; Bradshaw, Sawyer & O'Brennan, 2007), signalling the need for ongoing in-service professional development, as well as more education during the preparation stages of a teacher's career.

Giallo and Little (2003) in their exploration of student and graduate teachers found that preparedness and classroom experiences significantly predicted ratings of self-efficacy in managing behaviour, however, both cohorts felt 'only moderately prepared, and self-efficacious', with 85% indicating the need for additional training (p. 21). Lopata and Nowicki (2014) identified common issues amongst Canadian PSTs: lack of knowledge regarding the antecedents to bullying, holding inaccurate beliefs about bullying and lacking ability to identify those who bully. Each of these findings impacts the outcome and efficacy expectancies held by the PSTs, which in turn would impact their ability to step up to deal with bullying when needed in a school setting. Indeed, Craig and colleagues (2011, p. 3) noted that 'teachers who did not perceive bullying as serious, would be passive and ineffectual in addressing such behaviours'. Waasdorp and colleagues (2011) found that the norms and perceptions held about bullying were important aspects of a school's 'culture of bullying' (p. 128) and therefore the climate and ethos of the school to deal with it.

How PSTs fit into that climate/culture is of equal importance (Spears, Campbell et al., 2015). They have generally only been considered as part of the preparation of the workforce, to ensure they are 'industry-ready' when they graduate and can manage behaviours such as bullying appropriately. However, they also need to be seen as active agents and part of schools' intervention and prevention approaches and strategies *whilst on placement*, as it is here that they learn and rehearse techniques from their experienced mentors, in a specific educational cultural context, growing in skills and capacity over their entire training/programme (Spears et al., 2017).

The call for PSTs to learn more about bullying in their programmes has been made now for many years, from many educational cultural contexts, but it is not enough. Like all learning, it requires attention and rehearsal. Education training programmes offer significant opportunities throughout their degrees, by way of placement/practicum to do just that: in the contexts of real-world, school-based initiatives. Exploring the phenomenon as part of the degree-based programme is necessary, but not sufficient. Having the opportunity to *rehearse in situ, intersecting with real school policies and practices whilst being supported by experienced teaching staff* will provide PSTs with the lift in confidence and self-efficacy in identifying, addressing and dealing with student bullying (Spears et al., 2017).

Drawing Comparisons: An Emic-Etic Approach

According to Guillaume and Funder (2016), there are many ways to explore cultural similarities and differences, but three key approaches can be considered: absolutist, relativist or universalist. The absolutist approach looks for those characteristics which are common to us all as humans. In terms of understanding bullying, Guillaume and Funder suggest that this relates to those characteristics of bullying which are reported most frequently, regardless of culture: for example, the elements of Olweus' definition: a deliberate intent to harm, a power differential and repetition. An absolutist approach would also mean that measures developed in one cultural context could be readily imported into another. These are often referred to as *etic* approaches (Pike, 1967), where behaviours are examined from outside the cultural context. In contrast, relativists look for characteristics and behaviours moderated by culture (Guillaume & Funder, 2016) which are qualitatively different within cultures, and which are therefore not comparable across cultures. These are known as *emic* approaches which examine behaviour within a culture or system (Pike, 1967). The relativist approach requires that measures be constructed *within* cultural contexts (p. 215) so as to overcome methodological and cultural biases inherent when trying to import existing surveys and measures.

The universalist approach tries to understand the interactions between cultures and looks for both similarities and differences. This approach recognises that some measures would be imported across cultural boundaries to capture the universality of bullying behaviours, but that other, more qualitative methods would be needed to fully understand the idiosyncrasies of the cultures in question. In cultures where there is no single word for bullying, for example, using a standard survey/instrument to explore the universality of bullying as a phenomenon would sit alongside qualitative studies designed to understand the lived reality of such behaviours and the terms used to describe them within the particular context.

Schooling, whilst inherently national in cultural quality and tone, is also ubiquitous across all contexts, and is subject to national and transnational influences. Schooling is shaped by a world culture of values and beliefs about what education is and its functions, yet remains unique within its own context. In terms of understanding comparative education and schooling contexts, world culture theorists propose a global culture of schooling. Anderson-Levitt (2003), in considering whether there is a global culture of schooling, reflected on the differences in thought between anthropologists, who emphasise variation across countries, and also between districts/schools/classrooms and sociologists/world culture theorists, who argue that schools around the world are converging, becoming more similar over time, heading towards a single global model of common educational principles, policies and practices, yet with varying national characteristics.

In support of a global model of schooling, Anderson-Levitt (2003) cites increasingly commonly held views and ideals of education, where education is a universal human right, can have real and positive effects and is a contributor to productivity/economic growth and national development. Commonalities in basic organisation such as increasing female participation globally; mass compulsory education; quality assurance; performance-based management and accountability to centralised national ministries; and the collection of education statistics, such as high-stakes testing of students in core areas, as markers of how well or otherwise a society is performing are also noted. However, the reality is that schools vary in practice – in how these ideals, structures, principles and accountabilities play out in situ – and there are often emerging contradictions, tensions and differences as each nation tries to locate education to maximise its social, economic and political benefits.

The importance of this discussion is to consider not only how and in what ways Australia and India are similar, in a 'global theory of schooling' and universalist sense, but also how and where they are different, in an etic/emic sense, so that the implications of the findings from PSTs in these contexts, in relation to their knowledge and understanding of bullying, can be considered.

In many ways, India and Australia would seem to be vastly different sociocultural contexts, yet there are some areas of historical commonality which position these countries in similar ways. India, once colonised by the British, is a multilingual, multi-ethnic and pluralistic society, where there can be extreme differences between each region, across different religious beliefs and between different social strata, or castes. It is also one of the world's oldest cultures. Australia, by contrast, is a relatively recent multicultural society, founded upon European discovery and colonialisation only 200-plus years ago, but with an equally ancient and rich Indigenous people's culture, reaching back more than 45,000 years. Historically, both countries have been influenced by British culture: both have adopted variations of the British legal and educational systems; English is spoken in both contexts, and is specifically taught in schools in India. Similar to Australia, compulsory schooling exists in India for the first 10 years, and government and non-government schools are common to both.

Brislin (1976) noted that *emic analyses* in comparative research methodologies described behaviour in any one culture, taking account of what was valued as meaningful and important to that culture, whereas *etic analyses* aimed to generalise across cultures, taking into account broader human behaviours. An *emic–etic* distinction/metaphor in the cultural literature (Harris, 1976; Triandis & Brislin, 1984) suggests that culture-common (*etic*) and culture-specific (*emic*) aspects of concepts should be expected and sought. Whilst there are obvious cultural, social, economic and educational differences between countries, and indeed within communities, the similarities between them are also evident, making cross-comparative research highly relevant.

The current study employed surveys in two cultural contexts to explore PSTs' knowledge and understanding of bullying. Analyses and discussion are considered using an emic (within culture)/etic (across cultures) approach.

Methodology

An exploratory, mixed-method, cross-sectional survey design was employed. Questionnaires were developed from existing published studies, and included novel questions to gather culturally relevant knowledge about bullying. Surveys were checked by the key researchers in each region for clarity and relevance. Wording was also pre-tested in situ by a group of Indian teachers attending an in-service training. Opportunity and convenience sampling were employed to recruit PSTs (total N = 687) from teacher education programmes in two regions in India, Punjab (n = 209) and Tamil Nadu (n = 300), and two universities in Australia (n = 178). The Human Research Ethics Committee (HREC) of the University of South Australia granted approval to conduct anonymous surveys about bullying in both countries. The principals/heads of school/relevant authorities of each university were approached and consent was granted for PSTs to participate. Completion of the questionnaire indicated individual informed consent.

Procedure

Punjab: Data were collected by research teams who distributed hard copy surveys to PSTs from a high-ranking private education college (n = 70) in an urban setting, an urban government education college (n = 70) and a rural government education college (n = 69).

Tamil Nadu: The survey was also completed in English at two institutions in South India: a university (n = 200) and a college of education (n = 100). The students were from both bachelor and master of education courses. The (hard copy) questionnaire was distributed and data were collected under the personal supervision of the key researcher in that area.

Australia: PSTs from two universities (n = 178) were invited by email distribution lists to complete online surveys.

A coding sheet was developed, data entry was completed in each country and the data files were subsequently merged for analysis for use with the IBM SPSS Statistics, V 23 package. Qualitative responses to open-ended questions were reviewed by four independent researchers for trustworthiness and legitimacy of the ideas (micro themes), and macro themes were subsequently noted.

Results and Discussion

An emic (within cultures/culture specific) and etic (across cultures/culture common) analysis framework was employed to explore key similarities and differences: firstly, *within* sample as determined by geographic location – *emic*; and secondly, *across samples*, India and Australia – *etic*. Awareness, experience, perceptions of bullying, perceived capacity to deal with school bullying and sources of information about bullying were explored.

India: Emic – Culture Specific
Awareness and Experiences of Bullying   Table 11.1 shows whether PSTs had witnessed or were aware of bullying in a school setting. About half of Indian PSTs had witnessed or were aware of this, with nearly a quarter stating they were unsure. PSTs from the Tamil region were more likely to have not witnessed or been aware of school bullying, whilst those from the Punjab region were more likely to indicate they were unsure.

Table 11.1 *Geographic region by awareness of bullying problems in schools (numbers; percentages in parentheses)*

	PSTs' geographic region			
	Punjab PSTs	Tamil PSTs	All Indian PSTs	Australian PSTs
Yes	109 (52.2%)	127 (47.2%)	236 (49.4%)	106 (79.1%)
Unsure	64 (30.6%)	44 (16.4%)	108 (22.6%)	10 (7.5%)
No	36 (17.2%)	98 (36.4%)	134 (28.0%)	18 (13.4%)
Total	209 (100.0%)	269 (100.0%)	478 (100.0%)	134 (100.o%)

Punjabi versus Tamil, χ^2 = 26.7, df = 2. Cramer's V = −0.24. p < 0.001
Indian versus Australian, χ^2 = 38.0, df = 2. Cramer's V =−0.25. p < 0.001

Whilst there is no one word equivalent to *bullying* in India (see Chapters 4 and 13), a scan of the examples provided indicates that PSTs are aware of the type of behaviours and situations considered bullying in their contexts. For example:

> *He was never included in any of their entire class play* (Punjab, Male, 23 years).
> *He belonged to a lower caste and hence was not made a part of their team* (Punjab, Male, 23 years).
> *Someone daily punctured my friend's bicycle* (Punjab, Male, 22 years).
> *They will often lock him in the school toilet* (Punjab, Female, 22 years).
> *A lower-caste boy was made fun of by some upper-caste girls* (Punjab, Female, 23 years).
> *The fat boy beat the weak boy every time* (Tamil Nadu, Male, 27 years).
> *11th and 12th students ragging the junior students* (Tamil Nadu, Female, 21 years).

Table 11.2a shows whether Indian PSTs had experienced school bullying as a child or young person. Almost half of PSTs indicated they had been bullied, with a further quarter reporting they were 'unsure'. Uncertainty around their experiences in relation to bullying may reflect a lack of knowledge or clarity with regard to the formal definition of bullying and/or what actually constitutes bullying in their geo-sociocultural contexts. PSTs from the Punjab region reported they were more likely to have experienced bullying as a child, or were unsure, compared to those from Tamil Nadu. When frequency of self-reported childhood bullying experiences was examined in more detail (see Table 11.2b; data also available for

Table 11.2 *Geographic region by experience of childhood bullying (numbers; percentages in parentheses)*
(a) yes/unsure/no by Indian region

	PSTs' geographic region		
	Punjab PSTs	Tamil PSTs	All Indian PSTs
Yes	118	126	244
	(56.5%)	(44.7%)	(49.7%)
Unsure	65	56	121
	(31.1%)	(19.9%)	(24.6%)
No	26	100	126
	(12.4%)	(35.5%)	(25.7%)
Total	209	282	491
	(100.0%)	(100.1%)	(100.0%)

Punjabi versus Tamil, $\chi^2 = 34.3$, df = 2. Phi = -0.26. p < 0.001

(b) *more detailed breakdown by frequency, for all regions*

	PSTs' geographic region			
	Punjab PSTs $M = 4.50$ $SD = 1.19$	Tamil PSTs $M = 3.38$ $SD = 2.13$	All Indian PSTs $M = 3.73$ $SD = 1.95$	Australian PSTs $M = 2.94$ $SD = 1.39$
Almost every day	28 (22.8%)	78 (28.8%)	106 (26.9%)	6 (4.3%)
Most days	40 (32.5%)	39 (14.4%)	79 (20.1%)	22 (15.7%)
Once a week	28 (22.8%)	12 (4.4%)	40 (10.2%)	15 (10.7%)
Every few weeks	19 (15.4%)	9 (3.3%)	28 (7.1%)	24 (17.1%)
Only once or twice	8 (6.5%)	46 (17.0%)	54 (13.7%)	60 (42.9%)
Never	0 (0.0%)	87 (32.1%)	87 (22.1%)	13 (9.3%)
Total	123 (100.0%)	271 (100.0%)	394 (100.0%)	140 (100.0%)

Punjabi versus Tamil, $t(375.7) = 6.62$, $p < 0.001$, Cohen's $d = 0.65$
Indian versus Australian, $t(532) = -5.19$, $p < 0.001$, Cohen's $d = 0.47$

Australian PSTs), Punjab PSTs were *victimised* significantly *more often/ frequently* than PSTs from Tamil Nadu.

What is emerging through these data are the subgroup differences (northern/southern) within the broader notion of an Indian cultural context. The universality of experience of bullying exists for these PSTs, yet remains qualified by their individual understanding of the concept, and the different sociocultural sub-contexts of these two regions. In reality, their experiences are relativist: each is informed by their own socio-geographic contexts within the larger culture which makes up India. Again, the level of uncertainty regarding having been bullied or not could be an indicator that the notion of bullying per se may be unclear in this context, making it difficult to differentiate bullying from other non-bullying behaviours, such as conflict, for example.

One of the unique aspects of Indian culture relates to the role that caste and status play in society generally, whereby there are legitimate, ancient sociocultural power imbalances in play. India's constitution forbids negative public discrimination on the basis of caste, and upholds basic rights for all, including the right to equality and equal protection before the law (http://countrystudies.us/india/89.htm). There have been recent moves to break down barriers, yet the social system remains concerned with social rank and stratification in which individuals are born into certain castes which remain fixed for life. One's name, accent, local language, place of origin, profession and dress have all been markers of caste differences in India in the past, but this is slowly changing.

One function of the caste system is a hierarchical distribution of power, meaning that imbalances of power exist as the norm for most; thus bullying, which is inherently concerned with aggression and power imbalances, may not be perceived as unusual or unique in this regard. Being uncertain if you have been bullied, or indeed feeling that you never have been bullied is not so surprising in a context where there is no single word equivalent, and where power imbalance is the societal norm.

Perceptions of Bullying   Table 11.3 shows whether PSTs thought that bullying behaviour was a problem in schools. Almost two thirds of Indian PSTs thought it was, with one fifth unsure. More PSTs from the Punjab reported that bullying was an issue in Indian schools, compared to those from Tamil Nadu.

Table 11.4 shows data by government and private schools in India (data also available for Australian PSTs). PSTs in India were asked to consider their government (accessible to all) and private (fee for service)

Table 11.3 *Geographic region by perceptions of whether bullying is a problem in schools (numbers; percentages in parentheses)*

	PSTs' geographic region			
	Punjab PSTs	Tamil PSTs	All Indian PSTs	Australian PSTs
Yes	183	144	327	137
	(87.6%)	(49.0%)	(65.0%)	(90.7%)
Unsure	26	79	105	12
	(12.4%)	(26.9%)	(20.9%)	(7.9%)
No	0	71	71	2
	(0.0%)	(24.1%)	(14.1%)	(1.3%)
Total	209	294	503	151
	(100.0%)	(100.0%)	(100.0%)	(99.9%)

Punjabi versus Tamil, χ^2 = 90.6, df = 2. Cramer's V =−0.42. p < 0.001
Indian versus Australian, χ^2 = 38.7, df = 2. Cramer's V =−0.24. p < 0.001

Table 11.4 *Geographic region by perceptions of how frequently bullying happens in schools (numbers; percentages in parentheses), broken down by type of school (in India)*

	PSTs' geographic region						
	Punjab PSTs		Tamil PSTs		All Indian PSTs		Australian PSTs
	Government	Private	Government	Private	Government	Private	(All schools)
Almost every day	90 (43.1%)	16 (7.7%)	83 (30.5%)	51 (19.4%)	173 (36.0%)	67 (14.2%)	72 (61.5%)
Most days	73 (34.9%)	43 (20.6%)	98 (36.0%)	94 (35.7%)	171 (35.6%)	137 (29.0%)	26 (22.2%)
Once a week	31 (14.8%)	46 (22.0%)	21 (7.7%)	15 (5.7%)	52 (10.8%)	61 (12.9%)	11 (9.4%)
Every few weeks	13 (6.2%)	73 (34.9%)	13 (4.8%)	14 (5.3%)	26 (5.4%)	87 (18.4%)	6 (5.1%)
Only once or twice	2 (1.0%)	29 (13.9%)	36 (13.2%)	46 (17.5%)	38 (7.9%)	75 (15.9%)	2 (1.7%)
Never	0 (0.0%)	2 (1.0%)	21 (7.7%)	43 (16.3%)	21 (4.4%)	45 (9.5%)	0 (0.0%)
Total	209	209	272	263	481	472	117
	$M = 5.13$	$M = 3.70$	$M = 4.43$	$M = 3.85$	$M = 4.73$	$M = 3.79$	$M = 5.37$
	$SD = 0.95$	$SD = 1.19$	$SD = 1.64$	$SD = 1.83$	$SD = 1.42$	$SD = 1.58$	$SD = 0.97$
	100.0%	100.0%	100.0%	100.0%	100.0%	100.0%	100.0%

Notes: *Almost every day = 6; Never = 1*
Punjabi versus Tamil (Government), $t(448.2) = 5.9$, $p < 0.001$, Cohen's $d = 0.51$
Punjabi versus Tamil (Private), $t(453.6) = -1.06$, ns, Cohen's $d = 0.09$

school settings. The distinction between these schools is complex, and relates to differences between 'aided' (government funded) and 'unaided' schools in both the private and government sectors; student-teacher ratios; teacher salaries, training and accountability – as well as to schools which are 'recognised' or 'unrecognised': recognised schools have met the regulatory requirements of the state, and unrecognised schools have either not applied for or have not succeeded in gaining recognition (Goyal & Pandey, 2009).

Nearly three quarters thought that bullying occurred in Indian government schools either '*almost every day*' or '*most days*' compared to less than one third who thought it occurred so frequently in private schools. There was no difference between Tamil and Punjabi PSTs in terms of the overall bullying they perceived occurring within private schools, but Punjabi PSTs thought more bullying occurred more frequently in government schools overall, than did PSTs from Tamil Nadu.

PSTs' perceptions of the magnitude (scale, significance or importance) of the problem of bullying were examined on a scale from 0 (no problem) to 10 (major problem), with PSTs perceiving the problem as greater in government schools (see Table 11.5). Punjabi PSTs, however, perceived the magnitude of the bullying problem as higher/greater in *both* private and government schools, than did PSTs from the Tamil Nadu region.

Again, the universality of the perception of the magnitude of the problem of bullying in Indian schools was evident, but was qualified by system and region, suggesting that any prevention or intervention initiatives must really pay attention to the relative, specific needs of the school

Table 11.5 *Geographic region by perceptions of the magnitude of the problem of bullying in schools*

PSTs' geographic region						
Punjab PSTs		Tamil PSTs		All Indian PSTs		Australian PSTs
Government	Private	Government	Private	Government	Private	All Schools
209	209	298	300	507	509	148
$M = 8.01$	$M = 4.92$	$M = 5.51$	$M = 4.43$	$M = 6.54$	$M = 4.63$	$M = 6.58$
$SD = 0.95$	$SD = 1.43$	$SD = 3.30$	$SD = 2.72$	$SD = 2.88$	$SD = 2.29$	$SD = 1.68$

Notes: 0 = *no problem;* 10 = *major problem*
Punjabi versus Tamil Private, $t(474.8) = 2.64$, p < 0.01, Cohen's $d = 0.22$
Punjabi versus Tamil Government, $t(363.7) = 12.39$, p < 0.001, Cohen's $d = 1.03$

community and its context, rather than adopting a one-size-fits-all model across the country.

Capacity to Deal with School Bullying   Table 11.6 shows how informed, capable and confident PSTs felt about school bullying, by region.

Approximately half of the Indian PSTs reported they did not feel very informed, did not feel very capable/competent and did not feel very confident about dealing with school bullying incidents. This reinforces the real and pressing need to build Indian PSTs' capacity to competently identify and address bullying-related issues in their contexts. However, there was a strong and significant difference between the Punjab and Tamil PSTs. About three quarters of Tamil Nadu PSTs expressed at least some extent of being informed, capable/competent and confident, whereas very few Punjab PSTs did so.

Training and Professional Development   Table 11.7 outlines how PSTs are sourcing their information about bullying and reveals that for the Indian PSTs, very little education is being provided through their degree programmes. It is not surprising to see that many have indicated that general media and the Internet, including social media, were the most common sources of information about bullying, particularly for PSTs from the Punjab, who reported receiving no information from their university courses. This highlights a need for greater input from the education/ training organisations to help ensure credibility of information sourced. Given that the socio-geographic contexts of the north (Punjab) and south (Tamil Nadu) appear to have different needs and levels of knowledge, perceptions and experiences in relation to bullying, it would seem important that the education/training organisations in each context take some responsibility for ensuring that the PSTs are exposed to and equipped with relevant resources for the schools in which they will eventually teach.

Table 11.8 outlines PSTs' views on the importance of providing teacher training on strategies to deal with bullying. Nearly three quarters of participants thought this was necessary or essential, with more Punjabi PSTs thinking this than their counterparts from Tamil Nadu.

Collectively these results indicate that whilst there were some aspects of bullying which appear absolutist in nature: i.e. common across the Indian subcultures (Punjab and Tamil Nadu regions), as evidenced by the examples of bullying they provided and by their view of the need to train teachers in strategies to deal with bullying, within-country differences (relativist/culture specific) were evident in relation to knowledge, experiences and understanding of bullying. These findings highlight the need for a universalist approach to prevention and intervention in India

Table 11.6 *Geographic region by extent to which PSTs felt informed; capable/competent and confident about school bullying (numbers; percentages in parentheses)*

		PSTs' geographic region			
		Punjab PSTs	Tamil PSTs	All Indian PSTs	Australian PSTs
Informed	Very informed	0 (0.0%)	66 (22.0%)	66 (13.0%)	8 (5.4%)
	Informed	15 (7.2%)	171 (57.0%)	186 (36.5%)	85 (57.8%)
	Not very informed	194 (92.8%)	63 (21.0%)	257 (50.5%)	54 (36.7%)
	Total	209 (100.0%)	294 (100.0%)	509 (100.0%)	147 (99.9%)
Capable/Competent	Very capable/ competent	2 (1.0%)	67 (22.3%)	69 (13.6%)	7 (4.8%)
	Capable/competent	13 (6.2%)	176 (58.7%)	189 (37.1%)	87 (59.2%)
	Not very capable/ competent	194 (92.8%)	57 (19.0%)	251 (49.3%)	53 (36.1%)
	Total	209 (100.0%)	300 (100.0%)	509 (100.0%)	147 (100.1%)

Confident					
Very confident	3	79	82	7
	(1.4%)	(26.3%)	(16.1%)	(4.8%)
Confident	17	158	175	75
	(8.1%)	(52.7%)	(34.4%)	(51.0%)
Not very confident	189	63	252	65
	(90.4%)	(21.0%)	(49.5%)	(44.2%)
Total	209	300	509	147
	(99.9%)	(100.0%)	(100.0%)	(100.0%)

Notes:

Informed: Punjabi versus Tamil, $\chi^2 = 255.5$, df = 2. Cramer's V =−0.71. p < 0.001
Indian versus Australian, $\chi^2 = 22.8$, df = 2. Cramer's V = −0.19. p < 0.001
Capable/Competent: Punjabi versus Tamil, $\chi^2 = 268.9$, df = 2. Cramer's V = −0.73. p < 0.001
Indian versus Australian, $\chi^2 = 25.1$, df = 2. Cramer's V = −0.20. p < 0.001
Confident: Punjabi versus Tamil, $\chi^2 = 238.4$, df = 2. Cramer's V = −0.68. p < 0.001
Indian versus Australian, $\chi^2 = 20.0$, df = 2. Cramer's V = −0.17. p < 0.001

Table 11.7 *Geographic region by source of bullying information (numbers; percentages in parentheses)*

Source of Information	Punjab PSTs (n = 209)	Tamil PSTs (n = 300)	All Indian PSTs (n = 509)	Australian PSTs (n = 178)
University courses	0 (0.0%)	61 (20.3%)	61 (12.0%)	62 (34.8%)
Professional reading	63 (30.1%)	55 (18.3%)	118 (23.2%)	50 (28.1%)
General media (e.g. television)	177 (84.7%)	130 (43.3%)	307 (60.3%)	100 (56.2%)
Internet (including social media)	185 (88.5%)	53 (17.7%)	238 (46.8%)	85 (47.8%)
Family	87 (41.6%)	18 (6.0%)	105 (20.6%)	62 (34.8%)
Friends	134 (64.1%)	49 (16.3%)	183 (36.0%)	73 (41.0%)
Other	6 (2.9%)	21 (7.0%)	27 (5.3%)	61 (34.3%)

Notes: Multiple selections were possible.

Table 11.8 *Geographic region by importance of providing teacher training on strategies to deal with bullying*

	PSTs' geographic region			
	Punjab PSTs	Tamil PSTs	All Indian PSTs	Australian PSTs
Very necessary/ essential	148 (71.2%)	81 (34.3%)	229 (51.6%)	100 (86.2%)
Useful/necessary	52 (25.0%)	42 (17.8%)	94 (21.2%)	15 (12.9%)
No strong views	52 (3.8%)	32 (13.6%)	40 (9.0%)	0 (0.0%)
Not very necessary	0 (0.0%)	25 (10.6%)	25 (5.6%)	1 (0.9%)
Not at all necessary	0 (0.0%)	56 (23.7%)	56 (12.6%)	0 (0.0%)
Total	208 $M = 4.67$ $SD = 0.55$ 100.0%	236 $M = 3.28$ $SD = 1.59$ 100.0%	444 $M = 3.93$ $SD = 1.40$ 100.0%	116 $M = 4.84$ $SD = 0.43$ 100.0%

Notes: Not at all necessary = 1; Very necessary/essential = 5
Punjab versus Tamil, $t(295.9) = 12.59$, $p < 0.001$, Cohen's $d = 1.17$
Indian versus Australian, $t(546.7) = 11.73$, $p < 0.001$, Cohen's $d = 0.88$

which incorporates the similarities, but which simultaneously caters to the differences relevant and relative to the knowledge and understanding evident in each of those contexts.

Australia: Emic – Culture Specific
Awareness and Experiences of Bullying   After being provided with a definition of bullying, PSTs were asked if they had witnessed or were aware of bullying in schools (see Table 11.1). Nearly four fifths said they had. This is important as it relates to PSTs' ability to identify actual bullying behaviours in school settings, as distinct from simply knowing the definition. A scan of the examples provided indicated PSTs could readily identify bullying situations:

> *Exclusion and verbal abuse. I have seen physical violence between students as well* (Male, 30 years).
> *Leaving a child out regularly from play/conversation. Speaking negatively about the child in front of others and laughing* (Female, 40 years).
> *In some instances girls would get together and plan to wear their hair a certain way and tell certain girls but not all of them, so one girl would not be wearing the same hairstyle and therefore be left out of the group* (Female, 20 years).
> *I have witnessed a child from a low socio-economic background being bullied by a couple of children for how they were dressed and how their hair was cut; the reasoning behind the bullying was because the child was not up with the fashion even though she was dressed neatly* (Female, 43 years).
> *Antagonizing to the point of violence. Insults, cyberbullying in the form of sharing inappropriate pictures and derogatory language. Purposely excluding a student from classroom activities and outside activities* (Female, 23 years).

Table 11.2b outlines the frequency of childhood experiences of bullying. Nearly three quarters of the Australian PSTs responded and of those, nearly half reported having been bullied every few weeks or more often as a child or young person.

These data, as with the Indian data, represent adult reflections drawn across extended time frames, and not recent events. Whilst retrospective data can be problematic, Rivers (2001, p. 129) found that memory 'may be a useful indicator of reliability', cautioning that it should not replace longitudinal research. What the data do indicate however, is that very few Australian (or Indian) adults come through their childhood/adolescence untouched by bullying in our schools.

Perceptions of Bullying   As shown in Table 11.3, the overwhelming majority of PSTs felt that bullying was a problem in schools. This belief was supported by their perceptions of how often they thought bullying was occurring each term in Australian schools (see Table 11.4). More than four fifths thought that bullying was occurring most days or almost every day. Further, mean analysis (range 0 to 10) suggested that Australian PSTs felt the magnitude of the problem of bullying (its scale, significance and importance) was a serious concern in Australian schools (see Table 11.5).

These high levels of expectancy concerning the prevalence and magnitude of bullying in schools also relate to the conviction that one holds regarding successful prevention strategies or being able to intervene (Bandura, 1977). This expectancy in turn must impact PSTs' performance outcomes in terms of their confidence, competence, perceived efficacy and capacity to deal with bullying, both when on placement and when they graduate. This affirms that more needs to be done during their preparation to be teachers.

Capacity to Deal with School Bullying   As shown in Table 11.6, just more than a third of Australian PSTs reported they felt *not* very informed, or very capable/competent to deal with school bullying incidents, with nearly two fifths indicating they also did *not* feel very confident. The corollary of this, and on a somewhat positive note, was that around two thirds felt informed, capable and, to a lesser degree, confident. This does not necessarily mean this will translate into actual ability to deal with bullying in situ, and a need remains to support PSTs when on placement and when they emerge as commencing teachers.

Training and Professional Development   Table 11.7 indicates that approximately half of the Australian PSTs reported that their learning about bullying was informed by the general media and the Internet, rather than within their teacher education programmes. Whilst these avenues can provide valid sources of bullying-related information, it does raise questions about the level of digital literacy of PSTs to rely on locating and distinguishing evidence-informed sources of information from other less reliable sites. It is telling indeed that *all but one* PST felt that it was necessary or essential to have training during their degrees on strategies to deal with bullying (see Table 11.8).

Australian PSTs perceive bullying in schools is a problem, and it is occurring at high levels each term. Their reflections also indicate that most adults are likely to have had some experience of school bullying as a child or young person. They also firmly believe that there is a role for PST education to support them: to build their capacity and their efficacy to be able to deal with these behaviours on placement and when they graduate.

The final section examines these across contexts (etic) and provides an entry point for considering what is universally understood about bullying by PSTs in this study, and what is relative to the cultural contexts of each of these two countries.

India and Australia: Etic – Across Cultures

Many PSTs reported that they had experienced bullying as a child/young person. Of those who responded to this question, 93.5% from Punjab, 50.9% from Tamil Nadu and 47.8% from Australia indicated that they had experienced bullying *every few weeks or more often* (see Table 11.2b). This is a sobering finding, and speaks to the universality of this behaviour, and the likelihood that many will be influenced by it during their life course.

Collective Perceptions of Bullying in Schools   Table 11.3 showed a higher percentage of Australian PSTs perceived bullying as a problem in schools, compared to their Indian counterparts, who were significantly more likely to report that they were either unsure about bullying being a problem in their schools or did not feel that it was a problem. Australian PSTs also indicated that they perceived bullying as a more frequent issue in schools overall than their Indian counterparts (see Table 11.4). This could relate to their awareness, as a higher number of Australian PSTs reported they had witnessed or were aware of bullying in schools, in comparison to Indian PSTs (see Table 11.1). In terms of their perception of the magnitude of the problem (see Table 11.5), all PSTs reported that bullying was a serious problem, highlighting the universality of the issue for schools, yet the cultural contexts of the nature of the schooling systems and the geographic location in India seem pertinent.

After several decades of awareness raising and education about bullying in Australian school communities, this difference is not surprising and relates to several possibilities which have increased sensitivity and awareness in Australia, which are yet to be adopted in India: that the word *bullying* and the associated behaviours are well understood; that a consistent definition of the behaviour is used; and that most schools have an anti-bullying or well-being policy enshrined within the National Safe Schools Framework, which has provided a vision for schools through policy guidance since 2003 and expects all Australian schools to be 'safe supportive and respectful teaching and learning communities that promote student wellbeing' (MCEECDYA, 2011, p. 3). This national framework has been reviewed in 2017 and an updated version will be released to all Australian schools during 2018.

Capacity for Dealing with Bullying in Schools   There were significant relationships between country and the extent to which participants felt *informed, capable/competent* and *confident* to deal with bullying in schools (see Table 11.6). Whilst Australian PSTs were significantly more likely than Indian PSTs to report they generally felt informed, capable/competent and confident to deal with school bullying, Indian PSTs were significantly more likely to report either extreme: feeling *very* informed, capable/competent and confident, or the opposite, *not* feeling very informed, capable/competent and confident. As such, this suggests there may be greater variation amongst the Indian PSTs with regard to their perceived capacity to deal with school bullying, and speaks to the need for a unified approach across contexts and training.

Training and Professional Development   PSTs across both countries also tended to source information about bullying from informal avenues, particularly the Internet and social media, rather than through their institutions as part of their degree/training (Table 11.7). This finding highlights a double edge: that media and technology could potentially provide a relevant, accessible channel for delivering credible, accurate information to PSTs about dealing with school bullying; however, there is currently little in the way of ensuring the quality or relevance of information accessed through this medium generally, let alone for non-Western contexts. As most of the information available online generally relates to an understanding of bullying and cyberbullying derived from Western cultural settings/contexts, there is a need for culturally relevant websites and evidence-informed strategies for specific cultural contexts, so that the level and quality of information provided to that community is evidence-informed, relevant and relative to practitioners in those settings. Publication and dissemination of reputable websites to school communities must then form part of any budgetary consideration to ensure that PSTs are informed of their existence.

Whilst both cohorts acknowledged the importance of training, and most thought it was necessary or essential, more Australian PSTs felt it was essential to train educators to deal with school bullying (see Table 11.8).

Conclusions

PSTs are training to be teachers of, and responsible for, the next generations. Skilling them and building their capacity, efficacy and confidence to deal with bullying is important, not only for the students they will teach but also in terms of sustaining themselves in the profession, and for the continuity of existing programmes in schools. As school systems around the world increasingly become more similar, supporting a global cultural theory of schooling, dealing with bullying becomes a universal problem, with ISTs' and PSTs' roles critical in ensuring quality of education and equity of outcomes for every student.

Mishna and colleagues (2005) noted that the significance a teacher ascribes to incidences of bullying they witness shapes their approach and therefore their decision to intervene or not. This highlights the importance of providing PSTs with a thorough understanding of bullying as it is *universally* understood: as a negative behaviour premised upon a deliberate intent to harm, concerned with power differences between the parties and often repeated over time. It also highlights the need to *contextualise* understanding bullying to the relevant cultural and school context.

The sheer size and diversity of India's population means that a focus on socio-geographical subsets, such as those in this study (Punjab in the north and Tamil Nadu in the south) is important. In this way, absolute (culture common) and universal (interactions across boundaries) understandings of bullying could sit alongside context-specific (relativist) evidence to inform local education practices and sectors.

Listening to PSTs' views acknowledges them as important contributors to the bigger picture of prevention and intervention strategies. As summarised by PSTs:

All students have a human right to feel safe within the school environment. Effective training of teachers will hopefully ensure that most cases of bullying will not go unnoticed and appropriate solutions can be found (Australia, Female, 23 years).

Bullying can be stressful for the teacher too as they have a duty of care to their students, so they need to know what to do when faced with such a situation (Australia, Female, 21 years).

Training teachers in dealing with bullying incidents at school will protect children from the suffering and harassment that they face due to school bullying (Punjab, Male, 23 years).

Trained teachers can contribute in making schools safe for the pupils (Punjab, Female, 22 years).

Some limitations need to be noted. As a cross-sectional study, data were collected at a single point in time and the purposive and convenience sampling approach raises questions concerning response and non-response bias. As such, conclusions cannot be drawn in relation to a wider population, restricting any generalisations in relation to PSTs across all Indian and Australian states and jurisdictions. The survey was conducted in English, and in both online (Australia) and paper-and-pencil (Indian) formats, and language and technology barriers may have impacted the data quality. The language limitation meant that only

English-speaking participants from relevant colleges/universities could be recruited. In order to ensure consistency in delivery of the protocols/ instructions during the dissemination of surveys, however, the key researchers were closely involved.

This chapter represents a unique collaboration and contribution to knowledge about PSTs' understanding of bullying through a comparative study of PSTs in India and Australia. The implications of this study for prevention and intervention are clear: PSTs have an important role to play, and if they are to commit to the belief that they can do something about bullying, then they need to be mentored, trained and supported as part of an holistic approach. PSTs in Australia and India are quite similar in many ways: they want more education, more skills development and more information to grow their capacity to support students' well-being and learning outcomes.

References

Alvarez, H. K. (2007). The impact of teacher preparation on responses to student aggression in the classroom. *Teaching and Teacher Education, 23*(7), 1113–1126.

Anderson-Levitt, K. (2003). A world culture of schooling? In K. Anderson-Levitt (ed.), *Local Meanings, Global Schooling: Anthropology and World Culture Theory* (pp. 1–26). New York: Palgrave Macmillan.

Australian Bureau of Statistics (ABS). (2014). Schools Australia 4221.0 Table 40a Number of Full Time Students 2000–2014. Retrieved from www.abs.gov .au/AUSSTATS/abs@.nsf/DetailsPage/4221.02014?OpenDocument.

Australian Bureau of Statistics (ABS). (2013). Australian Demographic Statistics3101.0 Table 59. Estimated Resident Population by Single Year of Age, Australia, Retrieved from www.abs.gov.au/ausstats/abs@archive.nsf/log?ope nagent&3101059.xls&3101.0&Time%20Series%20Spreadsheet&126E206869 D54112CA257CA7000DD128&0&Sep%202013&27.03.2014&Latest.

Bandura, A. (1977). Self-efficacy: Toward a unifying theory of behavioural change. *Psychological Review, 84*, 191–215.

Barnes, A., Cross, D., Lester, L., Hearn, L., Epstein, M. & Monks, H. (2012). The invisibility of covert bullying among students: Challenges for school intervention. *Australian Journal of Guidance and Counselling, 22*(2), 206–226.

Bauman, S. & Del Rio, A. (2005). Knowledge and beliefs about bullying in schools. Comparing pre-service teachers in the United States and the United Kingdom. *School Psychology International, 26*(4), 428–442.

Bauman, S. & Del Rio, A. (2006). Preservice teachers' responses to bullying scenarios: Comparing physical, verbal, and relational bullying. *Journal of Educational Psychology, 98*(1), 219–231.

Begotti, T., Tirassa, M. & Acquadro Maran, D. (2017). School bullying episodes: Attitudes and intervention in pre-service and in-service Italian teachers. *Research Papers in Education*, *32*(2), 170–182.

Beran, T. (2005). A new perspective on managing school bullying: Pre-service teachers' attitudes. *Journal of Social Science*, *8*, 43–49.

Boulton, M. J. (1997). Teachers' views on bullying: Definitions, attitudes and ability to cope. *British Journal of Educational Psychology*, *67*(2), 223–233.

Boulton, M. J., Hardcastle, K., Down, J., Fowles, J. & Simmonds, J. A. (2014). A comparison of preservice teachers' responses to cyber versus traditional bullying scenarios: Similarities and differences and implications for practice. *Journal of Teacher Education*, *65*(2), 145–155.

Bradshaw, C. P., Sawyer, A. L. & O'Brennan, L. M. (2007). Bullying and peer victimization at school: Perceptual differences between students and school staff. *School Psychology Review*, *36*(3), 361–382.

Brislin, R. W. (1976). Comparative research methodology: Cross-cultural studies. *International Journal of Psychology*, *11*(3), 215–229.

Craig, K., Bell, D. & Lescheid, A. (2011). Pre-service teachers' knowledge and attitudes regrading school-based bullying. *Canadian Journal of Education*, *34* (2), 21–33.

Cross, D., Shaw, T., Hearn, L., Epstein, M., Monks, H., Lester, L. & Thomas, L. (2009). Australian covert bullying prevalence study (ACBPS). Retrieved from www.deewr.gov.au/Schooling/NationalSafeSchools/Pages/research.aspx.

Giallo, R. & Little, E. (2003). Classroom behaviour problems: The relationship between preparedness, classroom experiences and self-efficacy in graduate and student teachers. *Australian Journal of Educational and Developmental Psychology*, *3*(1), 23–34.

Goyal, S. & Pandey, P. (2009). *How Do Government and Private Schools Differ? Findings from Two Large Indian States*. South Asian Human Development Sector Report #30. Retrieved from http://datatopics.worldbank.org/hnp/files/edstats/INDwp09b.pdf.

Guillaume, E. & Funder, D. (2016). Theoretical and methodological issues in making cross-national and cross-cultural comparisons. In P. K. Smith, K. Kwak, & Y. Toda (eds.), *School Bullying in Different Cultures: Eastern and Western Perspectives* (pp. 211–228). Cambridge: Cambridge University Press.

Harris, M. (1976). History and significance of the emic/etic distinction. *Annual Review of Anthropology*, *5*(1), 329–350.

Huang, Y. Y. & Chou, C. (2013). Revisiting cyberbullying: Perspectives from Taiwanese teachers. *Computers & Education*, *63*, 227–239.

Intel Security. (2015). Teens, Tweens, Technology: India. Retrieved from http://apac.intelsecurity.com/digitalsafety/wp-content/uploads/sites/7/2015/10/Intel-Security_India-TeensTweensTechnology-2015-_National-Datasheet.pdf.

Kahn, J. H., Jones, J. L. & Wieland, A. L. (2012). Preservice teachers' coping styles and their responses to bullying. *Psychology in the Schools*, *49*(8), 784–793.

Kallestad, J. H. & Olweus, D. (2003). Predicting teachers' and schools' implementation of the Olweus bullying prevention program: A multilevel study. *Prevention and Treatment*, 6(1) October. No Pagination Specified Article 21. Retrieved from http://dx.doi.org/10.1037/1522–3736.6.1.621a.

Katz, I., Keeley, M., Spears, B., Taddeo, C., Swirski, T. & Bates, S. (2014). *Research on Youth Exposure to, and Management of, Cyberbullying Incidents in Australia: Synthesis Report* (SPRC Report 16/2014) (PDF) [431 Kb]. Sydney: Social Policy Research Centre, UNSW Australia.

Kochenderfer-Ladd, B. & Pelletier, M. E. (2008). Teachers' views and beliefs about bullying: Influences on classroom management strategies and students' coping with peer victimization. *Journal of School Psychology*, 46(4), 431–453.

Lester, L., Cross, D., Dooley, J. & Shaw, T. (2013). Bullying victimisation and adolescents: Implications for school-based intervention programs. *Australian Journal of Education*, 57(2), 107–123.

Lester, L., Waters, S., Pearce, N. & Spears, B. (2018). Pre-service teachers: Knowledge, attitudes and their perceived skills in addressing student bullying. *Australian Journal of Teacher Education*.

Li, Q. (2008). Cyberbullying in schools: An examination of preservice teachers' perception. *Canadian Journal of Learning and Technology/La revue canadienne de l'apprentissage et de la technologie*, 34(2). doi: http://dx.doi.org/10.21432/T2DK5G

Lopata, J. A., & Nowicki, E. A. (2014). Pre-service teacher beliefs on the antecedents to bullying: A concept mapping study. *Canadian Journal of Education*, 37(4), 1.

Microsoft Corporation Safety and Security Center. (2012). Worldwide online bullying survey. Retrieved from www.microsoft.com/en-us/download/details.aspx?id=30148.

Ministerial Council for Education, Early Childhood Development and Youth Affairs (MCEECDYA). (2011). National safe schools framework. Retrieved from https://docs.education.gov.au/system/files/doc/other/national_safe_schools_framework.pdf.

Mishna, F., Scarcello, I., Pepler, D. & Wiener, J. (2005). Teachers' understanding of bullying. *Canadian Journal of Education/Revue canadienne de l'éducation*, 28(4), 718–738.

Nicolaides, S., Toda, Y. & Smith, P. K. (2002). Knowledge and attitudes about school bullying in trainee teachers. *British Journal of Educational Psychology*, 72(1), 105–118.

Novick, R. M. & Isaacs, J. (2010). Telling is compelling: The impact of student reports of bullying on teacher intervention. *Educational Psychology*, 30(3), 283–296.

O'Moore, M. (2000). Critical issues for teacher training to counter bullying and victimisation in Ireland. *Aggressive Behavior*, 26(1), 99–111.

Pike, K. L. (1967). *Language in Relation to a Unified Theory of the Structures of Human Behavior* (2nd edn.). The Hague: Mouton.

Ramya, S. G. & Kulkarni, M. L. (2011). Bullying among school children: Prevalence and association with common symptoms in childhood. *Indian Journal of Pediatrics*, 78(3), 307–310.

Rigby, K. & Johnson, K. (2016). The prevalence and effectiveness of anti-bullying strategies employed in Australian schools. Retrieved from http://apo.org.au/n ode/66537.

Rigby, K. & Slee, P. (1999). Suicidal ideation among adolescent school children, involvement in bully–victim problems, and perceived social support. *Suicide and Life-Threatening Behavior, 29*(2), 119–130.

Rigby, K. & Smith, P. K. (2011). Is school bullying really on the rise? *Social Psychology of Education, 14*(4), 441–455.

Rivers, I. (2001). Retrospective reports of school bullying: Stability of recall and its implications for research. *British Journal of Developmental Psychology, 19*(1), 129–141.

Ryan, T., & Kariuki, M. (2011). A two year comparative analysis of cyberbullying perceptions of Canadian (Ontario) preservice educators. *Journal of the Research Center for Educational Technology, 7*(2), 100–111.

Smith, P. K., Kwak, K. & Toda, Y. (eds.) (2016). *School Bullying in Different Cultures: Eastern and Western Perspectives.* Cambridge: Cambridge University Press.

Spears, B., Campbell, M., Tangen, D., Slee, P. & Cross, D. (2015). Australian pre-service teachers' knowledge and understanding of cyberbullying: Implications for school climate. *Les Dossiers des sciences de l'éducation, 33*, 109–130.

Spears, B., Cox, G., Stretton, A. & Mattiske, J. (2017). *Existing Bullying and Wellbeing Resources and Future Needs: An Evidence-Informed Account.* Adelaide: University of South Australia.

Spears, B., Keeley, M., Bates, S. & Katz, I. (2014). *Research on Youth Exposure to, and Management of, Cyberbullying Incidents in Australia: Part A: Literature Review on the Estimated Prevalence of Cyberbullying Involving Australian Minors (SPRC Report 9/2014).* Sydney: Social Policy Research Centre, UNSW Australia.

Spears, B., Taddeo, C. M., Daly, A. L., Stretton, A. & Karklins, L. T. (2015). Cyberbullying, help-seeking and mental health in young Australians: Implications for public health. *International Journal of Public Health, 60*(2), 219–226.

Thomas, R. Y. A. N., Kariuki, M. & Yilmaz, H. (2011). A comparative analysis of cyberbullying perceptions of preservice educators: Canada and Turkey. *TOJET: The Turkish Online Journal of Educational Technology, 10*(3), 1–12.

Triandis, H. C. & Brislin, R. W. (1984). Cross-cultural psychology. *American Psychologist, 39*(9), 1006–1016.

Waasdorp, T. E., Pas, E. T., O'Brennan, L. M. & Bradshaw, C. P. (2011). A multilevel perspective on the climate of bullying: Discrepancies among students, school staff, and parents, *Journal of School Violence, 10*(2), 115–132.

Yilmaz, H. (2010). An examination of preservice teachers' perceptions about cyberbullying. *Eurasia Journal of Mathematics, Science & Technology Education, 6*(4), 263–270.

Yoon, J., Bauman, S., Choi, T. & Hutchinson, A. S. (2011). How South Korean teachers handle an incident of school bullying. *School Psychology International, 32*(3), 312–329.

12 Indian Perspectives on Bullying and Cyber Bullying

Documentary Interviews with Teachers and Educational Professionals from Punjabi and Tamil Nadu

*Alison Wotherspoon, Barbara A. Spears, Damanjit Sandhu and Suresh Sundaram**

The Indian-European Research Networking Programme in the Social Sciences brought together a team of academics from psychology, education and screen production, from 10 universities in 6 countries, to work on an interdisciplinary research project in India exploring understanding of *bullying, cyber bullying, pupil safety and well-being* in an Indian context. This project enabled a unique opportunity to create a series of documentary interviews with education professionals working in schools in the Punjab and Tamil Nadu, India. Excerpts from 4 major interviews, out of 18 filmed in 2014 during a number of meetings and school visits, are presented. Interviewees outline their perceptions of bullying relative to their educational contexts, describing the influence that diverse traditions, social norms, beliefs, religion, gender, locations and definitions, occurring between cultural groups within India, might have on how bullying behaviours are viewed and managed within school contexts.

For the first author as a non-Indian screen producer/film-maker, both personal reflexivity (how values, beliefs and interests influence the work) and epistemological reflexivity (how knowledge is generated through this process) (Creswell, 2013) are acknowledged and considered, particularly concerning any influence on the interpretation of findings and conclusions drawn. Reflexivity, then, is an individual's considered response to

* This research was funded by the Indian Council of Social Science Research (ICSSR, India) in association with the Economic and Social Research Council (ESRC, UK), the Agence Nationale de la Recherche (ANR, France), the Deutsche Forschungsgemeinschaft (DFG, Germany) and the Netherlands Organisation for Scientific Research (NWO, the Netherlands). The authors also wish to acknowledge funding contributed by the School of Humanities Creative Research Fund, Flinders University, and the Divisional Research Performance Fund of the Division of Education, Arts and Social Sciences, University of South Australia.

a situation/context and is a self-critical approach to reporting the findings (Creswell, 2013). This chapter demonstrates the role creative practice research (Collins, 2010) can play in exploring individuals' voices which adds richness to traditional research methodologies in the field of bullying and cyberbullying.

Participatory Action Research and Living Lab: Non-traditional Research Methodologies

Participatory Action Research (PAR) + Practice-Based Research = Documentary Film-Making

For an academic film-maker, participatory action research (PAR) and reflexivity play a significant role in practice-based research, especially in the production of documentary films, and effectively describes what occurs in the interviewing process (Wotherspoon, 2011). During the pre-production period of any film as much research as possible, within the limits of access, time and budget, is undertaken, but this cannot fully prepare the film-maker for filming in a country as diverse and culturally complex as India. Working within a multilingual, multicultural and plur-alistic country can result in a range of details and concepts being lost or misconstrued in translation. It is not possible to gain a full understanding of the range of cultural and religious norms in India in a limited number of weeks. Given these challenges, PAR and reflexivity become extremely useful qualitative research tools: they allow questions to be refined, re-evaluated and developed as a greater understanding is reached in the field. They allow for a film-maker/researcher to be fluid in their thinking and open to change.

PAR and reflexivity demand that the film-maker actively listens to what is being said, processes this new information quickly and critically in order for the interviews to continue and builds and extends on the newly acquired knowledge (Wadsworth, 1998). During the editing and post-production process this cycle continues as the film-maker interrogates the material gained in the field and structures it into a shape that is mean-ingful and unified. Working with the first footage raised questions that were developed in the subsequent two research and filming trips. This sequential and cyclical process of inquiry allowed a greater understanding of how bullying and cyberbullying are perceived and defined within the Indian cultural context. It also allowed for *personal* reflexivity, whereby the film-maker/researcher became aware of how little was known about Indian culture and society, in spite of the time spent in the field. It was apparent that whatever understanding was reached in these short immersive experiences would be limited and only introductory. There was also a recognition that questions about bullying that made sense in an Australian context were often inaccurate or irrelevant in an Indian one: *epistemological* reflexivity, highlighting the need for careful listening, processing and reflecting on what was said, how it was said and with what emphasis (Schön, 1983).

A Living Lab Approach: The Active Involvement of Practitioners and Researchers

A Living Lab approach (Henttonen et al., 2016; McPhee, Westerlund & Lemininen, 2012; Van der Walt et al., 2009), observes the living patterns of users, brings key actors together to explore a problem and possible solutions and places the user/informant from the culture centrally in the research process. This chapter presents and gives voice to some of the observations, thoughts, opinions and beliefs expressed by four key stakeholders who were interviewed in Annamalai Nagar, Tamil Nadu and Patiala, Punjab.

A Living Lab approach highlights the importance of employing alternative methods to access the insider perspectives from the cultural contexts of interest. This approach avoids a colonialist perspective, where outsider views are imposed; rather, through listening to informants, the knowledge base concerning the topic of concern, viz., bullying and cyberbullying, is extended cross-culturally. This approach enables the co-creation and co-generation of shared understandings of the different environmental, social and cultural contexts and practices with those trying to research or understand them (Mulder et al., 2008).

In the quest to extend knowledge about the cyber/bullying context in India, a Living Lab approach can thus serve two purposes: (1) as a *methodology* to explore the cultural context from an insider perspective, and (2) as a *development strategy for interventions* where the end users of the intervention, such as students engaged in an anti-bullying programme, are not merely participants/subjects in a research/evaluation process, but become central to the *co-design* of the intervention (Niitamo et al., 2006). Living Lab participants/informants, then, are not simply observed or recorded by others in a traditional sense, but *actively engage in a shared process with the researcher (in this case, the film-maker) where the co-creation and co-construction of shared meaning is articulated through their social interactions with each other and the researcher* (Niitamo et al., 2006).

This process disrupts the researcher's/film-maker's role from being the "director" of the participatory action research process to *becoming part of the process* where meaning is co-generated and co-constructed, enabling the outsider to gently enter the complexity that is the cultural context of interest. In positioning the informants as discussants of their own experiences, they are positioned as experts, capable of shaping and interrupting the Western understanding of bullying/cyberbullying which prevails in the literature. By bringing the informants' meaning and understanding to the foreground, Western understanding is broken down and reshaped, leading to the co-generation of new meaning around the conceptualisation of bullying in this cultural context.

The four interview excerpts reported in this chapter are with experts from professional backgrounds that include teaching, psychology, medicine, cyberbullying prevention and policing. All were working in the field of bullying prevention and cyberbullying education in India within their areas of expertise. Although at times words and definitions may not be agreed upon, may not actually exist or may be difficult to translate, there is a recognition and an understanding of behaviours that can be identified as bullying and cyberbullying, as well as the negative and damaging impact these have on young people in India. There is also a strong understanding of the need to quickly develop strategies for interventions that are appropriate and effective in an Indian context. The discussions and statements that follow reflect a sense of how the discussion and understanding of bullying and cyberbullying in India had developed by late 2014. It can be predicted that this knowledge has continued to develop and expand since these interviews took place. It is, however, useful to consider this snapshot of where the understanding of and issues surrounding bullying and cyberbullying was at the time. In this way, these excerpts from the interviews may act as a baseline for future discussion.

The Filming and Interview Selection Process

Altogether 18 interviews took place – 16 Indian and 2 European. These were not prearranged in pre-production or before reaching the location. Nine interviews took place in Annamalai Nagar and nine in Patiala, at conferences organised as part of the wider research project. Due to the limited space in this chapter only content from four Indian interviewees has been included.

A number of key questions and themes were identified before the filming took place (a priori) in Annamalai Nagar or Patiala, but the range of questions in each interview varied. It was acknowledged that the interviewees were the experts and their contribution to the filming process was as creative collaborators and co-researchers, in line with the Living Lab approach. Those interviewed were participants in the research events and visits to local and rural schools organised by the Indian researchers (the third and fourth authors of this chapter).

The interview excerpts reported here were selected on the basis of the depth of discussion and the knowledge shared. These four interviews were longer, and took the form of a conversation between professionals. The content discussed varied depending on who was being interviewed and their area of specialisation. Common questions asked of all included whether the term *bullying* was understood widely in India and how they defined bullying and cyberbullying. The filmmaker's background in researching and producing evidence-based anti-bullying educational resources provided the knowledge and understanding to investigate similar issues in the varying cultural and regional contexts of Tamil Nadu in the south and Patiala in the north. Previous experience teaching in high schools and universities allowed the film-maker to initiate discussions with the interviewees as peers (Wotherspoon, 2011). This enabled them, in turn, to reflect on and describe what bullying looked like in their schools, the impact it had on their communities and issues that were particular to an Indian context.

Practice in Action: Constraints and Opportunities

Two professional Indian film crews, organised by Dr Damanjit Sandhu in Patiala, Punjab, and Dr Suresh Sundaram in Chidambaram, Tamil Nadu, collaborated with the film director to film the interviews.

The four-man crew in Tamil Nadu came from the nearby city of Chennai, and consisted of a cameraman, sound recordist, gaffer and an additional junior crew member who was responsible for moving the lighting equipment. The Chennai crew came from a predominantly drama rather than a documentary background and their understanding of the need for urgency and recording sound at all times when filming documentary differed from that of the film-maker. It was unclear if this was due to them not normally working on documentary, or due to them being directed by a foreign woman. This at times led to missed opportunities for interviews due to the time it took the crew to get ready and the conflicting priorities about what was important to film. Consequently, the film-maker was unable to interview any Indian women at the conference held at Annamalai University. There were later opportunities to interview a female principal, as well as three female schoolteachers in Tamil Nadu, but these were very short interviews and although valuable, are not the focus of this chapter.

The interviews in Annamalai Nagar were made on the run, on the spur of the moment and under considerable time pressure, with people who had given an interesting presentation and who spoke reasonably good English but whom the film-maker had not met before. The interviewing process in Annamalai Nagar was challenging, as the film-maker was not familiar with the region, the culture or the school system and this resulted in more general and less focused interviews than those which occurred in the north.

In contrast, the three-man film crew in Patiala, from the nearby city of Chandigarh, were an experienced television crew who had worked with the film-maker before, and who understood the speed required in doc-umentary film-making. The interviews that occurred in Patiala were organised in part with the help of the local researchers with whom the film-maker had previously worked and had ongoing working relation-ships. Having had two previous research trips to Patiala made a significant difference to a general understanding of Punjabi issues and education. The interviewees chosen in Patiala were educational specialists who either were participants in the teaching workshop or taught at local schools. Although under some time pressure, the filming in Patiala was less rushed, and the film-maker was able to have pre-liminary discussions with the interviewees rather than effectively only meeting them for the first time when a camera was about to start recording them.

The Role Creative Practice Research and Living Lab Can Play and Contribute to Traditional Research Methodologies in the Field of Bullying

It is possible to glean a great deal of information from people when you are working in collaboration with them and they are reflecting upon or discussing their professional practice while sharing their lived experi-ences. During a filmed interview they share their knowledge and insights through stories, case studies and observations (Aufderheide, 2007). This material provides a rich source of information and their responses are often emotionally engaging as well as analytical. The documentary process, as well as the Living Lab methodology, recognises that the people being interviewed are the experts due to their knowledge and lived experiences. It is an extremely effective way to give voice to people who may not normally be asked to speak or may not usually be heard (Rabiger, 2009).

When researchers from India, Australia and the European Union started working together in the area of bullying and cyberbullying in India in 2013 there was a concern that this would be challenging due to there not being one single word for *bullying* in any Indian languages. A number of different terms described specific behaviours such as ragging or Eve teasing (see Chapter 1), but no one overarching word was shared or commonly understood (see also Chapters 4 and 13). What emerged out of these interviews in 2014 was that there is a *general understanding* of what the terms *bullying* and *cyberbullying* mean, and an increasing use of these English terms in contemporary India, especially by professionals working in the fields of education and psychology. This is especially true where work has been undertaken to educate communities and schools about the harmfulness of bullying on young people. Through these interviews it became apparent that the use of these terms and understanding of them is well known to many education specialists.

Insider Perspectives

The four interviewees represented here are Mr Rakshit Tandon, Dr Naina Sharma Uppal, Dr Sonam Dullat and Dr Arun Tipandjan.

Figure 12.1 Mr Rakshit Tandon is a consultant to the Internet and Mobile Association of India, as well as an advisor to the Uttar Pradesh and Haryana, Gurgaon Cyber Crime Department.

Figure 12.2 Dr Naina Sharma-Uppal is an Assistant Professor working in the Department of Distance Education in the subunit of Psychology at Punjabi University in Patiala.

Figure 12.3 Dr Sonam Dullat is an Assistant Professor in Psychology at SUS Tangori, in Patiala.

Figure 12.4 Dr Arun Tipandjan is a cognitive and cross-cultural psychologist working in Puducherry in southern India.

Prevalence, Definition and Understanding of Bullying and Cyberbullying

Rakshit's observation is that the term *cyberbullying* has been in common use for a considerable number of years. Coming from a background in software education, he was approached for help by a policewoman in 2004 to deal with a complaint from a young girl being cyberbullied in a chat room. After investigating this complaint and finding the culprit to be a young boy, Rakshit became aware of the need for young people to be educated about cyber safety.

He outlined the online context:

India had a population of 1.21 billion and . . . 875 million mobile users by October 2013 and that's increasing . . . when I go to schools, and I ask them the question, "How many of you are using internet on mobiles?", 90% of them stand up and raise their hands, and they say, "Yes, we have an access to internet on phones." So it's high, the penetration is high. And yes, it's not very expensive as well, to own internet on your smartphone. Even to own a smartphone, it's very economical today.

Rakshit then positioned his work with schools and government:

I realised that this younger generation, who is just very new to the chat, and Internet, and websites, . . . they really need to be trained on it . . . by 2008, we got the support of the government association Internet and Mobile Association of India.

And I reached out to seven, seven and a half lakh students in the country, more than 2,200 schools. More than 64 cities and 15 states of the nation.

A *lakh* is an Indian numbering unit equal to 100,000. Basing his estimates on his work in schools, Rakshit suggested that the frequency of cyberbullying among young people in India was:

Almost 30% [of] students, out of a crowd, if I say, 100 students are there in an auditorium that I'm addressing ... 30% have a negative problem faced [sic]. So they come up to me and say either their account was hacked or ... [or a] fake account [was] created on social media. They've been bullied with some personal stuff, somebody's misusing their picture, somebody's using their name and sending filthy messages. Sometimes it looks like a prank or it look(s) like some jealousy among each other, peers or something, but then it comes onto a public domain, ... it creates a problem.

In describing the challenges schools are facing in relation to cyberbullying, including the lack of consistency of approach between schools, parents and students, he indicated steps they are taking towards prevention and intervention, which is similar to elsewhere in the world:

Lot[s] of schools, they come to me directly ... anonymous pages being created on social media, [abusive] statements about teachers, about students and peers. So yeah, cyberbullying is, right now, very important. ... and [with the CBSE] we are creating content, ... we are creating train-the-trainer programmes for the schools, for the teachers, for the ICT and non-ICT teachers ... [for] cyberbullying and stalking and cyber safety.

In terms of young people feeling they could discuss issues such as bullying or cyberbullying with family, Rakshit described the following, which again resonates with what occurs elsewhere:

They feel very comfortable talking to me, [when they see my background and profile] ... with a special note that "please don't tell it to [my] family; I can't share it with my parents, they will kill me, they will beat me". And there's another fear in the child's mind ... The first solution of the parent would be, no online business now. No phones, no internet. So the student is scared. He doesn't want to cut off from – you can't cut off today's generation from this digital technology.

He elaborated in terms of parents' lack of understanding:

Now the problem is understanding. For him [student] it's serious when 500 odd friends are commenting negative[ly] about him ... But for the father? "What's Facebook? ... Who's writing somebody? Oh – ignore it. You'll be happy." But you don't understand the cycle of what he's going through when you go to the school and he's being bullied.

He went on to make the observation that:

parents feel very proud giving a smartphone to a person who's not even knowing what are the settings and securities, how to use it, good or bad . . . "I have a gadget." . . . They're very proud of it. So that's the role, what we're doing by conducting these workshops and going to schools and educating the teachers now.

This is not dissimilar to elsewhere, in that parents buy young people digital devices without fully understanding their capabilities or safety issues. Pride, however, is not an emotion generally linked with giving a child a smartphone in most other parts of the world. This potentially speaks to a level of social status bestowed on parents in this context, which is not commonly reported elsewhere.

This was also discussed by Naina, who noted that:

the parents think that our children are innocent, and they're not using such . . . devices which the other children are using. They would come and proudly say that "Thank God, my children [are] not doing it." But how much time are [you] giving to the child, how much do you know your child, and how much [do] you know about the technology? You're ignorant . . . So it's just like this . . . we do not acknowledge this fact, and then . . . we blame the school authorities, school authorities blame the teachers, sorry they blame the parents, that the parents are endorsing these things.

Rakshit also spoke of the disconnect between the ways children are educated by parents and teachers to follow the rules of society in general, yet, because of their lack of understanding about the online context, children were not receiving what they need to operate safely online:

You know what is missing? Missing is cyber hygiene and etiquette. So that's what the groundwork is. So they are living dual lives; they're living a real life and they're living a virtual life. For real life, we are preparing them. The parents are taking care, the school is taking care with talking, educating them. But when they live a virtual life, when they go onto the social media platform and they start making friends online, start writing, posting, nobody has told them the rules for that. And I think that's one of the reasons why cyberbullying is rising and it's an area of concern for the country right now.

Finally, in relation to the overlap noted internationally concerning bullying and cyberbullying flowing across the offline and online settings, Rakshit reflected that bullies and cyberbullies were in fact dissimilar.

Well, they are a mixture . . . the bullies in real life, on the playground or in the school campus, they're different. And the person who's doing online bullying . . . he has no demarcation, no specific demarcation. He can be anyone . . . So, in [a] case of cyberbullying you can't depend [on] who the normal bullies [are] in school, or the people who are beating you, snatching your tiffins from the junior or seniors. So they are different. And the cyberbullies are different.

The need for further education, for students as well as adults, in how to navigate safely in an online environment was also highlighted by Naina, who asserted that:

Everybody is using internet here in Punjab. Even in the villages, there is internet, and they [the villagers] know about the Facebook ... They're not that fluent with the English language, but they know that there is something Facebook. They all have their log-in IDs and they go to the cybercafes to get themselves registered for the Facebook. So somebody else is making their IDs, somebody else is giving them the password, a slip, and telling them that this is your password, this is your log-in ID so you can use it now ... So that is the status, that they are aware of it. And then what to post, what not to post, and how much to post, what information is required over there, what kind of pictures can they post. So it has become more, a kind of a social status over here. Did you have a Facebook at home? "Yes, I have." How many friends? "500." "Oh my god, you're really popular."

Having a Facebook is being like you're cool. But ... they're actually not aware about the usage of it, and about the repercussions it can cause ... how much effect this online abuse can cause a person psychologically, mentally. It's not being talked about ... I would say that it is rather a neglected issue over here.

Naina has conducted workshops in HIV/AIDS awareness and safe sex practices for young people and sex workers in the Punjab. In her experience, access to mobile phones and the internet has also exposed many very young Indian students to pornography.

The children have confessed that late [at] night they've been watching this kind of ... movies and they have downloaded [them] on the phone. The phone was taken by the father and then they got into trouble and then again blaming start[ed]. "My friend did it. I didn't know even about it. I don't, I swear upon God. I swear upon you I didn't do it. I didn't mean to do it. Somehow I don't know what I clicked and it was downloaded."

For Naina, as for Rakshit:

bullying, is definitely, it is prevalent here in India, and most of the students when we talk, when we go to the schools and say, "have you ever been bullied?", they can associate it, like if in case anyone has been verbally abused, or physically abused, or they do use the term "bully" for that. And even, I remember, one child said one thing, "my mother bullies me." Like it's the same kind, like if in case you're hurt, you're physically, you're emotionally, you're mentally, something which is damaging is considered to be a bully. Here even in the Indian culture, they use the word.

Naina went on to discuss the different forms bullying took across Indian states. The notion of beatings within families was mentioned by her, as well as a number of other interviewees. The relationship between beatings and what is recognised or called domestic violence or bullying seemed confusing when viewed from an outsider perspective. There was a notion that observing or experiencing beatings within families could lead to bullying outside of the home. Naina stated that:

In this diverse Indian culture ... and especially the places where there's more literacy, more education ... take the example of Kerala ... women even do not report of being bullied by the husband. But here in Punjab where there is more, you would say, a feudal kind of system, ... landlords are there, and there is a power assertion and they have the lands and agrarian society ... It is even more prevalent in Haryana, Rajasthan and Punjab ... the bullying of ... the women ... I would call it not as a domestic violence, I would say anybody can be ... bullied that way. So when they see the mothers being beaten up by the fathers or being bullied up, in the family, they somewhat vicariously carry that. When they see the father beating the mother, the mother beating the children, the child is definitely going to vent it out on some safer object, maybe, on a child who is a little safe, physically not that strong; he's physically weak. He might use his power assertion on him.

The role family plays in Indian society was repeatedly mentioned and a significant factor in all of the interviews, as was the fear many young people felt about how parents might react if they got into any form of trouble or were not succeeding at school.

Sonam reflected on the need for a greater recognition of bullying not being a phenomenon that is limited to schools. Sonam discussed the way in which the dynamics within the family and between siblings may actually result in bullying outside of it, and her belief that bullying, or as she described it *bullyism*, was on the rise in India.

Bullying in India ... it's not supposed to be meant that it is going to start from the school level itself. It has basically started from the home. So from their siblings, from your elder siblings, that is the fear that the children develop. And ... in some cases that fear takes the form of revenge, in certain cases, and that is the, basically, the growth of the bullyism ... in India the number of cases of bullyism is increasing day by day ... The reality check has to be done at every level, whether it [is] the ground level, whether it is at the primary school, the secondary school, or whether it's at, at any college or at the ... any university level.

Sonam continued, to observe that:

Bullyism also works at the workplace itself ... The higher officials, even your management, they ... also tend to bully people in a number of cases. And then there are other differences. People belong to different kinds of sects, and then because of these sects, because of the people belonging to different kinds of states, they have different kinds of notions. They think differently and because of that, they have the different definition of bullyism.

Arun also discussed the need to think about bullying outside of the school context.

One thing important that I want to tell the fellow researchers in [the] field of bullying, in [the] India context, identify the core issue ... What is prevalent in your ethnic cultural context, add that into universal applicability ... so, I would say much importance should be given to other person[s]. I mean teachers, parents, uncle[s], auntie[s], and these people because, in most of the bullying research, they reported ... only peer-group bullying, only students bullying other student[s].

Student[s] caus[e] harassment to other[s] ... This is a normal thing, but [who] are the other people who have already bullied that particular victim?

A consideration of how bullying is defined in an Indian context and whether there was consensus about its definition and the way in which it presents varied in a number of the interviews. For Arun, the phenomenon of bullying was not necessarily a traditional part of Indian culture.

Like other Western ... countries ... India do(es) experience bullying in the school ... Bullying has got its own, different shades in India, because bullying is not a construct which was present in [the] Indian context. Due to globalisation and other effects, ... bullying [takes] place in India.

When asked if he thought that there is a general understanding of the use of the word *bullying* in India, Arun's reply was that:

A new name has been given, and it's called as bullying. But it has been called by various names ... in various parts of India, as it got its own name, but bullying is a holistic terminology being used by the people who are doing research extensively, on [the] Western world.

He went on to observe that in India:

There are different forms. According to the ethnic background. For example, if you take [the] southern part of India, there are so many here hitting on the road, and stealing the bell of the cycle ... and ... taking away the ... air in the cycle. And these are the commonest, bullying things, and hitting one and stealing one's pencil box or ... eating ... food from the lunch boxes, these are common bullying ... we have certain cultures in the eastern population. I work with some of the universities in [the] northern eastern part of India ... so, there, the students used to complain that some senior students used to force them to eat something ... but it is not that common in other part[s] of India. There are so many different types of bullying behaviour[s] [that] happen in school, because India is a country of contrast[s]. We have different languages, different dialects, so, it's all different but it is all bullying.

A number of the interviewees went on to discuss the pressure on students to succeed academically. They spoke of how, in many families, parental expectations for children to achieve academically was immense. Given this, Arun identified that:

the teacher involvement in bullying is also very interesting ... in [the] Indian context, because there are so many things happening ... you can see the media, the social media ... The teacher giv[es] priorities to the students who [earn] very high grades in the schools, and this is a uniqueness, and these are the problems which have to be resolved, and any education, psycho-education, to change this type of attitude from the teacher's mind is also very important rather than only concentrating on the students who are studying.

Cultures Within: Family, Location and Change

For an outsider to gain an understanding of Indian society, understanding the role of the family within is critical. Many of the interviewees observed that changing employment patterns and an increasingly urbanised workforce is impacting the traditional notion of the family units in India and the relationship between the family and the community in many parts of the country. There was a belief by some that increasing numbers of couples were choosing to have only one child and that many children, especially those living in urban environments, were no longer being raised within traditional extended family structures. This in turn led to an increase in the number of children being isolated, with only gadgets for company after school and under the supervision of the family maid rather than a parent. The discussion of changing work and the increase of working mothers led to interesting observations about gender and bullying – which for many were clearly related.

For Sonam, the rise in bullying could be linked to the rapid changes India is going through and the shift from a traditionally collectivist society to one with an emphasis on the individual and an aspirational middle class:

Earlier I talked about India being a very diverse kind of a country. It is having people of different cultures. It is having people of different religions ... India is ... not an individualistic kind of a nation. It is basically [a] collectivistic kind of a nation ... We are forgetting ... who we are ... our own rules ... We are basically focusing upon the other things that are good, that are advanced, that are very good for the nations ... but we are forgetting about the things that are basically belonging to our own students ... If you go to any metros in India, like Delhi, Bombay, Bangalore, Kolkata, these students are ... bombarded with so much education, so much knowledge, so much advancement ... But students who are belonging to small cities, to small states, they do not know ... There is a difference between, in India ... people who can afford it, people who can't afford it. The middle ones, there is a major gap. And the middle people are basically having ... a competitive kind of a thing. Yes, we want to compete with this kind of a thing. What about this sect? They can't do it. They can't afford [it]. They can't even afford to have smart classes. They can't, they can't even afford to have something like technology ... They don't even know what counsellors are, what psychologists are. So ... because of these particular strata ... there are people who are being bullied each and every second, each and every day.

Naina also observed that:

In this decade ... there's been a drastic change in [the] Indian system as well, social system. The divorce rates are increasing ... nuclear families [are] on the rise ... the growing prices, inflation, ha[ve] resulted in both Mom and Dad going out for the work and children are left home. And what we can provide them is a domestic help, like taking care of the child. But that domestic ... is not aware of what the child is playing on the internet ... there's nobody to ask, "How was your day? How did you do?"

Sonam also discussed the impact parental involvement, or lack of it, has on children's lives.

There are mothers who do not even know what is going on in their own children's life, what is written in their own diary. And because of that, there are things that the students, they keep [to] themselves, and because of that particular thing, if the student is being bullied at one particular instance, the child is not going to tell his or her parents because the child does not consider his or her parents as his own. They basically think, "Okay, my mom is going to kill me. My mom is obviously going to blame me, because it's my fault."

She went on to conclude:

Basically what is happening today in India is that parents are not at all taking that much interest in children. And because of that, the children inhabit their own personal zone. And because of that, the incidence of the suicides, the incidence of the alcoholism, the incidence of the drug abuse is increasing.

What emerged from a number of the interviews was for the interviewees to extrapolate specific and local experience and perceive it as typical in a wider, more inclusive Indian sense. Many of the interviewees presented India as a homogenous society, which it is in the rule of law, but these generalisations were made with an acknowledgement of the significant cultural and religious differences between regions and states. The opinions each individual expressed reflected the class they were from, their educational backgrounds, their religious beliefs, whether they moved in circles with visible numbers of professional women and how widely they had travelled within India and abroad. There were, consequently, differing perspectives between the interviewees that corre-lated to geographic location and gender. In contrast to Sonam's state-ment, Arun asserted that India:

has got a close to family situation, family circumstances, family relationship and when-ever there is something happen[ing] in [the] Indian context in schools, [the] school context, the person immediately pass[es] this message to the mother, and the mother will go next day to the school and she may complain about this problem to the school there, or they will directly talk to the parents. This is the one thing which is essentially different from the Western concept, and India is different because the [amount] of bullying is ... a little less in India when compared to other countries, like in terms of cyberbullying, in terms of any type of bullying, for that matter. It's very [much] less because of the strong family functioning and the messages immediately conveyed out to the person who's bullying and the person who also already [has] been [a] victim.

For Arun, this involvement of families was very much linked to a rural community:

*It is happening more really in the rural setup where people live in . . . combined, joined
family system[s]. Because if you take . . . urban areas, the families are . . . isolated and
they are living in a nuclear system.*

Arun noted that:

*In rural schools, we have different types of bullying when compared to the urban schools
because . . . the families are intertwined and they . . . live very close in villages and . . .
students give respect to their elders and the problem of bullying is [a] little less when
compared to the urban schools because they're prone to more sophisticated technologies . . .
rural schools do experience bullying, but the intensity is very [much] less because of the
influence of family. Whereas, in urban [schools], the family is isolated and . . . everyone
has only got one child . . . the birth order and the number of children in the family, this is
also taken into consideration when doing research in India in terms of bullying and
harassment.*

*In rural [areas], most of the time . . . only one parent is working. In urban areas, both
the parents are working . . . and the isolation . . . also plays a vital role [in] creating this
type of bullying behaviour . . . if both the parents are working, it is very difficult to monitor
them. They are just simply given [a] laptop and they're given [a] tablet or some other
things . . . But, in rural areas, all the people are there around them. Rural children, they
are playing at the bank of the river or sometimes in temples or sometime in some
ground . . . because the village is very small and the boundaries are very limited. And
they are watched by some elders in the society, and [if] something is going on between the
students regarding bullying behaviour, they are well watched, and they'll be punished.*

*In former times, we had three, four, five, six siblings in the family. In [those] times, we
know the value of the siblings, the value of another person, maybe a brother or a sister,
younger or elder. They used to have discussion together. What is right, what is wrong.
A child, now, in urban settings, [is a] . . . single child to the parents, and they don't know
anyone to learn the socialisation skills . . .in India, the bullying experience and [a] single
child in the family . . . could be really an interesting area to be explored.*

He also discussed the changes in Indian schools and recalled that:

*In former times, in Indian school[s] there [were] moral educators. There [was] a period
called moral education that they [taught] dos and don'ts and soft skills, and modern
stories from our old age, books, and these [were] being taught by the people, and the
teachers of the morals. Nowadays, there is no moral lesson.*

*However, the government of India is taking necessary steps to introduce a counsellor to
all the schools . . . to identify the problems in schools and to make the students to [bring]
a kindness [into] the culture of the school, and to improve most academic performance.*

Conclusions

The interviewees revealed a deep understanding of bullying in an Indian
context coloured by their own personal understandings of the worlds they
inhabit as professionals. They also identified a range of areas within which
there is interest and need for future research. Working in collaboration

with non-Indian researchers highlights the need for research to be rooted in a deep, co-constructed understanding of the rich and complex nature of India as a nation whereby insiders enable outsiders to share their world views. This was well described by Naina, who concluded that:

> Yes, there's a drastic change because of, I think, the Internet. Like there's been globalisation, there's been ... loads of information ... flooding and we are getting away from the traditional book reading. Everything the child goes and search[es] on Google ... And then ... there's been a mix-up of the culture, that's a good thing as well, assimilation should be there. But at the same time, I feel that we all have one cultural identity; we need to retain that. To be ... at peace within ourselves, we all, the children, need to [be] rooted. They need to know ... what is actually their culture and what is [its] richness.

References

Aufderheide, P. (2007). *Documentary Film: A Very Short Introduction.* 1st edn. Oxford: Oxford University Press.

Collins, H. (2010). *Creative Research: The Theory and Practice of Research for the Creative Industries.* London: Bloomsbury Publishing.

Creswell, J. W. (2013). *Research Design: Qualitative, Quantitative, and Mixed Methods Approaches.* London: Sage.

Henttonen, K., Nisula, A. M., Blomqvist, K., Horila, A. & Takala, M. (2016). Factors motivating and influencing co-creation of social innovation: A Living Lab case. In *International Society for Professional Innovation Management.* (p. 1). ISPIM Innovation Symposium; Manchester: 1–15. Manchester: The International Society for Professional Innovation Management (ISPIM).

McPhee, C., Westerlund, M. & Leminen, S. (2012). Editorial: Living Labs. *Technology Innovation Management Review,* 2(9), 3–5. http://timreview.ca/arti cle/601. Accessed 26 February 2017.

Mulder, I., Velthausz, D. & Kriens, M. (2008). The Living Labs harmonization cube: Communicating Living Labs' essentials. *Electronic Journal for Virtual Organizations and Networks,* 10, 1–14.

Niitamo, V.-P., Kulkki, S., Eriksson, M. & Hribernik, K. A. (2006). State-of-the-art and good practice in the field of Living Labs. In *Proceedings of the 12th International Conference on Concurrent Enterprising: Innovative Products and Services through Collaborative Networks* (pp. 26–28). Milan.

Rabiger, M. (2009). *Directing the Documentary.* 5th edn. Amsterdam: Focal Press/ Elsevier.

Schön, D. A. (1983). *The Reflective Practitioner: How Professionals Think in Action.* New York: Basic Books.

Van der Walt, J. S., Buitendag, A. A., Zaaiman, J. J. & van Vuuren, J. J. (2009). Community Living Lab as a collaborative innovation environment. *Issues in Informing Science and Information Technology,* 6, 421–436.

Wadsworth, Y. (1998). What Is Participatory Action Research? Action Research International, Paper 2 www.aral.com.au/ari/p-ywadsworth98.html. Accessed 9 March 2017.

Wotherspoon, A. (2011). From Evidence to Screen: A Model for Producing Educational Content in the Twenty First Century. PhD Exegesis, Flinders University, Adelaide.

13 Exchanging Ideas
Anti-bullying Intervention Including Peer and Parent Support Strategies

Fran Thompson, Peter K. Smith, Catherine Blaya, Shubhdip Kaur and Suresh Sundaram

Bullying and anti-bullying intervention have been researched in Europe for more than 30 years; however, not only is little known about bullying in Indian schools, but even less is known about how bullying is tackled. One theme of the Indian-European Social Sciences Research network (IESSR, 2012–2015) was dedicated to exchanging ideas on anti-bullying intervention, including peer and parent support strategies. As there was little information about anti-bullying intervention in Punjabi and Tamil Nadu schools, a bespoke questionnaire, *The Bullying Questionnaire for Punjabi and Tamil Schools*, was designed to initiate this new area of research.

The first part of this chapter starts with the definition and description of bullying taken from European research and used in the introduction to the questionnaire. Had Punjabi and Tamil teachers witnessed this behaviour in their schools? And what words do they use in their own language to describe this type of behaviour? The responses of the Punjabi and Tamil teachers are discussed. In the second part of this chapter, we turn to anti-bullying intervention. Brief examples of European anti-bullying intervention taken from research in England and France are used as a starting point to explore interventions implemented in Punjabi and Tamil schools. Legislation, guidance, school policy and types of preventative and reactive intervention are covered here, including peer and parent support. Are there any similarities between the interventions used for bullying in England, France, the Punjab and Tamil Nadu? Are there other interventions used and thought effective? The last part of this chapter discusses the implications of the findings on an exchange of ideas. Were the Punjabi and Tamil teachers interested in finding out more about European forms of anti-bullying intervention which could be adapted and used in their schools? Likewise, could the anti-bullying interventions that Punjabi and Tamil schools use be adapted and used in European schools?

Methodology

Questionnaire

The *Bullying Questionnaire for Punjabi and Tamil Schools* (see Appendix 13.A) used English and French anti-bullying research as a basis for the items in the questionnaire, which included questions on guidance, policy and a range of interventions used to prevent and respond to bullying.
  Punjabi and Tamil teachers were asked:
- if they recognised the bullying behaviour described on the information sheet in their school
- which words they would use in their own language to describe this behaviour
- if they had received any guidance or information on bullying
- which interventions they used to prevent bullying
- which interventions they used to respond to bullying
- if they used peer support schemes to support bullied students
- if they would be interested in information on eight different aspects of intervention used in European schools
- if they had any comments

Questions 1–3 about witnessing bullying and accessing information on bullying used a simple three-point scale (yes/no/not sure) with a comment box for Punjabi and Tamil words for bullying. Questions 4–7 had lists of interventions with tick boxes for the teachers to indicate which they had used and comment boxes to qualify their answers. The last question was an open box for general comments. The questionnaire was in English.

Data Collection

Punjabi and Tamil Nadu schools were selected using convenience sampling; the researchers approached the school principals requesting permission for data collection and school selection was based on their acceptance. One hundred fifty teachers were recruited from 7 Punjabi schools and 149 teachers from 10 Tamil Nadu schools.
  Of the seven Punjabi schools, one in Alamdipur and two in Patiala were state-run, lower to middle socio-economic status (SES) schools, following the Punjab School Education Board, while the remaining four Patiala schools were privately owned, middle to upper SES schools, following the Central Board of Secondary Education (CBSE). All schools were urban except for the rural school in Alamdipur. Data collection took place at a two-day workshop held at the Punjabi University, Patiala. All teachers completed the questionnaire in a single group supervised by the Punjabi University research team.

Of the 10 Tamil Nadu schools, 9 were privately run, with one Government of India school. Six schools followed the CBSE with the remaining four schools following the Tamil Nadu Board of Secondary Education (TNBSE). All the schools were either rural or semi-urban. Data collection took place in each school supervised by the Annamalai University research team. Teachers were asked to complete the questionnaires in special sessions held during school time. However, in some schools teachers completed the questionnaires in their own time, which were collected the next day.

The Information Sheet of the Questionnaire: A Definition and Description of Bullying

European Definition of Bullying

To find out about bullying from Punjabi or Tamil teachers in the absence of an identified word in either language, an introductory information sheet with a brief definition of bullying taken from European research was included (Olweus, 1993; Smith & Sharp, 1994).

Bullying was defined as being distinctive in three main ways:
- there is an intention to harm
- the aggression is repeated
- there is an imbalance of power

A short description of bullying behaviour and types of bullying followed including the group dynamics which ranged from a dyad to a group, often with bystanders who witness the incident (Salmivalli et al., 1996). Different types of bullying were outlined including direct forms which can be physical (punching, kicking), verbal (name-calling, verbal abuse) and relational (excluding someone) (Smith et al., 1999). Additionally, indirect forms were included such as spreading nasty rumours about someone. As bullying often comes from difference, we listed a range of bias-based bullying including gender, race, religion, culture, sexuality and disability. Cyberbullying was also included – text messages, phone calls, social networking websites (Twitter, Facebook, Snapchat, WhatsApp), emails and online gaming platforms using smartphones, laptops and tablets can all be used to target cyber victims.

Witnessing Bullying in Punjabi and Tamil Nadu Schools

After reading the information sheet, teachers were asked if they recognised bullying behaviour in their schools. More Punjabi teachers (83%) reported witnessing bullying in their schools than Tamil teachers (58%).

Punjabi and Tamil Words for Bullying

When it came to identifying a word for bullying, more than half of both Punjabi (58%) and Tamil (55%) teachers either did not know of one, or were not sure one existed; 42% of Punjabi teachers and 45% of Tamil teachers identified a total of 14 words in Punjabi and 23 words in Tamil. These are listed in Table 13.1 (Punjabi) and Table 13.2 (Tamil). Punjabi and Tamil words for bullying were translated by the Punjabi University and Annamalai University research teams.

Of the 14 Punjabi and 23 Tamil words, only *panga lena* in Punjabi and *tunpuruttal* and *pakiṭivatai* in Tamil seemed to capture the three distinctive qualities of power imbalance, repetition and intention of the word *bullying*.

In Punjabi, *dhakeshahi* (show power or force over others), *badmaashi* (intimidate others) and *darana* (frighten someone) capture the power imbalance of bullying, whilst *pangebaazi* (habitually and intentionally troubling someone), *maar kutt* (intentionally having physical fights with others), *tang karna* (irritate others) and *panga lena* (occasionally troubling someone intentionally) reflect its repetitive and intentional aspects. Direct forms of bullying were captured by *kuttapa* (beating someone physically), which describes a physical attack, whereas *gaal kadni* (using foul language against someone), *dhamkian dena* (threatening someone)

Table 13.1 *Punjabi words for bullying reported by teachers (n = 54) in order of most selected*

Punjabi word	English version of Punjabi word	English translation
ਧੱਕੇਸ਼ਾਹੀ	*Dhakke shahi*	Show power or force over others
ਬਦਮਾਸ਼ੀ	*Badmaashi*	Intimidate others
ਪੰਗੇਬਾਜ਼ੀ	*Pangebaazi*	A habit of intentionally troubling someone
ਮਾਰ ਕੁੱਟ	*Maar kutt*	Intentionally have physical fights with others
ਤੰਗ ਕਰਨਾ	*Tang karna*	Irritate others
ਕੁਟਾਪਾ	*Kuttapa*	Beat someone physically
ਗਾਲ ਕੁਢਨੀ	*Gaal kadni*	Use foul language against someone
ਧਮਕੀਆਂ ਦੇਣਾ	*Dhamkian dena*	Threaten someone
ਮਜ਼ਾਕ ਉਡਾਨਾ	*Mazaak udana*	Make fun of someone
ਅਫਵਾਹ ਫੇਲਾਨੀਆਂ	*Afwah felaania*	Spread rumours against someone
ਬਦਨਾਮ ਕਰਨਾ	*Badnaam karna*	Defame someone
ਚੁਗਲੀਆਂ ਕਰਨੀਆਂ	*Chuglian karnia*	Bitch against someone
ਡਰਾਨਾ	*Darana*	Frighten someone
ਪੰਗਾ ਲੈਣਾ	*Panga lena*	Occasionally intentionally troubling someone

Table 13.2 *Tamil words for bullying reported by teachers (n = 68) in order of most selected*

Tamil word	English version of Tamil word	English translation
கேலி	*Kēli*	Teasing
தொந்தரவு	*Tontaravu*	Troubling others
சண்டை	*Caṇṭai*	Fighting
திட்டுதல்	*Tiṭṭutal*	Scolding
பகிடிவதை	*Pakiṭivatai*	Ragging
தாக்குதல்	*Tākkutal*	Hitting
தண்டனை நடத்தை	*Taṇṭippu naṭattai*	Punishing behaviour
எரிச்சல்	*Ericcal*	Irritating
கெட்ட வார்த்தை பயன்படுத்துதல்	*Keṭṭa vārttai payaṉpaṭuttutal*	Using bad words
அவமானப்படுத்துதல்	*Avamāṉappaṭuttutal*	Insulting others
ஏளனம்	*Ēḷaṉam*	Ridicule others
கிள்ளுதல்	*Kiḷḷutal*	Pinching
உதைத்தல்	*Kutaittal*	Kicking
குத்துதல்	*Kuttutal*	Punching
கீழே தள்ளுதல்	*Taḷḷutal*	Pushing
வலிமை காட்டுதல்	*Valimai kāṭṭutal*	Showing power
மோசமான வதந்திகளை பரப்புதல்	*Vatanti parapputal*	Spreading rumours
துன்புறுத்தல்	*Tuṉpuṟuttal*	Harassment
பட்ட பெயர் வைத்தால்	*Paṭṭā piyār vaithal*	Name-calling
ஒரங்கட்டுதல்	*Oraṉkaṭṭutal*	Sidelining
மிரட்டல்	*Miraṭṭal*	Intimidation
வாய்மொழி துஷ்பிரயோகம்	*Vāymoḻi tuṣpirayōkam*	Verbal abuse
வெறித்தனமான நடத்தை	*Veṟittaṉamāṉa naṭattai*	Sadistic behaviour

and *mazaak udana* (making fun of someone) describe forms of direct verbal attack. *Afwah felaania* (spreading rumours about someone), *badnaam karna* (defaming someone) and *chunglian karnia* (bitching against someone) capture indirect forms of verbal bullying.

In Tamil, *taṇṭippu naṭattai* (punishment), *valimai kāṭṭutal* (displaying power), *miraṭṭal* (intimidation) and *veṟittaṉamāṉa naṭattai* (sadistic behaviour) capture the power imbalance of bullying; whilst *tontaravu* (troubling others) and *ericcal* (irritating others) reflect its repetitive and intentional aspects. Direct forms of bullying were captured by *caṇṭai* (fighting), *tākkutal* (hitting), *kiḷḷutal* (pinching), *kutaittal* (kicking) and *taḷḷutal* (pushing), which describe various forms of physical attack, whereas *kēli* (teasing), *tiṭṭutal* (scolding), *keṭṭa vārttai payaṉpaṭuttutal* (swearing), *avamāṉappaṭuttutal* (insulting others), *paṭṭā piyār vaithal* (name-calling), *eḷaṇam* (ridiculing others) and *vāymoḻi tuṣpirayōkam* (verbal abuse) all describe various forms of verbal attack. Only *oraṇkaṭṭutal* (sidelining) captured the relational aspects of direct bullying. *Vatanti parapputal* (spreading rumours) was the only word reflecting an indirect form of verbal bullying. Two words, *tunpuruttal* (harassment) and *pakiṭivatai* (ragging), captured the power imbalance, intention and repetitive elements of bullying. *Pakiṭivatai/ragging* describes a particular form of physical and psychological bullying amongst Indian males and is similar to *hazing*, an initiation ceremony meted out to freshmen by older members of college fraternities in the United States (Nuwer, 1990).

When cross-referencing the words suggested for bullying by teachers with the terms suggested by the students in the Cartoon Task (see Chapter 4), *dhakeshahi, panga lena* and *tang karna* in Punjabi and *kēli* and *tunpuruttal* in Tamil were suggested by both teachers and students as terms for bullying. However, Tamil students used the word *cintutal* (humiliation) to describe bullying, which was not included in the teachers' terms.

Guidance and Legislation for Bullying in England and France

Although some anti-bullying intervention is common to both countries, the English and French governments are different in implementation.

In the past English schools received official anti-bullying guidance beginning with *Don't Suffer in Silence* (Department for Education, 1994, 2nd edn., 2000), which was superseded by *Safe to Learn* (DCSF, 2007). In the past decade government guidance for English schools has been drastically reduced to a series of Department for Education guidance booklets emphasising the statutory obligation of schools regarding behaviour management, including bullying (www.gov.uk/bullying-at-school/the-law). In 2017, the gov.uk webpage Bullying at School (www.gov.uk/bullying-at-school/the-l aw) includes guidance on (i) the law; (ii) reporting bullying; (iii) bullying outside school; and (iv) a definition of bullying. Schools are advised to report more serious forms of bullying (assault, theft, hate crimes) to the police and use legislation to '*prevent discrimination, harassment and victimisation within the school*' (www.gov.uk/discrimination-your-rights). Schools are inspected by the Office for Standards in Education (OFSTED) (www.gov.uk/government/organisations/ofsted) and rated for the behaviour management and safeguarding of their students. For further guidance, schools are advised to contact five UK charities. Government guidance now foregrounds the law for bullying. Legislation includes the Equality Act (2010) for prejudice-based bullying, the Children Act (1989) for safeguarding and the Public Order Act (1986) for harassing or threatening behaviour. The Communications Act (2003, section 127), the Malicious Communications Act (1988) and the Protection from Harassment Act (1997) can be used in serious cases of cyberbullying with section 33 of the Criminal Justice and Courts Act 2015 newly introduced for revenge pornography/sexting. By September 2016, more than 200 people had been prosecuted using this new law (www.bbc.co.uk/news/uk-37278264).

In France, the school system is centralised and anti-bullying guidance and policy are issued by the Ministry of Education to be implemented in all schools. By law, schools have to provide a safe environment for staff and children under Article L911-4 of the Code of Education, modified by the Education Act n°2015–177 of 16 February 2015. Since 2010, a national campaign has been launched against bullying and cyberbullying. The Ministry of Education provides resources to French schools (http://cache.media.eduscol.education.fr/file/violence/26/8/protocole_traitement_harcelement_213268.pdf). Subsequently, the No to Bullying website was created following the 2010 awareness-raising campaign (www.nonauharcelement.education.gouv.fr). Moreover, there is a website to provide information on positive school climate, including several guides for head teachers and teachers. The Education Act of 8 July 2013 (Education Act of 1 July 2013 – J. O. of 18 July 2013), published in the Education Official Bulletin n°30 of 25 July 2013, specifies that:

Tackling any form of bullying will be a priority for every single school. Intervention shall be designed by the whole educational community, adopted by the school council for primary education and by the board of governors for state secondary schools. The impact of interventions shall be evaluated on a regular basis and improved when necessary.

Legislation specifically targeting bullying in general is very recent, with only workplace bullying being prosecuted before 2014. Article 41222–33-2–2 of the Penal Code, created following Act n°2014–873 of 4 August 2014, stipulates that bullying someone can be punished by one year imprisonment and a €15,000 fine. This can include a two-year prison sentence and a €30,000 fine if the victim is (i) unable to attend school for at least eight days, (ii) under the age of 15, (iii) a vulnerable person (disability, pregnancy known by the perpetrator) or (iv) cyberbullied. The sentence can be increased to three years' imprisonment and a €45,000 fine for points (i) and (iv). Prior to its publication, this law has been used. In November 2013, a high school student was sentenced to eight months' imprisonment and a €5,000 fine, having created a Facebook profile and Skyblog account in the name of his former girlfriend. He was found guilty of impersonation in order to ruin her reputation by spreading sexual content. He was also referred for psychological therapy.

Guidance and Legislation for Bullying in the Punjab and Tamil Nadu

Legislation for ragging is the nearest Indian states come to a law against a serious form of physical bullying (see also Chapter 14). Ragging is the violence and humiliation meted out to younger students in schools and colleges and derives from the freshmen initiation ceremonies in the United States. Eight states in India, including Tamil Nadu, have passed anti-ragging laws. The Tamil Nadu Prohibition of Ragging Act (1997) dictates that anyone committing, participating in, abetting or propagating ragging can be expelled from college, imprisoned for up to two years and liable for a fine up to 10,000 rupees (www.snget.org/sngc/images/prohibition_ragging.pdf).

Although there is no specific state law against ragging in Punjab, all universities and higher education colleges must comply with UGC Regulations (2009) on ragging in higher institutions or have institution-specific regulations in place. Ragging is a punishable offence in all such institutions (http://indianlawwatch.com/practice/anti-ragging-laws-in-india/), with students obliged to submit an anti-ragging affidavit at enrolment. Although highly effective, these regulations work only in higher education, as anti-ragging laws and regulations have not been implemented in schools which are left to the jurisdiction of Punjabi local authorities.

Information and Guidance Reported by Punjabi and Tamil Teachers

More than half of Punjabi (59%) and a quarter of Tamil (27%) teachers reported that they had read information or guidance about bullying. When asked what kind of information or guidance they had read, both groups of teachers reported accessing information on the Internet and through the media, with Tamil teachers additionally identifying anti-bullying information (training, workshops, circulars, Central Board of Secondary Education guidance), counselling, psychology books, moral teachings and the law. Although fewer Tamil teachers reported reading guidance on bullying, they reported accessing a wider range of resources than Punjabi teachers.

Anti-bullying Intervention

Anti-bullying intervention has been researched in Europe for three decades. In England, the mapping of different types of intervention used by schools started with the Sheffield Project (1991–1994) and was followed up by a government-funded study of bullying interventions in England (Thompson & Smith, 2011). Since then there have been some meta-analyses of research evaluating anti-bullying interventions internationally (Cantone et al., 2015; Evans, Fraser & Cotter, 2014; Jiménez-Barbero et al., 2016; Ttofi & Farrington, 2011). In France, the evaluation of anti-bullying intervention is a more recent, rapidly growing area of research. Anti-bullying intervention can be divided broadly into four groups of strategies – preventative, reactive, peer support and parental involvement.

Interventions Used to Prevent Bullying in English and French Schools

Preventative strategies are designed to stop bullying and contribute to an anti-bullying ethos and positive school climate. In England and France, preventative strategies include whole-school, classroom and playground strategies.

In English schools, whole-school strategies include an *anti-bullying policy*, which needs to include a comprehensive definition of bullying, stating how the school community will prevent and respond to bullying (Smith et al., 2012). *Assemblies* provide an opportunity for the whole school community to share themed subjects presented by teachers and students and are considered the most consistent method of whole-school communication about a variety of subjects including bullying (Thompson & Smith, 2011). *Classroom strategies* can be used to tackle bullying in an age, gender and culturally appropriate way. These curricular strategies can be passive (e.g. literature, e-safety films) or more active (e.g. group work, interactive virtual environments). Lessons can be used to raise awareness of bullying and the school's anti-bullying policy (e.g. Personal, Social, Health and Economic education). *School councils* give elected student representatives the opportunity to meet regularly with members of school staff to discuss issues, including anti-bullying work (Thompson & Smith, 2011).

Playground strategies are used to prevent and respond to bullying outside the school building. Most direct forms of bullying (physical, verbal, relational) happen in the school grounds, so improving school grounds, having a school grounds policy and training lunchtime supervisors and peer supporters can be effective (Thompson & Smith, 2011). Some secondary schools have installed closed-circuit television (CCTV), which not only records and provides evidence of bullying, but can also act as a deterrent. However, CCTV can prevent adults in the schools from facing up to their supervisory responsibilities (Ott, 2007) and has been shown to be ineffectual in preventing crime (Welsh & Farrington, 2008).

In France, classroom strategies include a weekly 'class life' session that can be used to talk about bullying issues in secondary schools. In 2013, a national competition was launched for primary and secondary schools to design projects to fight bullying and cyberbullying. Students produce short videos or posters which are part of an overall prevention project to be implemented within the whole school community. A prize of €2,000 is awarded to the school to support the implementation of the project (http://eduscol.education.fr/cid72752/prix-non-au-harcele ment-2015–2016.html) with 10 national laureates participating in the annual award ceremony.

At a regional level, the *rectorats* (Local Education Authorities) have also launched a regional anti-bullying prize. Additionally, they provide schools with multidisciplinary teams of police officers, psychologists and educationalists called *Equipes Mobiles de Sécurité* (Mobile Safety Teams). These teams support head teachers on demand by delivering prevention training for issues such as cyberbullying and risk-taking. In secondary schools, the Education Committees for Health and Citizenship (CESC – *Comités d'Education à la Santé et à la Citoyenneté*) are in charge of designing prevention strategies. Committees are composed of the head of the school, all the health and welfare staff (e.g. nurses and social workers), voluntary teachers and representatives of external local agencies involved in the support of young people.

Interventions Used to Prevent Bullying Reported by Punjabi and Tamil Teachers

The range of preventative strategies reported by Punjabi and Tamil teachers is shown in Figure 13.1. There was a striking difference between the Punjabi and Tamil teachers' reports, with more Tamil teachers reporting using all the strategies than Punjabi teachers. The only excep-tion was in reporting the use of other forms of preventative strategies. The strategies reported more frequently by both groups of teachers were the use of whole-school information about bullying, specific lessons on bullying, using other forms of preventative strategy, having a designated member of staff to support victims of bullying and e-safety lessons. When asked to identify who provided support for bullied students, most Tamil teachers identified counsellors, with the principal and vice principal also

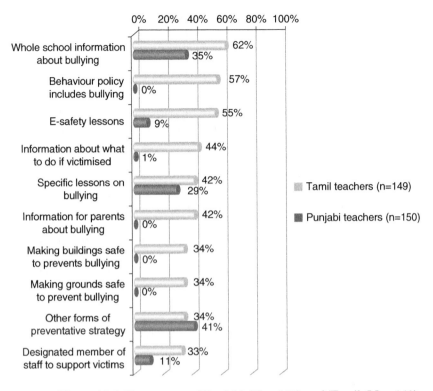

Figure 13.1 Percentages of Punjabi (N = 150) and Tamil (N = 149) teachers reporting different types of preventative strategies used in their schools

involved in some schools. Other members of staff identified by both Punjabi and Tamil teachers were physical education teachers and class teachers.

Around two-fifths of Tamil teachers reported that their schools provided information about what to do if someone is victimised, but only two Punjabi teachers reported the same. Four preventative strategies were only reported by Tamil teachers. These included using a behaviour policy which included bullying; providing information for parents about bullying; and making the school buildings, and the school grounds, safe to prevent bullying. Measures taken to make school buildings safe included the use of CCTV in the classrooms and corridors and the design of the school architecture ('*buildings are straight and visible; no hidden places*'). Measures used to make schools grounds safe included supervision by staff at break times, particularly physical education teachers, well-maintained grounds (*'soft land surfaces and safe boundaries'*), a good design (*'360 degree visible area'*) and activities (*'indoor and outdoor games'*).

When it came to reporting other preventative strategies, slightly more Punjabi teachers than Tamil teachers reported using other forms not listed in the questionnaire. Here was another striking difference. Punjabi teachers reported a more disciplinarian approach delivered by class teachers with the principal involved in serious cases. Making an example of and targeting bullying students by giving warnings and time out, making them *'stand on a bench'*, using *'non-physical punishments'* and *'complaining to parents'* were also used.

Tamil teachers reported a more educational, therapeutic approach, including counselling the students and providing guidance, teaching *'moral values and life skills'*; raising awareness through rallies, assemblies, videos, *'pictures and dramas'*; using cooperative activities such as sports, *'fun games'* and yoga. The closest that prevention came to a more punitive approach was close monitoring of and giving warnings to *'susceptible'* students. One Tamil teacher wrote: *'Emphasise good behaviour in the class through skits/talks etc. Develop empathy among students.'*

In summary, Tamil teachers used a wider range of preventative interventions for bullying than Punjabi teachers. Strategies common to both Punjabi and Tamil schools appear to be delivered through whole-school information (assemblies) and specific lessons on bullying (e-safety). Anti-bullying prevention in Punjabi schools also included making an example of the bully to show the consequences of bullying, whereas Tamil teachers used a softer approach based on counselling, awareness-raising and cooperative activities to inculcate an anti-bullying school climate.

Interventions Used to Respond to Bullying in English and French Schools

Reactive strategies are used to respond to bullying incidents. They range from empathy-creating strategies through restorative approaches (RA), which uses a series of diagnostic questions, to the use of sanctions or punishment for more serious cases. The common factor in all school-based strategies used to respond to bullying is adult mediation.

In England, effective reactive strategies are underpinned by a range of reporting systems for bullying (e.g. bully boxes, peer supporters, online reporting forms) and a centralised recording system (e.g. bullying records, either paper or e-records). Recording systems not only evidence the incidence of bullying in a school but also reveal, if used systematically, whether the interventions used to respond to bullying incidents work

(Thompson & Smith, 2011). Informal or formal interviews with students either individually or in a group are the first step in finding out what happened and underpin all reactive strategies.

In France, violence in schools has been recorded since the late 1990s. However, the surveys were based on head teachers' reports only, which constituted a bias, since the reported violent incidents were restricted to the ones that the adults knew. In 2011, with the support of the International Observatory of Violence in Schools, the Ministry of Education implemented Eric Debarbieux's *School Climate Questionnaire*, the first survey to ask students about their experience. Eighteen thousand students in Years 8 and 9 completed the questionnaire in 300 lower secondary state schools. In 2013 and 2015, the survey was repeated in 360 lower secondary state and public schools. The majority of students had an overall positive opinion of their schools, with 93% of the participants in 2015 stating that they felt well at school. In the 2014–2015 academic year, the prevalence of violent incidents had not increased compared to previous academic years and had stabilised. However, there were discrepancies between the types of schools, with vocational schools more affected by bullying than other schools with an increase from 2010 to 2014. Schools with a more socially deprived intake also reported more incidents than average schools (DEPP, 2015). A range of reactive interventions is now outlined, ranging from the least to most punitive.

The Method of Shared Concern and the Support Group Method

These two approaches are both empathy-creating, no-blame approaches to tackling bullying. Both methods use systematic forms of adult mediation. *The Method of Shared Concern* was developed in Sweden by Pikas (1989, 2002), as a counselling-based approach to school bullying. The bullying incident is deconstructed using a series of individual interviews with all involved (Rigby & Griffiths, 2010). In English schools using the Pikas method, it was described as an 'educative process' for those involved (Thompson & Smith, 2011). The *Support Group Method* (SGM) or *No Blame Approach* was developed by Robinson and Maines (2007) as a teacher-led, group-based strategy. It aims to change problematic behaviours, including bullying, by using peer pressure to elicit awareness in the bullying student of the harm and suffering caused to the victim. No punishments are involved and follow-up meetings are used to check on progress. In one evaluation, just over half of the participating schools rated the effectiveness of the method as 'very satisfactory' (Smith et al., 2007). Another study found that SGM was used most for relational and verbal bullying because of its non-confrontational and avoidance of 'punishment' (Thompson & Smith, 2011). In France, the method is being introduced into a few schools; Bellon and Gardette (2016) describe and promote the method, but without offering a genuine evaluation of the impact on bullying. As yet there are no evaluations of the impact of the method or of the way that school communities implement it.

Restorative Approaches

Restorative approaches have become increasingly popular in English and French schools to tackle bullying. These are a hierarchy of flexible responses, ranging from informal conversations through to formal facilitated meetings or conferences. In a national study, 77% of English schools reported using restorative approaches for bullying (Thompson & Smith, 2011). A series of diagnostic questions is central to this group of strategies:
- What happened?
- What were you thinking about at the time?
- What have your thoughts been since?
- Who has been affected by what you did?
- In what way have they been affected?
- What do you think needs to happen to make things right?

Restorative approaches emphasise the restoration of good relationships, rather than retribution, and can range from informal restorative circles to a formal restorative conference. To be effective, teachers practising restorative approaches need to be trained and the school needs to adopt a whole-school restorative approach (Thompson & Smith, 2011). Sanctions can be placed in a restorative framework and are used if students refuse 'to restore' or do not abide by the decisions reached. Restorative approaches are being increasingly used in English and French schools for all types of antisocial behaviour, including bullying.

In France, restorative approaches are endorsed by the Ministry of Education and are part of the resources found on its website (www.rese au-canope.fr/climatscolaire/fileadmin/user_upload/outilspdf/guide_justi ce_scolaire.pdf). Nationwide training in restorative approaches is delivered to school management teams in French schools. However, as the evaluation culture in the educational environment is recent, there is no evaluation of the strategies' effectiveness up to now.

Sanctions

Sanctions were found to be used more than any other strategy for bullying in English schools. Sanctions can range from a verbal reprimand/ticking off from the head teacher through to temporary or permanent exclusion from school. Sanctions are used to impress on bullying students that there are consequences for inappropriate behaviour and to demonstrate publicly that school rules and policies are to be taken seriously. Sanctions work best as a clear set of consequences expressed in the anti-bullying policy and mostly used within the framework of other strategies (e.g. restorative approaches) (Thompson & Smith, 2011).

In France, sanctions are organised in a similar way to England. However, schools having an anti-bullying policy with a clear protocol on responding to bullying are scarce and there is a genuine need for more progress here. Additionally, the idea that bullying students can be punished but also need support is not yet understood, with many parents unaware of who to go to for support or how they should respond if their children are involved in bullying as victims or perpetrators (Blaya & Dalloz, 2016).

Interventions Used to Respond to Bullying Reported by Punjabi and Tamil Teachers

The range of reactive strategies reported by Punjabi and Tamil teachers is shown in Figure 13.2. Again there was a striking difference between the Punjabi and Tamil teachers' reports. More Tamil teachers than Punjabi teachers reported using the full range of reactive strategies, with one exception: more Punjabi teachers reported using sanctions.

The strategies reported more frequently in both areas were informing and involving parents in responding to a bullying incident, the use of sanctions for serious bullying, interviewing the students involved in the bullying incident either separately or together and informally collecting information about the bullying incident.

When asked to qualify the types of sanctions used to respond to serious bullying, Punjabi teachers identified the use of physical punishments including a '*slap on the face*' and making students stand in the sun or in an awkward position for a long time. Fines, difficult tasks and repeated bouts of homework, complaining to the parents and expulsion were also reported for bullying students. Although Tamil teachers also reported using punishment, it was mostly of a milder kind: '*Serious bullying can be reduced by mild punishment; otherwise (they) won't realise their mistakes.*' Warnings, informing parents and a range of supportive strategies including counselling, guidance, monitoring and even medical examinations were offered to bullying students.

The remaining five reactive strategies were only reported by Tamil teachers: members of staff formally collecting and recording information

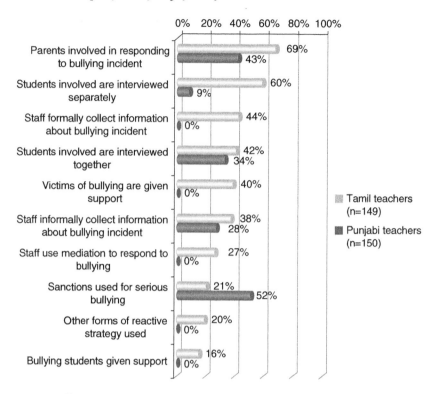

Figure 13.2 Percentages of Punjabi (N = 150) and Tamil (N = 149) teachers reporting different types of reactive strategies used in their schools

about the bullying incident, providing support to bullied students, using mediation, using other strategies and providing support to bullying students.

Tamil teachers described the types of mediation provided to bullied and bullying students as counselling, staff meetings, involving parents, encouraging compromise and problem-solving. One teacher described the mediation process as: '*analyse the incident and try to find reasons for the incident and solve the problem*'. Support for the bullied student involved counselling, teaching resilience ('*strengthening their mind*' and '*teaching braveness*'), giving extra staff support and reassurance including monitoring, holistic support ('*support physically, mentally or biologically*') and feedback from peers ('*peer groups report*'). Support for the bullying students included teaching social skills ('*Teach them soft skills. Encourage their desirable traits to overcome the other'*), creating a support group of *'parents, teachers, friends and relatives'*, counselling and extra educational support and guidance. One teacher encouraged *'strengthening them'*.

Only Tamil teachers reported using types of reactive strategies not listed in the questionnaire. These included involvement in group activities (*sport, self-defence, yoga*), raising awareness of bullying (*conducting moral classes, posters, rallies*), counselling, teaching values (*value talks*), monitoring students, identifying positive role models (*'give talks on great personalities who have overcome bullying'*), teaching social skills and meditation. One teacher reported engaging constructively with the bullying student as: *'list ... all [the] good positive ... behaviour of [the] bullying students and suggest that such a good student should not indulge in bullying behaviour'*.

In summary, Tamil teachers use a wider range of interventions to respond to bullying than Punjabi teachers. Although parental involvement in responding to a bullying incident is used in both Punjabi and Tamil schools, Tamil teachers identified it as their number one strategy. Punishment for serious incidents of bullying was reported most by Punjabi teachers, whereas only a minority of Tamil teachers reported using sanctions. Responding to a bullying incident by interviewing students either together or separately and collecting information about the incident informally was reported by both groups of teachers. Punjabi schools appear to adopt a more sanction-based approach to bullying, using a restricted range of interventions in contrast to the Tamil schools, which involve the parents and use a wider range of more therapeutic strategies.

Peer Support Interventions Used in English and French Schools

In Europe, peer support uses the knowledge, skills and experience of young people in a structured way to tackle bullying. Peer supporters are trained to deal with interpersonal conflicts, social exclusion and bullying in preventative and non-violent ways. Peer support schemes can also be used reactively, to respond to bullying incidents and support all involved. To be effective, peer supporters need to have a dedicated room for mentoring, ongoing teacher supervision and rolling recruitment; otherwise schemes can fail (Cowie & Wallace, 2000; Smith & Watson, 2004). Getting a good gender balance is often challenging, as there are usually more female recruits than males (Cowie & Smith, 2010).

Peer support schemes are popular in both English and French schools. In England, *buddy schemes* offer support and friendship to vulnerable students in everyday situations. Buddy schemes are particularly effective for students at transition or needing targeted support (Smith & Watson, 2004; Thompson & Smith, 2011). *Peer mediation* involves students in a problem-solving process. Student mediators can be trained in conflict resolution skills, including restorative approaches. English secondary school students thought that peer mediation schemes worked better if mediators were older and the bullied and bullying pupils were seen separately (Thompson & Smith, 2011). *Peer mentoring* aims to create a supportive relationship between two pupils, combining practical advice and encouragement. It is especially used for supporting a pupil at challenging times (e.g. transition, bereavement or bullying). Mentoring is most effective when agreed ways of working are clear and there is good staff supervision and support of the mentors (Cowie & Wallace, 2000; Smith & Watson, 2004).

In France, the main type of intervention used to respond to bullying is peer mentoring and peer mediation (Blaya & Cohen, 2016). Some secondary schools have set up peer mentoring schemes with the help of external agencies, based on research findings on the effectiveness of peer schemes (Bonafé-Schmitt, 2006; Condette-Castelain & Hue-Nonin, 2014).

Peer Support Interventions Reported by Punjabi and Tamil Teachers

Only Tamil teachers reported using peer support schemes in their schools. Peer mediation was reported most (46%), followed by peer mentoring (42%) and buddy schemes (33%). Other types of peer support included class monitors, including school counsellors: '*The representatives from all classes will take care of overall discipline of the students including bullying.*' As peer support schemes have been found to be one of the main ways students can be involved in anti-bullying work in Europe, this could identify an intervention to be explored by Punjabi schools.

Interventions Involving Parents Used in English and French Schools

This is a more recent area of anti-bullying research but is receiving increasing interest in both England and France.

Involving Parents in Preventing Bullying

Both English and French schools employ a range of interventions to educate parents about bullying. English schools use both *parent training information nights* and *teacher–parent/carer meetings*, which have been associated with more effective intervention programmes (Axford et al., 2015; Ttofi & Farrington, 2011). *Parent/carer evenings* can initiate discussions about bullying, including the signs, symptoms and associated risk factors. *Regular newsletters, consultation on policies, after-school clubs* and *support for parents of at-risk children* are some of the many ways schools try to involve parents (Farrington & Ttofi, 2009; Thompson & Smith, 2011). *Designated members of staff* (e.g. parent support advisors, family liaison officers, home school workers) can be appointed to liaise with parents with *family outreach programmes* helping to build community relationships. *Home school books, parents' leaflets, parents' questionnaires, assemblies for parents, parents' forums, parents' working groups* and *parents' evenings* have all evolved in order to instigate regular contact with parents (Thompson & Smith, 2011). Communication between school and parents is essential to preventative strategies in order for parents to recognise the symptoms of bullying and take early steps to report it.

In France, although the Education Act (2013) specifies that the whole school community, including parents, should be involved, families are informed of anti-bullying initiatives through their representatives at school or specific parents' evenings but are less involved as actors for change and prevention. However, information strategies are spreading and some Parents Cafés (i.e. sessions with parents to discuss issues from school life), include talks and conferences about school bullying (Debarbieux, 2016).

Involving Parents in Responding to Bullying

In England, research has identified how parents can be involved in responding to bullying (Axford et al., 2015). *Newsletters* or *booklets* and holding *parent–teacher meetings* can not only provide parents with information about the school's anti-bullying policy but also offer guidance on how to help their children deal with bullying. *Parenting skills classes* are targeted at parents with children who had been excluded or are at risk of exclusion for more serious cases of bullying. Parents can be directly involved in restorative approaches for bullying incidents participating in either informal meetings or more formal restorative conferences. However, schools often struggle to engage parents with parents' evenings poorly attended (Thompson & Smith, 2011).

Interventions Involving Parents Used in Punjabi Schools

Parental Group Therapy (PGT): A New Initiative

A study carried out at Punjabi University showed that parental involvement can significantly reduce cyberbullying incidents. Six hundred students from an urban school were interviewed by an Anti-Bullying Committee (ABC) consisting of six teachers and 12 senior school students. The ABC proved highly effective in encouraging students to reveal their 'never-disclosed' cyberbullying experiences. Thirty students involved in cyberbullying and 30 students with no involvement in cyberbullying were compared. Both cyberbullies and cyber victims were found to have weaker parent–child bonds. Whereas cyberbullies took out the frustrations of weaker parent–child bonds onto vulnerable peers (cyber victims), the cyber victims lacked a parent–child bond strong enough to discuss their cyber experiences with their parents, so as to prevent their further cyber victimisation (Sandhu & Kaur, 2016).

The study found PGT to be an effective intervention in reducing behavioural problems of both cyberbullies and cyber victims, as parents were educated about bullying and cyberbullying, including their children's cyberbullying experiences. Parents were helped to realise that in order to keep a check on their children's online activities, they themselves needed to increase their knowledge of the Internet and mobile phones. Deficits in parenting style, a lack of parent–child communication and need for strengthening parent–child bonds were addressed. In PGT, parents can reflect on their past parenting style, and are encouraged to adopt a more positive approach. This intervention significantly lowered cyberbullying incidents in schools, even six months after its completion (Sandhu & Kaur, 2016).

Exchanging Ideas

Information on Anti-bullying Intervention Used in English and French Schools

Based on European research, we identified eight aspects of anti-bullying intervention that might be of interest to Punjabi and Tamil teachers and adapted for their schools.
• **Bullying:** more detailed information on definition, types of bullying, group dynamics of bullying, causes of bullying and the impact of bullying on victims and perpetrators.

- *Developing an anti-bullying policy:* information on what the policy does, who to consult in the development of the policy (e.g. students, teachers, parents) and suggestions on what to include (e.g. definitions of bullying including types of bullying, how to report it and what action the school will take in response to a bullying incident).
- *Anti-bullying intervention guide:* a guide to the different types of preventative and reactive interventions with evidence of effectiveness and references to more detailed resources.
- *Peer support schemes:* an outline of peer support and the different types of schemes including what they aim to do and how effective they are.
- *Developing pupil voice:* an outline of the different initiatives used to give students a voice in their school e.g. school councils, student committees.
- *Involving parents in anti-bullying work:* a range of strategies and approaches used to engage parents in preventing and responding to bullying, including cyberbullying.
- *Reporting systems:* information on the different ways of reporting bullying from anonymous reporting (e.g. bully boxes, online reporting forms) to more direct, face-to-face reporting (e.g. peer support schemes, designated staff member).
- *Recording sheet:* an example of a sheet including what happened, who was involved, what action will be taken, what are the outcomes of that action and following up.

Interest Expressed by Punjabi and Tamil Teachers for Anti-bullying Information

The levels of interest expressed in different types of anti-bullying information are shown in Figure 13.3. Punjabi teachers expressed considerably higher levels of interest in all areas than Tamil teachers. Most Punjabi teachers were interested in general information on bullying, reporting systems, information on anti-bullying intervention and developing an anti-bullying policy. Around two-thirds were interested in information on bullying incident record sheets and peer support schemes, half were interested in information on involving parents in anti-bullying work and just over a quarter in developing pupil voice. One Punjabi teacher offered one possible explanation of the interest shown in the anti-bullying resources:

There is complete unawareness regarding school bullying. I even didn't know about this term before you came to our school. This is there in Indian society, but is not yet recognised. This is a heart-breaking truth ... Measures like this ... need to be done before this poisonous snake engulfs our schools. (Class 6 teacher, Punjabi school)

Around half of the Tamil teachers expressed interest in general information about bullying and developing an anti-bullying policy. Under half to a third were interested in peer support schemes and involving parents in anti-bullying work, with around a quarter interested in reporting systems, record sheets and information on interventions. Around two-fifths were interested in developing pupil voice.

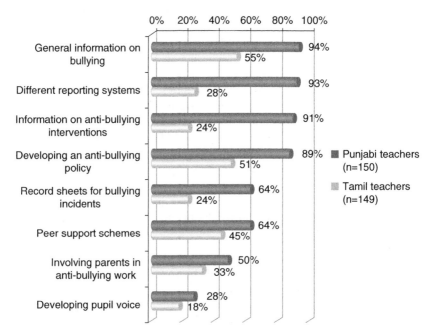

Figure 13.3 Percentages of Punjabi (N = 150) and Tamil (N = 149) teachers expressing interest in having more information on different types of anti-bullying intervention

In summary, Punjabi teachers expressed much higher levels of interest in information about European anti-bullying resources than the Tamil teachers. Reflecting on the previous data on preventative and reactive strategies, Tamil teachers employed a greater range of anti-bullying intervention, including preventative, peer support and reactive strategies than Punjabi teachers, so maybe they did not think it necessary. This could possibly explain our initial finding that Tamil teachers reported witnessing bullying less in their schools than Punjabi teachers because they do more about preventing it in the first place and more to respond to it when it happens. It is possible that making the Punjabi teachers aware of the range of anti-bullying intervention has raised awareness of bullying and prompted keener interest in this information. This is too small a study to conclude that Tamil schools are in better shape to tackle bullying than Punjabi schools, but the findings indicate a distinct difference between the two states in approach to and management of bullying behaviour.

What Have We Learned from Each Other?

Firstly, there are possible candidates for a word for bullying in both languages. Punjabi and Tamil Nadu teachers identified several words for bullying in each language, of which three Punjabi words (*dhakeshahi, panga lena, tang karna*) and two Tamil words (*kēli, tunpuruttal*) were the same as words identified by school students in the Cartoon Task (see Chapter 4).

In general, Tamil teachers reported using a bigger range of strategies than Punjabi teachers, although the questionnaire was far from exhaustive. There were similarities with English and French schools in both Indian states. The Punjabi teachers' practice of using sanctions for bullying is mirrored by English schools, with the exception of corporal punishment for serious bullying. Despite India ratifying the UN Convention on the Rights of the Child in 1992, children and young people experience physical punishment both at home and in school. More than two-thirds of parents surveyed by the Early Childhood Association (ECA) in Mumbai and Bengaluru reported hitting their children (ECA, 2016). Data from 3,000 children in Andhra Pradesh in 2009 concluded that physical punishment was endemic in schools, with 92% of younger students (7–8 years) and 68% of older students (14–15 years) witnessing corporal punishment in the previous week, while 77% of 7–8-year-olds and 34% of 14–15-year-olds reported being physically punished in school in the previous week (Morrow & Singh, 2014). Corporal punishment by teachers has been illegal in England only since 1986, and full legal prohibition is still to be achieved in France. There is still much more work to be done by both India and Europe to achieve the ambitions enshrined in the UN Convention on the Rights of the Child.

Although Tamil teachers reported using a similar range of interventions as English and French schools, theirs appeared to be a more therapeutic, non-punitive approach involving counsellors and parents in tackling bullying. Maybe there are lessons that Punjabi, English and

French schools can learn here. There is a rise in popularity of interventions, like *mindfulness* based in Buddhist and Hindu practices, being adopted in some English schools, indicating a gentler, proactive, peace-building approach which has been shown to improve student well-being (Kuyken et al., 2013; Weare, 2013).

Legislation for serious forms of bullying was common to all countries, with specific laws in France, Tamil Nadu and the Punjab and adapted legislation in England. It can be argued that a legal framework not only acts as an incentive for schools to take bullying seriously but equally acknowledges the status of victim. Supporters of legislation for bullying argue the importance of a powerful deterrent for bullying, as evidenced by the Department for Education guidance foregrounding legislation. However, others have reservations about legislating for bullying, arguing for promoting educating children and young people about values and respect for others rather than criminalising them (Cornell & Limber, 2015; Patchin & Hinduja, 2016).

This is a pilot study providing only a partial insight into Punjabi and Tamil schools' anti-bullying practice. With only a small sample of teachers from only 2 of the 29 states of India, questionnaires in English and a restricted range of questions on anti-bullying intervention, these findings have limited application. But it is a start. Further research needs to be done with a larger, stratified sample of schools with questionnaires in Punjabi, Tamil and English. More detailed items on the types of intervention used need to be included with more space for participants to qualify their answers. Student data on the efficacy of interventions also needs to be collected.

Even after three decades of research in Europe, bullying is still a problem in European schools. As forms of bullying change, so types of intervention must adapt. Researchers must be aware that just because particular intervention is effective in Europe does not mean it will translate to another culture. Equally, just because interventions in other cultures are not yet evaluated, does not mean they cannot be highly effective. At the very least, this research opened a dialogue on anti-bullying intervention.

I have been teaching since I was 25. Today I am 55. I have seen students fighting, bitching, hurting, ignoring, and harming each other in any way and up to any extent from the day I have joined this profession. But what I have not seen from day one is some kind of rescue work. I mean, no one knows how to control this newly labelled, old problem of our schools. But I am happy that at least some form of help, or efforts have started to come up [from the network project] for controlling this problem. (Class 8 teacher, Punjabi school)

References

Axford, N., Farrington, D. P., Clarkson, S., Bjornstad, G. J., Wrigley, Z. & Hutchings, J. (2015). Involving parents in school-based programmes to prevent and reduce bullying: What effect does it have? *Journal of Children's Services*, *10*, 242–251. http://dx.doi.org/10.1108/JCS-05-2015-0019.

Bellon, J.-P. & Gardette, B. (2016). *Harcèlement scolaire: le vaincre, c'est possible. La méthode Pikas : une technique éprouvée.* Paris: European Science Foundation.

Blaya, C. & Cohen, J. (2016). L'amélioration du climat scolaire en Europe et en Amérique du Nord: la mobilisation de tous pour la réussite scolaire et personnelle de chacun. In E. Debarbieux (ed.), *L'école face à la Violence – Décrire, expliquer, agir* (pp. 183–196). Paris: Dunod.

Blaya, C. & Dalloz, M. (2016). *Mon enfant est victime/auteur de harcèlement.* Paris: Soubeyran.

Bonafé-Schmitt, J.-P. (2006). La médiation scolaire par les pairs: Une alternative à la violence à l'École. *Spirale*, *37*, 173–182.

Cantone, E., Piras, A. P., Vellante, M., Preti, A., Danielsdottir, S., D'Ajola, E., Lesinskiene, S., Angermeyer, M. C., Carta, M. G. & Bhugra, D. (2015). Interventions on bullying and cyberbullying in schools: A systematic review. *Clinical Practice & Epidemiology in Mental Health*, *11* (Suppl. 1: M4), 58–76.

Condette-Castelain, S. & Hue-Nonin, C. (2014). *La Médiation par les élèves. Enjeux et perspectives pour la vie scolaire.* Dijon: Canopé.

Cornell, D. & Limber, S. P. (2015). Law and policy on the concept of bullying at school. *American Psychologist*, *70*(4), 333–343. http://dx.doi.org/10.1037/a003855.

Cowie, H. & Smith, P. K. (2010). Peer support as a means of improving school safety and reducing bullying and violence. In B. Doll, W. Pfohl & J. Yoon (eds.), *Handbook of Prevention Research* (pp. 177–193). New York: Routledge.

Cowie, H. & Wallace, P. (2000). *Peer Support in Action – From Bystanding to Standing By.* London: Sage.

DCSF (2007). Safe to learn: Embedding anti-bullying work in schools. www.antibullyingalliance.org.uk/tackling_bullying_behaviour/in_schools/law,_policy_and_guidance/safe_to_learn.aspx.

Debarbieux, E. (2016). *L'école face à la Violence – Décrire, expliquer, agir.* Paris: Dunod.

DEPP (2015). Note d'information n°49. Paris, Ministère de l'Education nationale, de l'Enseignement supérieur et de la Recherche.

DfES (2nd edn., 2000; revised 2002). *Bullying: Don't Suffer in Silence. An Anti-bullying Pack for Schools.* London: Her Majesty's Stationery Office.

Early Childhood Association (2016). *Survey on Bribing, Threatening and Keeping Secrets.* Mumbai: Early Childhood Association.

Evans, C. B. R., Fraser, M. W. & Cotter, K. L. (2014). The effectiveness of school-based bullying prevention programs: A systemic review. *Aggression and Violent Behavior*, *19*, 532–544.

Farrington, D. P. & Ttofi, M. M. (2009). School-based programs to reduce bullying and victimization: A systematic review. *Campbell Systematic Reviews*, 6, 1–148.

Jiménez-Barbero, J. A., Ruiz-Hernández, J. A., Llor-Zaragoza, L., Pérez-Garćia, M. & Llor-Esteban, B. (2016). Effectiveness of anti-bullying school programs: A meta-analysis. *Children and Youth Services Review*, 61, 165–175.

Kuyken, W., Weare, K., Ukoumunne, O. C., Vicray, R., Motton, N., Burnett, R., Cullen, C., Hennelly, S. & Huppert, F. (2013). Effectiveness of the Mindfulness in Schools Programme: Non-randomised controlled feasibility study. *British Journal of Psychiatry*, 203(2), 126–131. doi 10.1192/bjp.bp 113.126649.

Morrow, V. & Singh, R. (2014). *Corporal Punishment in Schools in Andhra Pradesh, India: Children's and Parents' Views*. Oxford: Young Lives.

Nuwer, H. (1990). *Broken Pledges: The Deadly Rite of Hazing*. Marietta, GA: Longstreet Press, Inc.

Olweus, D. (1993). *Bullying at School: What We Know and What We Can Do*. Oxford: Blackwell.

Ott, L. (2007). Pourquoi ont-ils brûlé les écoles?. In L. Mucchielli & V. Le Goaziou (eds.), *Quand les banlieues brûlent* (pp. 126–144). Paris: la découverte.

Patchin, J. W. & Hinduja, S. (2016). Deterring teen bullying: Assessing the impact of perceived punishment from police, schools and parents. *Youth Violence and Juvenile Justice*. http://journals.sagepub.com/doi/abs/10.1177/ 1541204016681057.

Pikas, A. (1989). A pure conception of mobbing gives the best for treatment. *School Psychology International*, 10, 95–104.

Pikas, A. (2002). New developments of the shared concern method. *School Psychology International*, 23, 307–326.

Rigby, K. & Griffiths, C. (2010). *Applying the Method of Shared Concern in Australian schools: An Evaluative Study*. Canberra: Department of Education, Employment and Workplace Relations. www.deewr.gov.au/schooling/national safeschools/pages/research.aspx.

Robinson, G. & Maines, B. (2007). *Bullying: A Complete Guide to the Support Group Method*. Bristol: Lucky Duck Publishing.

Salmivalli, C., Lagerspetz, K., Björkqvist, K., Österman, K. & Kaukiainen, A. (1996). Bullying as a group process: Participant roles and their relations to social status within the group. *Aggressive Behavior*, 22, 1–15.

Sandhu, D. & Kaur, S. (2016). Reducing cyber-bullying and problem behaviors among students through parental group therapy. *Pakistan Journal of Psychological Research*, 31(2), 383–401.

Sharp, S. & Smith, P. K. (eds.) (1994). *How to Tackle Bullying in Your School: A Practical Handbook for Teachers*. London: Routledge.

Smith, P. K., Howard, S. & Thompson, F. (2007). Use of the support group method to tackle bullying, and evaluation from schools and local authorities in England. *Pastoral Care in Education*, 25, 4–13.

Smith, P. K., Kupferberg, A., Mora-Merchan, J. A., Samara, M., Bosley, S. & Osborn, R. (2012). A content analysis of school anti-bullying policies: A follow-up after six years. *Educational Psychology in Practice, 28,* 61–84.

Smith, P. K., Morita, Y., Junger-Tas, J., Olweus, D., Catalano, R. & Slee, P. (1999). *The Nature of School Bullying: A Cross-National Perspective.* London & New York: Routledge.

Smith, P. K. & Sharp, S. (eds.) (1994). *School Bullying: Insights and Perspectives.* London: Routledge.

Smith, P. K., Smith, C., Osborn, R. & Samara, M. (2008). A content analysis of school anti-bullying policies: Progress and limitations. *Educational Psychology in Practice, 24,* 1–12.

Smith, P. K. & Watson, D. (2004). Evaluation of the CHIPS (ChildLine in Partnership with Schools) programme. Research report RR570, DfES.

Thompson, F. & Smith, P. K. (2011). The use and effectiveness of anti-bullying strategies in schools. DFE-RR098.

Ttofi, M. M. & Farrington, D. P. (2011). Effectiveness of school-based programs to reduce bullying: a systematic and meta-analytic review. *Journal of Experimental Criminology, 7,* 27–56.

Weare, K. (2013). Developing mindfulness with children and young people: A review of the evidence and policy context. *Journal of Children's Services, 8*(2), 141–153.

Welsh, B. C. & Farrington, D. P. (2008). Effects of closed circuit television surveillance on crime. *Campbell Systematic Reviews, 17.* www.crim.cam.ac.uk/people/academic_research/david_farrington/cctv.pdf.

APPENDIX 13.A

Bullying Questionnaire for Punjabi and Tamil schools

Indian-European Research Network

Bullying, cyberbullying, pupil safety and well-being https://sites.google .com/site/cyberbullyingeuindian/

Information sheet about bullying

The Indian-European Research Network is a group of academics from France, Germany, Netherlands, the Punjab, Tamil Nadu and the UK who are studying a distinctive form of aggression called bullying. Bullying has been researched in Europe for over 30 years. Please can you read the following information about bullying and then answer our questionnaire.
   Bullying is distinctive in 3 main ways:

o There is an **intention** to harm
o The aggression is **repeated**
o There is an imbalance of power.

Bullying can be between two people or can involve a group. Often there are bystanders, who witness the bullying.

Bullying can be **direct** e.g. physical (punching; hitting); verbal (name-calling; verbal abuse) and relational (exclusion from a group) or **indirect** (spreading nasty rumours).

It is often the differences between people that are used in bullying. These can be differences in:
o Gender
o Race
o Religion or culture
o Sexuality
o Disability

Cyberbullying is a more recent form of bullying. Victims can be cyberbullied by text message; phone calls; social networking websites (Twitter; Facebook; Snapchat; BBM; WhatsApp); emails and online games using smartphones; tablets and laptops.

Please now complete our questionnaire

Bullying questionnaire for Punjabi and Tamil schools

Please complete the following section and consent to the Indian-European Research Network using your data by typing your name in the <u>consent</u> box. Your data is anonymous and your school will not be identified in any publication or report. We would appreciate it if you can answer all the questions, but you are free to withdraw your participation at any time.

Position
School   **Consent**

Now, please answer the following questions about bullying.

Q1: Having read the information about bullying on the information sheet, have you witnessed bullying at your school?
☐ Yes   ☐ No   ☐ Not sure

Q2: If you have witnessed bullying in your school, do you have a word or words other than 'bullying' that you and your students use to describe this behaviour?

☐ Yes ☐ No ☐ Not sure

If yes, please write what this word is (or words are) here:

Q3: Have you read any information or guidance about bullying?

☐ Yes ☐ No ☐ Not sure

If yes, please tell us what information or guidance you have read:

Q4: Does your school do anything to prevent bullying happening?

☐ There is a school policy about behaviour which includes bullying and cyberbullying
☐ The whole school receives regular information about acceptable and unacceptable behaviour including bullying and cyberbullying (e.g. in school assembly)
☐ There are specific lessons about acceptable and unacceptable behaviour including bullying and cyberbullying
☐ There are lessons about how to stay safe on the internet/e-safety
☐ There is information about what to do if someone is victimised, bullied or cyberbullied
☐ The school buildings are made safe to prevent bullying – how?
☐ The school grounds are made safe to prevent bullying – how?
☐ There is a designated member of staff to support vulnerable children – who?
☐ The students' parents receive information about bullying and cyberbullying
☐ If you do anything else to prevent bullying – please specify:

Q5: If a student is bullied, how does your school respond to the bullying incident?

☐ A member of staff informally collects information about the bullying incident
☐ A member of staff formally collects and records information about the bullying incident
☐ The students involved are interviewed separately
☐ The students involved are interviewed together
☐ Parents are informed and involved in responding to a bullying incident
☐ A member of staff will use mediation to respond to incidents of bullying – please describe what they do:
☐ Serious bullying usually attracts a sanction or punishment – please tell us what this might be:
☐ The victims of bullying are given support – please tell us what this might be:
☐ Bullying students are given support – please tell us what this might be:
☐ If you do anything else to respond to bullying – please specify:

Q6: Do you have a scheme where students help to support bullied and/or vulnerable students in school?

☐ Buddy schemes (Older students who support vulnerable students in breaktimes and at transition when younger students move to secondary school).
☐ Peer mentor schemes (Older, trained students who are available to listen to and support bullied students, reporting more serious cases to a member of staff).
☐ Peer mediation schemes (Older, trained students who support bullied and vulnerable students with conflict management strategies, reporting more serious cases to a member of staff).
☐ If you have any other type of peer scheme – please specify:

Q7: Would you be interested in any of the following? Please tick any boxes.

☐ General information on bullying
☐ Different reporting systems for bullying
☐ Information on anti-bullying interventions
☐ Involving parents in anti-bullying work

☐ How to develop an anti-bullying policy
☐ A record sheet for bullying incidents
☐ Peer support schemes
☐ Developing pupil voice in your school

Q8: Any comments?

Thank you for completing our questionnaire. We will be putting summary findings up on our website: http://sites.google.com/site/cyberbullyingeuindian/

14 Bullying, Law and Pre-service Teachers' Perspectives
Australian and Indian Contexts

Colette Langos, Barbara A. Spears, Carmel Taddeo,
Lesley-Anne Ey, Toby Carslake, Alexander Stretton,
Damanjit Sandhu and Suresh Sundaram

Globally there has been much discussion concerning how the law and legislation might operate in relation to serious cases of bullying and cyberbullying. Some countries and states/provinces have enacted specific laws to prevent bullying, whereas others have sought to apply existing legislation (Campbell et al., 2010; Spears et al., 2014). In the United States, for example, 49 of the 50 states have an anti-bullying law in place to prevent bullying; however, little is known about their effectiveness.

In one study of the effectiveness of such laws, Ramirez and colleagues (2016) measured the impact of an anti-bullying law in Iowa in preventing bullying and improving teacher response to bullying, over three data points between 2001 and 2010 (pre-law, one year post and three years post). They found that after the law was introduced, there was an initial increase in reporting of bullying, largely due to heightened awareness, but it did eventually result in longer-term reductions in prevalence. However, what was not impacted was the extent to which teachers intervened in bullying incidents at school. Whilst teacher intervention was good, with most students reporting that they did intervene 'often or very often', there was a progressive decline in teacher intervention post-law introduction, i.e. the introduction of the law did *not* improve teacher intervention over time as expected.

This finding demonstrates a need to target what teachers actually do when a law is introduced, and how they are supported to interpret that law in the school setting. It also suggests to not solely rely on legal responses to generate change in school bullying. The importance of staff and leadership turnover in terms of prevention and intervention continuity over a five-year time frame is also highlighted through this study. Impacts occur to programmes, for example, with staff turnover as new teachers arrive and others leave, and the changing skill set available in the school to deal with bullying is altered (Spears et al., 2015).

Ramirez and colleagues (2016, p. 2) suggested that the theoretical basis underpinning the employment of anti-bullying laws is situated within socio-ecological approaches to prevention. They noted that activities related to anti-bullying laws, such as reporting, response strategies, disciplinary action, staffing and training, occur at various levels of the school/community ecology (Dresler-Hawke & Whitehead, 2009; Espelage, 2014). These are relevant to this chapter, as pre-service teachers (PSTs) are an important element of the total teaching ecology, and form part of staff rejuvenation and replacement strategies in schools, potentially impacting school climate through their arrival and capacity to respond to bullying, or lack of it (Spears et al., 2015).

Whilst there is a growing body of research concerning Western PSTs' capacity and competence to deal with bullying and cyberbullying (e.g. Bauman & Del Rio, 2005, 2006; Boulton et al., 2014; Nicolaides, Toda & Smith, 2002; Spears et al., 2015), little is currently known about Indian PSTs' attitudes to and knowledge or understanding of bullying and cyberbullying (see also Chapter 13), nor the legal contexts which oversee these behaviours within, and outside of, the school setting.

Currently in Australia, a matrix of existing civil and criminal laws operates to regulate serious behaviours related to bullying. At present, there is a dearth of literature exploring the laws governing bullying and cyberbullying in India. This chapter makes a significant contribution to the extant knowledge base by: (1) examining existing statutes and referring to relevant jurisprudence in relation to bullying, cyberbullying and other culturally relevant behaviours, such as ragging and Eve teasing, and (2) considering Indian and Australian PSTs' knowledge in relation to those legal contexts.

Issues of Definition

Before considering the legal contexts, and the views of PSTs, it is important to briefly reflect upon how bullying is defined and what it may mean for these contexts. Whilst it is often framed as a contested notion, there are three reliable elements upon which most researchers agree. Variations of Olweus' definition (1993, 1994) are most often quoted, identifying: *an aggressive behaviour perpetrated with the intent to harm the target; repeated over time; and characterised by real or perceived imbalance of power.* Whilst there are many subtypes of bullying, the common forms relate to physical, verbal, social/relational (psychological) and, most recently, cyberbullying behaviours. Debate also continues around the online/offline dichotomy and the overlap and interplay which occurs between them, and whether one is a continuation of the other, using digital means, or a new, unique form of bullying in its own right (see Smith, 2014, for review).

Relevant to this chapter are concerns about the cultural relevance of the definition. Coffin, Larson and Cross (2010), in their study of bullying in an Australian Aboriginal context, remind us that definitions are contextual, reliant upon the language and cultural patterns common to the settings in which individuals live, thus they determine how bullying is perceived and explained in that context. The role of 'voice' is therefore also important in understanding how these behaviours are construed in situ, and Spears and Kofoed (2013) argue for greater inclusion of voice when determining definitions, particularly in culturally and linguistically diverse settings.

This chapter now turns to the legal contexts in India and Australia relevant to schooling environments. Discussions surrounding the application of relevant laws are based on doctrinal methods of research. This methodological approach involves legal analysis of case law, legislation, regulations, parliamentary reports and other legal materials (Pearce, Campbell & Harding, 1987). Footnotes on these are gathered at the end of this chapter. Following this, a snapshot of relevant PST data from both cultural contexts is presented.

Indian Legal Context

Legal Framework Governing Bullying in Education Institutions

Bullying in Indian educational institutions (schools, colleges and universities) is not governed comprehensively by 'anti-bullying' laws. Applicable laws regulating instances of victimisation in these settings are detailed (primarily) in the Indian Penal Code 1860.[1] From a Western perspective, two forms of victimisation which may be labelled as bullying are 'ragging' and 'Eve teasing'. Both behaviours are prevalent in the Indian schooling and higher educational institution contexts (Ban on Ragging, 2007). Although there are nuances which delineate these behaviours from 'bullying' per se, it is useful to include ragging and Eve teasing when considering how Indian law regulates aggressive behaviours akin to bullying, especially given recent legislative changes.

Ragging

Recently, ragging has been identified as a category of aggressive behaviours carried out in the schooling context (Central Board of Secondary Education, 2015). Prior to this, it was deemed limited to the higher

---

[1] Indian Penal Code 1860 (India).

educational institution context (colleges, universities) (Jaishanker & Halder, 2009, pp. 579–582),[2] where it has been described as the 'offspring of bullying' and served as a 'means of ice-breaking between the juniors and seniors'.[3]

From a Western perspective, there are similarities and slight differences between 'bullying' and 'ragging'. Both encompass aggressive behaviours carried out to intentionally harm a victim. Harm in both contexts includes low-level emotional harm such as short-term annoyance, fear and grief, and extends to encompass protracted psychological injury. Both types of conduct involve an imbalance of power. A person's characteristics (e.g. height, intelligence, physical strength, age, gender, popularity and socio-economic status) can give a perpetrator perceived or actual power over a victim (Patchin & Hinduja, 2006). In India, caste and skin colour may also give rise to an asymmetric power relationship between peers. Notably, one key nuance between bullying and ragging relates to the aspect of repetition. In the bullying context, conduct is usually repeated. Instances of ragging may, however, involve only one isolated act, delineating ragging from bullying to a degree. Another point of distinction relates to the highly physical nature of ragging, unlike bullying, which may be relational, social, verbal or physical. Given the similarities between the behaviours, any dialogue around the regulation of bullying in India ought to therefore include ragging, *especially since it has been recently identified within the schooling context* (Central Board of Secondary Education, 2015).

Ragging has received significant judicial attention in India, particularly over the past 20 years (Garg, 2009).[4] The conduct is governed, to an extent, by legislation at the federal level, where it is likely to fall within the scope of various offence provisions of the Indian Penal Code.[5] The element which criminalises ragging usually relates to the 'assault' element of the conduct – the physical force applied.[6] In addition, several

---

[2] Anecdotal evidence based on discussions with university academics Dr Damanjit Sandhu, Annamalai University and Patalia University (Punjab, India) and Dr Suresh Sundaram (Tamil Nadu, India).

[3] Anecdotal evidence based on discussions with university academic Dr Damanjit Sandhu, Annamalai University and Patalia University (Punjab, India).

[4] *University of Kerala* v *Council, Principals, Colleges and Others* [2009] INSC 284 (11 February 2009).

[5] Indian Penal Code 1860 (India). See, for example, s 294 – obscene acts and songs; s 321 – voluntarily causing hurt; s 322 – voluntarily causing grievous hurt; s 326 – voluntarily causing hurt by dangerous weapons or means; s 339 – wrongful restraint; s 340 – wrongful confinement; s 350 – criminal force.

[6] Although s 294 – obscene acts and songs – does not require a physical act; an obscene song, ballad or uttering of words (without physical force) directed at the victim, in or near a public place, constitutes this offence. The requirement that the conduct is carried out in or near a 'public place' is an important element of this offence as it encapsulates the resulting harm; the public humiliation of the victim.

states also have enacted specific anti-ragging legislation prohibiting the conduct in higher educational institutions.[7]

The Supreme Court decision of *Vishwa Jagriti Mission through President* v *Central Government through Cabinet Secretary and Others*[8] (*Vishwa*) played a fundamental role in raising awareness of ragging in India among scholars, advocates and educational institutions generally.[9] The decision had a particularly profound impact on how Indian higher educational institutions respond to instances of ragging, given the primary role institutions have in managing student behaviour. Based on the *Report of the Committee to Curb the Menace of Ragging in Universities/Educational Institution* (University Grants Commission, 1999), the court issued directions, in the form of guidelines, for implementation by state governments and higher educational institutions.[10] These outlined a comprehensive prohibition/prevention/punishment approach.[11] Guidelines stipulated that non-complying institutions would be subject to University Grants Commission funding cuts.[12] Unfortunately, institutions implemented these measures to varying degrees, which limited the efficacy of the proposed approach/measures.[13]

Prompted by a further increase in ragging incidents, prevention and management strategies for higher educational institutions were reconsidered in 2006.[14] In 2007, the selected investigatory committee (the Raghaven Committee) filed *The Menace of Ragging in Educational Institutions and Measures to Curb It* (Raghaven Committee Report, 2007). The report delivered detailed findings on the nature of ragging (definition; scope); provided an overview of existing ragging measures, including a comparison of state anti-ragging legislation; and posited a series of recommendations for the strategic management of the conduct

---

[7] State legislation has been enacted in the following states: Andhra Pradesh, Maharashtra, Karnataka, Uttar Pradesh, Haryana, Tripura, Tamil Nadu, Assam, Kerala, West Bengal, Goa, Jammu and Kashmir, Himachal Pradesh and Punjab.

[8] AIR 2001 SC 2793.

[9] By virtue of the directions handed down in the decision itself (a decision of the Apex Court) and through the research findings and recommendations publicised in a report commissioned by the University Grants Research Council (the 1999 Report), which discussed forms of ragging, reasons for ragging, increase in prevalence of ragging and anti-ragging measures.

[10] *Vishwa Jagriti Mission through President* v *Central Government through Cabinet Secretary and Others* 2001 (3) SCR 540.

[11] Ibid.   [12] Ibid.

[13] The investigatory committee appointed in 2006 did not come across any serious effort to implement the guidelines of the Supreme Court in the manner intended (*The Menace of Ragging in Educational Institutions and Measures to Curb It* [2007], 3.09).

[14] *University of Kerala* v *Council of Principals and Colleges* SLP (C) No 24296–24299 of 2004, WP (Crl) No 173/2006 and SLP (C) No 14356/2005.

in Indian higher educational institutions specifically, and prevention of the conduct more broadly. As a result, the University Grants Commission Regulations on Curbing the Menace of Ragging in Higher Educational Institutions (the Regulations) came into force in 2009.[15]

The Regulations unequivocally prohibit ragging in all Indian higher educational institutions (University Grants Commission, 2009, s 6). In order to promote a uniform understanding, the Regulations provide a broad, comprehensive definition (University Grants Commission, 2009, s 3). Notably, from a Western perspective, most of the behaviours described would be understood as bullying, where the act is *repeated* (as opposed to an isolated event), where a *power imbalance* between the perpetrator and the victim is established and where an *intent to harm* can be inferred.[16]

Importantly, the Raghaven Committee Report noted the significance of adopting a holistic approach to curbing ragging in India. Although the focus of the 2007 Report related to the management of student behaviour in higher educational settings, the Raghaven Committee recommended *that human rights education programmes, which raise awareness of ragging, become compulsory in the* school *curriculum.*[17] Given that ragging is a learnt, arguably entrenched cultural behaviour in India, Nakassis (2013) argued for values-based learning in the early years of education, to highlight respect for privacy, diversity and equality as a way forward.[18]

The Committee recommended that the curriculum for the Bachelor of Education (B.Ed) and other teacher training courses include a mandatory learning module/unit on bullying.[19] This suggestion indicates an awareness that teachers play a fundamental role in managing and responding to

---

[15] University Grants Commission Regulations on Curbing the Menace of Ragging in Higher Educational Institutions (2009) F.1–16/2007 (CPP-II); *University of Kerala* v *Council, Principals, Colleges and Others* [2009] INSC 284 (11 February 2009), [3].

[16] Note, in relation to s 3(a): instances of long-term 'teasing' may be characterised as bullying, as conduct intended to harm another. Behaviour described in s 3(d) is very broad (low threshold). Peer-to-peer 'disruption' or 'disturbance' would need to be both aggressive and intentional to constitute bullying.

[17] Report of the Committee Constituted by the Supreme Court of India in SLP No 24295 of 2006, *The Menace of Ragging in Educational Institutions and Measures to Curb It* (2007), para 5.02. Unfortunately this recommendation was not reflected in the directions delivered by the Supreme Court in *University of Kerala* v *Council, Principals, Colleges and Others* [2009] INSC 284 (11 February 2009).

[18] Report of the Committee Constituted by the Supreme Court of India in SLP No 24295 of 2006, *The Menace of Ragging in Educational Institutions and Measures to Curb It* (2007), para 5.03.

[19] Ibid., 5.05. Reflected in the University Grants Commission Regulations on Curbing the Menace of Ragging in Higher Educational Institutions (2009) (India) s6.1 (d)(e).

bullying behaviours. This recommendation is reflected in University Grants Commission regulations.[20]

Since the publication of the Raghaven Committee Report, however, little is known about the extent to which Indian schools have implemented compulsory learning modules on ragging or bullying more generally. It is currently *not* mandatory for Indian schools to implement anti-bullying policies and there are *no uniform regulations* (Jaishanker & Halder, 2009; Srivastava, 2012, p. 20). However, there seems to be some movement in this direction.

In March 2015, the Central Board of Secondary Education disseminated a circular to schools within its jurisdiction[21] outlining interventions schools ought to consider implementing. Recommendations included: publishing a no-tolerance approach to bullying in school guidelines; constituting anti-bullying committees within schools; arranging counselling services within primary, secondary and senior secondary schools; educating parents; and implementing comprehensive guidelines for school behaviour management (Central Board of Secondary Education, 2015). *Additionally, the Central Board recommended that teacher training courses mandatorily include topics on sensitisation and prevention of bullying in schools* (Central Board of Secondary Education, 2015).

Whether these policy and legal changes and initiatives have as yet filtered through to current PSTs and teachers generally in India is unknown and requires ongoing investigation. Data for this project were collected in 2014, immediately prior to these legislative changes, thus this chapter (and Chapter 13) provides an important snapshot/baseline of PSTs attitudes and knowledge prior to the mandatory requirement to include topics on bullying.

Eve Teasing

Eve teasing, like ragging, is another culturally specific, 'highly prevalent' behaviour related to bullying in India[22] and is described as a 'social crime' which happens 'everywhere in schools and in homes irrespective of caste and creed' (Atthill & Jha, 2009, p. 166). It is a specific form of aggressive conduct perpetrated by males and is akin to sexual harassment in Western

---

[20] University Grants Commission Regulations on Curbing the Menace of Ragging in Higher Educational Institutions (2009) (India), s 6.1(k).

[21] The Board has jurisdiction over 15,799 schools in India (as of 9 March 2015) located in the Union Territory of Chandigarh, Andaman and Nicobar Island, Arunachal Pradesh, Sikkim, Jharkhand, Uttaranchal and Chhattisgarh.

[22] Anecdotal evidence: Dr Daman Sandhu, Annamalai University and Patalia University (Punjab, India).

situations. It is generally described as the sexual harassment of a woman occurring in a public place, and has been categorised into five forms: physical, verbal, psychological, sexual and harassment through objects (Halder & Jaishanker, 2011, p. 386).[23]

Tamil Nadu is the only state in India to enact specific legislation prohibiting the conduct (see Figure 14.1), originally, the Tamil Nadu Prohibition of Eve-Teasing Act 1997.[24] Notably, it was amended in 1998: the term *eve-teasing* was replaced with *harassment* and the Act was renamed The Tamil Nadu Prohibition of Harassment of Woman Act 1998.[25] Harassment (the legislature's interpretation of Eve teasing) is defined in the following way:

Figure 14.1 Street signage in Tamil Nadu concerning Eve teasing. Photo by Barbara A. Spears.

[23] *Deputy Inspector General of Police and Another* v S *Sumuthriam* 2012 (11) SCALE 420, [31].
[24] Tamil Nadu Prohibition of Eve-Teasing Act 1997 (Tamil Nadu, India).
[25] Tamil Nadu Prohibition of Harassment of Woman Act 1998 (Tamil Nadu, India).

any indecent conduct or act by a man which causes or is likely to cause intimidation, fear, shame or embarrassment, including abusing or causing hurt or nuisance or assault or use of force.[26]

Inherent in this definition is the element of power imbalance, which exists by virtue of a person's gender, where a male has a power differential vis-à-vis a female. Given that the aim of Eve teasing is to humiliate a female victim, it is likely that an intention to cause the victim harm will be inferred.[27] The definition is broad and is capable of encompassing conduct which could be construed as bullying where the conduct is repeated.

India has no specific federal law which governs Eve teasing. It is, however, possible to prosecute Eve teasing under several provisions of the Indian Penal Code.[28] The most applicable provision relates to s 509, which prohibits a man from uttering a word, making a gesture or doing an act 'intended to insult the modesty of a woman'.

In 2012 the Supreme Court of India considered the case of *Deputy Inspector General of Police and Another* v *S Sumuthriam*.[29] The Court condemned Eve teasing as a 'pernicious, horrid and disgusting practice'[30] and expressed the urgent need for specific uniform legislation.[31] Notably, the Court delivered multiple directions in the form of guidelines (for urgent implementation by the states) aimed at curtailing instances of Eve teasing.[32] Situational crime prevention measures included deploying plain-clothed female police officers to public places such as bus stands, railway stations, metro stations, cinema theatres, shopping malls, parks, beaches, public service vehicles and places of worship to monitor and supervise incidents of Eve teasing,[33] including installing closed-circuit television in strategic positions.[34] The Court ordered that women's helplines be established in various cities within three months[35] and that

---

[26] Ibid., s 4(a).

[27] The wording of the provision indicates that the threshold for 'harm' is low; the inclusion of 'nuisance' describes an almost trivial reaction.

[28] Indian Penal Code 1890 (India) s 509 – word, gesture or act intended to insult the modesty of any woman; s 354 – assault or criminal force to woman with intent to outrage her modesty; s 294 – obscene acts and songs; Criminal Law Amendment Act 2013 (India) s 354A – sexual harassment; s 354B – using force with intent to disrobe a woman (amends Indian Penal Code).

[29] *Deputy Inspector General of Police and Another* v *S Sumuthriam* 2012 (11) SCALE 420. The Supreme Court of India has considered sexual harassment in *Vishaka and Others* v *State of Rajasthan* (1977) 6 SCC 241.

[30] *Deputy Inspector General of Police and Another* v *S Sumuthriam* 2012 (11) SCALE 420, [31].

[31] Ibid., [30]. Note, no uniform legislation has been enacted to date.   [32] Ibid., [32].

[33] Ibid., [32 (1)].   [34] Ibid., [32(2)].

[35] Ibid., [32(5)]. Helplines have been established. See, for example, 'Helplines against eve-teasing, ragging,' *The Tribune* (Himachal), 3 July 2015 www.tribuneindia.com/news/himachal/community/helpline-against-eve-teasing-ragging/62023.html.

boards (billboards) cautioning against Eve teasing be exhibited in all public places (see Figure 1).[36] Notably, however, no specific measures for implementation in schools were issued as part of the Court's directions. The implementation of the 2015 recommendations for curbing bullying, issued by the Central Board of Secondary Education, would go some way towards addressing Eve teasing in schools. As a form of victimisation, the conduct would fall within school bullying guidelines as unacceptable conduct.[37] Again, it is not known whether these recommendations have trickled down to PSTs or indeed practising teachers and schools and warrants further investigation.

Cyberbullying

To date, no specific cyberbullying law has been enacted in India. Rather, some instances of cyberbullying are captured by existing federal law provisions, where the conduct falls within the scope of an offence. The statutes of particular relevance include the Information Technology Act 2000[38] (ITA), Information Technology (Amendment) Act 2008[39] (ITAA) (which amends the ITA by providing for a range of new offences) and the Indian Penal Code.

The ITAA came into force in 2009 and amended the principal Act (the ITA). As a result, particular forms of cyberbullying are criminalised. For example, s 66 C, which provides for the offence of 'identity theft', may govern instances of 'impersonation' (where the perpetrator dishonestly uses a victim's electronic signature, password or unique identifications feature).[40] Dissemination of pornography and child pornography is governed by s 67A and s 67B of the ITA (by virtue of the ITAA). This regulates cyberbullying known as 'harassment' where a victim is repeatedly sent sexually explicit (pornographic) material either directly (e.g. a victim's personal email account or mobile phone) or indirectly (e.g. to a social media platform or website) (this conduct is also known as Internet trolling) (Langos, 2013, pp. 52–53). These provisions also may regulate cyberbullying known as 'denigration' by way of an image of a sexual or intimate nature (Langos, 2013, pp. 55–58). This form of cyberbullying

---

[36] *Deputy Inspector General of Police and Another* v *S Sumuthriam* 2012 (11) SCALE 420, [32(6)].

[37] Note also that the University Grants Commission (Promotion of Equity in Higher Educational Institutions) Regulations 2012 (India) enacted to address discrimination in higher educational institutions encompass gender victimisation. Thus, Eve teasing in colleges and universities is prohibited.

[38] Information Technology Act 2000 (India) (ITA).   [39] Ibid.

[40] Information Technology (Amendment) Act 2008 (India) (ITAA) s 66C. Note that a similar provision is provided for in Indian Penal Code s 416 – Cheating by personation.

involves the distribution of an image of a sexual (depicting the subject engaging in a sexual act) or intimate (depicting the subject's genital or anal area, or using a toilet) nature, which identifies the subject (shows the subject's face or otherwise identifiable features) and is disseminated without the subject's consent. Where the materials published or transmitted are not sexually explicit, they may still be prohibited. Section 67 of the ITA is a broader provision which captures 'obscene' material in electronic form more generally (material need not be 'sexually explicit').[41] This provision potentially governs any form of cyberbullying which involves transmission of material containing lewd content via mobile phone SMS, email, post to social media platform or website.

Eve teasing in the cyber context is highly likely to constitute cyberbullying, particularly where it occurs in a public online forum, such as social media, a publicly viewable website or via email or SMS text message with multiple recipients. The act is repeated by virtue of the public nature of the forum (Langos, 2012).[42] 'Online' Eve teasing is not governed by a specific law. However, such conduct may fall within the scope of section 509 of the Indian Penal Code.[43] The law may be infringed where a perpetrator has morphed a victim's image to be sexually suggestive (to 'insult the modesty' of the victim), or where comments 'insulting the modesty' of a female victim are posted. There also may be scope to punish perpetrators who post video footage capturing an act(s) intended to 'insult the modesty' of a female victim, where the 'posting' of the video without consent is considered 'an act' for the purposes of the offence. There is, therefore, potential for the provision to regulate instances of 'happy slapping'[44] where the victim is female.

Age of Criminal Responsibility in India

Although federal legislation governing some instances of bullying (specifically ragging and Eve teasing) and cyberbullying exists, a perpetrator

---

[41] ITA s 67.

[42] In a cyberbullying context, 'repetition' does not necessarily involve several instances. In instances where a perpetrator posts an electronic communication to a public forum, such as a public blog, a social media forum or a video-sharing website, it is no longer necessary for the victim to fall subject to a series of acts to satisfy the element of 'repetition' in this context. 'Repetition' occurs by virtue of the public online forum in which the behaviour occurs.

[43] Indian Penal Code 1860 (India) s 509 – Word, gesture or act intended to insult the modesty of a woman.

[44] 'Happy slapping' involves the filming of a physical assault on a victim and the subsequent distribution of the film to humiliate the victim publicly.

may be of an age where the law deems the person incapable of forming criminal intent (*mens rea*). In India a child under the age of seven cannot be prosecuted. A child between the ages of seven and 12 is presumed incapable of committing a crime because of a lack of understanding of the differences between right and wrong, and consequential lack of *mens rea*, although a rebuttable presumption exists.[45] A child over the age of 12 is considered capable of committing a crime having attained the developmental maturity to be held fully responsible for their actions under the criminal law.[46] The Juvenile Justice (Care and Protection of Children) Act 2000 applies to all children under the age of 18.[47] This means that young people charged with offences when aged between 12–18 years at the time of the offence[48] will be heard by the Juvenile Justice Board (as distinct from an adversarial adult court).

It is apparent that there are initiatives to bring bullying, ragging, Eve teasing and cyberbullying to the notice of the legal and schooling communities in India, in ways which might serve to protect vulnerable children and keep them safe in school settings. Whether and how PSTs might make sense of these are presented after the brief review of Australian legislative responses.

Australian Legal Context

Scholars have examined criminal and civil legal frameworks governing bullying and cyberbullying in Australia in detail (Campbell, Butler & Kift, 2008; Katz et al., 2014; Langos, 2014a). As such, the purpose of this section is to provide the reader with an overview of potentially applicable laws, and to consider the laws PSTs ought to be familiar with prior to their appointment within the teaching profession.

Criminal Law

There is no single body of criminal law governing the whole of Australia (Findlay, Odgers & Yeo, 2014, p. 7). Australian states and territories are responsible for their own criminal laws. The Commonwealth government may enact federal criminal legislation pursuant only to the powers vested

---

[45] The older the child, the more easily the presumption may be rebutted – although the threshold for rebuttable is high.

[46] There have been no amendments to the Juvenile Justice Act prohibiting ragging (or bullying).

[47] Juvenile Justice (Care and Protection of Children) Act 2000 (India).

[48] Note that children between the ages of seven and 12 may be prosecuted under the Act. The prosecution must establish that the child has the developmental maturity to be capable of forming *mens rea*.

in the Commonwealth Constitution.[49] At present, no specific bullying or cyberbullying offence exists per se. Rather, a complex matrix of state and federal laws can criminalise bullying and cyberbullying behaviours falling within the scope of existing offences (Katz et al., 2014; Langos, 2014a; Spears et al., 2014).

Age of Criminal Responsibility

The common law doctrine of *doli incapax* applies to youths (juvenile) aged between 10 and 13 years in all Australian jurisdictions.[50] Once a youth is aged between 14 and 17 years, the youth is taken to have attained the developmental maturity to be held fully responsible for their actions under the criminal law. This is important to note given that bullying and cyberbullying are prevalent amongst young people.

All Australian states have their own juvenile justice systems. By way of example, the design of the South Australian model is founded on a tiered system of pre-court diversion. As such, youths under the age of 18 are afforded special protections on account of their youth and welfare needs. Most instances involving bullying or cyberbullying warranting police involvement are resolved through formal warning or family conferencing rather than through a formal hearing.

State Law

It has been well documented that state offences governing 'unlawful threats',[51,52] 'assault'[53] or 'stalking'[54] may regulate instances of traditional (face-to-face) bullying. These provisions may, equally, govern cyberbullying – online manifestations of conduct falling within the scope of these provisions (Katz et al., 2014; Langos, 2014a; Spears et al., 2014). State 'filming offences'[55] may have particular application in relation to a range of specific cyberbullying behaviours involving the non-consensual distribution of visual content (images or film).

South Australia has recently enacted laws which better regulate cyberbullying behaviours colloquially known as non-consensual

---

[49] Australian Constitution s 51.

[50] *Doli incapax* is a rebuttable legal presumption that a youth 10–13 years of age is incapable of crime under statute or the common law because of a lack of understanding of the differences between right and wrong, and consequential lack of *mens rea*.

[51] South Australia is used as the jurisdiction of choice.

[52] For example, the Criminal Law Consolidations Act 1935 (SA) s 19.

[53] For example, ibid., s 20.   [54] For example, ibid., s 19AA.

[55] For example, the Summary Offences Act 1953 (SA) Part 5A.

'sexting',[56] 'revenge porn'[57] and 'happy slapping'.[58,59] One of the most important features of the Summary Offences (Filming and Sexting Offences) Amendment Act 2016 (SA), which came into operation October 2016, is that it criminalises threats to distribute an invasive image/film (depicting the subject engaged in a sexual act or using a toilet or the subject's breasts or bare genital region).[60] Given that repeated threats of this kind can be regarded as bullying, the law serves as a novel legislative response to a behaviour which is prevalent as a result of the pervasive nature of technology. The new law also enables police to charge a young offender with a non-indictable offence for non-consensual distribution of such material.[61] Given the sexual nature of images and film involved in sexting and dissemination of revenge porn, state child pornography offences could apply where the subject of the image or film is under the age of 17 years.[62] Charging a young person with possession and/or dissemination of child pornography for consensual or non-consensual sexting is arguably inappropriate given the very serious consequences of conviction (Langos, 2014b). Police now have an alternative offence to turn to when a criminal response to publishing visual content of a sexual nature is warranted.

Federal Law

Federal law has a role to play in the regulation of cyberbullying.[63] The provision which has the greatest relevance, capturing a broad range of cyberbullying behaviours, governs 'harassing, menacing or offensive' material transmitted electronically.[64] A perpetrator commits this federal indictable offence if he or she uses a carriage service ('making a telephone call, sending a message by facsimile, sending an SMS message, or sending a message by email or some other means of using

---

[56] Described as an electronic communication(s) containing sexual material, such as suggestive or provocative text, or images that are nude, nearly nude or sexually explicit (Salter, Crofts & Lee, 2013), 301.

[57] Involves image-based exploitation. Occurs where a person formerly in an intimate relationship with the subject of a private (sexually explicit) image/film distributes the image/film without consent as an act of revenge (once a relationship has come to an end).

[58] Involves the filming of a physical assault on a victim and the subsequent distribution of the film to humiliate the victim publicly.

[59] The Summary Offences (Filming Offences) Act 2013 (SA) introduced new offences to the Summary Offences Act 1953 (SA); the Summary Offences (Filming and Sexting Offences) Amendment Act 2016 (SA) made further amendments to the Summary Offences Act 1953 (SA).

[60] Summary Offences Act 1953 (SA) s 26D.   [61] Ibid., s 26DA.

[62] Criminal Law Consolidation Act 1935 (SA) s 63 and s 63A; *R v Marcus James Empen* (Unreported, District Court of South Australia, Rice J, 22 August 2014).

[63] Australian Constitution s 51(v).   [64] Criminal Code Act 1995 (Cth) s 414.17.

the Internet')[65] to menace, harass or cause offence to a victim.[66] This provision is broad in scope given that the prohibited conduct need only reach a threshold of being 'offensive'. As such, the provision potentially captures a wide range of cyberbullying. Notably, the offence requires the prosecution to prove that the perpetrator was aware that his or her conduct could be viewed as harassing, threatening or offensive. This means that it may be possible for an eccentric or unreasonable perpetrator (not capable of forming an awareness of risk) to escape conviction.

In 2016, the Criminal Code Amendment (Private Sexual Material) Bill 2016 was introduced to the Parliament of Australia, largely in response to and in recognition of 'the community's increased use of telecommunications to engage in harmful and abusive behaviour of a sexual nature and the harm that can be caused' (Commonwealth Parliament, 2016). The proposed offence prohibits non-consensual distribution of private sexual material[67] using a carriage service where distribution causes the subject depicted in the material distress or harm or there is a risk of causing the subject distress or harm.[68] The offender would need to be able to form an awareness of a substantial risk of causing the subject depicted in the private material distress or harm. The Bill was withdrawn in 2017, following the second reading of the Bill, leaving prosecutors without an alternative federal offence tailored more specifically to managing some forms of cyberbullying, particularly revenge porn or non-consensual sexting.

Ragging and Eve Teasing

Ragging and Eve teasing are not discrete behaviours prevalent in the Australian education context or wider community. If they were, both would be largely encompassed by existing Australian criminal laws. Given the physical nature of ragging, 'assault' provisions provided for under state laws would be particularly significant. In relation to Eve teasing, equally, state laws are likely to govern the conduct. For example,

---

[65] Commonwealth Parliament, Explanatory Memorandum, Crimes Legislation Amendment (Telecommunications Offences and Other Measures) Act (No 2) 2004 (Cth) s 474.15.

[66] Consideration of the meanings of the terms *harass, threaten* and *offensive* suggests that the term *offensive* is given the broadest meaning and relates to resentful displeasure.

[67] Defined as material depicting the subject engaging in a sexual pose or sexual activity (whether or not in the presence of other persons); or in a manner or context that is sexual; or a sexual organ or the anal region of the subject; or the breasts of the subject who is female, or who is transgender or an intersex person who identifies as female; and a reasonable person in the position of the subject would expect the material to be kept private.

[68] Criminal Code Amendment (Private Sexual Material) Bill 2016 s 474.24E.

in South Australia the offence of 'disorderly or offensive conduct or language'[69] could encapsulate less serious instances, whilst 'assault' provisions may govern the more heinous forms of Eve teasing which result in physical harm. Online manifestations of Eve teasing would be subject to the host of state and federal laws enacted to govern instances of technological misuse.

Civil Laws in Australia

Tort of Negligence

Another significant facet of the law relevant in a bullying and cyberbullying context relates to the duty of care owed by school authorities. At common law, schools owe students a duty of care to prevent and respond appropriately to instances of both on- and off-campus bullying. State legislation too may have a role to play in this regard. For example, in South Australia, the Civil Liability Act 1936 (SA) prescribes that a school authority must take 'reasonable precautions' against risk of harm – effective implementation of school anti-bullying policies and response measures may be particularly relevant in establishing the taking of 'reasonable precautions'. A successful negligence claim hinges upon proof of the victim sustaining a recognised psychiatric illness[70] as a result of the school's negligence (Spyrou, 2015).

Defamation

Pursuing a claim for defamation can, in some instances, be a useful avenue of legal redress for a victim of bullying where the perpetrator makes repeated defamatory (slanderous) statements about the victim to a third party.[71] It may be relevant in relation to cyberbullying given the unprecedented growth of online platforms, such as social media, publicly accessible blogs and websites and video-sharing websites. It is important to note, however, that civil actions can incur significant associated legal costs. Further, where a perpetrator does not have assets (highly like when the perpetrator is a young person), there may be little financial incentive for a victim to pursue a claim for compensatory damages.

---

[69] Summary Offences Act 1953 (SA) s 7.   [70] Civil Liability Act 1936 (SA) s 53(2).
[71] Defamation Act 2005 (SA).

Self-Regulation on Social Media

If content posted on social media sites is not illegal,[72] content is not regulated by the law per se. Thus, content posted to social media is largely self-regulated. When individuals sign up to use social media (e.g. Facebook, Twitter), they agree to set terms and conditions of use in the form of a Statement of Rights and Responsibilities or Terms of Use Agreement. A user must agree before being able to 'sign up for' (access and use) the site. This is a contractual agreement between the user and the social media provider. As such, violation of any of the terms of the contract enables the social media provider to sever the agreement – remove infringing content and terminate its contract with the user. Users themselves have the ability to make use of the inbuilt safety tools provided by the social media site. For example, Facebook give users the power to report offensive content and for administrators to vet messages before they go online and to block certain users from posting content. A practical issue of concern for victims of cyberbullying via social media relates to the provider's delayed response. User-end reports of abuse often prove not to be a 'quick fix' for content removal. To that end, the Office of the eSafety Commissioner was established.[73]

eSafety Commissioner

The Office of the eSafety Commissioner (https://www.esafety.gov.au) functions as a central point of contact for online safety issues for all Australians. It operates as a civil enforcement mechanism which has particular relevance for managing serious instances of cyberbullying targeting children, image-based abuse and removing illegal content.[74] The website provides a user-friendly reporting portal, as well as a range of self-help resources. Once a complaint is received the instance is investigated and assessed.[75] Factors such as the nature of the material, the age of the target and the statutory classification of the social media service are taken into account. To that end, one of the Commissioner's primary roles is to communicate with social media services where cyberbullying material (material an ordinary, reasonable person would consider seriously threatening, intimidating, harassing or humiliating where the material[76]) is not removed and request its removal. Whether social media providers

---

[72] Illegal as deemed under state or federal criminal law provisions or the Broadcasting Services Act 1992 (Cth).
[73] Enhancing Online Safety Act 2015 (Cth).
[74] Office of the eSafety Commissioner: www.esafety.gov.au/about-the-office/role-of-the-office.
[75] Enhancing Online Safety Act 2015 (Cth)., s 19.   [76] Ibid., s 5.

can be compelled to remove the material will depend upon how the service is classified under the legislation.[77] Where the service is a 'tier 1' service, the Commissioner can, within 48 hours of a request for removal being made, provide the service with a written notice requesting removal, but has no direct removal powers.[78] Where the service is a 'tier 2' service (e.g. Facebook), the Commissioner can, within 48 hours of a request for removal being made, provide the service with a written notice requesting removal. Failure to remove the content can result in the service entering into an enforceable undertaking or the issuing of a court-ordered injunction and/or fine.[79]

Arguably the most useful aspect of this regime is the statutory power conferred upon the Commissioner to communicate with social media services to *request the removal of cyberbullying material* and, where circumstances permit, *enforce* content removal. The more expediently harmful online content is removed, the less public humiliation need be endured by an Australian child targeted by the material. It is imperative that teachers have a sound understanding of this regime so that they are empowered to direct students in their care who are victims of cyberbullying to the resources available or suggest to parents that they assist with the complaints process.

Pre-service Teachers, Bullying and the Law

Laws provide a community with parameters on how members of that community ought to behave, and inform as to the types of conduct which fall foul of acceptable standards. Knowledge of laws provides victims of conduct deemed a crime with just deserts (criminal law) and facilitates legal redress in instances where a legal right has been infringed (civil law). Teachers are placed in a special position of power and care over schoolchildren and students in higher education contexts. Not only are they responsible for facilitating the communication of knowledge, they also provide students in their care with guidance on behavioural norms in the classroom and, to an extent, beyond the school gates. In order to manage bullying behaviours, whether online or offline, teachers ought to be empowered with regard to the laws which govern these behaviours. Having a comprehensive understanding of legal frameworks and the corresponding avenues of redress will enable teachers, and indeed PSTs, to make informed decisions about *appropriate disciplinary action* and when the matter should be *reported to the police* for investigation, and

---

[77] Social media services will be classified as a tier 1 or tier 2 service – ibid., Part 4.
[78] Ibid., s 29(2).   [79] Ibid., s 35(1), s 36, s 46–48.

provide some initial guidance as to *where victims in their care may be able to seek external assistance.*

The following section provides insight into PSTs' understanding of bullying and the law in India and Australia. The data provide useful perspectives as to whether PSTs currently have a sound understanding of legal frameworks and whether they feel confident about responding to instances of bullying and cyberbullying.

Methodology

This study employed an exploratory, mixed-method, cross-sectional survey design. Questionnaires were developed from various existing published studies, and included novel questions to gather culturally relevant knowledge about bullying. Australian PSTs were invited by email distribution lists to complete online surveys (N = 178), and Indian PSTs, from two states (Punjab and Tamil Nadu), completed hard copy versions in English, in the presence of a local researcher (N = 510). A coding sheet facilitated data entry on both continents, and the data files were subsequently merged and entered into the IBM SPSS Statistics package, V 23. Qualitative responses to open-ended questions were reviewed by four independent researchers for trustworthiness and legitimacy of the ideas (micro themes), and macro themes were subsequently noted. (For fuller details on the sample and procedure, see Chapter 13.)

The Human Research Ethics Committee of the University of South Australia granted approval to conduct anonymous surveys about cyber/bullying in both countries. The principals/heads of school/relevant authorities of each Indian university/training college were approached and consent was granted for PSTs to participate. Completion of the questionnaire indicated individual informed consent.

Results and Discussion

Qualitative Open text boxes in the surveys enabled participants to respond and expand on key questions concerning their understanding of bullying, why they thought it occurred and whether there should be a criminal law against it. Data were analysed thematically (Braun & Clarke, 2006), within and across each group, to gather insights into the lived realities of each cohort. Exemplar quotes are included to illustrate some of the emerging key themes.

Overall, when asked *why bullying occurs*, a plethora of reasons were provided across all contexts which had remarkable similarity relating to being targeted due to interpersonal differences, social and socio-economic differences and cultural differences. A view held by many related to cultural diversity/status:

> *Because of stratification in society* (Punjab, Male, 22 years).
> *Diversity will always make for bullying* (Australia, Male, 20 years).
> *Bullying occurs because too many people don't understand how to accept people's differences* (Australia, Female, 19 years).
> *Culture favours it . . . stronger expected to dominate the weak* (Punjab, Female, 23 years).
> *Belonging to a lower caste is the cause of being bullied* (Punjab, Female, 22 years).
> *Education system, caste, religion . . .* (Tamil Nadu, Male, 23 years).
> *A lack of understanding for diversity in our country, especially for others' situations* (Australia, Female, 21 years).

Others tapped into the more specific elements relating to bullying per se, for example power, repetition and deliberate intent to harm:

> *When people need to feel that they have power over others* (Australia, Female, 22 years).
> *Repeated, negative behaviour* (Tamil Nadu, Female, 32 years).
> *Students from high-class families show off their status by teas[ing] students from lower castes* (Punjab, Male, 23 years).

Comments relating to academic status were noteworthy, suggesting power and status comes with good academic performance:

> *Sense of inferiority among academically poor students leads them to low confidence . . . that's why they become the victims of bullying* (Punjab, Female, 23 years).

In addition were those who felt that bullying was under-recognised or not recognised at all:

> *[It is] a non-recognised menace* (Punjab, Male, 23 years).
> *Awareness is important* (Tamil Nadu, Male, 36 years).

In relation to whether there should be a criminal law addressing bullying, there was considerable variation of responses both in support and against. Quotations that follow capture the essence of the core responses: that having a criminal law will make no difference, will be preventative and teach children something, will make adults take greater responsibility for their children's behaviours or will uphold children's rights.

> *I cannot see that a juvenile criminal record would be of any use in reforming the behaviour of bullies. Furthermore I doubt criminal convictions for bullying are unlikely to prevent recidivism. However, I see considerable value in adopting a restorative justice approach to rebuilding relationships in bullying cases* (Australia, Female, 31 years).
> *If there is a criminal law against . . . some students may think twice before bullying* (Australia, Female, 44 years).

The laws should only be applied to adults, such as parents and teachers who failed to control . . . their children (Punjab, Male, 23 years).

A specific law against bullying is required to make the bullies realise the consequences of their wrongdoings. It is necessary to tell the bullies that they cannot escape the consequences of their wrong actions. Moreover, making and implementing a law against bullying will contribute in making schools safe and a happy place for the children (Punjab, Male, 21 years).

There should be a specific criminal law which regulates bullying because the rights of children need to be upheld (Australia, Female, 20 years).

Some see no need for a specific law:

I don't think we need a specific criminal law regulating bullying, as it should be covered in other laws (Australia, Female, 45 years).

Fundamentally, though, this final sentiment provides some insight into the dilemma concerning the use of criminal law and bullying amongst children:

Students are not criminals (Tamil Nadu, Male, 24 years).

Quantitative   Although cross-cultural differences might be anticipated, nuances within the Indian cultural setting (Punjab/north and Tamil Nadu/south) were evident. This was not unexpected, given there are currently no mandatory or uniform bullying regulations or policies in India. Teachers' awareness of bullying and understanding of approaches for dealing with bullying incidents has been shown to be a key factor in building teacher confidence to intervene in incidents of bullying (Ahtola et al., 2012), hence, the knowledge and confidence which PSTs bring to the profession regarding bullying-related laws were examined.

Within the Indian context, results indicated the level of awareness of bullying-related laws was statistically associated with geographic region, with PSTs from the Tamil region significantly more likely to have an awareness of bullying related laws (see Table 14.1).

Results from the Indian context also revealed a significant association between region and support for bullying-related laws. Although PSTs from the Punjab region were less likely to be aware of bullying-related laws, they were more likely to be in favour of a specific criminal law that regulates bullying (see Table 14.2), and also were similarly more likely to be supportive of a specific criminal law that regulates cyberbullying (see Table 14.3).

The need for and the value of bullying laws, including an explicit cyberbullying law, is, however, a contested issue amongst stakeholders (Katz et al., 2014). There is potential for personal experiences of bullying, in particular, to shape an individual's position on the matter. This significant association was evident in the current study, with Indian PSTs

Table 14.1 *Awareness of bullying-related law by geographic region in India (numbers; percentages in parentheses)*

	Awareness of bullying-related laws	
	Yes	No
Punjab PSTs	1	208
	(0.7%)	(65.2%)
Tamil PSTs	143	111
	(99.3%)	(34.8%)

$\chi^2 = 166.7$, df = 1, Phi = 0.60. p < 0.001

Table 14.2 *Geographic region in India by support for criminal law which regulates bullying (numbers; percentages in parentheses)*

	Support for criminal law which regulates bullying	
	Yes	No
Punjab PSTs	162	22
	(54.4%)	(19.1%)
Tamil PSTs	136	93
	(45.6%)	(80.9%)

$\chi^2 = 41.7$, df = 1. Phi = 0.32. p < 0.001

Table 14.3 *Geographic region in India by support for criminal law which regulates cyberbullying (numbers; percentages in parentheses)*

	Support for specific criminal law that regulates cyberbullying	
	Yes	No
Punjab PSTs	191	18
	(55.8%)	(18.8%)
Tamil PSTs	151	78
	(44.2%)	(81.3%)

$\chi^2 = 41.4$, df = 1. Phi = 0.31. p < 0.001

who had been victims of bullying at school more likely to support a law against bullying (see Table 14.4). Furthermore, Indian PSTs who supported a law against bullying also supported a law specific to cyberbullying (see Table 14.5).

Scrutiny of PSTs in the Australian context revealed no significant associations between awareness of laws and a PST's perceived capability/competence or confidence in dealing with school bullying. Consistent with findings from the Indian subsample, Australian PSTs who supported a law for bullying also supported a law specific to cyberbullying (see Table 14.6).

Table 14.4 *Indian pre-service teachers' experience of bullying by support for criminal law that regulates bullying (numbers; percentages in parentheses)*

	Support for criminal law which regulates bullying	
	Yes	No
Indian PSTs who had been victims of bullying	158 (54.7%)	36 (31.3%)
Indian PSTs who had not been victims of bullying	53 (18.3%)	45 (39.1%)
Indian PSTs who were unsure if they had been victims of bullying	78 (27.0%)	34 (29.6%)

$\chi^2 = 24.2$, df = 2. Cramer's V = 0.25. p < 0.001

Table 14.5 *Indian pre-service teachers' support of a criminal law which regulates bullying by support for criminal law that regulates cyberbullying (numbers; percentages in parentheses)*

	Support for a criminal law which regulates cyberbullying	
	Yes	No
Indian PSTs who support a criminal law which regulates bullying	269 (87.9%)	21 (22.3%)
Indian PSTs who do not support a criminal law which regulates bullying	37 (12.1%)	73 (77.7%)

$\chi^2 = 155.1$, df = 1. Phi = 0.62. p < 0.001

Table 14.6 *Australian pre-service teachers' support of a criminal law which regulates bullying by support for a criminal law which regulates cyberbullying (numbers; percentages in parentheses)*

	Support for a criminal law which regulates cyberbullying	
	Yes	No
Australian PSTs who support a criminal law which regulates bullying	67 (80.7%)	4 (22.3%)
Australian PSTs who do not support a criminal law which regulates bullying	16 (19.3%)	17 (81.0%)

$\chi^2 = 29.4$, df = 1. Phi = 0.53. p < 0.001

Table 14.7 *Country of origin by attitudes towards schools' role in managing and responding to school bullying (numbers; percentages in parentheses)*

	Schools' role in managing and responding to school bullying	
	Schools don't have a role	Schools have a role
Australia PSTs	0 (0.0%)	108 (21.6%)
Indian PSTs	114 (100.0%)	391 (78.4%)

$\chi^2 = 30.0$, df = 1. Phi = −0.22. p < 0.001

Australia and India Comparisons

When reflecting on where the responsibility lies for addressing bullying in school settings, there is an imperative to understand PSTs' views on the matter, as it speaks to their future capacity to prevent and actively respond to the issue. Results highlighted significant differences both cross-culturally and within the Indian cultural context. Specifically, a significant association was evident between country of origin and a school's role in managing and responding to school bullying (see Table 14.7).

Whilst Australian PSTs were more likely to indicate that schools did have a role in managing and responding to school bullying, Indian PSTs

Table 14.8 *Indian geographic region by attitudes towards schools' role in managing and responding to school bullying (numbers; percentages in parentheses)*

	Schools' role in managing and responding to school bullying	
	Schools don't have a role	Schools have a role
Punjab PSTs	0	208
	(0.0%)	(53.5%)
Tamil PSTs	114	181
	(100.0%)	(46.5%)

$\chi^2 = 103.9$, df = 1. Phi = −0.46. p < 0.001

were less likely to feel that schools had a role to play. Examination of these views by Indian geographic region revealed that PSTs from the Punjab region were more likely than PSTs from the Tamil region to indicate that schools had a role to play in addressing school bullying (see Table 14.8).

This is interesting, given that PSTs from Tamil Nadu reported a greater awareness of bullying-related laws, yet appear more likely to exonerate schools from having a role in addressing school bullying. It is possible that PSTs from the Tamil Nadu region feel that the issue is one which lies within the legal rather than educational domain, and is a finding that potentially aligns with the study by Ramirez and colleagues (2016). This will be important to follow up now that there are changes to the laws in India and the Central Board of Secondary Education (2015) *recommendation that teacher training courses mandatorily include topics on sensitisation and prevention of bullying in schools*. There are important opportunities here to explore and discuss the place of preventative bullying measures that focus on an educative process, as opposed to reactive response, which potentially could align more closely to legal interventions.

PSTs in both contexts clearly need to engage more with the legal frameworks in place so that they can enhance their capacity to successfully intervene and provide accurate information when they move out into schools as graduate teachers, to be able to make informed decisions about *appropriate disciplinary action* and when the matter should be *reported to the police* for investigation, and to provide some initial guidance as to *where victims in their care may be able to seek external assistance.*

Strengths and Limitations

A particular strength of this research is that it is the first time that a comparative study has explored Australian and Indian PSTs' understanding of bullying and the relative legal context in each jurisdiction. Successfully employing a mixed-method approach across two different cultural contexts has enabled a comprehensive exploration of the issue within and between the two settings: Australia and India (Tamil Nadu and Punjab). Dedicated efforts were taken to appropriately contextualise scenarios for each cultural setting (not reported in this chapter), which along with research processes and protocols was validated by colleagues from India.

Furthermore, the doctrinal research methodology employed in this study provided the basis for analysing the operation of potentially applicable laws and means of legal redress relevant to bullying and cyberbullying. Having a sound understanding of the statutory requirements of identified laws and the operation of common law doctrines underpins the legitimacy of research which explores how particular conduct is governed by way of the law. The comprehensive exploratory legal research conducted so as to inform the analysis presented in this study is a strength. What is important to keep in mind is that the question as to whether a particular instance of bullying or cyberbullying infringes upon a law or provides a victim with civil redress must be considered in light of the specific facts of each case – there is no definitive 'black or white' answer.

There are also some limitations of the study that need to be noted. As a cross-sectional study, data have been collected at a single point in time. Additionally, given the nature of the sampling approach (purposive and convenience), there is potential for response and non-response bias, and as such, conclusions cannot be drawn regarding the representativeness of the sample. This further restricts any generalisations being drawn in relation to PSTs across all Indian and Australian states and jurisdictions.

Limited access to digital resources and possible language barriers also needed consideration. In recognising that technology was not easily accessible in some Indian locations, surveys were disseminated via two different modes: Indian PSTs completed print surveys, whilst Australian PSTs completed surveys online. Every endeavour was made to ensure consistency in the delivery of the protocols/instructions during the dissemination of surveys; however, there may have been language difficulties when completing the survey for the Indian PSTs, as the survey was completed in English. This language limitation did impact recruitment and sample selection as only PSTs from English-speaking training colleges/universities could participate.

Conclusions and Recommendations

Overall, this study has shed light on two countries' legal contexts in regard to bullying and cyberbullying, and PSTs' views and understanding in relation to the law. The preparation of new teachers in terms of their knowledge and understanding about bullying and the laws pertaining to the same as they step into the profession in future years is paramount, particularly if they are to feel confident and competent in their ability to operate in and around the legal requirements of their relevant systems. One clear recommendation relates to empowering teachers and PSTs through the provision of accurate and relevant legal knowledge and advice, so that they can make informed decisions about appropriate disciplinary action and when the matter should be reported to police for investigation, and how to provide initial advice and guidance as to where victims in their care may be able to seek external assistance.

References

Ahtola, A., Haataja, A., Kärnä, A., Poskiparta, E. & Salmivalli, C. (2012). For children only? Effects of the KiVa antibullying program on teachers. *Teaching and Teacher Education, 28*(6), 851–859.

Atthill, C. & Jha, J. (2009). *The Gender-Responsive School: An Action Guide.* London: Commonwealth Secretariat.

Bauman, S. & Del Rio, A. (2005). Knowledge and beliefs about bullying in schools. Comparing pre-service teachers in the United States and the United Kingdom. *School Psychology International, 26*(4), 428–442.

Bauman, S. & Del Rio, A. (2006). Preservice teachers' responses to bullying scenarios. Comparing physical, verbal, and relational bullying. *Journal of Educational Psychology, 98*(1), 219–231.

Boulton, M. J., Hardcastle, K., Down, J., Fowles, J. & Simmonds, J. (2014). A comparison of preservice teachers' responses to cyber versus traditional bullying scenarios: Similarities and differences and implications for practice. *Journal of Teacher Education, 66*(2), 145–155. doi: 10.1177/0022487113511496.

Braun, V. & Clarke, V. (2006). Using thematic analysis in psychology. *Qualitative Research in Psychology, 3*(2), 77–101.

Campbell, M., Butler, D. A. & Kift, S. (2008). A school's duty to provide a safe learning environment: Does this include cyberbullying? *Australian and New Zealand Journal of Law and Education, 12*(2), 21–32.

Campbell, M., Cross, D., Spears, B., & Slee, P. (2010). *Cyberbullying – Legal Implications for schools.* Occasional Paper #118. Melbourne, Victoria: Centre for Strategic Education.

Central Board of Secondary Education (India). (2015). Guidelines for prevention of ragging and bullying in schools. (Circular No. Acad.-17/ 2015, 9 March).

Coffin, J., Larson, A. & Cross, D. (2010). Bullying in an Aboriginal context. *Australian Journal of Indigenous Education, 39*(1), 77–87.

Commonwealth Parliament. (2004). Explanatory Memorandum, Crimes Legislation Amendment (Telecommunications Offences and Other Measures) Bill 2004 (Cth).

Commonwealth Parliament. (2016). Explanatory Memorandum, Criminal Code Amendment (Private Sexual Material) Bill 2016 (Cth).

Dresler-Hawke E. & Whitehead, D. (2009). The behavioural ecological model as a framework for school-based anti-bullying health promotion interventions. *Journal of School Nursing, 25*(3), 195–204.

Economic and Political Weekly (2007). Ban on ragging. *Economic and Political Weekly, 42*(22), 2033.

Espelage, D. L. (2014). Ecological theory: Preventing youth bullying, aggression, and victimization. *Theory Into Practice, 53*(4), 257–264.

Findlay, M., Odgers, S. & Yeo, S. (2014). *Australian Criminal Justice.* (4th edn.). South Melbourne: Oxford University Press.

Garg, R. (2009). Ragging: A public health problem in India. *Indian Journal of Medical Sciences, 63*(6), 263–271.

Halder, D. & Jaishankar, K. (2011). Cyber gender harassment and secondary victimization: A comparative analysis of the United States, the UK, and India. *Victims and Offenders, 6*(4), 386–398. doi.org/10.1080/15564886.2011.607402.

Jaishanker, K. & Halder, D. (2009). Cyberbullying amongst school students in India. In K. Jaishanker (ed.), *International Perspectives on Crime and Punishment* (pp. 579–600). Newcastle: Cambridge Scholars Publishing.

Katz, I., Keeley, M., Spears, B., Taddeo, C., Swirski, T. & Bates, S. (2014). *Research on Youth Exposure to, and Management of, Cyberbullying Incidents in Australia: Synthesis Report* (SPRC Report 16/2014) (PDF) [431 Kb]. Sydney: Social Policy Research Centre, University of New South Wales Australia.

Langos, C. (2012). Cyberbullying: The challenge to define. *Cyberpsychology, Behaviour and Social Networking, 15*(6), 285–9.

Langos, C. (2013). Cyberbullying, Associated Harm and the Criminal Law (Doctoral Thesis). University of South Australia, Australia.

Langos, C. (2014a). Regulating cyberbullying: A South Australian perspective. *Flinders Law Journal, 16*(1), 73–109.

Langos, C. (2014b). Sexting: Time for some changes to the law? *Bulletin, 36*(10), 18–20.

Nakassis, C. (2013). Youth masculinity, 'style' and the peer group in Tamil Nadu, India. *Contributions to Indian Sociology, 42*(2), 245–269.

Nicolaides, S., Toda, Y. & Smith, P. K. (2002). Knowledge and attitudes about school bullying in trainee teachers. *British Journal of Educational Psychology, 72*, 105–118.

Olweus, D. (1993). *Bullying at School: What We Know and What We Can Do.* Malden, MA: Blackwell Publishing.

Olweus, D. (1994). Bullying at school: Basic facts and effects of a school based intervention program. *Journal of Child Psychology and Psychiatry*, 35(7), 1171–1190.

Patchin, J. W. & Hinduja, S. (2006). Bullies move beyond the schoolyard: A preliminary look at cyberbullying. *Youth Violence and Juvenile Justice*, 4(2), 148–169.

Pearce, D., Campbell, E. & Harding, D. (1987). *Australian Law Schools: A Discipline Assessment for the Commonwealth Tertiary Education Commission.* Canberra: Australian Government Publishing Service.

Raghaven Committee Report. (2007). Report of the Committee Constituted by the Hon'ble Supreme Court of India in SLP No 24295 of 2006. *The Menace of Ragging in Educational Institutions and Measures to Curb It.*

Ramirez, M., Ten Eyck, P., Peek-Asa, C., Onwuachi-Willig, A. & Cavanaugh, J. E. (2016). Evaluation of Iowa's anti-bullying law. *Injury Epidemiology*, 3(1), 15. doi: 10.1186/s40621-016-0080-9.

Salter, M., Crofts, T. & Lee, M. (2013). Beyond criminalisation and responsibilisation: 'Sexting', gender and young people. *Current Issues in Criminal Justice*, 24(3).

Smith, P. K. (2014). *Understanding School Bullying: Its Nature and Prevention Strategies.* London: Sage Publication.

Spears, B. A., Campbell, M., Tangen, D., Slee, P. T. & Cross, D. (2015). Australian pre-service teachers' knowledge and understanding of cyberbullying: Implications for school climate. Special edition on school climate and cyberbullying. *Les Dossiers des sciences de l'éducation*, 33, 109–130.

Spears, B. & Kofoed, J. (2013). Transgressing research binaries: Youth as knowledge brokers in cyberbullying research. In P. K. Smith & G. Steffgen (eds.), *Cyberbullying through the New Media: Findings from an International Metwork* (pp. 201–221). London: Psychology Press.

Spears, B., Taddeo, C., Swirski, T., Keeley, M., Katz, I., Collin, P., Daly, T. & Bates, S. (2014). *Research on youth exposure to, and management of, cyberbullying incidents in Australia: Part C – An evidence-based assessment of deterrents to youth cyberbullying* (SPRC Report 11/2014) (PDF) [357 Kb]. Sydney: Social Policy Research Centre, UNSW Australia.

Spyrou, P. (2015). Civil liability for negligence: An analysis of cyberbullying policies in South Australian schools. *University of South Australia Student Law Review*, 1, 34–51.

Srivastava, S. (2012). Pessimistic side of information and communication technology: Cyberbullying and legislature laws. *International Journal of Advances in Computer Science and Technology*, 1(1), 14–20.

University Grants Commission. (1999). *Report of the Committee to Curb the Menace of Ragging in Universities/Educational Institutions.* New Delhi: University Grants Commission.

Part IV

Commentaries from North America

15 Looking below the Surface
A Canadian Perspective on Cyberbullying in Schools and Universities

Wanda Cassidy, Chantal Faucher, and Margaret Jackson

Like the other jurisdictions discussed in this book, Canada also faces the challenges of peer-to-peer bullying and cyberbullying in schools and universities. As noted by the editors in Chapter 1, bullying using information and communication technologies (ICT) increasingly has been a focus of research internationally, particularly with students at the middle and secondary school levels, and more recently in the post-secondary context.

Many studies already exist on bullying at the school level in Canada (Cénat et al., 2015; Hymel & Swearer, 2015; Roberge, 2011), fewer at the post-secondary level (Twale & DeLuca, 2008). While a relationship has clearly been established between bullying and cyberbullying (Beran & Li, 2007; Cassidy, Jackson, & Brown, 2009), in the present chapter we focus primarily on cyberbullying because of its growing prevalence in Canadian schools and universities and the notable lack of research accorded to it to date at the university level. However, our own recent research has indicated that cyberbullying at the university level appears to be a growing problem in and of itself (Faucher, Cassidy, & Jackson, 2015).

This chapter therefore discusses the nature, extent, challenges, impact, solutions, and policy responses to cyberbullying in Canada at the both the school and university, with a focus on student-to-student cyberbullying. Where possible, connections are made with research undertaken in India and the challenges identified there, with an aim to learn from each other's experiences and gain insights in non-hierarchical, culturally sensitive ways (see Chapter 2).

Canadian Educational Context

Chapter 1 briefly outlines the educational and societal milieu of the countries who participated in the research described in this book, to provide context for the ensuing discussion on bullying and cyberbullying. We provide a similar abridged description of the Canadian context here.

In Canada, responsibility for education rests with the 13 provincial/territorial governments, not the federal government, with provincial governments delegating some responsibility to local school districts. Schools must follow their provincially mandated curriculum from kindergarten to grade 12, although school districts may add local courses or programs. Funding comes from local district taxes as well as provincial coffers. Most students (93%) are enrolled in free public schools that are offered in either English or French, although the government also funds a portion of the budgets of independent or private schools (Van Pelt et al., 2015). Special needs students and languages learners are incorporated into mainstream classes, with help from aids and pull-out sessions. The number of students in a class is mandated by labour agreements or by provincial legislation, and varies somewhat from province to province; for example, in British Columbia, kindergarten is capped at 20, grades 1 to 3 at 22, and 4 to 12 at 30. Teachers generally do not supervise lunch and recess breaks; this responsibility is contracted out to other adults. Corporal punishment in schools was banned by the Supreme Court of Canada in 2004, although the practice fell into disfavour well before that date.

All universities in Canada are publicly funded through provincial coffers, except for a handful of smaller religious institutions and one small secular private university. Universities also charge tuition fees, which vary from institution to institution.

Any discussion of cyberbullying in Canada should be seen in the context of Canada's increasingly culturally and linguistically diverse population. Although English and French are the official languages, approximately 22% of Canadians speak a first language other than English or French (Statistics Canada, 2016). One in five Canadians self-identify as a visible minority, with approximately 7 million out of 36 million Canadians born outside of the country (Statistics Canada, 2011). Of note are the 1.2 million Canadians who claim their heritage from India, with approximately 30,000 new immigrants from India settling in Canada each year, primarily in British Columbia and Ontario (Statistics Canada, 2016). Immigrants from India are the largest immigrant group after the Philippines.

This ethnic diversity is evident primarily in Canada's major cities. In the Vancouver school district, for example, 25% of the 50,000 students are designated English as a Second Language learners, 60% speak one of 126 languages other than English at home, and 4% are Indigenous from 600 bands or nations (Vancouver School Board, 2017).

Defining and Researching Cyberbullying

Researchers in Canada tend to use the term *cyberbullying* as the umbrella term to describe online behaviour that is offensive, derogatory, exclusionary, unwanted, and hurtful (Beran et al., 2015; Cassidy, Faucher, & Jackson, 2013; Deschamps & McNutt, 2016; Li, 2010; Mishna et al., 2014), although researchers such as Shariff (2015) note that this term may be too broad, suggesting that it is important to distinguish cyberbullying from online flirty fun, sexual harassment, child pornography, morphing, or extortion. The term *cyber aggression* is also used by some (Shapka & Law, 2013), as well as *cyber harassment* (Beran et al., 2012), to cover all negative online interactions, of which cyberbullying is only one subcategory. This conceptualization compares favourably to Blaya's (2013) use of *cyberviolence* as the umbrella term, as discussed in Chapters 5 and 6. Canadian researchers generally interpret Olweus' (1993) bullying requirements of repetition and power imbalance broadly, in that one negative posting on social media can be circulated widely and repeated over and over, and technology can be used as a tool to wield power.

In studies that we conducted in British Columbia schools (Cassidy, Brown, & Jackson, 2011, 2012a, 2012b; Cassidy et al., 2009; Jackson, Cassidy, & Brown, 2009a, 2009b) and at Canadian universities (Cassidy, Faucher, & Jackson, 2014, 2017; Cassidy, Jackson, & Faucher, 2015; Faucher et al., 2015; Faucher, Jackson, & Cassidy, 2014, 2015), we used the following definition, while also giving participants specific examples of actions and behaviour. We also identified various forms of technology that could be used to cyberbully, including text messages, blogs, Facebook, YouTube and other video-sharing sites, chats, Twitter, email, game servers, Skype, etc.

Cyberbullying uses language or images that can defame threaten, harass, bully, exclude, discriminate, demean, humiliate, stalk, disclose personal information, or contain offensive, vulgar or derogatory comments. Cyberbullying is intended to harm or hurt the recipient.

This definition is similar to Griggs' (2010), used in the France-India university study and quoted in Chapter 6. Like the other jurisdictions discussed in this book, no standard tool or instrument is used in Canada to assess cyberbullying. Researchers tend to use self-reports as the primary mechanism: paper and online surveys, focus groups, and interviews.

Cyberbullying in Canadian Schools and Universities

Nature and Venues

The venues students use to cyberbully in Canada are similar to India and elsewhere; perpetrators use whatever technology is available to send vulgar or hurtful messages or post obscene photographs of victims without their permission – messages designed to mock body shape, size, and looks (see Chapters 1, 5, 6). As new ICT platforms are developed, the opportunities expand: for example, in our first study of cyberbullying among adolescents aged 11 to 16, MSN and email were used most often (Cassidy et al., 2009; Jackson et al., 2009b); now it is the more popular Facebook, Instagram, Twitter, YouTube, and group gaming sites (Beran et al., 2015; Cassidy et al., 2013). At the university, course chat rooms are also a site for cyberbullying (Blizard, 2016; Faucher et al., 2014).

In Chapters 5 and 6, Blaya and colleagues discuss the problem of Internet addiction experienced by Indian youth in schools and universities. Studies in Canada and elsewhere (Cassidy et al., 2013; Ybarra & Mitchell, 2004) demonstrate a strong positive relationship between the amount of time spent online and a greater risk of cyberbullying perpetration or victimization. Similar to India, Canada is "wired", with 99% of Canadian youth having access to the Internet (Johnson, 2013), so the opportunities to bully online are ever present.

Prevalence

The few studies that have taken place in India show a high rate of cyberbullying among youth and young adults. Chapter 1 highlights a 2015 study conducted by Intel Security, which placed India above the other three countries surveyed (Australia, the United States, Singapore) in terms of percentage of children aged 8 to 16 who have cyberbullied others over social media (22%). Singh (2012) describes a Microsoft study which revealed an even higher rate of 52%, third highest among 25 countries, including Canada (see Chapters 1 and 5).

Canada is a large and geographically diverse country, so many of the studies of adolescents are localized to a particular region, except for one randomized national study of 1,001 youth aged 10 to 17 conducted by Beran and colleagues (2015), which found that 14% of youth had been cyberbullied in the previous month, while 7% admitted to cyberbullying others. Other studies with similar age groups, but with different time periods, show a range of victimization between 18% and 50% and perpetration from 25% to 36% (Cassidy et al., 2009; Cénat et al., 2015; Li, 2006; Mishna et al., 2010; Wade & Beran, 2011).

Our study of peer-to-peer cyberbullying at four universities from three provinces in Canada indicated that 25% of those surveyed had been victimized over the previous 12 months – 12% by friends and 14% by strangers – while 5% admitted to participating in cyberbullying (Faucher et al., 2014). These percentages are lower than what is reported in France, where Berthaud and Blaya (2014, 2015) found that 51% of university respondents were victims at least once during the previous 12 months and 14% had cyberbullied others (see Chapter 6).

Of course, as cautioned in the previous chapters, direct comparison of findings between (or within) countries is problematic due to different instruments being used and different understandings of what is deemed cyberbullying behaviour, as well as cultural differences. Also, as noted in Chapters 5 and 6, few scientific studies have been done to date in India with most of the statistics emanating from non-academic sources.

Motivation and Targets

Studies in Canada (Cassidy et al., 2011; Jackson et al., 2009b; Shariff & Churchill, 2010), like studies elsewhere (Cassidy et al., 2013; Kowalski, Limber, & Agatston, 2012; Smith, 2012), show that cyberbullying among adolescent females typically occurs within so-called friendship groups, with one or more girls targeting others to gain a higher position in the group hierarchy. A study by Canadian researchers Currie, Kelly, and Pomerantz (2009) found that meanness tends to bestow high status and be associated with being popular among peers, even though those girls may be mean and unlikeable.

Relational aggression (Crick & Grotpeter, 1995) is less common among boys in school, with boys targeted with sexual pictures and jokes, and innuendoes about their sexual orientation (Cassidy et al., 2009, 2011). Students who do not fit the norm of dress, behaviour, or looks may be especially vulnerable to being victimized (Cassidy et al., 2009; Faucher et al., 2015). The few studies that have been done in India concur with this motivation: the concept of "groupism" described in Chapter 1, and the study done by Srisiva, Thirumoorthi, and Sujatha (2013), which noted appearance and skin colour/complexion as common reasons for being targeted.

Among those who know each other, targeting because of interpersonal reasons (the target is not liked or retaliation for something the target did) dominates the reasons perpetrators give for cyberbullying at school and university. There is also a percentage of students who said they did it "for fun"; 9% at the school level (Cassidy et al., 2009), and in the top three of reasons provided by male undergraduates who admitted to cyberbullying (Faucher et al., 2014). Shariff (2015) found that 60% of adolescents she surveyed did it for fun, with respondents claiming that sarcasm, jokes, threats, humiliation, and passing of embarrassing intimate images were part of the everyday life of the teenager, and not harmful to others at the receiving end.

This behaviour lends credence to the power and control theoretical model (Pence & Paymar, 1993) that we use in our research, where someone perceived as weaker is targeted (compare "ragging" behaviour at Indian colleges described in Chapter 1), or someone is made weaker due to the behaviour of others who make them a target.

The behaviour of adolescents in school and young adults in university also must be viewed within the wider context of societal and cultural hierarchies and practices. The previous chapters raise these issues: in India, the caste system and postcolonial structures are noteworthy. In Canada, issues of income inequality (Conference Board of Canada, 2017), white privilege (McIntosh, 2012), and racial and religious discrimination, particularly in relation to Indigenous and Muslim populations (Banting & Kymlicka, 2010; Mishna & Van Wert, 2015; St. Denis, 2007), create and help maintain hierarchies and may directly or indirectly support bullying behaviour.

Gender Issues

Gender differences are not consistent in the international cyberbullying literature, pointing to the need for specific jurisdictions to conduct their own local research to determine what is happening. Chapter 6 draws attention to several studies that demonstrate this inconsistency: female university students in Portugal were more likely to be the aggressors and the victims (Francisco et al., 2015), whereas male students in China (Hong et al., 2007) and in Turkey (Dilmaç, 2009) were more involved as perpetrators. In India, female and male students were equally cyberbullying victims (Kaur, Kaur, & Sandhu, 2014).

In Canada, females volunteer to participate in cyberbullying research (surveys, interviews, focus groups) at a much higher rate than males, perhaps indicating a greater interest in the topic or more willingness to disclose. For example, in our university study, 74% of survey respondents were females, although a similar number of females (24%) compared to males (25%) reported being cyberbullied in the previous 12 months. Male undergraduates, however, were targeted more relentlessly and viciously than females (Faucher et al., 2014, 2015), although females reported more serious impacts than males at both the university and school levels (Cassidy et al., 2017; Faucher et al., 2014; Shariff & DeMartini, 2016). At the school level, more girls (21%) than boys (15%) were targeted, with relational aggression being the prime motivator (Jackson et al., 2009b).

Socio-economic and Ethnicity Issues

As Blaya, Kaur, and Sandhu discuss in Chapter 5, more research is needed to assess the influence that culture, socio-economic status, and ethical values play in cyberbullying. The authors note that socio-economic statuses do not seem to be a major factor in European cyberbullying studies to date, or if differences do exist, they are marginal at most. In our studies of cyberbullying at the school level, which encompassed schools at the high and low ends of the socio-economic ladder, we found no differences in the nature, extent, or targets when comparing those schools. Instead, differences depended on the school leadership at each school, whether the administrators were proactive in addressing cyberbullying issues, whether education and dialogue among all stakeholder groups occurred, and whether the school culture as whole tolerated bullying behaviour (Cassidy et al., 2011, 2012a, 2012b).

For example, two elementary schools (kindergarten to grade 7), located a kilometre apart and in the same middle to high socio-economic area, had radically different approaches to countering cyberbullying, even though both schools had experienced a serious incident just prior to our research being conducted. At School A, the principal redirected the perpetrators into leadership roles, while astutely talking with them about the motivation for their behaviour; plus, she also engaged the whole student body in longer-term solutions that fit their school. At School B, the principal suspended the perpetrator for a few days, then brought him back into the same classroom with the target, while imposing a code of silence among the staff and students.

Similarly, ethnicity was not a major factor in any of our studies at school or university, even though other studies have found that minority groups are sometimes targeted (Finn, 2004; Molluzzo & Lawler, 2012; Wensley & Campbell, 2012; Wang, Iannotti & Nansel, 2009). Canadian researchers Shapka and Law (2013) found that parental control played a role in slightly lower incidents of adolescents of East Asian background involved in cyber aggression compared to students from European backgrounds, although East Asian students were more likely to be motivated to engage in cyber aggression for proactive rather than reactive reasons.

Perhaps one explanation for ethnicity not being a major factor in the Canadian research to date is that much of the research in Canada takes place in the major cities, which are highly multicultural. As researchers, we would be interested in assessing whether there are differences between rural and urban areas, or whether certain areas that report community-based discrimination have higher incidents of cyberbullying. Also, since social status, hierarchical positioning within groups, sexual orientation, gender, and (sometimes) appearance and unpopularity are factors in cyberbullying, it would be helpful to research the intersectionality (Dhamoon, 2011) of these factors as possible contributors to victimization.

Impacts and Negative Effects

Cyberbullying victims report relatively similar impacts, no matter the location in the world. Research from various jurisdictions (see Chapters 1, 5, and 6), including India (Kaur et al., 2014; Kaur & Sandhu, 2015) and Canada (Beran et al., 2015; Cassidy et al., 2009, 2017; Mishna et al., 2014), documents impacts related to mental health (depression, anxiety, panic attacks, self-esteem issues, feeling helpless, suicidal ideation), physical health (sleeplessness, headaches, stomach upset, eating disorders), school (avoidance, academic decline, dropping out), relationships (loneliness, inability to make friends), and anger (wanting revenge). A Canadian study by Beran and colleagues (2012) also noted self-harm and drug use as a result of being cyberbullied at school.

Of note is the similarity of impacts across the age spectrum, whether a student is age 12 in middle school, or age 20 as an undergraduate young adult. These impacts also compare to the negative effects reported by Canadian university faculty members who had been cyberbullied (see Blizard, 2016; Cassidy et al., 2017). It appears that the impacts cross age, status, and maturity.

Chapter 1 also draws attention to the negative influences bullying and cyberbullying have on observers and the bullies themselves, as well as the overall school climate. We observed this impact in our studies at the school level: there was a palpable culture of silence in schools where victims and observers had no voice, and where known bullies were either feared or revered (Cassidy et al., 2012a, 2012b).

Reporting and Responses

Studies in India describe a culture that attributes bullying behaviour to growing up, where victims generally do not report, and teachers tend to ignore the incidents. Rarely are there systemic responses (see Chapter 1). The documentary interviews in Chapter 12 illuminate reasons why Indian youth generally do not tell their parents, and why parents tend to be in the dark about their children's negative online behaviour.

These findings resonate with studies among adolescents done in Canada. Victims generally suffer in silence or tell a friend, with fewer than half informing their parents and even fewer reporting the incident to school authorities (Cassidy et al., 2011, 2013). Shariff and Churchill (2010) found that 50% of teens did not report being cyberbullied because they might be labelled "a rat", be subject to retaliation, or have their access to technology curtailed.

Parents generally were unaware of the extent of their children's behaviour. In our study (Cassidy et al., 2012a), only 11% of parents of middle school children knew that their child had been on the receiving end of cyberbullying, while fewer than 1% knew their child was a perpetrator, even though 32% of the children of those parents said they had been victimized and 36% claimed to be perpetrators. Similarly, most teachers and school administrators were unaware of the problem, with many stating that it was the parents' responsibility and not theirs, since much of the cyberbullying took place on the home computer (Cassidy et al., 2012b). Craig, Bell, and Lescheid (2011) found that pre-service teachers in Ontario were less likely to intervene in cyberbullying incidents compared to physical forms of face-to-face bullying, since they regarded cyberbullying as less serious and less impactful.

Administrators at university are even less likely to know about cyberbullying incidents on campuses, as they are further removed from the day-to-day lives of their students, and adult students are even less likely to report to parents or to authorities (Cassidy et al., 2017; Faucher et al., 2014, 2015). Even when reporting does occur, chairs and department heads may be at a loss to know what to do unless clear policies and procedures are in place, which to date in Canada, only exist in a few universities (Faucher et al., 2015).

Solutions and Interventions

As Blaya and colleagues note in Chapter 5, there is little scientific evidence that demonstrates the effectiveness of intervention programs in changing students' behaviour and reducing harm. In Canada, provincial Ministries of Education have developed anti-bullying programs and safe-school policies, which are implemented inconsistently in schools across the provinces (Nosworthy & Rinaldi, 2013). Some programs include a cyberbullying component, yet no comprehensive evaluation measures have been implemented to assess the effectiveness of these programs. While Canadian researchers associated with PrevNet (Promoting Relationships and Eliminating Violence Network) have conducted research to assess face-to-face bullying programs, no intervention studies have been published to date (to our knowledge) related to cyberbullying (see www.prevnet.ca).

Participants in studies at Canadian schools and universities suggest very similar solutions, whether the respondents are students, educators, or parents. These include: more effective education about cyberbullying, clear anti-cyberbullying policies that are developed collaboratively with all stakeholders and communicated widely, better reporting mechanisms (younger students want anonymous reporting), more support for victims, and improvement in the wider culture of the institution, including modelling appropriate behaviour in the home and school (Cassidy et al., 2011, 2012a, 2012b, 2013; Faucher et al., 2014, 2015; Ryan, Kariuki, & Yilmaz, 2011).

One approach, which seems to be relatively ineffective, particularly on its own, is that of punishment. Punishment rarely uncovers the reasons behind the behaviour, nor does it mend relationships between the parties. The authors of Chapter 12 discuss two different approaches taken by schools in the Punjab region of northern India and in the Tamil region in the south: the former stressed consequences and punishment, making an example of the bully, while the Tamil region adopted a whole-school preventive and intervention approach that included lessons on bullying, support for victims, and cooperative activities to improve school climate. Sue Montebello and Christie Whitley, two prominent British Columbia educators featured in the award-winning documentary *Dare to Care: Transforming Schools through the Ethics of Care* (Hawley & Van Poelgeest, 2008), discuss the importance of an ethic of care (Noddings, 2002, 2005, 2006) response to bullying behaviour – one that encourages listening to all relevant voices, responding in ways that are respectful and insightful, and prioritizing relationships, restoration, and community-building in short- and long-term ways.

The authors of Chapter 7 purport that evaluation studies of intervention programs show that, in part, bullying is resistant to intervention. This perspective, coupled with the discussion in Chapter 2, encourages interventionists to take a macro or more holistic view of cyberbullying, to see it as a broader sociocultural problem, rather than just an individualistic or psychological phenomenon. Unfortunately, bullying behaviour is endemic in the wider culture, practised by too many teachers, parents, religious authorities, politicians, celebrities, and others who are in a position to mentor, influence, and guide our youth. There is often a tug-of-war between the micro-cultures of particular schools or environments that seek to develop positive, respectful cultures and the wider community or society that pushes against these initiatives. In her extensive body of work to promote an ethic of care in schools, Noddings (2002, 2005, 2006) admonishes those committed to fostering a kinder, more caring school culture to model and practise the behaviour they would like students to emulate, to encourage open and respectful dialogue, and to confirm positive practices and behaviour when evident (see also Beck & Cassidy, 2009; Cassidy & Bates, 2005; McDowell, 2011; Montabello, 2008).

It is important to address what is seen in school and university behaviour as well as what is unseen, but brewing beneath the obvious. Sensoy and DiAngelo (2012, p. 16) incorporate an appropriate visual, that of an iceberg, taken from the website of the Indiana Department of Education (2017) to portray what is seen and unseen in regards to cultural (mis) understandings. Most of the iceberg is underneath the water, but is nonetheless significant and (sometimes) threatening. Transferring this model to cyberbullying, there is a need to address the deeper macro issues that lie beneath the surface if anti-cyberbullying programs are to be effective and far reaching.

Policy and Legislation

Relevant legislation at the federal level in Canada, like India (Chapters 1 and 14), was motivated, in part, following two high-profile cyberbullying cases. Although the Canadian Criminal Code already addressed issues of harassment and defamatory libel, no specific legislation targeted cyberbullying. In 2012, 15-year-old Amanda Todd committed suicide after being tricked into posing semi-nude online, then blackmailed and threatened with exposure. In 2013, 17-year-old Rehtaeh Parsons was sexually assaulted and filmed, with the pictures widely circulated online to classmates. She too committed suicide. In 2015, the Canadian Parliament passed Bill 13, which made it illegal to distribute intimate images of a person without their consent. Although some advocates see this as a positive sign, many decried that it only addressed one aspect of cyberbullying (visuals), and stressed sanctions rather than education (Broll & Huey, 2015; Coburn, Connolly, & Roesch, 2015).

Another high-profile case, involving the University of Calgary and twin brothers who were students there, also drew attention to the issue of cyberbullying, but for different reasons. The Pridgen brothers developed a Facebook page mocking one of their instructors. Eight other students from the class joined in. The Pridgen brothers were found guilty of non-academic misconduct by the university and penalties were imposed, including suspension, but the brothers took their case to Court of the Queen's Bench of Alberta, claiming their right to freedom of expression under the Canadian Charter of Rights and Freedoms. The court ruled in their favour and reinstated the brothers, and although the University of Calgary appealed the decision to the Alberta Court of Appeal, the decision of the lower court was upheld (*Pridgen* v. *U. of Calgary*, 2012 ABCA 139).

At the provincial level, possibly to mitigate against workplace liability, several provinces have implemented workplace safety legislation, including measures to prevent and address bullying and harassment. British Columbia, for example, has WorkSafe BC, which requires that all schools and universities have anti-bullying policies in place and conduct staff training.

Some would argue that the law too often lags behind the needs of society (Waddams, 2016), while others argue that legislation does not necessarily promote desired behaviour. The law is a tool of last resort, a "stick" to enforce compliance, but not necessarily to change attitudes (Taylor, 1968). Legislation, like the policies in schools and universities, however, can reflect an intention and can serve to educate community members towards a desired end.

Discussion: Next Steps

The discussion in Chapter 2 of bullying as a sociocultural problem requiring interventions at both the macro and micro levels resonates with us as Canadian researchers. From our perspective, prevention and intervention approaches need to look at the wider impact societies and communities have on cyberbullying behaviour, as well as the smaller cultures (Holliday, 1999) of individual schools and post-secondary institutions with different leadership styles, varying degrees of student voice, and different approaches to fostering kinder, more respectful cyber interactions.

The micro-culture of the family also influences cyberbullying behaviour. In Canada, it is important to recognize the impact that families from diverse cultural and language groups may have on the way cyberbullying is defined and understood (Chapter 2), as well as possible tensions between cultural norms of behaviour and expectations outlined in Canadian laws and policies. Unlike the United States, which has been described as a melting pot of cultures, Canada's tradition is that of a cultural mosaic (Peach, 2005), where cultures are encouraged to keep their own traditions and practices (Canadian Multicultural Act, 1985).

Canada may be slightly less individualist and more collectivist (see discussion, Chapter 2) than the United States (Lipset, 1990), yet cyberbullying statistics involving students in Canada are comparable to findings emanating from the United States (Beran et al., 2012; Hinduja & Patchin, 2012; Hymel & Swearer, 2015; Kowalski et al., 2012; Wang et al., 2009).

The ethnic diversity of Canadian society, as well as its large land mass and urban/rural split, points to the need for more localized prevention and intervention programs, rather than "one size fits all" initiatives (Shapka & Law, 2013).

There certainly are important takeaway messages to be gleaned from the chapters in this book. A few examples: Canadian researchers are encouraged to be clear about their definitions of cyberbullying (Chapter 1), to embrace newer methodologies like the use of visuals and symbols (Chapters 4 and 10), and to extend the network of those being researched to the media, senior policy developers, and other influential community members (Chapter 12). That latter chapter also stresses the need for collaboration in undertaking research which is deeply rooted in co-constructed understandings of the rich and complex nature of India, but encourages as well the sharing of world views, now facilitated by technology. Chapter 13 emphasizes the need to focus upon preventative strategies to bullying, given the success the Tamil teachers had with parental involvement and peer support programs, and a gentler, proactive, peacebuilding approach – in comparison with the Punjabi teachers' focus on reactive sanctions. Finally, Chapter 11 highlights what is truly needed in other jurisdictions, that is, not only an awareness of and information about bullying, but also the training required to obtain clarity in individuals' knowledge and understanding for a best practices outcome.

It is also important to conduct longitudinal studies. For example, although cyberbullying occurs at both the school level and at postsecondary, is it the same youth who continue their bullying behaviour through to university, or does the university attract a different population of cyberbullies (and victims)? Also, to what extent are particular intervention methods successful, in the short as well as the long term? An emphasis towards building more respectful and caring school and university cultures may be the more difficult challenge (the part of the iceberg below the surface) than addressing immediate incidents that come to the fore. We propose that the ethic of care theoretical orientation has much to offer in addressing both micro and macro cyberbullying issues facing schools and universities, whether in Canada, India, or elsewhere.

References

Banting, K. & Kymlicka, W. (2010). Canadian multiculturalism: Global anxieties and local debates. *British Journal of Canadian Studies, 23*(1), 43–72. doi: 10.3828/bjcs.2010.3.

Beck, K. & Cassidy, W. (2009). Embedding the ethic of care in school policies and practices. In K. te Riele (ed.), *Making Schools Different: Alternative Approaches to Educating Young People* (pp. 50–64). Thousand Oaks, CA: Sage Publications.

Beran, T. & Li, Q. (2007). The relationship between bullying and cyberbullying. *The Journal of Student Wellbeing, 1*(2), 15–33.

Beran, T., Mishna, F., McInroy, L. B., & Shariff, S. (2015). Children's experiences of cyberbullying: A Canadian national study. *Children & Schools, 37*(4), 207–214. doi: 10.1093/cs/cdv024.

Beran, T., Rinaldi, C., Bickham, D., & Rich, M. (2012). Evidence for the need to support adolescents dealing with harassment and cyber-harassment: Prevalence, progression, and impact. *School Psychology International, 33,* 562–576. doi: 10.1177/0143034312446976.

Beran, T., Stanton, L., Hetherington, R., Mishna, F., & Shariff, S. (2012). Development of the bullying and health experiences scale. *Interactive Journal of Medical Research, 1*(2), e13. doi: 10.2196/ijmr.1835.

Berthaud, J. & Blaya, C. (2014). Premiers résultats de l'enquête française Cyberviolence à l'université. *Adjectif, Analyses et Recherches sur les TICE.* Retrieved from www.adjectif.net/spip/spip.php?articles279.96.

Berthaud, J. & Blaya C. (2015). Pratiques numériques, perception de la violence en ligne et victimation chez les étudiants. *Recherches en éducation, Hors série, 7,* 146–161.

Blaya, C. (2013). *Les ados dans le cyberspace. Prises de risque et cyberviolence.* Bruxelles: De Boeck.

Blizard, L. (2016). Faculty members' experiences of cyberbullying by students at one Canadian university: Impact and recommendations. *International Research in Higher Education, 1,* 107–124. doi: 10.5430/irhe.v1n1p107.

Broll, R. & Huey, L. (2015). "Just being mean to somebody isn't a police matter": Police perspectives on policing cyberbullying. *Journal of School Violence, 14*(2), 155–176. doi: 10.1080/15388220.2013.879367.

Cassidy, W. & Bates, A. (2005). "Drops outs" and "push outs": Finding hope at a school that actualizes the ethic of care. *American Journal of Education, 112*(1), 66–102.

Cassidy, W., Brown, K., & Jackson, M. (2011). Moving from cyber-bullying to cyber-kindness: What do students, educators and parents say? In E. Dunkels, G.-M. Franberg, & C. Hallgren (eds.), *Youth Culture and Net Culture: Online Social Practices* (pp. 256–277). Hershey, PA: IGI Global Press.

Cassidy, W., Brown, K., & Jackson, M., (2012a). "Making kind cool": Parents' suggestions for preventing cyber bullying and fostering cyber kindness. *Journal of Educational Computing Research, 46*(4), 415–436. doi: 10.2190/EC.46.4.f.

Cassidy, W., Brown, K., & Jackson, M., (2012b). "Under the radar": Educators and cyberbullying in schools. *School Psychology International, 33*(5), 520–532. doi: 10.1177/0143034312445245.

Cassidy, W., Faucher, C., & Jackson, M. (2013). Cyberbullying among youth: A comprehensive review of current international research and its implications and application to policy and practice. *School Psychology International: Special Issue on Cyberbullying, 34*(6), 575–612. doi: 10.1177/0143034313479697.

Cassidy, W., Faucher, C., & Jackson, M. (2014). The dark side of the ivory tower: Cyberbullying of university faculty and teaching personnel. *Alberta Journal of Educational Research, 60*(2), 279–299.

Cassidy, W., Faucher, C., & Jackson, M. (2017). Adversity in university: Cyberbullying and its impacts on students, faculty and administrators. *International Journal of Environmental Research and Public Health, 14*, 888–906. doi: 10.3390/ijerph14080888.

Cassidy, W., Jackson, M., & Brown, K. N. (2009). Sticks and stones can break my bones, but how can pixels hurt me? Students' experiences with cyber-bullying. *School Psychology International, 30*(4), 383–402. doi: 10.1177/0143034309106948.

Cassidy, W., Jackson, M., & Faucher, C. (2015). Gender differences and cyberbullying towards faculty members in higher education. In R. Navarro, S. Yubero, & E. Larrañaga (eds.), *Cyberbullying across the Globe: Gender, Family, and Mental Health* (pp. 79–98). Basel, Switzerland: Springer.

Cénat, J. M., Blais, M., Hébert, M., Lavoie, F., & Guerrier, M. (2015). Correlates of bullying in Quebec high school students: The vulnerability of sexual-minority youth. *Journal of Affective Disorders, 183*, 315–321. doi: 10.1016/j.jad.2015.05.011.

Coburn, P. I., Connolly, D. A., & Roesch, R. (2015). Cyberbullying: Is federal criminal legislation the solution? *Canadian Journal of Criminology and Criminal Justice, 57*(4), 566–579. doi: 10.3138/cjccj.2014.E43.

Conference Board of Canada (2017). Income inequality. Retrieved from www.conferenceboard.ca/hcp/provincial/society/income-inequality.aspx.

Craig, K., Bell, D., & Leschied, A. (2011). Pre-service teachers' knowledge and attitudes regarding school-based bullying. *Canadian Journal of Education, 34*(2), 21–33.

Crick, N., & Grotpeter, J. (1995). Relational aggression, gender, and socio-psychological adjustment. *Child Development, 66*, 710–722. doi: 10.2307/1131945.

Currie, E., Kelly, D., & Pomerantz, S. (2009). *Girl Power: Girls Reinventing Girlhood.* New York: Peter Lang.

Deschamps, R., & McNutt, K. (2016). Cyberbullying: What's the problem? *Canadian Public Administration, 59*(1), 45–71. doi: 10.111.capa12159.

Dhamoon, R. (2011). Considerations on mainstreaming intersectionality. *Political Research Quarterly, 64*(1), 230–243. doi: 10.1177/1065912910379227.

Dilmaç, B. (2009). Psychological needs as a predictor of cyber bullying: A preliminary report on college students. *Educational Sciences: Theory and Practice, 9*(3), 1307–1325.

Faucher, C., Cassidy, W., & Jackson, M. (2015). From the sandbox to the inbox: Comparing the acts, impacts, and solutions of bullying in K-12, higher education, and the workplace. *Journal of Education and Training Studies, 3*(6), 111–125. doi: 11114/jets.v3i6.1033.

Faucher, C., Jackson, M., & Cassidy, W. (2014). Cyberbullying among university students: Gendered experiences, impacts, and perspectives. *Education Research International, 2014*, 1–10. doi: 10.1155/2014/698545.

Faucher, C., Jackson, M., & Cassidy, W. (2015). When online exchanges byte: An examination of the policy environment governing cyberbullying at the university level. *Canadian Journal of Higher Education, 45*(1), 102–121.

Finn, J. (2004). A survey of online harassment at a university campus. *Journal of Interpersonal Violence, 19*(4), 468–483. doi: 10.1177/0886260503262083.

Francisco, S. M., Veiga Simão, A. M., Ferreira, P. C., & Martins, M. J. D. D. (2015). Cyberbullying: The hidden side of college students. *Computers in Human Behaviour, 43*(0), 167–182. doi: 10.1016/j.chb.2014.10.045.

Grigg, D. (2010). Cyber-aggression: Definition and concept of cyberbullying. *Australian Journal of Guidance and Counselling, 20*(2), 143–156. doi: 10.1375/ajgc.20.2.143.

Hawley, M., & Van Poelgeest (Producers/Directors). (2008). *Dare to Care: Transforming Schools through the Ethics of care.* Vancouver, BC: Life Is Short Entertainment.

Hinduja, S. & Patchin, J. (2012). Cyberbullying: Neither an epidemic nor a rarity. *European Journal of Developmental Psychology, 9*(5), 539–543. doi: 10.1080/17405629.2012.706448.

Holliday, A. (1999). Small cultures. *Applied Linguistics, 20*(2), 237–274. doi: 10.1093/applin/20.2.237.

Hong, Y., Li, X., Mao, R., & Stanton, B. (2007). Internet use among Chinese college students: Implications for sex education and HIV prevention. *Cyberpsychology & Behavior, 10*, 161–169. doi: 10.1089/cpb.2006.9973.

Hymel, S. & Swearer, S. (2015). Four decades of research on school bullying. *American Psychologist, 70*, 293–299. doi: 10.1037/a0038928.

Indiana Department of Education, Office of English Language Learning & Migrant Education (2017). The iceberg concept and culture. Retrieved from www.doc.in.gov/englishlanguagelearning.

Jackson, M., Cassidy, W., & Brown, K. (2009a). Out of the mouths of babes: Students "voice" their opinions on cyber-bullying. *Long Island Education Review, 8*(2), 24–30.

Jackson, M., Cassidy, W., & Brown, K. (2009b). "You were born ugly and youl die ugly too": Cyber-bullying as relational aggression. *In Education: Special Issue on Technology and Social Media, Part 1, 15*(1), 68–82. www.ineducation.ca/article/you-were-born-ugly-and-youl-die-ugly-too-cyber-bullying-relational-aggression.

Johnson, M. (2013). Connected, mobile and social: The online lives of Canadian youth. *Transition Magazine, 43*(3), 5–9.

Kaur, K., Kaur, S., & Sandhu, D. (2014). Cyber bullying: An emerging threat to pupil well-being. *International Journal of Social Sciences Review, 2,* 374–377.

Kaur, K. & Sandhu, D. (2015). Studying depression and loneliness amongst the victims of cyber bullying. In M. Irfan, R. Sultana, H. Shafiq, M. Singh, & K. Singh (eds.), *Mental Health, Religion and Culture: A Psychological Paradigm* (pp. 10–18). Patiala: 21st Century Publications.

Kowalski, R., Limber, S., & Agatston, P. (2012). *Cyberbullying: Bullying in the Digital Age* (2nd edn.). Malden, MA: Wiley-Blackwell.

Li, Q. (2010). Cyberbullying in high schools: A study of students' behaviors and beliefs about this new phenomenon. *Journal of Aggression, Maltreatment & Trauma, 19*(4), 372–392. doi: 10.1080/10926771003788979.

Lipset, S. (1990). *Continental Divide: The Values and Institutions of the United States and Canada.* London: Routledge.

McDowell, K. (2011). Who cares? Who doesn't? An exploration of perceptions of care based on the experiences of secondary school students from different economic groups. (Unpublished doctoral dissertation). Simon Fraser University, Burnaby, BC, Canada.

McIntosh, P. (2012). Reflections and future directions for privilege studies. *Journal of Social Issues, 68,* 194–206. doi: 10.1111/j.1540–4560.2011.01744x.

Mishna, F., Cook, C., Gadalla, T., Daciuk, J., & Solomon, S. (2010). Cyber bullying behaviors among middle and high school students. *American Journal of Orthopsychiatry, 80*(3), 362–374.

Mishna, F., Schwan, K., Lefebvre, R., Bhole, P., & Johnston, D. (2014). Students in distress: Unanticipated findings in a cyber bullying study. *Children and Youth Services Review, 44,* 341–348. doi: 10.1016/j.childyouth.2014.04.010.

Mishna, F. & Van Wert, M. (2015). *Bullying in Canada.* Oxford: Oxford University Press.

Molluzzo, J. C. & Lawler, J. P. (2012). A study of the perceptions of college students on cyberbullying. *Information Systems Education Journal, 10*(4), 84–109.

Montabello, S. (2008). Journeying into the heart of schools: Dwelling in time, place and intimacy. (Unpublished Doctoral Dissertation). Simon Fraser University, Burnaby, BC, Canada.

Noddings, N. (2002). *Educating Moral People: A Caring Alternative to Character Education.* New York: Teachers College Press.

Noddings, N. (2005). *The Challenge to Care in Schools: An Alternate Approach to Education* (2nd edn.). New York: Teachers College Press.

Noddings, N. (2006). Educational leaders as caring teachers. *School Leadership & Management. 26*(4), 339–345. doi: 10.1080/13632430600886848.

Nosworthy, N. & Rinaldi, C. (2013). A review of school board cyberbullying policies in Alberta. *Alberta Journal of Educational Research, 58*(4), 509–525.

Olweus, D. (1993). *Bullying at School: What We Know and What We Can Do.* Oxford: Blackwell.

Peach, C. (2005). The mosaic versus the melting pot: Canada and the USA. *Scottish Geographical Journal*, *121*(1), 3–27. doi: 10.1080/00369220518737218.

Pence, E. & Paymar, M. (1993). *Education Groups for Men Who Batter: The Duluth Model.* New York: Springer.

Roberge, G. D. (2011). Countering school bullying: An analysis of policy content in Ontario and Saskatchewan. *International Journal of Education and Policy Leadership*, *6*(5), 1–14.

Ryan, T., Kariuki, M., & Yilmaz, H. (2011). A comparative analysis of cyberbullying perceptions of preservice educators: Canada and Turkey. *Turkish Online Journal of Educational Technology*, *10*(3), 1–12.

Sensoy, Ö. & DiAngelo, R. (2012). *Is Everyone Really Equal? An Introduction to Key Concepts in Social Justice Education.* New York: Teachers College Press.

Shapka, J. D. & Law, D. M. (2013). Does one size fit all? Ethnic differences in parenting behaviors and motivations for adolescent engagement in cyberbullying. *Journal of Youth and Adolescence*, *42*(5), 723–738. doi: 10.1007/s10964-013-9927-2.

Shariff, S. (2015). *Sexting and Cyberbullying: Defining the Line for Digitally Empowered Kids.* New York: Cambridge University Press.

Shariff, S. & Churchill, A. H. (eds.). (2010). *Truths and Myths of Cyber-bullying: International Perspectives on Stakeholder Responsibility and Children's Safety.* New York: Peter Lang.

Shariff, S. & DeMartini, A. (2016). Cyberbullying and rape culture in universities: Defining the legal lines between fun and intentional harm. In H. Cowie & C.-A. Myers (eds.), *Bullying among University Students: Cross-National Perspectives* (pp. 172–190). London: Routledge.

Singh, P. V. (2012, June 27). 53 percent kids in India bullied online: Microsoft survey. *Governance Now.* Retrieved from www.governancenow.com/views/thi nk-tanks/53-percent-kids-india-bullied-online-microsolft-survey.

Smith, P. K. (2012). Cyberbullying and cyber aggression. In S. R. Jimerson, A. B. Nickerson, M. J. Mayer, & M. J. Furlong (eds.), *Handbook of School Violence and School Safety: International Research and Practice* (2nd edn.) (pp. 93–103). New York: Routledge.

Statistics Canada (2011). *National Household Survey: Data Tables.* Retrieved from www12.statcan.gc.ca/nhs-enm/2011/dp-pd/dt-td/index-eng.cfm.

Statistics Canada (2016). *Census Datasets.* Retrieved from www12.statcan.gc.ca /datasets/index-eng.cfm?Temporal=2016.

St. Denis, V. (2007). Aboriginal education and anti-racist education: Building alliances across cultural and racial identity. *Canadian Journal of Education*, *30*(4), 1068–1092. doi: 10.2307/20466679.

Srisiva, R., Thirumoorthi, R., & Sujatha, P. (2013). Prevalence and prevention of school bullying – A case study of Coimbatore City, Tamilnadu, India. *International Journal of Humanities and Social Science Invention*, *2*, 36–45.

Taylor, R. (1968). Law and morality. *New York University Law Review, 43,* 611–647.

Twale, D. J. & DeLuca, B. M. (2008). *Faculty Incivility: The Rise of the Academic Bully Culture and What to Do about It.* San Francisco, CA: Jossey-Bass.

Vancouver School Board (2017). Our district. Retrieved from www.vsb.bc.ca/abo ut-vsb.

Van Pelt, D. N., Clemens, J., Brown, B., & Palacios, M. (2015). *Where Our Students Are Educated.* Vancouver, BC: Fraser Institute.

Waddams, W. (2016). *Introduction to the Study of Law.* (8th edn.). Toronto: Carswell.

Wade, A. & Beran, T. (2011). Cyberbullying: The new era of bullying. *Canadian Journal of School Psychology, 26*(1), 44–61. doi: 10.1177/0829573510396318.

Wang, J., Iannotti, R. J., & Nansel, T. R. (2009). School bullying among adolescents in the United States: Physical, verbal, relational, and cyber. *Journal of Adolescent Health, 45*(4), 368–375. doi: 10.1016/jadohealth.2009.03.021.

Wensley, K. & Campbell, M. (2012). Heterosexual and nonheterosexual young university students' involvement in traditional and cyber forms of bullying. *Cyberpsychology, Behavior, and Social Networking, 15*(12), 649–654. doi: 10.1089/cyber.2012.0132.

Ybarra, M. & Mitchell, K. (2004). Online aggressors/targets, aggressors, and targets: A comparison of associated youth characteristics. *Journal of Child Psychology and Psychiatry, 45*(7), 1308–1316. doi: 10.1111/j.1469–7610.2004.00328.x.

16   Bullying and School Climate in the United States and India

Dewey Cornell and Kathan Shukla

This book provides valuable insight into the challenges of creating a safe and supportive school climate in Indian schools through research comparing Indian students with students from Europe, Australia, and other nations. This chapter comments on some key findings from this research and extends the discussion to a relevant body of research by our group at the University of Virginia in the United States.

In the United States, bullying has become recognized as a serious national concern actively being addressed by federal and state governments (Cornell & Limber, 2015). The US National Crime Victimization Study found that 28% of students aged 12–18 report being bullied at school during the school year (Robers, Kemp, & Truman, 2013). Nearly 20% of female and 18% of male high school students reported being bullied on school property in the past 12 months according to the Youth Risk Behavior Survey (Kann et al., 2014). Another study of a nationally representative sample of sixth through tenth graders found prevalence rates of approximately 13% for having been the victim of physical bullying, 37% for verbal bullying, 41% for social or relational bullying, and 10% for cyberbullying in the past two months (Wang, Iannotti, & Nansel, 2009).

Studies reported in this book confirm that peer aggression is a ubiquitous international problem that demands attention in all schools. As in other nations, Indian students report high levels of being teased, harassed, threatened, and, in some cases, physically assaulted. Specific forms of peer aggression are recognized as serious problems in India, such as the public sexual harassment of girls and the hazing of beginning college students described in Chapter 2. Indian students in different regions reported specific forms of peer aggression that are especially problematic, such as stealing food from a classmate's plate or making fun of someone for poor grades. It is important to recognize regional differences in particular forms of peer aggression that reflect socioeconomic and cultural influences.

Bullying, as well as other discriminatory behavior, may occur more frequently in social groups where there are large disparities in social status. As suggested in several chapters, the caste system in India might contribute to the prevalence of bullying. Although Indian law bans discrimination based on caste, the hierarchical nature of this system may promote attitudes conducive to bullying. For example, students were reported to tease or insult those from lower castes.

In order to deal effectively with the problem of bullying and other forms of peer aggression, it is necessary to examine the broader socio-ecological system in schools. The assessment of school climate allows educators to identify key socio-ecological factors and target areas for school improvement. In this chapter, we discuss our work examining the influence of positive school climate on bullying in the United States and its implications for India. However, first we describe some of the challenges and limitations we have identified in our research on the measurement of bullying.

The Hazards of Measuring Bullying

There is some question whether peer aggression, and bullying in particular, occurs at a higher rate in India than in other nations. International comparisons are fraught with measurement problems, since there are no terms such as *bullying* that can be found across languages. Several teams of researchers (e.g., Chapter 4) have made valiant efforts to construct measures that bridge language differences and recognize culturally specific forms of aggression. Although these studies yield fascinating results, and suggest high rates of peer aggression in several regions of India, there is reason to be cautious about inferring national trends. International and regional comparisons may be confounded by socioeconomic factors, especially the high rates of poverty in India, and by differences in how students understand and respond to surveys.

Understandably, studies of India have relied on relatively small samples that do not represent the diversity of Indian peoples. The incredible size and complexity of India make any generalization about rates of peer aggression or bullying doubtful. With more than 1.3 billion inhabitants, India is comprised of 29 states and seven union territories, each with distinctive cultural and historical characteristics. The Census of India of 2001 identified 122 major languages and the government recognizes 22 official languages (Office of the Registrar General & Census Commissionaire, India, 2017).

A common problem in studying peer aggression is the difficulty of defining and measuring bullying. Although English is widely used in India, especially in higher education and government, many Indian languages do not have a term that closely corresponds to Western conceptions of bullying. For example, Punjabi has no translation for *bullying*, and the most similar terms are *dhakeshahi* for showing off one's power and *baar baar tang karna* for repetitive harassment (Chapter 4).

Academic definitions distinguish bullying from other forms of peer aggression with three criteria of intentionality, repetition, and power imbalance. However, students in India as well as other countries do not necessarily use these criteria in identifying themselves as victims of bullying. In the Skrzypiec and colleagues study (Chapter 3) only one quarter of the Indian students who said they have been seriously bullied also reported experiences that conformed to the academic criteria for bullying. A critical question is whether student reports of bullying are consistent with the academic definition used by researchers and often presented on written surveys.

Definitional Problems. We conducted two studies in the United States in which school counselors investigated student reports of bullying by interviewing students and their classmates in order to determine whether bullying consistent with the academic definition actually occurred (Cornell & Mehta, 2011; Phillips & Cornell, 2012). In these studies students were presented with a standard written definition of bullying that included the three criteria. In both studies, school counselors found that students tended to be over-inclusive in their reports of bullying. Students who claimed to be victims of bullying often failed to use the power imbalance criterion and reported other forms of peer conflict as bullying (Cornell & Mehta, 2011). Only about half (56%) of the students who marked on a confidential (not anonymous) survey that they were victims of bullying could be confirmed as actual victims of bullying. In many cases the students were involved in peer conflicts that did not meet the criteria for bullying.

In another study, students were presented with a standard definition of bullying and asked to identify peers in their school who were victims of bullying (Phillips & Cornell, 2012). Counselors again found that peer reports were often overly inclusive. The proportion of students who could be confirmed as victims of school bullying ranged from 43% for students with two peer nominations to 90% for students with nine or more nominations (Phillips & Cornell, 2012). Some of the nominated students were experiencing other forms of conflict or distress, and some had been bullied in the past but were no longer being bullied. Although there is no method to determine with certainty whether a student is being bullied (the school counselors might not have been correct in all of their assessments), these studies made clear that students often use a broad definition of bullying that does not match the academic definition used in bullying research.

In a third study, we tested the effects of using a written survey definition of bullying on bullying prevalence rates (Huang & Cornell, 2015). This study used a large sample of Virginia high schools in which students completed an anonymous, online school climate survey that contained a series of questions about bullying. In the first part of the study, 7,717 students in 59 high schools were asked three general questions regarding whether they had been bullied in the past month and in the past year, or had bullied someone else in the past year, and four more specific questions whether they had been victims of physical, verbal, social, or cyberbullying. However, half of the students in each school were randomly assigned to receive a survey with a standard definition of bullying before answering the questions and half received no definition of bullying. The results were a lesson in humility for bullying researchers who construct carefully worded definitions of bullying in order to obtain precise data on its prevalence: there were no statistically significant differences between the two groups on the school prevalence rates for any form of bullying. In other words, it did not matter whether students were given a survey definition of bullying or simply asked about bullying with no definition.

We also tested whether the order of questions about bullying had an impact on school prevalence rates (Huang & Cornell, 2015). In a separate sample of 9,585 students attending 60 high schools, half of the students in each school were asked three general questions about being bullied (e.g., "Have you been bullied in the past year?"), followed by four more specific questions (e.g., "Have you been verbally bullied?"), and in the other half of the sample the specific questions were presented first, followed by the general questions. Students who were asked the specific questions first reported higher rates of being bullied in the past year on all four of the specific questions but not on the general questions. There was a 29% to 76% increase in bullying prevalence when the specific questions were asked before the general questions. One interpretation of these findings is that asking questions about specific forms of bullying yields higher endorsement rates and primes students to report higher rates on the more specific questions about bullying. Although it is not possible to say which order of questions yields the most accurate prevalence rates, it is evident that the order of questions about bullying matters.

Exaggeration. Finally, we have investigated whether some students might intentionally exaggerate their involvement in bullying. Several studies have found that a small group of students will intentionally provide dishonest answers to survey questions, perhaps in an effort to be mischievous or rebellious (Fan et al., 2006). Other students might answer surveys in a rapid or careless manner that increases the endorsement of low-frequency items such as questions about bullying. One strategy to detect students who are dishonest or careless in answering survey questions is to include validity questions, such as "I am telling the truth on this survey" (Cornell et al., 2012). Our studies have found that self-report rates of bullying others and being a victim of bullying, as well as other infrequent behaviors (such as using drugs and bringing weapons to school) are inflated by a small group of students who admit they are not answering the survey truthfully (Cornell, Lovegrove, & Baly, 2014; Cornell et al., 2012; Jia et al., 2016). For example, one study found that a small (12%) group of students who admitted they answered the survey untruthfully provided rates of bullying that were much higher than students who reported that their answers were truthful. Failure to screen out this small group inflated the total sample rates of bullying victimization by 8.8% and bullying others by 29.7%. Rates for other problem behaviors were also inflated, such as carrying weapons (38.6%) and smoking marijuana (18.5%).

A further problem is that because students who exaggerate their involvement in bullying also endorse other problem behaviors, the correlates of bullying are also inflated. For example, we found that failure to screen surveys for invalid responders can produce inflated correlations between bullying and drug use, suicide attempts, fighting, and bringing weapons to school (Jia et al., 2016). These results suggest that some of the negative outcomes associated with bullying found in the research literature may be inflated by the use of unscreened survey data.

One implication of these studies is to recognize that student reports are not objective measures of bullying and should be interpreted with caution. Validity screening does not eliminate all dishonest responses, but there is evidence that it improves data quality and gives more realistic prevalence rates (Cornell et al., 2012; Jia et al., 2016). Researchers are also advised to use questions about bullying that employ terms and ideas familiar to the students rather than attempt to import concepts that may be foreign to their perceptions and experiences. Academic definitions of bullying seem to have little impact on student responses.

Although comparisons across regions and nations may be dubious, repeated surveys within the same school, using terms and concepts familiar to the students, may yield helpful information about local conditions in individual schools. These results might not be regarded as precise measures, but as indices that can be tracked over the years. A survey can be useful in drawing attention to the problem of bullying, and in helping to assess local intervention efforts. Peer nomination surveys are one way to help schools identify a group of students who may be victims of bullying (Cornell & Huang, 2015). However, the final determination of bullying in a school is best made on a case-by-case basis with direct interviews and observations conducted by experienced educators and counselors.

This research summarizes some critical measurement problems related to bullying. In the next section, we focus on school climate because it is one of the most consistent predictors of bullying and other problem behaviors. The assessment of school climate offers educators a tool for understanding school conditions and developing school improvement plans.

School Climate

School climate has become an important focus of attention in improving student learning and achievement. In school climate research, the idea is to understand the network of socio-ecological factors in a school and how they affect student outcomes ranging from bullying to academic achievement. Once the climate is understood, educators can focus on the malleable factors that can be manipulated to produce desirable student outcomes.

The concept of school climate covers a wide range of organizational, educational, interpersonal, and safety aspects of school experiences. The US Department of Education (2013, p. 2) defined school climate as "a multi-faceted concept that describes the extent to which a school community creates and maintains a safe school campus, a supportive academic, disciplinary, and physical environment, and respectful, trusting, and caring relationships throughout the school community." A positive school climate has been linked to safer school conditions and higher student achievement (Cohen et al., 2009). Students experiencing a positive school climate tend to report less bullying and peer victimization (Cornell, Shukla, & Konold, 2015; Gottfredson et al., 2005; Konold et al., 2014), less disciplinary suspension (temporary removal) from school (Bradshaw, Mitchell, & Leaf, 2010; Gregory, Cornell, & Fan, 2011), lower rates of risk behaviors (Klein et al., 2012; Shukla, Cornell, & Konold, 2016), and more desirable psychological and behavioral outcomes (Kuperminc, Leadbeater, & Blatt, 2001) than those who experience a more aversive school climate. The prevalence of bullying and other forms of peer aggression in a school can be regarded as a prime indicator of a poor school climate that is detrimental to student learning and achievement and leads to higher dropout rates (Cornell, Gregory, Huang, & Fan, 2013).

Authoritative School Climate. Our research has focused on a conceptual model of school climate referred to as an *authoritative school climate*.

This model identifies key features of a positive school climate that are associated with lower rates of student risk behavior and aggression. This developing theory of school climate is derived from work by Baumrind (1968) on authoritative parenting that stimulated a large body of child development research (Larzelere, Morris, & Harrist, 2013). Parenting researchers have found that authoritative parents manifest a combination of high expectations (also called "demandingness") and emotional support (also called "responsiveness") for their children. High expectations are often measured as strict discipline, but can refer to high expectations in other domains such as academic achievement. Parents are less effective when they have high expectations but are not supportive (authoritarian), when they are emotionally supportive but lack high expectations (permissive), or when they are lacking in both expectations and support (disengaged or neglectful). Although there is no reason to believe that an authoritative school climate is completely homologous with authoritative parenting, it has been an illuminating avenue of study.

The authoritative school climate theory posits that two domains of school climate are key to a safe and effective school (Gregory & Cornell, 2009; Pellerin, 2005). The first domain encompasses high disciplinary and academic expectations for students, which has been referred to as the *demandingness* or the *structure* of the school climate. In a structured school, teachers and other school staff members enforce discipline in a strict but fair manner, and they communicate high academic expectations for all students. The second domain concerns the responsiveness or *supportiveness* of teacher–student relationships. In a supportive school, teachers and other school staff members interact with students in a respectful, caring, and helpful manner.

Our group developed the Authoritative School Climate Survey to measure the structure and supportiveness of a school from both student (Konold & Cornell, 2015; Konold et al., 2014) and teacher/staff perspectives (Huang & Cornell, 2016; Huang et al., 2015) using large statewide samples of Virginia middle and high schools. Three studies found that an authoritative school climate (characterized by high scores on scales measuring structure and support) was associated with positive student behavioral adjustment. A study of 39,364 seventh and eighth grade students attending 423 schools found that higher disciplinary structure and student support were associated with lower levels of teasing and bullying, as well as fewer self-reports of being victimized in general (Cornell et al., 2015).

A second study, of 47,888 students in grades 9–12 attending 319 high schools, found that students attending schools with an authoritative school climate had lower levels of student-reported alcohol and marijuana use; bullying, fighting, and carrying weapons at school; less interest in gang membership; and fewer suicidal thoughts and behaviors (Cornell & Huang, 2016).

A third study, of 9,134 teachers in 389 middle schools, compared student perceptions of school climate with teacher reports of how much verbal and physical aggression they experienced from their students (Berg & Cornell, 2016). There was consistent evidence that teachers felt safer and experienced lower levels of student hostility and aggression in authoritative climate schools. In other words, in schools characterized by students as having strict but fair discipline and teachers who were supportive and concerned about their success, the teachers found that they were treated with respect by their students and did not experience the incidents of verbal abuse, threatening behavior, or in some cases, physical assault, that occurred in schools with a less structured and supportive climate. Some educators may hold outdated beliefs that teachers and school administrators must be punitive and controlling in their interactions with students in order to maintain school discipline and order, but these findings suggest the opposite. When educators convey concern, respect, and warm encouragement to their students, school discipline is strengthened and teachers experience less hostility and aggression from their students.

The value of the authoritative school climate was not limited to certain kinds of schools, such as schools with higher-income students or schools in urban versus rural locations. All three of these studies controlled for student demographic variables of gender, race, grade, and parent education level as well as school demographics of enrollment size, racial/ethnic minority composition, and percentage of low-income students.

Other studies found that higher disciplinary structure and student support were associated with positive academic outcomes such as higher student engagement in school, higher course grades, and higher educational aspirations in both middle school and high school samples (Cornell, Shukla, & Konold, 2016), as well as lower high school dropout rates (Jia, Konold, & Cornell, 2015). Once again, these findings were generalized across schools of demographically diverse student populations.

School Climate Interventions. School climate has become a central target of school improvement efforts in the United States. Federal programs have encouraged states to develop measures of school climate and to implement programs that make schools safer and more supportive environments for all students (Centers for Disease Control and Prevention, 2009; Cohen, 2014; Dynarski et al., 2008).

The authoritative school climate model offers educators some promising avenues for school improvement. The key components of disciplinary structure, high academic expectations, and supportive teacher–student relationships are malleable and full of potential. In other words, interventions can be developed in schools to improve disciplinary fairness, raise academic expectations, and place more emphasis on positive teacher–student relationships.

Some of the leading school improvement programs in the United States can be examined from an authoritative school climate perspective. For example, the Positive Behavioral Interventions and Supports (PBIS) approach to school improvement encourages educators to establish schoolwide expectations for student behavior that stress positive goals (e.g., "Be respectful to others") and implement a reward system to reinforce positive behavior among students. Moreover, PBIS emphasizes the adoption of a uniform and consistent approach to reinforcing desired student behavior by all teachers and school staff members (Bradshaw, 2013).

Another intervention, My Teaching Partner-Secondary (MTP-S), focuses on coaching secondary school teachers to improve their interactions with students (Mikami et al., 2011). Consistent with the authoritative school climate model, MTP-S aims to develop respectful and emotionally supportive relationship between teachers and students. MTP-S research revealed positive effects on improving peer relations and lowering disruptive behavior (Mikami et al., 2011).

In conclusion, school climate research in the United States is thriving and the knowledge base continues to expand. Perhaps due to these efforts, the prevalence of bullying has decreased over the past decade in the United States (Waasdorp et al., 2017). Although many schoolwide interventions for improving school climate and student safety have been developed in the United States, there has been little examination of school climate in India.

School Climate as a Path to School Improvement in India

India has made impressive gains by focusing on the expansion of its school systems and developing its educational infrastructure. The basic education system, which consisted of around 200,000 schools in 1950, expanded to more than 1.1 million in 2010. This enormous school system, in combination with adult literacy programs, has led to significant improvement of literacy rates (from 18% in 1947 to 73% in 2011). A free meals program is credited with increasing enrollment in village schools from 22.3 million students in 1990 (Govinda & Josephine, 2004) to more than 193 million in 2010–2011 (Mehta, 2012). However, the quality of educational experiences in these schools remains a serious challenge for policymakers and educators. More specifically, student safety continues to be an issue of critical concern because many Indian children and adolescents are exposed to high levels of physical violence at home and at school.

According to a study by the Ministry of Women and Child Development Government of India (2007), "two out of every three children are physically abused" (p. vi) across different social contexts. In addition, students experience violence in the form of corporal punishment in their schools. Nearly 65% of children attending school reported experiencing corporal punishment at school and 62% of these victims were in government and municipal schools (Ministry of Women and Child Development Government of India, 2007). Accounts of students being physically or verbally abused by their teachers or their peers at school are reported in the news media across Indian states (e.g., Outlook Web Bureau, 2017). Authorities have long recognized that adverse conditions in schools, generally the absence of a safe and supportive school climate, lead to high dropout rates (see, e.g., Kumar, 1992; World Bank, 1997). The problem of school dropout was especially prevalent among socioeconomically deprived groups and first-generation learners.

Massive central as well as state government efforts have been made to improve Indian schools, but no established system exists to empirically examine whether these efforts are changing the schooling experience of children and producing more positive outcomes. Overall, there is a national need to examine the climate of Indian schools and evaluate the effectiveness of school improvement programs. It is important to understand the broader schooling experiences of students – how they are treated in the schools, whether they perceive disciplinary practices as fair and consistent, and whether there is a culture of equity and nondiscrimination in the schools. If students have positive relationships with their peers and teachers, they could have a deeper engagement with the schools, which in turn could facilitate their academic achievement and reduce the probability of dropping out.

Although there is no literature testing the efficacy of the authoritative school climate theory in India, the combination of higher disciplinary structure as well as higher support systems could enhance students' schooling experience. It is important to note that, except for students in some expensive private schools, students in India do not have access to school counselors or psychologists. The mental health professional workforce is largely absent from India's education system.

The Indian family structure tends to be highly hierarchical. Children are mostly excluded from decision-making and expected to obey older family members without questioning. Similar expectations prevail in schools, where students are expected to be obedient followers of their teachers and administrators. The cumulative effect of this strict disciplinary structure in home as well as in school could create emotional distress in students. It is not surprising that academic stress is one of the most prominent reasons for committing suicide among Indian students. In 2015, approximately 1,360 children and adolescents committed suicide for "Failure in Examination" (National Crime Records Bureau, 2016). Authoritative school climate theory highlights the importance of support systems along with disciplinary structure. Thus, using this theory, if interventions are developed to establish and maintain strong support systems for students in schools, they may be able to cope more successfully with high academic expectations. Perhaps policymakers could explore ways for including the human resource of school psychologists and counselors in the education system to provide much-needed support systems to students. School administrators and teachers could integrate supportive mechanisms for dealing with their students as practiced in US schools and schools in other nations. Pre-service and in-service programs for teachers could place more emphasis on: (1) the supportive role of a teacher; (2) teacher–student relationships based on mutual trust and respect; and (3) implementing disciplinary policies in a consistent and fair manner.

Moreover, it seems critical to investigate whether students feel there is equitable discipline and support in schools across cultural and socioeconomic groups. School climate research presents an empirical mechanism for examining disparities in students' perceptions of their schooling experience based on their socioeconomic group. Our recent study (Shukla et al., 2016) employed a person-centered approach to analysis and examined within-school heterogeneity in students' perceptions of their school climate in 47,631 US high school students. Four latent profiles of student perceptions were identified: positive climate, medium climate–low bullying, medium climate–high bullying, and negative climate. The results indicated that the positive climate class contained more white students (60.7%) and fewer black or African-American students (15.7%) compared to the negative climate class (51.6% white and 21% black). In other words, students of the same school perceived their school climate differently and white students were more likely to report a positive climate than black students on average. Another study revealed that although perceptions of school climate differed between white and black groups, a positive school climate related to lower peer victimization and higher engagement in a similar manner for all students irrespective of their racial membership (Konold et al., 2017). Such empirical investigation across diverse Indian groups defined by caste, economic class, religion, language, and gender can be of great value. It could help school administrators to be more mindful of the within-school variation in schooling experiences of students from different socioeconomic backgrounds. Policymakers should recognize that a more positive school climate is one that is equitable across groups and provides support mechanisms for marginalized groups.

In conclusion, the authoritative school climate theory presents a useful means of investigating some of the pressing issues related to bullying and other student experiences in Indian schools. In relative terms, schools in India tend to be safer for students than other contexts like the home and the neighborhood. The study on child abuse by the Ministry of Women and Child Development Government of India (2007) concluded: "[this] study has indicated beyond doubt that schools as compared to other situations are the safest place for children and therefore efforts should be made to increase the enrollment and retention of children in school" (p. 124). Almost 19% of the world's children are in India. If Indian schools could provide a safe and supportive climate to all children, it will be a major achievement for the entire world.

References

Baumrind, D. (1968). Authoritarian vs. authoritative parental control. *Adolescence, 3*, 255–272.

Berg, J. K. & Cornell, D. (2016). Authoritative school climate, aggression toward teachers, and teacher distress in middle school. *School Psychology Quarterly, 31*, 122.

Bradshaw, C. P. (2013). Preventing bullying through Positive Behavioral Interventions and Supports (PBIS): A multitiered approach to prevention and integration. *Theory into Practice, 52*, 288–295.

Bradshaw, C. P., Mitchell, M. M., & Leaf, P. J. (2010). Examining the effects of schoolwide positive behavioral interventions and supports on student outcomes: Results from a randomized controlled effectiveness trial in elementary schools. *Journal of Positive Behavior Interventions, 12*, 133–148.

Centers for Disease Control and Prevention. (2009). *School Connectedness: Strategies for Increasing Protective Factors among Youth*. Atlanta, GA: US Department of Health and Human Services. Retrieved from www.cdc.gov/he althyyouth/protective/pdf/connectedness.pdf.

Cohen, J. (2014). School climate policy and practice trends: A paradox. *Teachers College Record*, 1–5.

Cohen, J., McCabe, L., Michelli, N. M., & Pickeral, T. (2009). School climate: Research, policy, practice, and teacher education. *Teachers College Record, 111,* 180–213.

Cornell, D., Gregory, A., Huang, F., & Fan, X. (2013). Perceived prevalence of teasing and bullying predicts high school dropout rates. *Journal of Educational Psychology, 105,* 138.

Cornell, D. & Huang, F. (2015). School counselor use of peer nominations to identify victims of bullying. *Professional School Counseling, 18,* 191–205. doi: http://dx.doi.org/10.5330/2156-759X-18.1.191.

Cornell, D. & Huang, F. (2016). Authoritative school climate and high school student risk behavior: A cross-sectional multi-level analysis of student self-reports. *Journal of Youth and Adolescence, 45,* 2246–2259.

Cornell, D., Klein, J., Konold, T., & Huang, F. (2012). Effects of validity screening items on adolescent survey data. *Psychological Assessment, 24,* 21–33. doi: 10.1037/a0024824.

Cornell, D. & Limber, S. (2015). Law and policy on the concept of bullying at school. *American Psychologist, 70,* 333–343.

Cornell, D., Lovegrove, P. J., & Baly, M. (2014). Invalid survey response patterns among middle school students. *Psychological Assessment, 26,* 277–287.

Cornell, D. & Mehta, S. (2011). Counselor confirmation of middle school student self-reports of bullying victimization. *Professional School Counseling, 14,* 261–270. doi: http://dx.doi.org/10.5330/PSC.n.2011-14.261.

Cornell, D., Shukla, K., & Konold, T. (2015). Peer victimization and authoritative school climate: A multilevel approach. *Journal of Educational Psychology, 107,* 1186.

Cornell, D., Shukla, K., & Konold, T. (2016). Authoritative school climate and student academic engagement, grades, and aspirations in middle and high schools. *AERA Open, 2*(2), 2332858416633184.

Department of Education. Retrieved from http://ies.ed.gov/ncee/wwc.

Dynarski, M., Clarke, L., Cobb, B., Finn, J., Rumberger, R., & Smink, J. (2008). *Dropout Prevention: A Practice Guide* (NCEE 2008–4025). Washington, DC: National Center for Education Evaluation and Regional Assistance, Institute of Education Sciences, United States.

Fan, X., Miller, B., Park, K., Winward, B., Christensen, M., Grotevant, H., & Tai, R. (2006). An exploratory study about inaccuracy and invalidity in adolescent self-report surveys. *Field Methods, 18,* 223–244. doi: 10.1177/152822X06289161.

Gottfredson, G. D., Gottfredson, D. C., Payne, A. A., & Gottfredson, N. C. (2005). School climate predictors of school disorder: Results from a national study of delinquency prevention in schools. *Journal of Research in Crime and Delinquency, 42,* 412–444.

Govinda, R. & Josephine, Y. (2004). *Para Teachers in India.* New Delhi: National Institute of Educational Planning and Administration.

Gregory, A., & Cornell, D. (2009). "Tolerating" adolescent needs: Moving beyond zero tolerance policies in high school. *Theory Into Practice, 48,* 106–113.

Gregory, A., Cornell, D., & Fan, X. (2011). The relationship of school structure and support to suspension rates for black and white high school students. *American Educational Research Journal, 48,* 904–934.

Huang, F. & Cornell, D. (2015). The impact of definition and question order on the prevalence of bullying victimization using student self-reports. *Psychological Assessment, 27,* 1484–1493. http://dx.doi.org/10.1037/pas0000149.

Huang, F. & Cornell, D. (2016). Multilevel factor structure, concurrent validity, and test-retest reliability of the high school teacher version of the Authoritative School Climate Survey. *Journal of Psychoeducational Assessment, 34,* 3–14. doi: 10.1177/0734282915570278.

Huang, F., Cornell, D., Konold, T., Meyer, P., Lacey, A., Nekvasil, E., Heilbrun, A., & Shukla, K. (2015). Multilevel factor structure and concurrent validity of the teacher version of the Authoritative School Climate Survey. *Journal of School Health, 85,* 843–851.

Jia, Y., Konold, T., & Cornell, D. (2015). Authoritative school climate and high school dropout rates. *School Psychology Quarterly, 31,* 289–303. http://dx.doi.org/10.1037/spq0000139.

Jia, Y., Konold, T., Cornell, D., & Huang, F. (2016). The impact of validity screening on associations between self-reports of bullying victimization and student outcomes. *Educational and Psychological Measurement, 45,* 2246–2259. doi: 10.1007/s10964-016-0424-3.

Kann, L., Kinchen, S., Shanklin, S. L., Flint, K. H., Hawkins, J., Harris, W. A., Lowry, R., O'Malley Olsen, E., McManus, T., Chyen, D., Whittle, L., Taylor, E., Demissie, Z., Brener, N., Thornton, J., Moore, J., & Zaza, S. (2014). Youth risk behavior surveillance – United States, 2013. *MMWR Surveillance Summaries*; 63(SS-04): 1–168.

Klein, J., Cornell, D., & Konold, T. (2012). Relationships between bullying, school climate, and student risk behaviors. *School Psychology Quarterly, 27,* 154.

Konold, T. & Cornell, D. (2015). Measurement and structural relations of an authoritative school climate model: A multi-level latent variable investigation. *Journal of School Psychology, 53,* 447–461.

Konold, T., Cornell, D., Huang, F., Meyer, P., Lacey, A., Nekvasil, E., Heilbrun, A., & Shukla, K. (2014). Multi-level multi-informant structure of the Authoritative School Climate Survey. *School Psychology Quarterly, 29,* 238–255. doi: 10.1037/spq0000062.

Konold, T., Cornell, D., Shukla, K., & Huang, F. (2017). Racial/ethnic differences in perceptions of school climate and its association with student engagement and peer aggression. *Journal of Youth and Adolescence, 46,* 1289–1303.

Kumar, K. (1992). *What Is Worth Teaching?* New Delhi: Orient Longman.

Kuperminc, G. P., Leadbeater, B. J., & Blatt, S. J. (2001). School social climate and individual differences in vulnerability to psychopathology among middle school students. *Journal of School Psychology, 39,* 141–159.

Larzelere, R. E., Morris, A. S., & Harrist, A. W. (2013). *Authoritative Parenting: Synthesizing Nurturance and Discipline for Optimal Child Development.* Washington, DC: American Psychological Association.

Mehta, A. (2012). *Elementary Education in India: Progress towards UEE: Analytical Report 2010–11*. New Delhi: National University of Educational Planning and Administration. Retrieved from www.dise.in/Downloads/Publ ications/Publications%202010–11/AR%202010–11/DISE-analytical-tables-provisional-2010–11.pdf.

Mikami, A. Y., Gregory, A., Allen, J. P., Pianta, R. C., & Lun, J. (2011). Effects of a teacher professional development intervention on peer relationships in secondary classrooms. *School Psychology Review, 40*, 367–385.

Ministry of Women and Child Development Government of India. (2007). Study on child abuse: India 2007. Retrieved from http://wcd.nic.in/child abuse.pdf.

National Crime Records Bureau. (2016). *Accidental Deaths and Suicides in India 2015*. New Delhi: Ministry of Home Affairs, Government of India. Retrieved from http://ncrb.nic.in/StatPublications/ADSI/ADSI2015/adsi-2015-full-repo rt.pdf.

Office of the Registrar General & Census Commissionaire, India. (2017). *Abstract of Speakers' Strength of Languages and Mother Tongues –2001*. Ministry of Home Affairs, Government of India. Retrieved from www.censusindia.gov.in/Censu s_Data_2001/Census_Data_Online/Language/Statement1.aspx.

Outlook Web Bureau. (2017, August 12). Shocking corporal punishment: UP school headmaster filmed viciously beating students with a cane. *Outlook*. Retrieved from www.outlookindia.com/website/story/shocking-cor poral-punishment-up-school-headmaster-filmed-viciously-beating-stude/ 300295.

Pellerin, L. A. (2005). Applying Baumrind's parenting typology to high schools: Toward a middle-range theory of authoritative socialization. *Social Science Research, 34*, 283–303.

Phillips, V. & Cornell, D. (2012). Identifying victims of bullying: Use of counselor interviews to confirm peer nominations. *Professional School Counseling, 15*, 123–131. doi: http://dx.doi.org/10.5330/PSC.n.2012-15.123.

Robers, S., Kemp, J., & Truman, J. (2013). *Indicators of School Crime and Safety: 2012*. NCES 2013–036/NCJ 241446. Washington, DC: National Center for Education Statistics.

Shukla, K., Konold, T., & Cornell, D. (2016). Profiles of student perceptions of school climate: Relations with risk behaviors and academic outcomes. *American Journal of Community Psychology, 57*, 291–307.

Shukla, K. & Wiesner, M. (2016). Relations of delinquency to direct and indirect violence exposure among economically disadvantaged, ethnic-minority mid-adolescents. *Crime & Delinquency, 62*, 423–445.

US Department of Education. (2013). *Directory of Federal School Climate and Discipline Resources*, Washington, DC: US Department of Education. Retrieved from https://safesupportivelearning.ed.gov/sites/default/files/3_App endix%201_Directory%20of%20Federal%20School%20Climate%20and%2 0Discipline%20Resources.pdf.

Waasdorp, T. E., Pas, E. T., Zablotsky, B., & Bradshaw, C. P. (2017). Ten-year trends in bullying and related attitudes among 4th-to 12th-graders. *Pediatrics*, e20162615.

Wang, J., Iannotti, R. J., & Nansel, T. R. (2009). School bullying among adolescents in the United States: Physical, verbal, relational, and cyber. *Journal of Adolescent Health, 45*, 368–375.

World Bank. (1997). *Primary Education in India*. Washington, DC: The World Bank.

17   Editorial Reflections

Peter K. Smith, Suresh Sundaram, Barbara A. Spears,
Catherine Blaya, Mechthild Schäfer and
Damanjit Sandhu

The research on which this book is based presented a number of challenges. One was the obvious one associated with the nature of cross-cultural research: of a variety of Western researchers working with and alongside Indian researchers, all coming from quite different cultural and educational backgrounds. Another challenge was that Indian pupils are probably much less familiar with taking school-based survey questionnaires relating to their attitude or behaviour towards others in their environment than most Western pupils now are (Chapters 4, 7). But even amongst the Western researchers contributing to the research project and to this book, there are noticeably different research emphases. Broadly, and in collaboration with the Indian teams, the English and French teams pursued a rather pragmatic approach, exploring foundational aspects of pupil and teacher experiences through use of both longer surveys and shorter questionnaires, including a survey on cyberbullying and online behaviours in tertiary education (French team) and examining linguistic issues with a cartoon test (English and other teams). The Dutch and German teams, using peer nominations as well as questionnaires, pursued a more theory-driven approach, influenced by evolutionary ideas such as the adaptiveness of some bullying behaviours or socio-psychological approaches to group dynamics. The Australian team approached the task more qualitatively, putting emphasis on the lived experiences of pupils and practitioners in the Indian contexts, through use of PhotoStory and Living Lab interviews, as well as questionnaires.

Amongst the researchers contributing to the research project and to this book, these noticeably different research emphases raise an overarching challenge: whether the partly separate endeavours can lead to a fuller, more comprehensive picture of bullying and school social relationships in India, compared to Europe, than could have been done by Indian researchers exploring their own contexts, alone.

The main themes arising from the research explicated in this book are:

- India, like every other country examined to date, faces challenges with bullying and cyberbullying; whilst these problems may seem to be higher in India than in many other countries, such a conclusion must be tempered by many methodological considerations or might even be wrong.
- The problems of bullying and cyberbullying intersect with other areas such as peer aggression, risk-taking, sexting and Internet addiction.
- There are important similarities and differences between bullying and cyberbullying in India, and in the participating Western countries.
- There is a growing awareness of the need for interventions against bullying, including cyberbullying, in India, and experiences in Western countries may be of some help in taking these forward in an Indian context.

We consider these issues in turn in this final chapter.

India, like every other country examined to date, faces challenges with bullying and cyberbullying; whilst these problems may seem to be higher in India than in many other countries, such a conclusion must be tempered by many methodological considerations or might even be wrong

That India has a problem with bullying and cyberbullying is no surprise. Large-scale pupil self-report surveys such as Health Behaviour of School-Aged Children (HBSC) have found average rates, across many countries, of around 12% being bullied and around 10% bullying others; this refers to being bullied at least two or three times a month, over the previous couple of months. The 2009/2010 survey has a data set from 38 countries, mostly European, but also including the United States, Canada, the Russian Federation, Armenia and Ukraine (Currie et al., 2012). Being bullied (victim rates) overall, ranged from ca. 3% to 28% across countries. The most recent survey, 2013/2014 (Inchley et al., 2016), has data from 42 countries, and overall victim rates ranged from ca. 3% to 30%; this survey for the first time included two extra questions on being a victim of cyberbullying, for which victim rates varied from ca. 1% to 10%.

The literature reviewed in Chapters 1 and 3 generally suggests higher figures for bullying and cyberbullying in India, but many factors affect prevalence rates. Different studies use different criteria, for example regarding definition of bullying, frequency criteria and the time reference period asked about (Chapter 1). Country differences may also be affected by aspects such as social desirability in responding, and the proportion of untruthful students (Chapter 16). Another issue, especially when the term *bullying* is used in a definition or survey question, is how the word *bullying* is translated into non-English languages. From the study reported in Chapter 4, it appeared difficult to find a term in Tamil, and especially in Punjabi, which corresponded closely in meaning to *bullying*. In fact in Punjab, the English word *bully* appeared the best (but not exact) fit for schools where English is widely used. Finally, even in schools where English is widely used, the understanding of the questionnaires appeared to be a challenge to a number of pupils. For example, in Tamil Nadu, pupils had a choice of Tamil or English questionnaires (Chapter 7), and language difficulties might have resulted in either over- or underreporting despite translation efforts by peers and researchers.

Direct comparisons are necessary to give much credence to the supposed higher rates of bullying in India. Unfortunately, India does not feature in the large cross-national surveys that provide bullying data (Smith et al., 2016). It is not an OECD country, and it is not represented in HBSC, Trends in International Mathematics and Science Study (TIMSS) or the Programme for International Student Assessment (PISA). It does provide data to the World Health Organization–based Global School Health Survey (GSHS), but unlike most countries the survey in India did not include questions on bullying (see www.who.int/chp/gshs/IIH2007_public_use_codebook .pdf?ua=1).

The Microsoft Survey of online bullying referred to in Chapter 1 (see www.microsoft.com/en-us/download/details.aspx?id=30148) found high rates of being a cyber victim or cyber bully in India, higher than in the United Kingdom or Germany (of the countries represented in this book). This survey found China to have the highest rates for both cyber victim and perpetration. However, Wright and colleagues (2015a), comparing cyber victimisation and perpetration in China, India and Japan, found rates to be highest in India (for both boys and girls).

This book presents a few other direct comparisons. The peer nomination study reported in Chapter 8, comparing India (Punjab and Tamil Nadu) with Europe (the Netherlands and Germany), found more bullies and more boy victims in India, and more girl defenders in Europe. However, the peer nomination studies reported in Chapters 7 and 9 did not find more bullies in Tamil Nadu than in Germany. In higher education, the questionnaire study reported in Chapter 6 found more cyber victimisation (negative experiences on the Internet) in India (Punjab and Tamil Nadu) than in France. Thus, the evidence does tend to point to higher rates in India, but not totally consistently. Given the variations within Western countries, and also the likely variations within different regions of India, it may be premature to say that rates are higher in India, but clearly they are high enough to be of considerable concern and warrant ongoing investigation.

The problems of bullying and cyberbullying intersect with other areas such as peer aggression, risk-taking, sexting and Internet addiction

Bullying is usually defined in terms of aggressive behaviour which also is repeated and where there is an imbalance of power (Olweus, 1999; Smith, 2014). While fairly widely accepted, this definition is sometimes criticised as imprecise or narrow, especially but not only so far as cyberbullying is concerned (Bauman, Underwood & Card, 2013). As the study reported in Chapter 3 shows, pupils often may not use the repetition and imbalance of power criteria. If they are not used, we are talking about peer aggression (or cyber aggression) rather than bullying as defined by most researchers. This obviously affects prevalence rates (Chapter 3). The study of higher education students reported in Chapter 6 also grappled with the issue of studying cyberbullying, or more generally 'negative experiences' on the Internet. Finkelhor, Turner and Hamby (2012) argued the case for putting more effort into studying aggression and victimisation generally, rather than within the stricter definition of bullying.

Bullying behaviour intersects with risk-taking, as shown in Chapter 9 and as might be predicted from the theory that bullying behaviour can be adaptive in terms of displaying status and ultimately attracting sexual partners (Ellis et al., 2012). On the Internet, cyberbullying intersects with behaviours such as sexting and Internet addiction (Chapters 5, 6). These problem areas are clearly of concern in India, as in Western countries.

There are important similarities and differences between bullying in India, and in the participating Western countries

With English as a commonly spoken language in India, *bullying* is widely recognised as a phenomenon. In terms of similarities, it is clear that it is possible to assess bullying using adapted Western instruments such as self-report questionnaires (Chapters 3, 5) and the participant role scale (Chapters 7, 8, 9), albeit with some adaptation for the Indian context. Furthermore, sex differences in roles appear to be similar (boys more often bullies, girls more often defenders). There are similar social status correlates of these roles in India (Punjab and Tamil Nadu) and Europe (the Netherlands and Germany) (Chapter 8), and similar relations with risk-taking (the Netherlands and Punjab) (Chapter 9). As pointed out in Chapter 15, many findings are also similar to those in Canada.

However, these similarities should not distract us from important differences between India and Western countries. Even leaving aside issues of definition, and of terms for bullying in Indian languages, the types of bullying phenomena described are somewhat different. Although terms such as *ragging, Eve teasing* and *groupism* (Chapter 1) can certainly be understood by Westerners, they have a distinctive importance in Indian discussions of bullying and peer aggression. Different scenarios of bullying were also apparent in revising the cartoon test for suitability with Indian pupils (Chapter 4). New cartoons included taking someone's food at dinner, sneering at kinds of food eaten, insulting someone for being in a lower caste and shunning someone who always gets bad marks. These would not be typical scenarios in Western schools. Indeed, in many Western schools there would be more risk of being bullied from always getting good marks than from always getting bad marks.

An important difference highlighted in Chapter 8 is the great degree of sex segregation in many Indian schools, which is generally supported as normative by schools and teachers. This impacts the types of bullying likely to be experienced, and the way that participant roles (such as defender) are enacted. Interesting comparisons might be made with the generally smaller number of same-sex institutions in Western countries, and how co-education affects participant role distributions.

Many factors affect differences between countries, and the EU Kids Online model (Livingstone, Haddon, Görzig & Ólafsson, 2011) mentions cultural values (e.g. power distance, individualism/collectivism and peer attachment), education system (e.g. class groupings, structure of school day, break time supervision), technological infrastructure (e.g. penetration of smartphones, Internet), regulatory framework (e.g. school policies, legal aspects, anti-bullying initiatives) and socio-economic stratification (e.g. income, health, crime). Some of these are discussed in Chapter 2, including, for example, the Hofstede cultural value dimensions (Hofstede, Hofstede & Minkov, 2010). Wright, Kamble and Soudi (2015b), in India, found individualism was related positively, and collectivism negatively, to peer victimisation and aggression perpetration, moderated by levels of peer attachment.

What remains important is that schools everywhere are microcosms which reflect the cultural values of their communities. Bullying *within*

India also needs to be understood in relation to all these factors, as it is a religiously, socially and culturally diverse country in its own right, as reflected by the two distinct states/communities which participated in this research: Tamil Nadu and Punjab.

There is a growing awareness of the need for interventions against bullying, including cyberbullying, in India, and experiences in Western countries may be of some help in taking these forward in an Indian context

As shown in Chapters 11, 12 and 13, there is considerable awareness of the issues around bullying amongst professionals, schools, teachers and also pre-service teachers in training. There is also a desire expressed by many pre-service teachers for more information and resources on the topic (Chapter 13). Currently, many get information from social media and the Internet rather than from training (Chapter 11).

Some specific suggestions for taking things forward in Indian schools are given in Chapter 13. Some interesting differences emerged in this study between Punjab and Tamil Nadu. Sample sizes are limited, so these might be school differences rather than regional differences, but the indications were that, as far as reactive approaches to bullying incidents are concerned, schools and teachers in Punjab favoured more disciplinary approaches to bullying, whereas schools and teachers in Tamil Nadu favoured more counselling-based approaches. This issue is far from settled in Western countries, where the balance between disciplinary and counselling-based approaches to dealing with bullying incidents remains under discussion (Garandeau, Poskiparta & Salmivalli, 2014; Rigby, 2010). Compared to Punjab, schools and teachers in Tamil Nadu also appeared to be more in favour of peer-support schemes. These too have had both critics and proponents in Western countries (Smith, Cowie & Salmivalli, 2012; Ttofi & Farrington, 2011), with much depending on the type of scheme used (Palladino, Nocentini & Menesini, 2016).

Chapter 14 discusses the legal situation regarding bullying and cyber-bullying in India. This varies by state, and there are some laws on ragging and Eve teasing, but, it seems, nothing specifically on cyberbullying. The situation is also very varied in Western countries, including arguments about whether specific laws on cyberbullying are needed (Campbell & Zvarsnik, 2013; Katz et al., 2014). We know little about how effective legal approaches are, but a couple of studies from the United States (Hatzenbuehler et al., 2015; Ramirez et al., 2016) suggest some reductions in bullying and cyberbullying rates at a state level when anti-bullying laws were introduced.

Besides reacting to incidents, and having an appropriate legal framework, Chapter 16 argues the importance of developing an authoritative school climate. This has had some success in schools in the United States in reducing bully and victim rates. It could be a worthwhile approach to pursue in Indian schools. Schools may also need to engage more with parents. Western studies have demonstrated the overlap between harsh or abusive parenting, sibling bullying and school bullying (Lereya, Samara & Wolke, 2013; Wolke, Tippett & Dantchev, 2015). One lesson already learnt from Western studies, which surely will be true for India too, is that tackling bullying is not easy and cannot be achieved by isolated actions: a sustained effort at different levels of the ecological model (society, schools, families, peers, individual) is going to be necessary (Hong & Espelage, 2012).

Interventions in schools need to be feasible (rather than complicated and expensive), contextualised (Benbenishty & Astor, 2005), evidence-based with a clear aim (to reduce bullying), but still processed step by step in order to react to elements that do work, and change those that don't work as expected. They are best developed in consultation with teachers and other interested parties. This includes pupils, with the importance of pupil voice particularly brought out in Chapter 10. It is important too that any intervention initiatives in Indian schools are thoroughly evaluated. Good evaluations will be multi-method (qualitative and quantitative), use multiple informants (individuals, peers, teachers), have a longitudinal design and have suitable control groups (ideally, a randomised control design trial). They will assess fidelity (is the intervention properly carried out?) and include a follow-up after any external intervention has ceased (sustainability) (Smith, 2017). It has taken a while to get such interventions going in (mainly) Western contexts, but a number of high-quality evaluations are now available (Jiménez-Barbero et al., 2016).

The challenges in reducing bullying and cyberbullying and improving school climate in Indian schools are considerable, and initially depend on establishing the nature of the problem. This book takes some first steps towards establishing an evidence base with cross-cultural comparisons, and thinking about how to employ that new knowledge to underpin initiatives aimed at improving the experiences of children and young people in India who might be victimised through bullying and cyberbullying. Whilst much can be learned from efforts in other, often Western, contexts, the differences in the Indian context (and indeed within different states in India) must be considered at the forefront.

Meaningful change takes time. In the United Kingdom, it took some 10–15 years to bring about a deep cultural shift in how bullying was seen and dealt with, by schools but also by politicians and society at large (Smith, 2016). In France, it was not until 2010 that bullying was taken seriously (Debarbieux, 2016); since then, a national anti-(cyber)bullying school framework has been designed and all schools are to set up prevention and intervention strategies (Blaya & Dalloz, 2016). In the United States, a study in the state of Maryland has found a rather steady decrease in indicators of bullying over a 10-year period from 2005 to 2014 (Waasdorp, Pas, Zablotsky & Bradshaw, 2017). In Australia, the National Safe Schools Framework is undergoing its third revision (2003, 2011), aimed at supporting children's and young people's safety and well-being at school. Things can change, but they need evidence to do so. We hope that this volume has provided evidence which can be considered and which can contribute in some ways to productive change in Indian schools, so that children and young people are kept safe from the negative impacts of bullying and cyberbullying.

References

Bauman, S., Underwood, M. K. & Card, N. A. (2013). Definitions: Another perspective and a proposal for beginning with cyberaggression. In S. Bauman, J. Walker & D. Cross (eds.), *Principles of Cyberbullying Research: Definition, Methods, and Measures* (pp. 41–45). New York: Routledge.

Benbenishty, R. & Astor, R. A. (2005). *School Violence in Context: Culture, Neighborhood, Family, School, and Gender.* New York : Oxford University Press.

Blaya, C. & Dalloz, M. (2016). *Mon enfant est victime/auteur de harcèlement.* Paris: Soubeyran.

Campbell, M. & Zvarsnik, A. (2013). Should cyberbullying be criminalised? In P. K. Smith & G. Steffgen (eds.), *Cyberbullying through the New Media: Findings from an International Network* (pp. 65–82). Hove: Psychology Press.

Currie, C. et al. (eds.) (2012). *Social Determinants of Health and Well-Being among Young People. Health Behaviour in School-Aged Children (HBSC) Study: International Report from the 2009/2010 Survey.* Copenhagen: WHO Regional Office for Europe.

Debarbieux, E. (2016). *L'école face à la Violence – Décrire, expliquer, agir.* Paris: Dunod.

Ellis, B. J., del Guidice, M., Dishion, T. J., Figueredo, A. J., Gray, P., Griskevicius, V., Hawley, P. H., Jacobs, W. J., James, J., Volk, A. A. & Wilson, D. S. (2012). The evolutionary basis of risk taking behavior: Implications for science, policy, and practice. *Developmental Psychology, 48,* 598–623.

Finkelhor, D., Turner, H. A. & Hamby, S. (2012). Let's prevent peer victimization, not just bullying. *Child Abuse & Neglect, 36,* 271–274.

Garandeau, C. F., Poskiparta, E. & Salmivalli, C. (2014). Tackling acute cases of school bullying in the KiVa anti-bullying program: A comparison of two approaches. *Journal of Abnormal Child Psychology*, *40*, 289–300.

Hatzenbuehler, M. L., Schwab-Reese, L., Ranapurwala, S. I., Hertz, M. F. & Ramirez, M. R. (2015). Associations between antibullying policies and bullying in 25 states. *JAMA Pediatrics*, *169*(10), e152411.

Hofstede, G., Hofstede, G. J. & Minkov, M. (2010). *Cultures and Organizations: Software of the Mind*. New York: McGraw-Hill.

Hong, J. S. & Espelage, D. L. (2012). A review of research on bullying and victimization in school: An ecological system analysis. *Aggression and Violent Behavior*, *176*, 311–322.

Inchley, J. et al. (eds.) (2016). *Growing Up Unequal: Gender and Socioeconomic Differences in Young People's Health and Well-Being: Health Behaviour in School-Aged Children (HBSC) Study: International Report from the 2009/2010 Survey*. Copenhagen: WHO Regional Office for Europe.

Jiménez-Barbero, J. A., Ruiz-Hernández, J. A., Llor-Zaragoza, L., Pérez-Garćia, M. & Llor-Esteban, B. (2016). Effectiveness of anti-bullying school programs: A meta-analysis. *Children and Youth Services Review*, *61*, 165–175.

Katz, I., Keeley, M., Spears, B., Taddeo, C., Swirski, T. & Bates, S. (2014). *Research on Youth Exposure to, and Management of, Cyberbullying Incidents in Australia. Synthesis Report (SPRC Report 16/2014)*. Sydney: Social Policy Research Centre, UNSW Australia.

Lereya, S. T., Samara, M. & Wolke, D. (2013). Parenting behavior and the risk of becoming a victim and a bully/victim: A meta-analysis study. *Child Abuse & Neglect*, *37*, 1091–1108.

Livingstone, S., Haddon, L., Görzig, A. & Ólafsson, K. (2011). *Risks and Safety on the Internet: The Perspective of European Children: Full Findings*. London School of Economics and Political Science: EU Kids Online.

Ministerial Council for Education, Early Childhood Development and Youth Affairs (2011). *National Safe Schools Framework: All Australian schools are safe, supportive and respectful teaching and learning communities that promote student wellbeing*. Retrieved from https://docs.education.gov.au/system/files/doc/other/national_safe_schools_framework.pdf.

Ministerial Council on Education, Employment, Training and Youth Affairs (2003). *National Safe Schools Framework*. Retrieved from www.mdc.wa.edu.au/assets/About-Us/Policies/Safe-Schools-Framework.pdf.

Olweus, D. (1999). Sweden. In P. K. Smith, Y. Morita, J. Junger-Tas, D. Olweus, R. Catalano & P. Slee (eds.), *The Nature of School Bullying: A Cross-National Perspective* (pp. 7–27). London & New York: Routledge.

Palladino, B. E., Nocentini, A. & Menesini, E. (2016). Evidence-based intervention against bullying and cyberbullying: Evaluation of the NoTrap! program in two independent trials. *Aggressive Behavior*, *42*(2), 194–206. doi: 10.1002/ab.21636.

Ramirez, M., Ten Eyck, P., Peek-Asa, C., Onwuachi-Willig, A. & Cavanaugh, J. E. (2016). Evaluation of Iowa's anti-bullying law. *Injury Epidemiology*, *3*, 15. doi: 10.1186/s40621-016-0080-9.

Rigby, K. (2010). *Bullying Interventions in Schools: Six Basic Approaches.* Camberwell, Victoria: Australian Council for Education Research.

Smith, P. K. (2014). *Understanding School Bullying: Its Nature & Prevention Strategies.* London: Sage Publications.

Smith, P. K. (2016). Research and practice in the study of school bullying. In K. Durkin & R. Schaffer (eds.), *Blackwell Handbook of Developmental Psychology in Action* (pp. 290–310). Oxford: Blackwell.

Smith, P. K. (2017). School-wide interventions for bullying: What works? In P. Sturmey (ed.), *Wiley Handbook of Violence and Aggression, Volume 3: Societal interventions.* New York: Wiley.

Smith, P. K., Robinson, S. & Marchi, B. (2016). Cross-national data on victims of bullying: What is really being measured? *International Journal of Developmental Science, 10,* 9–19.

Smith, P. K., Salmivalli, C. & Cowie, H. (2012). Effectiveness of school-based programs to reduce bullying: A commentary. *Journal of Experimental Criminology, 8,* 433–441.

Ttofi, M. M. & Farrington, D. P. (2011). Effectiveness of school-based programs to reduce bullying: A systematic and meta-analytic review. *Journal of Experimental Criminology, 7,* 27–56.

Waasdorp, T. E., Pas, E. T., Zablotsky, B. & Bradshaw, C. P. (2017). Ten-year trends in bullying and related attitudes among 4th- to 12th-graders. *Pediatrics, 139,* e20162615.

Wolke, D., Tippett, N. & Dantchev, S. (2015). Bullying in the family: Sibling bullying. *The Lancet Psychiatry, 2,* 917–929.

Wright, M. F., Aoyama, I., Kamble, S. V., Li, Z., Soudi, S., Lei, L. & Shu, C. (2015a). Peer attachment and cyber aggression involvement among Chinese, Indian, and Japanese adolescents. *Societies, 5,* 339–353. doi: 10.3390/soc5020339.

Wright, M. F., Kamble, S. V. & Soudi, S. P. (2015b). Indian adolescents' cyber aggression involvement and cultural values: The moderation of peer attachment. *School Psychology International, 36*(4) 410–427. doi: 10.1177/0143034315584696.

Index

academic achievement, 7, 24, 27,
341–342, 345
addiction to the Internet. *See* internet
addiction
ADHD, 179, 182
age of criminal responsibility, 295, 297
anonymity, 4, 7, 85, 88, 133, 154
anti-bullying policy, 13, 15, 17, 229, 263,
269, 273, 275–276, 284
Australian Covert Bullying Prevalence
study, 209
authoritative school climate, 341–342, 349
awareness and experiences of bullying, 227

*Bullying Questionnaire for Punjabi and Tamil
schools*, 255–256, 281
bully-victim, 26, 235

capacity for dealing with bullying in schools,
223, 228, 230
cartoon figures, 30
cartoon test, 62, 64–67, 79, 352, 356
caste, 8, 33–34, 39, 66–68, 218–220, 288,
291, 304, 322, 337, 347, 356
child maltreatment, 38, 40
collectivism, 31
competitive altruism hypothesis, 147–148,
161, 163
ConRed, 90
coping with bullying, 197, 205
corporal punishment, 13–14, 16, 19,
277, 318
COST Action IS0801, 87
cross-cultural differences, 40, 124, 170,
174–175, 178, 180, 305
cross-national comparison, 118
cyber aggression, 4, 5, 85, 88, 90–91, 98,
100, 106, 115, 124, 334, 355, 361
cyber harassment, 92, 109
Cyberbullying in higher education, 107–108
cyberstalking, 4, 108–109, 126

CyberTraining project, 88
cyberviolence, 21, 84–86, 90–91, 98, 107,
121–123, 330

defender, 130, 137, 139, 142–144, 148–149,
151–152, 154–156, 158, 163–164, 168,
171, 178, 182, 354–356
defining culture, 27
definition of bullying, 4, 10, 24, 46, 56, 61,
64, 72, 78, 80, 84–87, 90, 95, 101, 103,
112, 126, 151, 171, 190, 195–196, 203,
214, 218, 227, 229, 244, 248–249, 255,
257, 260, 263, 274, 286, 287, 289–290,
293, 319, 332, 338–339, 349, 353,
355–356, 359
Digital India, 83
disability, 12, 14, 16, 17, 257, 261
dominance, 7, 8, 23, 130, 132, 142, 144,
148, 153–154, 156, 158–159, 163–165,
168, 178, 182–183

ecological model, 312, 358
Ecological Systems Theory, 26
emic, 63, 214–217, 233
ethnicity, 323
etic, 63, 213–217, 228–229, 233
EU Kids Online, 61, 79, 84, 86–88, 101,
102, 105, 112, 356, 360
European Commission, 88
eve-teasing, 9, 30–31, 124, 196, 204–205,
286–287, 291–296, 299, 356, 357
Evolutionary psychology, 146

Facebook, 11, 67–68, 92, 94, 97, 102–103,
110, 245, 247, 257, 261, 282, 301–302,
319–320, 327
family, 28, 36–40, 42–43, 84, 87, 91, 101,
113, 117, 119, 122, 149, 167, 184–185,
193–194, 198, 206, 226, 245, 248,
250–252, 273, 297, 328, 331, 346,
359, 361

362